Little Ice Cream Boy

Little Ice Cream Boy

JACQUES PAUW

PENGUIN BOOKS

PENGUIN BOOKS

Published by the Penguin Group
Penguin Books (South Africa) (Pty) Ltd, 24 Sturdee Avenue, Rosebank,
Johannesburg 2196, South Africa
Penguin Group (USA) Inc, 375 Hudson Street, New York, New York 10014, USA
Penguin Group (Canada), 90 Eglinton Avenue East, Suite 700, Toronto, Ontario,
Canada M4P 2Y3 (a division of Pearson Penguin Canada Inc)
Penguin Books Ltd, 80 Strand, London WC2R 0RL, England
Penguin Ireland, 25 St Stephen's Green, Dublin 2, Ireland (a division of
Penguin Books Ltd)
Penguin Group (Australia), 250 Camberwell Road, Camberwell, Victoria 3124, Australia
(a division of Pearson Australia Group Pty Ltd)
Penguin Books India Pvt Ltd, 11 Community Centre, Panchsheel Park,
New Delhi – 110 017, India
Penguin Group (NZ), 67 Apollo Drive, Mairangi Bay, Auckland 1310, New Zealand
(a division of Pearson New Zealand Ltd)

Penguin Books (South Africa) (Pty) Ltd, Registered Offices:
24 Sturdee Avenue, Rosebank, Johannesburg 2196, South Africa

www.penguinbooks.co.za

First published by Penguin Books (South Africa) (Pty) Ltd 2009

Copyright © Jacques Pauw 2009

ISBN 978 0 143 02592 4

Typeset by CJH Design in 9.5/14.5 pt News
Cover design Michiel Botha
Cover photograph: Larissa Degen
Printed and bound by Paarl Print, Cape Town

For my mother, who died during the writing of this book.
She was always my most avid critic and supporter.
Shortly before her death, she read the first few pages.
She declared them vulgar, obscene and unfit for publication.

Author's Note

This is better than fiction, I said to myself when the full extent of the atrocious activities of the gang emerged. This was real-life pulp at its very best. In fact, if this *was* fiction, people might say it's too fantastic, too far-fetched; implausible.

The year was 1996 and I was watching a video of the theatrical funeral of a Johannesburg diamond smuggler and robber which took place in Port Elizabeth. The ostentatious white coffin contained the mangled remains of the chubby hoodlum who had crashed his Honda Blackbird on a highway, going 300 kilometres an hour.

At the time of the crash the hood was on trial for South Africa's biggest diamond robbery. The gang had targeted a family of diamond diggers in the former Western Transvaal who, over a period of ten years, had hoarded their very best stones as insurance against the ANC's expected land grab. The gang pretended that they were diamond buyers and when the diggers produced their ten million rand collection of stones, one of the hoods grabbed it, jumped into a hotted-up BMW and took off.

The wailing widow was slumped over the coffin, her bottle-blonde mane falling stylishly across its lid. Most of the mourners had completed little more than primary school and their gangster attire was a dead giveaway – poodle haircuts (middle partings with a rat's tail hanging down the back of the head), black leather and lots of gold. There were murderers, thieves, robbers, fraudsters and smugglers among them.

One was a childhood friend, fellow robber and convicted murderer. He grew up as one of sixteen children in a railway house in Randfontein, where he slept on the dirty washing. Somewhere down the years he had had one leg amputated below the knee.

The most notorious member of the gang was a former police-man, convicted killer and apartheid assassin. But he was not present. He was smoking crack in his brothel in Johannesburg. He was a co-accused in the diamond robbery and his bail conditions confined him to the city limits. I had spent countless hours talking to him in his brothels in Johannesburg's northern suburbs.

The gang moved like a spectral ogre between the criminal underworld of drug dealing, prostitution, robbery and murder, and South Africa's official death squads.

At the time of the gangster's death I was producing a seventy-five minute television documentary on the activities of the gang which had ruled the Johannesburg underworld in the late eighties and early nineties. The gang members were just some of the characters I encountered and their shenanigans were just some of the stories I investigated in a journalistic career that has taken me to places where ordinary people don't venture and which brought me face to face with spine-chilling individuals who dutifully and unquestioningly served apartheid and killed in its name.

The first was former Vlakplaas death squad commander Dirk Coetzee, who I smuggled out of the country in 1989 in order to write his story. I spent a great deal of time with him – in South Africa, Zambia, Mauritius and London.

He was followed by a throng of assassins and hitmen who came to me with their confessions in the early nineties. On the one hand, they hoped that confessing might absolve them from future criminal prosecution or retribution by an ANC government and, on the other, they had scores to settle with their superiors and the politicians who had abandoned them. Investigative journalists feast on outcasts who have a score to settle.

One of the most bizarre confessions came from the bowels of the maximum security section of the Weskoppies psychiatric hospital in Pretoria. A puny man with delirious eyes – he was a master torturer – told me how Vlakplaas commander Eugene de Kock had built a bomb into a Walkman cassette player and sent it to Dirk Coetzee in Zambia. I was with Coetzee in Lusaka when he received the parcel. He refused to accept it, and it was sent back to South Africa. It blew up Coetzee's lawyer.

When I finally came face to face with De Kock several years later, he was incarcerated in Pretoria Central Prison and facing life imprisonment. I took him an extra-hot Nando's chicken as a gift because I wanted him to continue to talk to me.

There were others, like CCB[1] operative Pieter Botes who told me on his smallholding outside Pretoria how he had made a 'little sauce' out of the arm of anti-apartheid activist Albie Sachs – today a Constitutional Court judge. He blew him up with a car bomb in Maputo, Mozambique.

And how can I forget a Sunday afternoon on a bushveld farm in the Limpopo province when security policeman Paul van Vuuren – a member of a death squad that electrocuted their victims with a generator – told me: 'Shooting a human being or a buck is basically the same.'

Many of the death squad operatives weren't just state-sanctioned hitmen; they merrily mixed profit and patriotism, but they were really nothing more than common criminals.

And then there was Ferdi Barnard, a menacing-looking desperado who flaunted hoodlum garb and a macho swagger. For a long time he was one of the most feared men in the country, both as a CCB assassin and as a gangster of Herculean proportions.

One Friday afternoon in 1996, Barnard confessed to me, in a chemical cloud of crack, that in 1989 he had shot and killed anti-apartheid activist David Webster with a shotgun in front of his home in Troyeville. I made a statement to the Transvaal Attorney General and eventually testified against him in the Pretoria High Court.

Eugene de Kock and Ferdi Barnard between them were convicted of about ten murders, as well as crimes that ranged from theft to robbery to fraud. Both are in prison for life. Dirk

---

[1] Civil Co-operation Bureau, a military death squad.

Coetzee is also a convicted killer, but he received amnesty and remains a free man.

I have documented the exploits of these cut-throats in three works of non-fiction, the last being *Dances with Devils* at the end of 2006.

Barnard's story and the death squad saga somehow refuse to leave me. The last time I saw Barnard was at the end of 2007 when I visited him in the medium security section of Pretoria Central. He greeted me like a long-lost brother and invited me to attend his wedding in prison.

All the men I have mentioned here were simultaneously terrifyingly normal and utterly deranged. Beneath their veneer of normality lurked deeply damaged psychopaths who showed their victims absolutely no mercy or compassion.

There is something of each of them in this book. Although names have been changed, many of the incidents are all too real. Other events and characters have been invented in order to fill out the storyline. I have, however, tried to stay close to the truth, portraying the characters as genuinely as possible.

Little Ice Cream Boy is an attempt to expose the sordid underbelly of white gangland at a time when life was cheap and gangsters furthered their deviant careers under the protective shield of apartheid.

This – to steal the title of one of my previous books – was life in the heart of the whore.

Prologue

My cell is hardly as big as a king-size bed. I would say it's slightly bigger than a shithouse. I'm no globetrotter, but imagine spending the rest of your life in the stuffy, jam-packed economy class section of a Boeing. No way of getting out of it; I'm as stuck as a pig in a slaughterhouse.

On my left lurks a murderer. On the seat next to me a rapist parks. Behind me a robber snoozes. In front of me a habitual crook dozes. Imagine shitty-looking male attendants with shitty attitudes, carrying batons and wearing shitty-coloured uniforms that spread like boxing gloves over their *boeps*. Breakfast is black tea and stale bread with a gob of white margarine; lunch a heap of salt-less *pap*, bread and jam. Dinner is a swanky banquet of boiled chicken neck, more *pap* and beetroot drowning in vinegar. Worst is: it's a flight to nowhere.

The cabin just gets stuffier and more frenetic. *Sif* gangsters with tattoos of skulls and daggers, golden nuggets in their choppers and murder in their hearts, pull hidden home-made daggers from under their seats. The toilets get filled to the brim with shit, inmates piss against the walls, and in the bathrooms demented psychotics skulk with blades concealed in toothbrushes. The attendants wring your last buck from you for an extra chicken neck.

And so you whirl and spin until your head explodes. You stick your fingers in a goon's bloodshot eyes. You grab a baton and swing it about until you feel and hear bones crush and splinter under its weight. You scheme of diving through a little window and tumbling towards the open spaces that beckon far, far below. But you're stuck.

Welcome aboard Bomb Airlines on a flight to eternity. I've been on a plane like this for fourteen years and I'm still going fucking nowhere. Best of all: I have to spend three lives in here. Fortunately, I have only one. I call it Bomb Airlines because the Medium Security Section of Pretoria Central Prison is known as The Bomb. Like thousands of convicted criminals before me, I was ferried in leg and hand irons in the back of a yellow van to the solid yellow-brick fortress where under the watchful eyes of swivelling cameras I was ushered through the fort-like wooden gateway. Then I heard the clang of steel doors behind me. That was the moment when I was reduced to fuck all; the moment I became the property of the state.

As a new arrival, I was stripped of everything: my clothes, my liberty, my dignity. I had to hand in my black court suit at the reception office and was issued with an olive green prison outfit. Some time later they changed the colour to orange, which reduced me to a cranky-looking Oros man. A warder escorted me up the polished steps and through impenetrable steel doors that led to the innards of the dungeon. Many, many years ago the steps were carved from sheer rock but thousands upon thousands of shuffling and despondent feet have hollowed out their surfaces. In those steps are ingrained the pain and filth and waste and despair of all of us who have passed into this torture chamber.

I've got a cell that's nothing more than a concrete bed cemented to the floor, a steel cupboard, a chair and a tiny table. It's decorated with a few books, a transistor radio and photographs of my beloved fiancée and my family on the table and on the wall. Talk about the wall. It's not just dirty, it's rotten and filthy. It makes me think that a jailbird got stuck as he tried to escape through the barred window up near the ceiling. As he hooted and howled like a madman for someone to come get him down, he shat all over the wall. I've tried to clean it but the dirt clings to the surface. That's the story it seems, of this multi-storey shrine to crime.

There is a sticker outside my cell, alongside the steel gate. On it is my name and number. In here it's like the army of old because whatever you do – eat, wash, phone, shit (I wish I could say fuck) – someone always wants to know: name and number! Name and number! It rolls off my tongue: G J Goosen, 2745534. Below my name and number are the misdemeanours I'm in for. Three murders, attempted murder, armed robbery, assault with intent to do grievous bodily harm, theft, malicious damage to property and unlawful possession of arms and ammunition. I often look at the sticker and realise: Jesus Christ, there's not space for anything else! That's why my sentence had to be squeezed into the right-hand corner. Just two words: 'Three Life'. That's for the three murders. The judge slammed another thirty-five years on me for the rest but I suppose that's unimportant when a silly cunt wearing a red robe has condemned you to rot for ever in this shithole. It's strange, though, that that sticker is also my guardian and my protector. Anyone who's had one look at that sticker knows: fuck with 2745534 and he'll whack your ass so hard that you'll never be able to walk, fuck or shit again. That's why I have a single cell. I'm regarded as dangerous and, in Correctional Services jargon, I am 'potentially harmful to other prisoners'. I like the aura of fear that surrounds me.

That's maybe why I have no buddies. I mostly despise those

who seek my attention. Caged with me in C Section of The Bomb are several loony right-wingers who planted bombs throughout the country, as well as police death squad commander Eugene de Kock. It sometimes seems as though apartheid's death squads have descended on to C Section for a reunion or a picnic. We joke that we seriously reduced the country's problem of overpopulation but are getting fuck all credit for it.

Eugene is a dark, brooding character who's a bit of a nutter because every other day he claims he has inside information about amnesty for birds like us. It's obviously bullshit because we're still in The Bomb. These right-wingers are scum and I want nothing to do with them. They sometimes corner me in The Three Ships – that's what we call the eating hall, named after the famous restaurant at the former Carlton Hotel – and talk shit. This afternoon they parked across from me and wanted me to sign some silly petition for political amnesty that they intend to send to the Union Buildings. They think because I whacked a leftie commie – or anti-apartheid activist as they're called these days – I'm on their side. Well, they're wrong. I told them straight that their piece of paper is worthless because *grootbaas* Mbeki decided long ago that they'll rot inside and there's fuck all they can do about it. One of them gabbled something to the effect that the white man must never *hensop* to the communists and we must stand together and hold hands. I tuned him I want fuck all to do with any of them and got up and walked back to my cell.

Across the passage is a communal cell with thirty-five birds, although there's hardly room for twenty. They're all coloureds and blacks and members of the 26s and 27s and 28s. Most are in for murder, robbery or rape, often all three. I'm not sure who's a 26 or a 27 or a 20-whatever. One 20-something gang rapes while the other steals and the third one kills, but the distinction is not important because they're all a bunch of fucking hooligans. Their brains have been fried by white pipes and tik and whatever other shit they pump into their carcasses – many will say I'm the last one to speak – and they feel fuck all for anyone. They're tattooed from toe to head and I know you're not going to believe me, but in the showers I've personally seen tattoos on their dicks. They don't mess with me and always grin from ear to ear when they spot me. These goons love to smile, especially the generals and the lieutenants among them who flash the gold nuggets that have replaced their missing teeth. The ordinary troopers just have to live with the gaps in their choppers. They usually greet me like a long-lost brother: 'Howzit, china!' I always wave back, careful not to piss them off.

We call their cell Auschwitz. And with good reason because most of the murders and assaults in C Section are schemed in that pit. Need a thug to whack a bird or a jailer or teach someone a lesson he'll never forget? You hire your bruiser in Auschwitz and pay in money, booze, drugs or sex. An inmate who recently bought an Okapi knife in Auschwitz paid the general in goods – by organising a birdie from the juvenile section for a night of canoodling. A jailer himself delivered the tender piece of jail-meat. I know it because I saw it. There's a small barred window at the top of the cell doors through which the jailers spy on birds to make sure they're asleep and not busy with hanky-panky or whatever. From my little window I can see Auschwitz's door and, believe me, the traffic in and out of that nest is worse than Commissioner Street at five o'clock on a Friday afternoon. Booze and drugs and food and guns and knives and boys are delivered throughout the day and night. Jailers pop in for a Klippies or Red Heart and Coke and a chunk of steak.

Veggeneraal Taliep Carstens commands Auschwitz. I don't know which 20 he runs but he's a diabolical son of a bitch. One of his eyelids flops over the eyeball – courtesy of a knife stab – while the other is permanently bloodshot. He has a scar under his right eye – the open one – and his skin looks as though he was attacked with rough sandpaper. His body swarms with tattoos of skulls and daggers and hearts and numbers. What that indicates I do not know, except that in order to win his rank he definitely had to kill again and again and again. Life in Auschwitz is sweet – except for those who are carted in for the pleasure of the generals and, if they reckon it is deserved, for their troopers.

These goons pick and choose their cell mates. A Nigerian drug dealer – nabbed with two dozen cocaine bullets in his ass – was thrown into Auschwitz but lasted less than a day. The goons remodelled his face so badly that he was transferred to another cell the next morning. And guess where the Nigee – we call him Abasanjo – is parking now? With the right-wingers! They complained in The Three Ships the next day that he suffered from 'excessive body odour' and said they were taking their gripe to the highest level. They were going to plead 'cultural incompatibility'.

'Not another fucking petition!' I said and laughed. Suffice to say that Abasanjo is still parking with the white loonies.

I have only one reason to survive The Bomb and to hope for parole one day: a middle-aged doll with a coiffed hairdo – sprayed as stiff as a cock on his honeymoon night. She's the only thing that makes my life (barely) bearable in this hellhole. Her name is Debbie and I've promised her that I've renounced my former life and want to start afresh with her. I'm still not sure why or how this angel breezed into my life.

One day, about three years ago, I received a letter from a Debbie du Preez who said she was an ordinary woman from Roodepoort. She had seen me on television, read about me and decided to write me a letter. I would also like to visit you, she said. God Jesus, I thought as I sat with the letter in my hand, is this some wacky stiletto scrubber who gets off on fantasies about being tied to the bars and thrown around from one corner to the other and being shagged silly by a jailbird with a menacing dick? And why write to *me*? She could only have read blood-curdling things about me. A well-known journo (I still have a little score to settle with the bitch) recently wrote a book (it's standing on my bookshelf) where she describes her interactions with me and says she had to dig deep into her Oxford Thesaurus to find words to describe Gideon Goosen. She obviously dug very deep because she paints me as 'abominable, depraved, offensive, repugnant, repulsive, monstrous, loathsome, odious, execrable, detestable, despicable'.

Have you ever heard anything like that? Would you let your mommy (Debbie is a divorcee and mother of three) visit Gideon Goosen? No fucking way in hell! I didn't answer the first letter, but then a second arrived. There was something about the way she spoke to me: soft, gentle, caring and understanding. It was as though she'd known me for a long, long time. She even knew I had a fourteen-year-old daughter named Charmaine (she was just a few months old when I went in) who lives with my mother in Roodepoort. She offered to visit the child, make sure she has everything she needs, and bring her to Pretoria to visit me. My dad died shortly after I went in and my mother is too old and frail to make the weekly trips to Pretoria.

Debbie had a small, womanly handwriting and the paper smelt of perfume. When was the last time I had savoured the scent of a woman? It was a far cry from the Mum for Men and Shield for Sportsmen that envelop many an inmate. I was intrigued, and even charmed, although I remained suspicious. When I was a smart-ass gangster with a poodle-cut hairstyle, leather garb, gold chains, black Ray-Bans and a 9mm Glock, I was swamped by trophy bimbos. These scrubbers lapped up the excitement and danger of gangland and were all too eager to squander my blood-earned booty and gloat in my infamy. I was scared that Debbie had a similar, peculiar attraction to me because she knew I was in for life.

I nonetheless decided to write back. I wrote down my address. There's a standard procedure for writing letters and it has to follow this order: Prisoner no 2745534. Gideon Johannes Goosen. C Section, Medium Security, Pretoria Central Prison. This is so the jailers know where the letters come from when they check out their contents at head office in Andries Street. You therefore have to be careful when you write stuff like thanking your folks for the bottle of Klippies they'd smuggled in courtesy of a brotherly warder. I know many birds who got into mega trouble because they couldn't keep their mouths shut and wrote all kinds of shit in their letters. Others take the piss out of the jailers by writing bullshit about prison breaks and drugs and whatever. Just the other day a platoon of heavy dudes with machine guns – recces or Task Force or whatever – marched into C Section to shake our cells. Some dude had written to someone about a robber who was greasing the palm of a jailer to jump him out. A clever censor – and believe me there are not many – picked it up. I heard afterwards it was just a scheme to get the dude out of C Section.

I'm no letter writer and I stared for a long time at my name and number before writing: 'Dear Debbie'. And then I paused again. What do you say to a broad you've never seen before? Problem is, there's actually fuck all happening in The Bomb. That's apart from the odd fight or escape or death or rape or whatever and I'm sure she didn't want to know about any of that. So I started with: 'How are you? I hope you are fine. With me it's going well and I have no complaints.' Boring shit like that. The letter was less than a page long.

Within a week she had written back. Then I discovered that Debbie had deposited money into my prison account – an account you use to buy pies, cold drinks, sweets and toiletries at the tuck shop. Why have you done this? I asked her in my next letter. Because you're a very special person and deserve to be pampered, she wrote back. Fucking hell, I thought! It gave me a warm and wonderful feeling.

Debbie announced that she was going to pay me a visit. I was nervous as hell because I didn't know what she looked like or what to expect. I showered early on the morning of her visit and ironed my orange prison uniform. I felt slightly embarrassed about meeting her in my orange outfit. The only other place where you'd expect to see someone in such garish attire is in a fucking madhouse or a circus. I also had a nasty bruise on my forehead, the result of a brawl earlier that week. Some coloured goon a few cells away was busted with a half-jack of Klippies and told the jailers that I was his supplier. The bastard had been bugging me for some time and although the jailers didn't swallow his shit, I decided to teach him a lesson. I cornered him in the bathroom the next morning, bashed his head against the wall and when he went down, I emptied my tube of toothpaste in his choppers and forced him to swallow every last drop of Colgate. Of course he repaid me in kind. The next day another goon, armed with a short iron rod, jumped me from behind in the library. The jailers leapt in and broke up the brawl, but by then I had a bash on my forehead.

A jailer came to my cell, announced that I had a guest, and escorted me to the visitors' section. Debbie was waiting for me on the other side of the glass barrier. I was still a C Class prisoner then because of the tiffs I'd been involved in and the disturbances I'd caused. I couldn't receive contact visits. So there she was: a spick and span cookie with a hairdo. For a moment I thought about turning around and doing a duck. I don't know what I'd expected: a bottle-blonde with a red mouth and big tits perhaps? Of course I'd forgotten that all these years in The Bomb had turned me into a bit of a wasted old fart. I'm skinny and turning grey and there's little left of the macho gangster I used to be – except for the bruise on my forehead.

I forced myself to sit down on the other side of the glass. 'What happened to you, Gideon?' she asked. She had a soothing, motherly voice.

I laughed and said: 'I was in combat.'

'I thought you'd finished with that?'

'Sometimes a man has to defend himself. It's rough in here.'

She shook her head and said: '*Siestog*. We'll have to get you out of here. This is no place for a decent human being.'

'I'm afraid that's going to take some time.'

'You're much thinner than I thought,' she said.

'All the steak and chips,' I said.

We both laughed. 'I'll pay some more money into your account. You have to eat better.'

'You don't have to,' I said.

'I want to,' she responded.

As some point both of us fell silent, probably to give us time to take each other in. Her green, almost turquoise eyes, their corners lined with tiny creases, glowed serenely. Her mouth was wide and soft and her prominent nose gave her a no-nonsense aura. As I've said, her hair was neatly styled and she was wearing a flowered dress. A string of pearls adorned her neck. If I had come across Debbie fifteen years ago, I wouldn't have spared her a second glance. She looked too much like a high school teacher and even, I thought with a shock, a bit like my own mother a decade or two ago.

But I wasn't twenty-five either. Long gone were the days when I measured a bimbo by her knockers or required her to have fucked at the Olympic Games before I set my sights on her. Debbie was a comely woman and – let's get one thing straight – when you're a down-and-out convict encased in a clown's attire you don't decline the attention of any broad, not even those who look like dogs. Not that Debbie looked like a dog at all. Of course not! She was actually quite lovely. The hour-long visit seemed to pass in a matter of minutes. We spoke and laughed and generally talked shit. At some point she told me she had recently become a grandmother and has had three husbands. My fucking hell, I thought, I was making eyes at a granny!

When Debbie left, she pressed her manicured hand against the glass partition as though she was reaching out to touch me. I pressed mine against hers and, with the glass separating us, we said goodbye. I swear I could feel her warmth and energy flowing into me.

After her first visit I kept thinking how different Debbie was from the nasty slivers of meat that once surrounded me. The last broad to complicate my life was Sharné Labuschagne, ironically also the one who later ratted on me and contributed more than any other person to getting me locked up here. When I met her in the middle eighties, she was an eighteen-year-old red-haired hooker from the wrong side of Nigel – and, believe me, they don't come much lower than that. But she was cute and fresh and flashing an amazing pair of titties. I first cast my eyes on her in the presidential suite of a larney hotel and it was love at first sight. I literally had to take up arms to make her mine. I whacked the brothel boss who had enslaved and pimped her and threw him down a big, black hole. She only became mine and decorated my bed on a more permanent basis when I had a bullet hole in my chest.

You will hear a lot more about Sharné. Suffice to say now that when I was arrested in the winter of 1994 she was a wretched bag of bones and bore no resemblance to the sweetmeat I had scraped up off the pavement. She had dark circles under her eyes, her teeth were decaying from far too many crack pipes, her tits sagged and her bottle-blonde mane was greasy and unkempt. But, my God, did she have a memory! When she took the stand against me, she implicated me in the finest detail in knock after knock, robbery after robbery and even murder after murder. As she concluded her orgy of a testimony, she said: 'I hate him because I was his possession. He turned me into his personal drug and sex slave. I want to hurt him like he hurt me.'

I couldn't believe it! I wanted to jump up and inform the court that a slave she might have been, but my God she never once objected to anything. She merrily participated in whatever carnal or narcotic challenge I threw at her. Crack pipes, coke lines, threesomes, foursomes – whatever I tossed at Sharné, she lapped it up and revelled in the attention.

Sharné's venom nonetheless fucked me up. As I was escorted into Maximum Security, I realised how true it was that hell hath no fury like a woman scorned and that pillow talk is the most lethal of all romantic activities. It has betrayed many a villain and landed countless criminals behind bars. I had told Sharné far too much, but how could I have known at the time that a fucked-out-of-her-skull crack tart was going to remember all that shit?

My letters to Debbie grew longer and more intimate and her visits became more frequent. I started to become far more conscious of my appearance. After years of inactivity I ventured to the prison gym and started pushing weights. I paid the prison barber – one of the goons from Auschwitz – ten rand to trim my hair properly and square-cut it at the back.

'Hey, china,' the toothless hood wanted to know, 'is all this titivating for that cookie who visits you every Saturday?'

'Bugger you, man,' I tuned him back. 'If you call her a cookie again, I'll *bliksem* your last remaining tooth out.'

'But hey, china, man,' he laughed, 'she's quite advanced in years, hey?'

'I wouldn't say that,' I responded. 'It's just that she's nicely grown up.'

'Since when do you dig such vintage models?'

'She's like a Merc,' I said. 'She just gets better with time.'

He laughed. 'As long as you don't forget to change the clutch plate and the spark plugs!'

Debbie brought my mother and Charmaine to visit me. I've never really known my child. In the few months before I went in, I'd hardly looked at her. I was so fucked out of my skull that I have almost no memory of my child. In all the years I'd been in The Bomb, I had seen her maybe twice a year. I'd never wanted Sharné to have this child in the first instance. I'm not even sure that Charmaine is mine. Sharné was a bit of a floozie and her hunger for crack turned her into a slut who fucked for the first team. Throughout her pregnancy she was as high as a kite and when I dropped her at Johannesburg Hospital to pop, she was goofed out of her skull. I was convinced that whatever she brought into the world would be scarred and disfigured. I was astonished to see a child with ten toes, ten fingers and with eyes an acceptable distance apart.

After the birth, I took Sharné back to my house where she continued to cook crack (and smoked half the stuff herself). Charmaine was nothing but a bundle of nuisance that howled at the top of her voice and shat in her nappies. That's about all I remember. The cops nailed me shortly afterwards.

I looked at Charmaine standing behind Debbie and my mother. She didn't say anything, just gawked at the orange man on the other side of the glass. My child was a budding beauty. She looked a bit like her mother in her heyday: the same deep blue eyes and Angelina Jolie-like lips. Debbie said she had my facial bone structure but I couldn't see it. I realised then that if I ever sit down and cry, it won't be about the human heads I've reduced to pulp or the scores of people I've fucked up, nor even about the time I've wasted in The Bomb. It will be for this delicate and adorable young girl who will always carry the burden of having a murderer for a father and a hooker for a mother – neither of whom wanted her and ignored her from the moment she escaped that crack-lined womb.

My mother had become an old woman, her wrinkled face testimony to a life of anguish and loss and neglect. The last time I had touched her was many years ago on the day that I was sentenced to life. As the judge gathered his papers and left the courtroom, I turned around to look at my parents. My mother stood up, put her arms around me and kissed me on my lips. She wept as they led me down the steps to the cells. I was gone, probably for ever. My father died a few months later. Since then, my mother has had two strokes, the last one less than a year ago.

I have long forgotten what it is like to cry, but I confessed my pain to Debbie in my letters. It's never too late to right a wrong, she wrote back. Be the best father you can be, even from where you are. Remember that the night is at its darkest just before the suns rises in the east, she said, and that the greatest glory in living lies not in never falling, but in rising every time you go down.

One Saturday afternoon, I slipped into Auschwitz for a brandy and Coke and a piece of boerewors that jailer Van Deventer had barbecued at his home earlier that afternoon before delivering it in a Tupperware dish to Taliep. The goons were celebrating the release on early parole of two of their troops who were going home the following Monday. One had killed his brother-in-law in a family brawl and stabbed his wife in the neck, while the other had shot dead a fellow goon in a gang fight. They were monstrous characters who were both feared and loathed. Yet they'd served hardly half their time.

'What on fucking earth did these dudes do to get out of here?' I asked Taliep as he sliced off another chunk of the delicious sausage with his Okapi knife. He skewered the meat and held it out to me. As I stuck it in my mouth, he said: 'A clean prison record and the blessing of Pastor van Heerden.'

Many birds bribe jailers like Van Deventer to expunge blemishes from their prison files.

'But how did they get the pastor's blessing?' I asked Taliep. 'Grease him?'

'No, asshole, they go to church. And so should you.'

'I don't dig Jesus,' I said. 'He's done fuck all for me.'

'Doesn't matter, china. Spending time on your knees goes down well with the parole board,' Taliep said as he rolled a joint between his fingers. A flame illuminated his shrivelled face. He took a long draw and passed the joint to me.

'You should try it, china. It looks good on your file.'

The next morning I went to church for the first time in about thirty-five years. Taliep and the whole of Auschwitz were not just in church, they were occupying the first two rows of the prison chapel. I couldn't help thinking that if these muggers ever manage to sneak in through the pearly gates, they'd clean out the Saviour's house and nick his crown from his head! Taliep waved at me and signalled me to sit next to him. I declined and slipped into the back row. Pastor van Heerden preached that even those of us incarcerated in The Bomb could be as free as birds if we just accepted God as our saviour and salvation.

'Hallelujah!' Taliep trumpeted.

'Hallelujah!' the rest of his goons bawled.

Taliep followed it up with 'God is great!'

'Oh yes he is!' agreed his choir.

They thundered as one: 'God our saviour!'

As the orange congregation rose to sing 'Praise the Lord the King of Angels', the goons stuck their arms in the air and swayed from side to side. Taliep was easily the smallest bird in The Bomb, but his voice thundered above the rest. Since then I've been a converted Christian à la Taliep. Every Sunday, I park in the third row of the chapel, just behind the goons, and sing and pray and 'Hallelujah!' occasionally. I even had a one-on-one with Pastor van Heerden when I fibbed about God's greatness and how grateful I was that Jesus died on the cross for my sins.

Debbie was delighted to hear that I've turned into a kind of Jesus freak. She is a devout churchgoer and wrote to me that sometimes one had to be dead to be able to live again.

The church-thing worked. Just a few weeks after my first church appearance, some jailer with brass on his shoulder announced that I'd been upgraded to an A Class bird. Not only did it mean more telephone time, books, watching TV and more visitors, but also contact visits. Imagine: contact visits! I would be able to touch Debbie! For eighteen months we'd been kind of feeling one another up through the glass. Every time we'd pressed our hands together against the glass, I could feel her energy and warmth and hope flowing into me. The thought of actually putting flesh on flesh overawed me. For many nights before my first contact visit I tossed around in my bed and wondered what Debbie felt like. I've stared for countless hours at her hands – soft and caring, with her nails immaculately kept. I've often yearned to take them and wrap them in my warmth and love.

Love! How do you love through glass? Ever thought about it? I tried never to think about loving Debbie. It just seemed so fucking pointless. But the thought that we could touch, if only holding hands in the visitors' section, filled me with both anguish and excitement.

Have I ever loved? I'm not sure. I thought I loved Sharné but once I had her I didn't want her any longer. I've certainly had scores of bitches for a night or two or three but I think the only thing I loved about them was how they succumbed to my power and authority. I loved the way they obeyed my every wish and command. In turn, they just loved to swoon in my arms and bask in the glory of a supreme hood.

And touching? Well, obviously I touched them in every way proper and improper. But did I feel anything? I don't think so. My most intimate fling with flesh might have been a sordid thug I once strangled with my own hands. I've smashed in many faces with my fists, but I've wrung to death only one soul. The guy kidnapped one of my hookers, tied her up, raped her and pushed a broken bottle into her. She died next to the road. My bouncers picked him up and brought him to my haunt at the back of the club. He was tied up and gagged. I checked him up and down. It's sometimes a difficult choice: how to whack a dude. A baseball bat or a pellet through his loaf would have messed up my fluffy carpet. There was only one way of doing it. I stepped forward and put my hands around his throat and squeezed as hard as I could. His neck artery pumped frantically against my fingers. I squeezed harder and harder. After the first frantic attempt to get blood to his brain, his pulse became slower and slower and then there was nothing. When I took my fingers away, he slumped to the floor. Don't get me wrong: I whacked him with a song in my heart. But I'll always remember the beat of his pulse as I squeezed every last fucking bit of life out of him.

I'm not sure why I'm telling you this because this whacking never made it to the charge sheet and I don't want to stand in the dock again. Let me get back to Debbie. One spring morning in September, a warder called me for my weekly visit. I had hardly slept the previous night and was shivering with fear and anxiety. My prison uniform was freshly ironed, I had sprayed on an extra layer of Mum For Men and must have brushed my teeth at least three times. We walked past the visitors' section with its glass partitions and out into an open courtyard where the A and B birds could fraternise with their folks.

Debbie stood waiting for me. She looked more beautiful than ever before and had a smile on her face. I walked into her arms and our bodies melted together. It was as simple as that. Birds are generally allowed to hug their broads and get a hello and goodbye smack. Smooching is out of bounds. But of course they always find a way of slipping one another a tongue.

I pressed my mouth against Debbie's, and we stood like that for quite a while. Not open mouths or anything like that, but I was sure I could feel a stir somewhere inside me. I hadn't felt a tingle like that for quite some time. I've never really thought about shagging Debbie. It just didn't occur to me that it would ever be possible. Above all, she was not the kind of gal that you just take and have your way with.

We spoke little for the rest of the hour, but sat close together, our fingers entwined. Her hands were warmer and more tantalising than I'd ever imagined.

I was in love.

That night in my cell in The Bomb, I grabbed a pen and my feelings for her poured out.

My beautiful friend, my soulmate and the bright, shining light in this dark, lonely world I'm living in, you are my love, my life and my universe, and I want to spend the rest of my life with you. You are to me the most precious and rarest of diamonds that this world has ever seen.

The love I have for you is no ordinary love, but a burning, smouldering, eternal flame.

Dream of our love,
Gideon

One

Mom says the sixteenth of August 1966 was a dry, bleak and windy day on the Transvaal highveld. That was also the day she brought me into the world. She told me many years later that Dad had wrapped her in blankets on the back seat of the Valiant station wagon and rushed her to the Krugersdorp General Hospital to pop me out.

It was an exhausting birth, she said, and it was hours before the sister finally pulled me out and lifted me by my ankles. I dangled like a dead rabbit in the air and then she smacked me on my back. I huffed and puffed and then bawled in a high-pitched voice that echoed around the bare walls of the delivery room.

'I knew you were going to be a stubborn child,' Mom said. 'It was a difficult birth. You just didn't want to be in this world. And once I had you out, you wouldn't stop screaming.'

She said nothing helped. No amount of dummies, breast or solace succeeded in silencing me. Even when my tummy was full and Mom was cuddling me against her bosom, I fired off a yelp and erupted into a torrent of tears. Nothing deterred me. I was what Mom called a *koliekbaba* – a colicky baby. Then Dad made a wondrous discovery. One weekend we were on our way to a bushveld farm outside Potgietersrus in the old Transvaal. I was only two months old and lying fast asleep on my mother's lap on the front seat of the Valiant station wagon. This was long before the fuss about kids wearing seatbelts or toddlers being strapped into baby chairs secured to the back seat. As Dad turned into the Caltex garage in Warmbaths to fill up, I stirred to life. I stared wide-eyed at him and as the car jerked to a standstill, I started bawling uncontrollably. Unperturbed, Dad ordered Sipho – all his life he called black men Sipho, why I don't know but that's how it was – to put in fuel. As he pulled away and headed towards the main road, I fell silent. Dad looked at Mom and stopped the car. I opened my mouth wide and wailed. When he pulled off again, I snuggled up to Mom and my eyes closed.

They had found the secret to dealing with my colic.

In the days and months to come, I grew up in the Valiant station wagon. Mom and Dad, armed with a flask of strong black coffee and a half-jack of Klippies, took turns to drive me around Krugersdorp, usually down Voortrekker Street, left at the traffic light and down Ontdekkers Way past Roodepoort. I lay in dreamland in a plastic basket on the back seat. Those were the good old days when the Siphos had to be off the streets at night so the suburbs were quiet and safe.

As you might have gathered, I grew up in Krugersdorp, a rather dreary town west of Johannesburg. People who lived there called it shit like 'an industrial hub' or the 'gateway to the Witwatersrand goldfields'. The place was better known for unruly hordes of white trash that gathered every now and then at the Paardekraal Monument where they hoisted the *Vierkleur* and vowed to fuck up each and every Sipho.

But when I was growing up, Krugersdorp was the best place

in the world and I vowed never to leave it. My chest swelled at the thought of the town being named after the great president Paul Kruger, a guy with a long beard who took up arms against the English. I learned in school that a very important gathering of Boer leaders took place at Paardekraal, where they pledged never to surrender to the rooinekke. Hence the importance it gained in later years for Eugene Terre'Blanche and his AWB dregs.

We lived in a middle-class suburb in a neat three-bedroom house with a manicured garden. We had nothing to do with the low-class whites and pissed on the trailer-park scum of the town. These people had nothing else to do but hang around in bars and pick fights. Their daughters had a bun in the oven by the time they were sixteen, while the sons often had their first taste of prison food not long after their eighteenth birthday. On Sunday afternoons they roared and revved their Cortina Big Sixes through town and gathered at the local roadhouse where they drank Coke-floats. Dad warned us against the roadhouse, saying it was a nest of dagga smokers.

I was the second of three brothers. Family photographs show us standing like organ pipes with ice cream cones in our hands on the beach at Margate where we holidayed every December. In fact I had *two* ice creams in my hand. Mom told me that I had a nasty habit of roaming the beach searching for fathers and mothers buying cones for their kids. I would literally follow Sipho with his white box as he zigzagged through the blaze of umbrellas and beach towels and as soon as a deal went down, I would rush forward, pull a forlorn look and politely beg the uncle or auntie for a lolly. If they refused, I burst into a torrent of tears which usually resulted in me walking off with a cone in my hand and a smile on my face.

Dad snapped a photograph of me in my bathing trunks on the beach. I was bawling my heart out, although I already had an ice cream in one hand. Maybe I was trying to solicit a second. This photograph was in a frame in my parents' bedroom and was one of Mom's most prized possessions. When in later years I fell foul of the law and landed in prison, Mom would often say: 'I wonder what happened to my little ice cream boy?'

'I'm not little any more, Mom,' was my usual response.

'I wish you were.'

We were, at least on the face of it, a normal family. Karel was two years older than me and I towered over Pieter, although I was barely a year his senior. My younger brother was a bit of a retard. According to Karel he was born with the umbilical cord wrapped around his neck and as a result had suffered a shortage of oxygen. I have no idea how accurate this assessment was or where Karel got it from, but I worshipped the earth on which he moved and lapped up his every utterance. He was a whizz in every respect: faster, smarter and wiser than anyone I knew.

Pieter, on the other hand, was sickly, feeble and a sissy. He had been in a remedial class from his earliest years at school, but failed grade two. He still sucked on a dummy and peed and shat in his pants when he was eight years old. He didn't play sport and spent most of his time in the bedroom listening to *Die Geheim van Nantes* and other soaps on Springbok Radio. We also caught him playing with a doll that he had nicked from one of his cousins. Karel had burst into the garden shed and there was Pieter sitting on the floor, dressing or undressing his doll. He wrestled the plaything from his brother, saying, 'You're a moffie! Only moffies play with things like this.' He gleefully handed the doll to Dad who ripped it apart, threw it in the dustbin and dragged Pieter to the bedroom where he received the hiding of his life.

'And what sort of thing is a moffie?' I later asked Karel.

'It's a horrible thing. A boy who digs other boys,' he responded.

I was amazed. 'But I also dig boys!'

'*Ja*, but not like that. A moffie doesn't like girls.'

'But girls are ugh! Does that mean I'm a moffie?'

While Pieter was a mommy's boy, Karel and I were boyish and rugged and therefore more in tune with Dad. Don't get me wrong: I loved Mom dearly and I have only fond memories of her.

She was a homely woman who always wore her hair in a bun at the back of her head. She was a housewife and, according to dad, a damn good one at that. The house was always spotless and I grew up with the smell of floor and wood polish in my nose.

It's amazing how childhood memories flood back when you're locked away in a hole like Pretoria Central. There's too much time to think. The worst times are Sundays when a yearning for home and loved ones invades your mind. That's probably why the worst mischief in The Bomb is cooked up on the Sabbath. That's when the birds drink, smoke, fight, fuck, steal, whatever. I might well have been over in Auschwitz this afternoon having a Klippies if it wasn't for the fact that I'm sitting in my cell digging up my childhood memories.

I was properly homesick at lunch this afternoon. They threw the usual Sunday shit of boiled pork, samp and carrots at us. I craved Mom's Sunday lunch – standard fare of roast leg of lamb with rich brown gravy. It was always served with rice, baked potatoes, *boerboontjies* and *strooppampoen*. My favourite was the *boerboontjies* which I drenched in gravy and gobbled up.

I've mentioned that Karel and I were closer to Dad, who was a rugger-bugger-no-fucking-bullshit-nonsense Afrikaner. He was as mean and prickly as barbed wire. In my earlier years I was in awe of him, not only because he was a policeman and worked at nailing the baddies, but also because he was a fanatical sportsman.

Dad's life was consumed by sport. He had double provincial colours: for boxing and for rugby. He played lock forward for Transvaal and rugby was a religion in our home. The bar in the corner of the lounge was a kind of Transvaal rugby museum. On the wall were two framed rugby jerseys: one worn by Dad in a Currie Cup Final (they lost) and a Springbok jersey that one of his rugby friends sported against the All Blacks in 1949 (the Boks routed them).

It was not unusual for Dad to include the fortunes of Transvaal or the Springboks when he said grace at table. 'Father, bless the meal on the table and bless those of us who are in need,' he would start, and then continue: 'And, dear Father, bless our boys and make them strong enough to withstand any challenge they meet.'

Dad was a security police captain and a merciless and stubborn disciplinarian. He had a ruddy complexion – he downed at least half a bottle of Klippies every day – which was further marred by his crooked nose, clearly the result of far too many straight jabs that found their target. When he lost his temper, his face bulged like a toad's and changed from ruddy to bright red. This was the sign for all of us to get the fuck out of his proximity. Karel was lightning fast and would dart for the front door with me following close on his heels.

That left Pieter and my mother to bear the brunt of his wrath. Dad detested his last-born and the mere sight of Pieter seemed to make his blood boil. Nothing helped, not even when he had stopped shitting in his pants or tried to be less of a pansy by playing rugby or cops and robbers with us. How many times did I not witness Dad's oversized hairy hands swatting my little brother off his thin white legs?

And Mom? Well, unfortunately she always seemed to be in the way. She was very protective of Pieter and tried to shield him from Dad and landed up getting a hiding herself. To this day I believe that Dad really loved Mom, but he simply couldn't control his rage. It was devastating to see my mother getting fucked up by my father, especially when I couldn't do anything about it and loved both of them so much.

Mom, I have to say, took her beatings with grace. Even when a multitude of punches thumped down on her, she never whined. She kept her cool and afterwards sneaked into our room to comfort the three of us sitting wide-eyed on our beds.

I was ten years old when Karel said to me one night: 'Dad has to go to court.'

I understood court to be a place for murderers and criminals. 'Why?' I wanted to know. 'What has he done?'

'They say he killed a *houtkop*.'

A *houtkop* was a derogatory name for a black, or a kaffir as most people called them in those days.

I'm hesitant to use the so-called k-word these days because people brand you a racist and say you hate them and you can get fucked up for it. Back then there was nothing improper about it. In fact they had many other names as well. Some people referred to them as Bantus and, as you know, Dad called them Siphos. Karel and most of our friends tagged them *houtkoppe*.

'Why *houtkoppe*?' I once asked him.

'Because you have to bash their heads very hard in order to crack them,' he replied.

Mom later explained to us why Dad had to go to court. She said that his job was not just to nab criminals, but also to ask them questions so that they could be taken to court and sent to prison. While Dad was doing exactly that, she said, this Sipho had dived through the window, landed on his head and died.

'It must have been a *moer* of a dive,' cracked Karel.

'Yes, well, he's dead and now Dad must go to court to explain what happened. Don't worry, everything will be fine.'

Dad wriggled himself into a suit the next morning, strapped a tie decorated with yellow flowers around his neck and got into the Valiant. That night, as he brooded with a brandy next to the radio, listening to evening prayers, Karel and I approached him warily and asked him what had happened in court.

His eyes were bloodshot and he glared at us without saying a word. I looked at his boxer's hands and took a step back. He lifted his hand, but instead of *klapping* us, he said: 'Gideon, Karel, come here.' He put his glass on the side table, grabbed Karel and me by the arm, and pulled us closer to him. He had never done that before.

'You two laaities must know something,' he said in a boozy slur. 'I did it for you. There're people who want to take this country away from us. Sipho wants to put his children in your place in school. He wants to go to Margate for a holiday and force you to work for him. You'll be Sipho's slave.'

Karel asked: 'Are you talking about terrorists, Dad?'

'Yes, I am, son. Terrorists and communists. One and the same thing.'

I was acquainted with terrorists and communists, although my reference was a cheesy comic-book warrior by the name of Captain Caprivi. Karel had a whole collection of Captain Caprivis hidden in a drawer – along with two *Scope* magazines that were jam-packed with bikini babes with knock-out knockers. His Bible and Sunday school exercise books were stacked on top.

My favourite Captain Caprivi adventure was titled 'Attack on the Vaal Dam'. Some dudes plotted to blow up the Vaal Dam near Johannesburg and starve the city's whites of water. Guess who was behind this dastardly scheme? Who else but Mother Russia in the personae of Comrade Colonel Kasparov and Comrade Captain Boris? Their troopers were a platoon of *houtkoppe*, dressed in gardener-like overalls and armed with machine guns. One of them carried a suitcase in which the bomb was hidden.

As the saboteurs plotted their way to the dam, Captain Caprivi, dressed only in cam pants and army boots, burst on to the scene. Two bullet belts were draped across his hairy chest. In one hand he clutched his shooting iron, in the other a long steel knife. With a 'Take this, you damned communist!' the good Captain broke Kasparov's neck, booted Boris off the wall and mowed the *houtkoppe* down. It didn't look as though they were very good shots. He disarmed the bomb seconds before it was due to explode.

'Dad, are they like the people in Captain Caprivi?' I dared to ask.

Karel kicked my shin. Dad stared menacingly at me. 'I saw one at the barber the other day,' I countered. 'Captain Caprivi threw them off the dam wall.'

'Yes, something like that,' Dad said as he put his hand on my shoulder. 'One day, you two boys will also have to go and fight these terrorists.'

My face lit up. 'Like Captain Caprivi, Dad?'

'Yes, sort of.'

It was a fantastic prospect. Karel and I were already playing Captain Caprivi on an almost daily basis. Karel had made the role of Captain Caprivi his own while I played Corporal Strydom, his trusted and merciless adjutant. We usually dragged Pieter from the house to play Comrades Boris or Kasparov. He steadfastly refused to be a *houtkop*. My little brother made the perfect terrorist or communist because he couldn't run fast and was hopeless at hiding himself and we mercilessly hunted him down in the open veld behind our house. Our favourite action was to tie him to the bluegum tree in the backyard and interrogate him. The game almost always ended with Pieter in tears and Karel taunting him as a sissy and a moffie.

Karel had a friend whose brother was in the army and had recently returned from the border in South West. I remember him sitting with his big, black machine gun on the bed while we sat in a circle on the carpet at his feet. He recounted spellbinding experiences of tracking and hunting down terrorists. He called them Swapos, a term I didn't understand, except that they were black and bad.

'When you shoot a Swapo, it doesn't look like the movies at all,' he said.

'What *does* it look like?' we asked simultaneously.

He held a big bullet in the air. 'Can you imagine what happens,' he trumpeted, 'when I pump this into your head?'

'What?'

'It disappears. You have a head no more.'

For the week that Dad was in court, Karel, Pieter and I prayed like never before. We had a standard prayer we recited before bedtime every night. Kneeling next to our beds with our hands clasped in front of us, we repeated one after the other: 'Dear Jesus, I'm a child small and frail, make my heart clean and pure.' With Dad being in shit, we added: 'And dear Jesus, please don't let Dad go to prison. Amen.'

It worked. The judge found that Dad was not guilty and that nobody was to blame for the *houtkop*'s death. When he came home that night, he was pissed out of his skull but instead of turning on Pieter and Mom as he often did when he was plastered, he was cheery and carrying a box of fish and chips in his hand. The next morning there was a big photograph of Dad in the newspaper. It showed him beaming from ear to ear, posing with his thumbs in the air. The headline announced: 'Top cop off the hook.'

On the Saturday following Dad's reprieve, a troop of policemen descended on our house for a celebration party. Earlier that morning, Dad had bought piles of boerewors and chops and several bottles of Klippies and Coke. Karel played barman and I helped Dad with the fire and the meat. Pieter was told that it was an adult bash and so he had to stay in his room or help his mother in the kitchen.

Dad had shown Karel exactly how to pour a respectable brandy and Coke, a so-called *drie-vinger*. He had to count one-two-three at a sluggish pace – that made the glass about half full – and top it up with Coke. Karel was a busy boy, running to and fro filling empty glasses.

'This is how real police coffee should taste!' more than one cop happily exclaimed.

By the time the meat was sizzling on the coals and Mom and Pieter brought out the *pap-en-sous*, the guests were plastered. The army of shirtless cops, their *boepe* hanging over their khaki pants, was a peculiar sight. Some lounged around on the stoep, others played touch rugby on the lawn, while some frolicked drunkenly with one another in the inflatable children's pool.

This was equal to the best school jamboree I'd ever been to. Dad was a hero and revered by his colleagues, who agreed that he deserved a medal. Saying grace before the guests tucked in, Dad made special mention of God's grace in opening the judge's eyes and enabling him to see the light. When Dad opened his eyes, they were wet. It was the first time that I had seen the big man so close to tears.

By the time the mound of chops and sausage was reduced to a pile of bones, satisfied burps echoed around the stoep and Gerhard Viviers' comforting voice was announcing the kick-off of the rugby test match between the All Blacks and the Springboks in Bloemfontein. Viviers was a legendary radio commentator, as celebrated as any of the players.

I was ten years old at the time and had no clue that the 1976 All Blacks tour to South Africa was plagued with controversy. The tour almost coincided with the student uprising in Soweto, although many white South Africans regarded the unrest as nothing more than a silly tiff between communist-inspired agitators and our boys in blue, who fortunately had matters tightly under control.

As Springbok captain Wynand Claasens led the boys in green and gold on to the pitch, Dad ordered us to bring Springbokkies, an alcoholic concoction devised to affirm one's support for the national rugby team. Dad had earlier explained to Karel how to make it: a generous tot of peppermint liqueur topped with a layer of cream liqueur with another coat of the green stuff on top. It (more or less) resembled the colours of the Springbok rugby jersey. Being ardent supporters ourselves, Karel and I both secretly swallowed a Springbokkie. Karel was the first to imitate the grown-ups and tossed the concoction to the back of his throat. His eyes just about popped out of their sockets and he had to bend over to hold on to his breath. I followed suit and, although I don't want to boast, I handled it far better than Karel. Apart from being short of breath for a second or two, I was fine. I was clearly a born boozer.

It was a calamitous day for the Springboks. Grim-faced and clutching their 'police coffee' to their chests, the policemen listened in disgust as the All Blacks routed their more favoured adversaries. The mood around the transistor had by then turned ugly and the conversation moved on to the international campaign against our country. The All Black tour had led to an African boycott of the Olympic Games in the same year and throughout the world hordes of filthy *takhaar* protesters armed with placards were urging the All Blacks to go home. Dad and his friends were openly baying for the blood of whoever was complicit in the Boks' defeat: the New Zealanders, hippies, terrorists, communists, *houtkoppe*.

'Fucking barbarians!' said one cop.

'They just want our country,' said another.

'This is a bloody communist plot to get our minerals,' Dad said as he took a deep gulp of his police coffee. 'They're behind the trouble in the *lokasies*.'

Everybody nodded their heads in agreement. A thin-lipped, bespectacled man sporting a cravat and a jacket spoke: 'The communists won't rest until they have shackled all of us.'

Dad had told us earlier that this dude was a colonel and the commander of their unit. As such, he had to be treated with utmost respect and Karel had to keep his glass filled to the brim. I didn't quite understand what the colonel was saying, but Karel whispered in my ear: 'It's the terrorists and the *houtkoppe*. They're part of it.'

Karel and I were listening open-mouthed to the wisdom being flaunted right in front of us. 'That's right, Colonel,' said Dad, 'it's only by the grace of the Almighty God that we are still free to pray, braai our meat and listen to the rugby.'

A sturdy cop with a pinkish complexion and a bald head clambered to his feet and held his police coffee in the air. 'I want to propose a toast,' he babbled, 'to Hendrik Goosen and what he has done for us. I thank God he's in our midst today.'

'I will drink to that,' said the colonel and got to his feet. 'Not that there was ever any doubt about the outcome. We look after our men.'

As the cops downed their blackish concoctions, lifted their glasses and held them towards Dad, my chest just about burst with pride. There was no doubt that he had simply done his duty. It wasn't his fault that the *houtkop* had dived through the window and met his Maker with a thud on the pavement.

'Let me show you what we do to the troublemakers,' Dad said and marched into the house. He returned with a thick brown file under his arm. He slammed it down on the table and flipped it open. The policemen assembled around it.

'*Jissus God*, Hendrik,' ejaculated a cop. 'You really clobbered him, hey?'

'You really fucked him up!' said another.

Karel and I wrestled our way through the sea of burly forearms and ballooning waists. On the table in front of us were four photographs. Television had just arrived in the country and although I had watched action movies like Clint Eastwood's 'Dirty Harry' and 'The Green Berets', this was different. It was real.

'It's the *houtkop* that fell through the window,' Karel whispered in my ear.

The dead man's eyes were stretched wide open. His skull had shattered and mushy, sticky stuff spilled on to the pavement. His fleshy lips were slightly parted and a thin line of blood trickled out of his mouth. Another picture showed him lying on his side with his hands shackled behind his back. I was so startled and so scared that I could hardly breathe.

'What a beautiful sight,' laughed a cop.

'Is this a terrie, Dad?' Karel dared to ask.

'That's what a terrie looks like, my son,' Dad said. 'A beautiful terrie!'

Everybody laughed. 'The only good terrie is a dead terrie!' echoed another policeman. I stared at the photographs until Dad closed the file and Karel pulled me away. By then the cops had lost interest and wandered off for another police coffee.

As I got into bed later that night, the image of the *houtkop* rumbled like an angry volcano in my head. I woke up in a pool of sweat. Throughout my dreams this man, things dribbling out of his head and his eyes like saucers, chased me through the house, down the aisle at church, and across the rugby field at school. I swerved and veered and ducked and dived, but he stayed on my heels.

The image stayed in my head for a long time afterwards.

Two

The photograph of the dead *houtkop* caused us endless shit. Karel had nicked one of the pics and showed it to his mates at school. Karel was in standard six and I was still in primary school. He recounted with glee how Dad sculpted this bad Sipho into a good Sipho and, as far as I could gather, the treasured possession substantially enhanced his stature. Boys bought him chips at the tuck shop and, with the picture in his hand, he chased girls around the playground.

He also terrorised his little brother by shoving the photograph in his face. To our amusement, Pieter burst into tears and pulled his pillow over his head. 'Moffie,' Karel accused him, adding: 'If you ever tell Dad about this, you will look like this Sipho.'

We should have known better. Pieter couldn't keep his mouth shut and blurted everything out to Mom who in turn alerted

Dad. Dad strode into the house that afternoon without greeting anyone and summoned Karel, Pieter and me to our room. He was flushed and he reeked of brandy. Armageddon was about to be unleashed on us.

'Where's it?' Dad demanded. Tears welled up in my eyes. 'Where the fuck is it?' Dad thundered.

Karel hesitantly produced the photograph. With a long, slow thump Dad *klapped* him to the floor. His upper lip was split open and blood seeped out of it. By then Pieter and I were bawling our lungs out. Dad turned to me. 'Do you know anything about this?' He didn't wait for an answer and smacked the side of my head.

I collapsed, screaming, on to my bed. Pieter sat on the floor, shrieking at the top of his voice.

Dad took off his belt and walked back to Karel. 'Bend over,' he ordered. Karel bit down on his lower lip in order not to cry. Without waiting for him to oblige, Dad lifted the belt above his head and thrashed it down on his body. 'You want to get me into shit, hey?' he shouted as the blows rained down on Karel, who didn't utter a sound. I didn't want to watch the carnage and covered my face with my hands.

Dad turned to me. I pushed my face into my pillow as the leather crashed down on my buttocks. I didn't count the blows but there were many more than six. Eventually he stopped and, seconds later, the volume of Pieter's wailing grew as Dad turned on his youngest son.

Mom's voice cut like a knife through the room. 'Leave him, Hendrik!' she demanded. 'He had nothing to do with this!'

I lifted my head and saw Mom standing in the doorway. Dad looked up, clicked his tongue contemptuously and continued pelting Pieter, who was screaming blue murder.

My mother took a few steps forward and as Dad reached the top of his backswing, she grabbed the belt and said in a piercing voice: 'That is enough!'

For a moment Dad gawked at Mom, his expression one of astonishment. He probably couldn't believe that his dutiful spouse was challenging his authority in front of his kids. Mom was a tiny woman and Dad towered like a beast over her. He regained his composure and, without saying a word, he pulled back his hairy hand and smashed it into her face. She flopped backwards and landed on her back. I swallowed my tears and stared at Mom lying in a heap on the floor. Pieter had also stopped crying. Dad took one long look at her, pointed his finger at Pieter and said: 'I'm not finished with you yet.'

Then he walked out of the room.

It took Mom a few minutes to struggle to her feet. She held her hand against her cheek where a blue tennis ball was fast appearing. Pieter was crying again and holding on to her skirt. Without saying a word, she kissed him on his head and shuffled out of our room. We didn't see her again that night.

There was no breakfast on the table the next morning and we had to get dry bread and milk for ourselves. Dad was sound asleep on the couch, an empty Klippies bottle on the floor next to him. Mom did not emerge from her room.

When we came home from school that afternoon Mom was waiting for us with two packed suitcases. 'We're leaving,' she announced. There was a swelling the colour of a ripe plum on her left cheek.

'Where to?' Karel wanted to know.

'We're going to Aunt Magdalena,' she said. 'She's coming to fetch us in a few minutes.'

'Why are we going there?' Karel asked.

'We're going to live there for a while,' Mom said. 'We can't stay here.'

I could feel my heart sinking into my shoes. 'Why not?' I asked.

'Because your father will kill us.'

Karel shook his head and said: 'I'm not going. I'm staying here.'

Pieter walked towards Mom and took her hand. It was clear that he'd made up his mind to go with her.

'There's no way I'm going,' Karel said and turned to me.

I was torn. I looked at Mom standing hand in hand with

Pieter next to the two suitcases. She was in a wretched state and her eyes were filled with tears. Every few seconds she touched the bruise on her cheek and I realised that she must have been in extreme pain.

'I'm going to phone Dad,' said Karel and started walking towards the lounge.

'Please don't phone your father, Karel,' Mom pleaded. 'Do you want him to really kill me?'

Karel stopped, turned around and said: 'Well, I'm not going anywhere.' He looked at me and said: 'And neither are you. This is our home and we're not leaving Dad alone.'

My mind had been made up for me. Minutes later, Mom and Pieter were gone. Karel and I waited apprehensively for Dad to come home. As we expected, he erupted like a volcano. His face turned the colour of ripe strawberries and he clenched his fists and shouted: 'That fucking bitch! She and her little bastard child!' He let out a snort of disgust. 'I'll fucking kill them!'

Dad poured himself a stiff brandy and Coke and got on to the phone. Karel and I stood wide-eyed as Dad ranted and raved for the next ten minutes, spitting out words we'd never heard before. When he finally slammed down the phone, he turned around and said: 'You know what? She can fucking stay where she is! I don't want her back.'

It was Karel who finally said: 'Dad, we haven't eaten yet.' He took us to the kitchen, opened a tin of bully beef, threw four eggs into a pan and cut two thick slices of bread. The eggs were dry and rubbery but we were hungry and wolfed them down. Dad filled up his glass and flopped into his Lazyboy where he brooded until he fell asleep.

For the first time ever there was nobody to put us to bed. As we got into our pyjamas, I said to Karel: 'We have to say our prayers.'

'No, we don't,' he said as he slid into bed. 'Mom's not here.'

The household was in chaos. By the third day of Mom's leaving, I could no longer face bully beef. There were no cooked breakfasts or yummy lunch boxes, the beds were left unmade and our school uniforms were dirty and wrinkled.

Without Mom to pep him up, Dad was tumbling off the rails. He was drinking more and more heavily and by eight or nine every night he had passed out in his Lazyboy. Karel, who was already smoking secretly, also started taking sips of Dad's brandy and Coke every time he had to fill up his glass. The two of us finished Mom's Old Brown Sherry that was standing in the bar next to the bottle of Klippies.

'This place looks like a whorehouse after a police raid,' Dad growled one morning. 'It can't go on like this. I have to persuade Mom to come back. Otherwise we have to get a servant.'

Two days later, an elderly black woman knocked on the back door. 'Morning, *kleinbaas*,' she said to me. 'My name is Martha. And how is the *kleinbaas* this morning?'

I stared at her without responding and called Dad. I'd never had any interaction with a black woman before because we'd never had a servant. Dad was always vehemently against a servant working in the house. He said he wasn't going to let a pair of black hands cook his food or bring up his children. They also steal, he said. In those days, black women were generally referred to as *meide*, which was sort of the female equivalent of kaffir. Although father referred to black men as Siphos, he didn't have a similar name for women.

We simply referred to Martha as our *meid*. Father inspected her pass in order to make sure that she was legally entitled to work in Krugersdorp and warned her that he was a policeman and should anything disappear from the house, he would lock her up and throw away the key. When we came home that afternoon, we were met by the smell of floor polish and the aroma of roasting meat. Martha was a mighty fine housekeeper.

Dad was wooing Mom to come back. He started visiting her at Aunt Magdalena where she and Pieter were staying and one day he even took her a box of chocolates. According to Karel, who always seemed to know everything, Dad had promised to stop drinking and never to beat her or us again. Mom and Pieter visited us twice to pick up clothes and to make sure we were okay. We were delighted to see her and she held us to her for a long time. When we finally pulled away, she had tears in her eyes.

'You look neglected,' she said as she looked us up and down.

'We're fine, Mom,' Karel assured her.

'Are you saying your prayers every night?'

'Of course, Mom,' Karel lied. We had stopped saying prayers the day Mom absconded and hadn't been to Sunday school since.

Although Karel and I were delighted with Martha's cooking skills, Mom was disgusted when she found a layer of dust on the Lowry organ that dad had bought her on their tenth wedding anniversary.

'It's clear that the *meid* doesn't know how to clean,' she said. 'I'll have to come back.'

'When?' I wanted to know.

'Another week or two,' she said. 'As soon as Dad and I have sorted things out.'

Karel and I were less delighted to see Pieter, who was glued to Mom's dress and didn't let her out of his sight. When she took Martha aside for a dressing-down on the state of the house, Karel asked Pieter: 'And so, do you enjoy playing dolls with your cousins?'

Pieter looked at his feet and didn't answer. 'If it wasn't for you, this shit would never have happened,' snarled Karel.

Pieter still didn't respond but his lower lip quivered. As he turned around and walked after Mom, Karel said: 'You stupid fucking moffie.'

A week later Mom and Pieter returned. Everybody was delighted, except Martha who was unceremoniously told to leave and not come back again. For a week or two, everything was hunky-dory. Dad drank less and was courteous and even loving towards Mom. Even the usually irksome Pieter was, in Karel's words, 'Not pissing in his panties all the time.'

Where did I fit into all of this? I suppose I was the quiet one, forever lurking in Karel's shadow. But then – and thank God for that – I avoided the attention that poor Pieter drew to himself. I was average in everything and excelled at nothing. I was in the B Class and got around sixty per cent for most subjects.

When I was arrested many years later and journalists flocked to Krugersdorp to probe my past and search for the reasons for what the judge labelled my 'animalistic behaviour', hardly anyone could remember me.

My highlights at school? There weren't many, but the one that stood out was scoring the winning try for the first rugby team when I was in standard five, my last year in primary school. It pleased Dad immensely and elevated me to celebrity status for a week or so.

I was a tall, skinny fellow and only started gaining weight at around sixteen. Because of my frail frame, I couldn't stand up to my classmates physically and was a rather mediocre rugby player. I always played second team and in an effort to find my niche, I changed from position to position. I was fullback until someone kicked a high ball on me. I didn't just miss the ball, but the wind was knocked out of me and I was trampled into the dust. I eventually went to hide in the scrum, at hooker nogal! As Dad said: in the heart of the oven!

I preferred the hooker position for two reasons. One was that it was an easy place to hide. You never had to touch the ball and thus avoided being tackled. The second was that although I had limited ball skills, I had a lightning-fast hook foot. My team often stole the opposition's throw-in at the scrums, not because we were necessarily stronger, but as a result of my foot raking the ball to our side. I even acquired a nickname: Mamba.

I just couldn't get into the A Side. The headmaster's son was the first team's hooker and however fast my foot flashed, I was the second choice. This all changed when our first team – under 13A – reached the finals of the West Rand schools rugby league. The headmaster's son got sick, and the coach (apprehensively) promoted me to the A Team. In the week preceding the match, the local paper published a team photograph. Dad joked, saying that the Goosens had been in the paper twice: him for fucking up the *houtkop* and me for playing in the finals!

I don't remember much of the match. I plodded around the field, upheld my nickname by turning over two or three of their scrums, but as always managed to avoid touching the ball. That was until the final minute. The score was even at nine-all. There was a line-out on the opposition's try-line. It was their throw-in. As hooker, I was standing at the front of the line-out. Their lock raked high into the air to grab the ball, but he failed to gather it cleanly and knocked it back towards his side.

Their scrumhalf couldn't pick up the ball and knocked it on. By then I was doing not much more than standing around watching the commotion. As a result of the scrummie's handling error, the ball rolled in my direction. The next moment, the egg-shaped leather ball was lying right in front of me, in their goal area!

I dived. I hovered for a moment or two in space, and then came crashing down on top of the ball. Several of their forwards piled on top of me and just about knocked me senseless. But it didn't matter, because I'd scored a try. And what was more, the winning try! I staggered to my feet with the ball in my hand. My team mates descended on me, hugging and embracing me.

As we walked off the field, I noticed two people. One was Dad, standing up and waving his hands. The other was a short, rather plump girl with a pair of black pigtails. Her name was Linda Botes and she was in the same class as me. She looked straight at me and for a moment our eyes locked.

I had been in love with her for ages but never had the guts to ask her to *kys* – an Afrikaans word for a pre-teen love affair. My new post-rugby match status changed all of that and gave me new impetus to make her mine. The Monday following the rugby final, the headmaster spoke of the winning try at weekly assembly. He said: 'Gideon, stand up so that we can see you.'

My hands sweaty, I got to my feet. The school cheered and the headmaster said: 'Son, that was the finest dive I've ever seen!'

It was time to make my move. As school ended and we filed out of class, I pressed a note into Linda's hand. 'Will you be my girlfriend?' I had written a similar note probably a hundred times during the year but never had the guts to give it to her. The next day there was a folded piece of paper on my desk. It was from Linda, and I opened it with quivering hands. It contained one word: 'Yes.' That letter became one of my most treasured possessions and I kept it in my Bible.

Our love affair consisted of tenderly goggling at each other during school breaks. We never really spoke. What was there to talk about?

Then Linda wrote me another letter. 'Would you like to visit me on Friday afternoon at our plot?'

There were several problems with Linda. The first was that she was a *maplotter*, an Afrikaans word for a poor white who lived on a smallholding. That meant that she and her family came from the wrong side of town. They were part of a settlement of poor whites that squatted on a batch of smallholdings on the outskirts of Krugersdorp. The smallholdings were usually unkempt and overrun by chickens and pigs and car wrecks.

And then she looked coloured. Today we would say she was olive-skinned and exotic but in those days people with brown skins were frowned upon. It was generally accepted that their daddies or forefathers had bonked the servant. It didn't matter to me but I had to keep my love business secret.

The third problem was that Linda and her family were members of the Apostolic Church. Our *Nederduits Gereformeerde*, or Dutch Reformed Church looked down on the Apostolics. They were generally regarded as a bunch of downtrodden happy-clappies who played drums and guitars in church and only baptised their children once they had grown up. They stood, so to say, right at the back of the queue to heaven.

But I wrote back 'yes', upon which I got another letter. Linda said I could go home on the bus with her. Her father would take me home later in the afternoon. I didn't sleep that night.

The next morning, I pinched one of Karel's seven-single records: 'Love is a Beautiful Song' sung by Dave Mills. I thought I would take it with me in case the family had a hi-fi. Many *maplotters* might not have had enough to eat, but they all had powerful Sonys and Cortina Big Sixes.

It was one of the most beautiful afternoons of my life. She first showed me around the smallholding while an army of little brothers and sisters loitered behind us. Their yard was neat and organised and didn't smell of pig shit as I had expected. Her father was an avid dove breeder, while her mother farmed turkeys.

'Christmas lunch,' she said. Those were amongst the only words we spoke that afternoon. We later sat in the lounge where her mom – a jovial auntie with a broad smile – served cupcakes and Oros. A big Sony was indeed displayed in the corner. I pulled out the seven-single. She took it without a word and put it on the turntable.

Love is a beautiful song
La-la, la-la-la, la-la

As Dave Mills chirped away, our eyes met. We were unaware of the world around us; of the little heads peeking around the door to see what we were up to or her mom bringing more cake and cold drink. This was true love and I was convinced it would last for ever.

It didn't. In fact it was very short-lived. The next morning, Karel discovered his seven-single was gone. In my state of love I had left the record behind at the smallholding. Karel knew it was me and although I tried to run away, he tackled me to the ground and tortured the truth out of me. Although I begged him to keep it between us, he gleefully babbled out my secret at the dinner table that night.

'And who is this Linda?' Dad demanded to know.

'Her surname is Botes, Dad,' I said.

'Hmm,' he pondered. 'And Karel said you visited her yesterday.'

'Yes, Dad.'

'And where do they live?'

I couldn't lie. 'Luipaardsvlei, Dad.'

'On the plots?'

'Yes, Dad.'

Dad looked up from his plate and said: 'I don't want you to go there again.'

I could feel my heart breaking. But I also knew that it was fatal to argue with Dad. I simply looked down at my plate and said: 'Yes, Dad.' As if that wasn't bad enough, Karel added gleefully: 'And they're Apostolic, Dad.'

My love affair was in jeopardy. To make things worse, I was shortly afterwards humiliated in the most excruciating manner by the most revolting kid in school. Gerhard Keulder was an overweight red-faced *maplotter*. His parents were really down and out and he was ridiculed terribly because he was so podgy. I had always kind of pissed on him but he really stirred my wrath when I discovered that he was also in love with Linda.

When Gerhard heard that Linda and I had a thing going, he turned nasty. It headed for a showdown when he pulled her hair at the end of class, just before break, and she burst into tears. I was never a fighter at school and was generally regarded as a bit of a namby-pamby, but I had no option but to challenge Gerhard to a fight there and then. My classmates, all rooting for me, formed a circle around us. Linda stood a few metres away, clearly expecting her beau to demolish this vermin in our midst.

I hoisted my fists and started dancing around Gerhard. 'Come on, fight!' I said and pushed out a right hand that landed slightly short of his chest. Gerhard slowly raised his fists. The fight was on.

I was still contemplating my next move when something startling happened. It was as though somebody had ignited a bomb cracker in Gerhard's arse. To this day I don't know what spurred him into action. Maybe he was inflamed by years of belittlement and had decided that he'd had enough.

I never even saw it coming. Gerhard's fist exploded against the side of my cheek. It wasn't unusual for me to be *klapped* in my face. Dad did it often enough, but almost every time I knew it was coming and I could brace myself and it was, after all, well, Dad. This was wholly unexpected. But it was the second blow that did the real damage.

I must have dropped my fists – something that Karel had taught me many times before was an absolute no-no during a bout. Gerhard's second punch landed slap-bang on my nose. I staggered back, blood streaming from my punctured orifice. I could feel the tears welling in my eyes. The fight was over. I kept my eyes shut and held my hands over my nose in an effort to stop the bleeding. I could hear my classmates laughing and jeering. My love affair was on the rocks.

Fortunately, Karel was flying our flag and was a born bruiser. He never lost any contest. Most of the town's feuds were settled on a Friday afternoon at the vlei on the edge of town where the combatants would take up fists in the presence of a crowd of ebullient supporters and onlookers. It was usually a free-for-all as they got into one another with fists, elbows, heads, knees, teeth and boots.

The fight I remember best was the one with Paul Reyneke. This dude wasn't just any skivvy, but the son of Dominee Reyneke, our preacher. We attended his sermons every other Sunday if Mom managed to rouse Dad from his slumbers.

The quarrel between the two had its roots in Paul's sister, a hottie by the name of Elsa. She had most of the boys' blood boiling with her long, white legs that she knew exactly how to flaunt, while her angelic face was adorned by a pair of green eyes and framed by wavy brown locks. Elsa was in fact the only good reason to go to church. The Reyneke family always parked in the bench right behind the elders and throughout the sermon my eyes were fixed on her.

Karel and Elsa were both in their first year in secondary school and were in the same class. Like the rest of us, he was besotted with her and had asked her several times to *kys*. He had told me more than once: 'I'm still going to play *stinkvingertjie* with her!'

'Sis, man!' I responded. I had an idea what this was but I couldn't quite comprehend such a vile activity. 'What's *stinkvingertjie?'*

He just laughed and made up-and-down movements with his middle finger. 'You'll see. Just wait.'

Elsa had always rejected Karel's advances and apparently told her schoolmates that the Goosens were drunks and losers. This infuriated Karel and so he terrorised Elsa. When he took the photograph of the dead Sipho to school, Elsa was one of the girls he chased around the playground. He threw itchy powder – Think-Pink fibreglass – down her back in the classroom and emptied a bottle of writhing earthworms into her school bag.

The spat between the two of them reached a climax when they bumped into one another at break. Karel told her to stop thinking that she pissed eau de cologne and that she was better than the rest of us. According to Elsa, he also attempted to touch her breast. She ran to Paul who challenged Karel to settle their score on Friday at the vlei.

News of the bout spread fast and about twenty children assembled at the vlei for what promised to be the fight of the month. Paul had brought a whole entourage with him that included Elsa, who was still in her school uniform and as beautiful as ever. I was Karel's only backer and held his jacket as he loosened up.

Paul was two years older than Karel and two or three inches taller. He was brimming with confidence as he faced Karel and lifted his fists. Without even looking at Paul or taking up a proper position, Karel took off and belted him with a right in his stomach – or slightly below. Paul folded double, his face showing his agony. Karel kicked him in the ribs. As he fell, Karel was on him, punching his head, his face, all over his body. When he got up, Paul's face was a mess and he was groaning with pain.

Karel was about to walk away when he looked at Elsa, took a few steps back and kicked Paul's face as hard as he could. He smiled, took his jacket from me and said: 'Come, *boet*, let's go home.'

When I glanced back over my shoulder, Elsa was kneeling next to Paul. She was crying. I felt an urge to run back and comfort her.

Dominee Reyneke knocked on our door early that evening. Karel had broken Paul's nose and cracked a rib. Dad invited him in, mother made coffee and Karel was summoned to the lounge to explain his violent conduct. Karel looked as though butter wouldn't melt in his mouth. He said that Paul had challenged him and he had merely defended himself. In the end, his only punishment was that he had to go on his knees and endure an excruciatingly long prayer from Dominee Reyneke in which he begged the Lord to bless Karel with the love of Abraham, the patience of Job and the wisdom of Solomon.

After the dominee left, Dad patted Karel on his shoulder and said: 'Well done, son. We Goosens don't take shit from anybody.'

Three

My insipid little brother was blessed with an exceptional gift: he could sing. Mom called Pieter her Little Nightingale. It was astonishing what crystal-clear sounds emerged from his tiny throat. He was only ten when he performed the main role in the school operetta. He played Moon in *Skrikkeljanie*, a fable of love, hate and revenge amongst the planets and the stars. Pieter appeared on stage in a blue satin costume with a yellow moon draped across his chest. Venus was Moon's bride but unfortunately she towered over him like an oak over an acorn. The wedding ceremony bordered on the farcical, but when Moon opened his mouth to serenade his new number, he evoked a standing ovation.

Mom announced at the dinner table: 'Pieter has been selected for the Drakensberg Boys' Choir.'

'What's that?' Karel asked. I was astounded that Pieter, who was grinning widely, could have been selected for anything. His life had been a model of mediocrity.

'It's the top boys' choir in the country,' said Mom. 'There's a music school in the Drakensberg where the boys learn to sing and then they tour the whole world.'

She explained that a choirmaster from the Drakensberg School had attended the operetta and heard Pieter sing. He immediately offered him a scholarship.

'But what about his learning problems?' asked Karel.

'They said they'll provide remedial education.'

Dad, who hadn't even looked up from his plate of bobotie, spoke for the first time: 'Over my fucking dead body!'

Pieter's grin was wiped off his face and Mom looked perplexed. 'But Hendrik, why not? It's a fantastic opportunity.'

'Over my dead body will any of my children attend that school.'

'Why not?' asked Mom again.

'It's a nest,' said Dad.

'Of what?'

'Homosexuality,' he said. 'And many other unholy things.'

'What do you mean, Hendrik?' asked Mom.

'It's a well-known fact,' said Dad as he stuffed another forkful of bobotie into his mouth, 'that the school is full of moffies.'

'Oh nonsense!' exclaimed Mom. 'You're talking nonsense!'

Dad threw down his knife and fork. 'It's not fucking nonsense!' he thundered, slamming his fist on the table. 'And don't you dare talk to me like that!'

He thrust his finger at Pieter and continued: 'You are not going anywhere! And that's final!'

Pieter burst out crying. 'Stop it!' ordered Dad, but the volume of his sobbing simply increased. 'You're not a fucking baby!' he bellowed.

By then Pieter was wailing uncontrollably. Dad rose menacingly to his feet, grabbed him by the collar and dragged him out of the dining room. We could hear the fracas in the bedroom as dad *klapped* him.

When he strutted back into the dining room, Mom was also crying. Dad gave her one glance, pointed at the door and ordered: 'Maria, go to the bedroom! I'm not listening to your shit any longer!'

As my mother left the dining room, Dad looked at Karel and me and said: 'And you two: eat!' He stuffed more food into his mouth and continued: 'What on earth have I done to deserve that little shit?'

The choir story was just another example of how stony-hearted and merciless Dad was towards Pieter. He just couldn't do anything right. Dad made no secret of the fact that as far as he was concerned his youngest son was a pain in the arse. Pieter was a puny, fragile boy with not a hell of a lot of marbles upstairs and therefore he was an embarrassment in front of other people. He didn't take part in sport, preferring to sing, play with dolls and bake cakes with Mom. Dad resented him. I thought things couldn't get worse – but they did.

The following Saturday around lunchtime, Dad announced: 'I'm going out.'

'Where're you going, Hendrik?' Mom asked.

'The Leopard,' he said. 'I'm going to listen to the rugby.'

The Leopard was the nickname for the Luipaardsvlei Hotel, a Krugersdorp landmark and institution. Dad was a regular at The Leopard and this caused endless shit between him and Mom. She insisted that she didn't want her husband to mingle with the scum that frequented the establishment and that it sent the wrong signal to the kids. Dad maintained that he frequented The Leopard purely to listen to the rugby. After all, he said, one of my Transvaal rugby jerseys is on display in the bar.

He wasn't fooling anybody. Rugby is a winter sport and Dad fraternised the hotel throughout the year. Furthermore, a game of rugby lasted for only eighty minutes but Dad usually came home from The Leopard long after we had gone to bed.

Perched in the shadow of the station, The Leopard embodied the Krugersdorp of the sixties and seventies. It was as vulgar, smutty and tasteless as the rest of the town. The hotel was a meeting place for white trash and its bar was widely known as Bloedrivier – a reference to the famous nineteenth-century Battle of Blood River where the Voortrekkers routed the Zulus. The bar derived its name from the bloody brawls that erupted at weekends and its red carpet was simply a means of concealing the stains of the blood that got spilt in the process.

Rugby jerseys, caps, flags and knickers hovered over the heads of patrons and barflies. Nobody ever stayed at The Leopard apart from the hookers who paraded around the station area. Rooms were rented out on an hourly basis, mainly for the convenience of the hookers and their predominantly married, churchgoing and God-fearing clientele.

By nine that night, Dad was still not home and Mom was growing increasingly agitated. It was time for us to go to bed when Mom announced: 'This is nonsense. I'm going to fetch him.'

Mom's car was being serviced, so she ordered a taxi. By then Pieter was bawling his heart out and refused to stay at home with his two brothers. Mom said he could go with her but had to stay in the car while she fetched Dad. Karel and I protested that if Pieter could go, so should we. In the end, all four of us piled into the taxi and headed for downtown Krugersdorp.

'Stay in the car,' Mom ordered as we pulled in at The Leopard, its name emblazoned in red neon lights. Cortina Big Sixes and Holden Camaros, with aluminium mags and fluff on their dashes, lined the street outside while Abba pumped from inside The Leopard's bowels. Mom got out of the taxi and trotted towards Bloedrivier's double swing doors.

'I'm going too,' said Karel and before Pieter or I could protest, he was out of the car. We followed and as Mom burst through the doors, we were just metres behind her. We ignored the sign that said 'Nobody under 18 years'.

My first impression of Bloedrivier was twofold. I'd never seen a place so embellished with colour. Everything was red: the carpets, the walls, the lights, the people's faces. Then there was the smell, a nauseous potpourri of spilt, foul booze, trashy perfume, disinfectant, vomit, smoke, and maybe even blood.

And then there were the people. Mom had always warned us against these ponytailed Zephyrs in their bell-bottoms, sleeveless shirts and platform shoes. If you didn't grow up in a place like Krugersdorp you wouldn't know why we called them Zephyrs. A Zephyr was actually a car, on a par with a Big Six or a Camaro or a Ford Fairmont. Zephyr wrecks were strewn across the smallholdings of Krugersdorp where they stood on bricks with their bonnets in the air.

The Bloedrivier women had red lips and their miniskirts crept up their thighs. I gaped at them and they gaped back. We must have been an uncanny sight: an auntie with a bun, wearing a light blue nylon dress that covered her knees, a pair of flat shoes on her feet. Behind her were her three urchins, barefoot and dirty after a day's play outside. Mom had not yet realised that we had followed her and she ventured deeper into Bloedrivier. We were close on her heels.

Karel was the first to see it. Like a goldfish suffering from a lack of oxygen, he gulped once or twice and then his mouth slowly fell open. His eyes popped out of his head, and so did mine when I turned around. In a corner of Bloedrivier was a little stage that was, like the rest of the place, covered with a red carpet. In the middle of the stage was a silver pole. Poking out from both sides of the pole was a pair of balloonlike tits, their nipples covered with shiny stars.

Those milk cans were much bigger than any in the *Scope* magazines in Karel's drawer. They bounced up and down lazily, as though they had a life of their own. They were attached to a near naked woman who was just about wrapped around the pole. Apart from the nipple caps, she was wearing only white boots and a skimpy pair of red panties. She was making circular movements with her hips, as though she was rubbing her guava against the metal. I'd never seen a naked or half-naked woman before and had never dreamt that bare flesh could be so titillating.

By then, my mother had spotted us and was scuttling around

to cover our faces and get us out of Sodom and Gomorrah. Karel and I bobbed and weaved in order to feast our eyes on the pole lady for a few extra seconds. Suddenly, Pieter shrieked at the top of his voice: 'There he is! There he is!'

He was pointing at a table a few yards from the stripper. There was Dad, and he was in a peculiar position. A floozie with a mane of bottle-blonde hair was slumped on his lap. Their faces were partly obscured because they were in a feverish embrace. Their mouths and lips were sucking and gobbling one another up. I couldn't believe my eyes. But it was undisputedly one of Dad's hairy hands caressing the broad's back. The other was pushing her face even deeper into his mouth.

My mother froze and Karel and I tore our gazes away from the stripper. Pieter scurried forward, his hand and finger pointing at the couple. 'It's Dad! It's Dad!' he shrieked, his voice rising above the blaring jukebox.

It was only then that Dad pulled his tongue out of the tart's wet red mouth. Imagine his shock! One moment he was in an illicit carnal heaven, the next he was confronted by the missus and his three laaities.

Dad reacted as though a thunderbolt had struck him in his ass. With one swoop he lifted the slut, who was rather plump, from his lap and slammed her down on the chair next to him. He rose slowly from his seat and looked menacingly at his feeble son who was pointing him out to everyone in the bar. Pieter, realising that he was within an arm's length of a wounded beast, turned around and scrambled back on his spindly legs to the safety of Mom. By then, Bloedrivier had come to a standstill.

'What the fuck are you doing here?' thundered Dad, his eyes bloodshot, as he waddled towards us. Mom didn't answer.

By now a group of patrons had assembled around us. 'You're in shit, Hendrik!' said one.

'So deep you'll never get out of it,' hooted another.

What happened next was like a slow-mo horror movie. 'You miserable little fuck!' Dad snarled as he grabbed Pieter by his shirt collar and lifted him off the ground. He held him for a second or two in the air and then dropped him on to the floor where he gurgled once or twice before bursting into tears. He turned to Mom, poked his finger in her face and said: 'And you go fucking home where I will deal with you!'

My mother stood her ground, looked Dad straight in the eye and calmly said: 'Come, Hendrik. We can't stay here. Look at the kids.'

By then the whole of Bloedrivier had assembled around us. Some were rooting for Dad. '*Jissus*, Hendrik, don't take any shit from her!'

Others stuck up for Mom. 'Come on, Hendrik, you're a spectacle. Go home!'

A new player entered the ring: the thickset, powder-faced slut with the golden locks. She was clearly a nasty piece of work. She grabbed Dad's arm, pulled at him and said: 'Fuck her, Hendrik! She's not worth it! Let's go!'

I could see it coming: one of those wide, backhander strokes that had floored us many times. Her head snapped back as Dad knocked her into the arms of one of the bystanders. The guy held her for a moment before dropping her on the red carpet where she lay spreadeagled, out cold. At that moment, two or three bouncers, all of them bigger and in far better shape than Dad, pounced on him. But not for nothing had Dad been a boxing champion and his fist crashed into the face of one of the bouncers. He ducked a blow from another before thrusting his fist into his belly.

Women whooped and yelled while several men joined in the fracas. In a joint like Bloedrivier any excuse was good enough reason to break the place down. Within seconds it had turned into a confusion of entangled bodies, arms and legs. Fists were swooshing through the air. Dad was somewhere underneath the pile of human garbage and it was impossible to see in what state he was.

All this lasted no more than a few seconds and by then Mom had assembled her flock and was pulling us out of Bloedrivier. One or two of the patrons assisted her in getting us through the swing doors.

'What about Dad?' Karel protested.

'Your father can look after himself,' Mom said as she pushed us into the taxi.

As we sped off, blue lights were pulling in at The Leopard.

Dad didn't come home that night. He spent it in prison. Early the next morning two of his police friends brought him home. Dad's clothes were torn and grimy and he clearly hadn't closed an eye. By the time he had washed and changed, the thin-lipped colonel had arrived at our house. He took Mom and Dad into the lounge and closed the door. When they emerged half an hour later, Mom said: 'You don't have to worry. Everything is going to be okay.'

Dad had promised not to visit The Leopard again and to drink less.

According to Karel, he also agreed to enlist at Alcoholics Anonymous and attend their meetings twice a week. The slut at The Leopard had been coming on to him, he said, and as far as he was concerned she posed no threat to his marriage vows.

It was all bullshit. Dad went to AA only once. He said he wasn't an alky and didn't have a problem. He continued drowning his ghosts in Klippies and Coke and it wasn't long before he was back at The Leopard.

Dad never forgave Pieter for giving him away and continued to pick on him for stupid little things. He was like a rock that seemed to have embarked on a mission to crush his family. It took me a long time to realise he was a cunt, no better than any of the Zephyrs in Bloedrivier or the trash that roamed the plots. Back then, however, Hendrik Goosen was just Dad. He bought us nice things and looked after us. The fact that he was a drunk and beat up his family had become, well, normal. We were what I call a *bo-blink-onder-stink* kind of family. While everything on the surface appeared to be hunky-dory, the underneath was stinking and rotten.

Mom, frail and fearful, was incapable of standing up to Dad. Pieter crept more and more into his shell and was in tears much of the time. Even Karel, who still recorded reasonable marks at school and excelled at sport, was showing cracks. He was nicking Dad's Klippies and Mom's sherry, smoked like a chimney, and was increasingly embroiled in brawls both in and out of school.

I think by now you've grasped this never-ending cycle of aggression and fury that was my early life. It was as though my family was doomed to misfortune. Disaster and calamity followed us wherever we went. In the end, something had to give. Break off. Crack, crash and shatter.

It came in the person of my little brother.

There's a family photograph standing on the table in my cell. It was taken around the time of Dad's brawl at The Leopard and Karel's demolition of Paul Reyneke. It was the spring of 1980 and I had just turned fourteen and was in standard six. By then, Krugersdorp would have woken up from its drab and dreary winter slumber and the jacarandas might already have been in bloom. Purple-coloured clouds would have massed in the afternoons and the chatter of weaver birds at my window would have woken me at dawn every morning.

I often look at this photograph. Karel and I are standing in front of Mom and Dad. It is obviously a happy day. My brother and I are beaming from ear to ear. Even Dad offers a smirk to the photographer and holds a glass of Klippies and Coke in the air. My mother is wearing her gardening hat and a wide shadow masks her face. But there's a fifth person in the picture. It is Pieter, who looks as if he is hiding under my mother's dress. He has his arms around her waist and half his face is obscured. It is almost as though he isn't really part of the picture – or the family.

My mother brought the picture to the prison a few years ago, along with a pile of books and magazines.

'Why are you giving me this picture?' I asked her.

She looked at me for a while and then said: 'It's the last family picture that was ever taken.'

I didn't answer her. She said: 'Pieter died just after this.'

I am now forty-two years old. For the last twenty-eight years of my life I have thought about my little brother virtually every single day. His death runs like a black highway through my memory.

Around the time the picture was taken, Pieter's teacher paid Mom and Dad a visit. Pieter was told to go to his room while Karel and I listened to the conversation around the corner in the dining room. Pieter was then just about to turn thirteen but was only in standard three. It looked as though he was about to fail again, said the teacher. Pieter couldn't cope in a normal school and it was advisable that he continue his education in a place for children with learning disabilities.

'Over my dead body,' said Dad. 'He's going nowhere. There's nothing wrong with him.'

It was amazing, though, added the teacher, that he had an almost normal IQ.

'He doesn't study,' said Dad.

'Maybe there are problems at home,' said the teacher.

'There're no problems,' Dad said bluntly. 'The boy doesn't study.'

'What do we do then?' asked the teacher.

'I promise you, Miss,' said Dad, 'that Pieter will pass standard three.'

'And how are you going to achieve that?'

'Leave it to me,' said Dad. That was the end of the meeting and the teacher left. As soon as Dad had closed the front door, he turned on his heel and marched to our bedroom where Pieter was lying on his bed. Dad slammed the door behind him. Mom was still standing in the lounge, wringing her hands, her mouth half-open as though she wanted to say something. Dad had decided to clobber his youngest son through standard three. He was convinced that there wasn't a problem that his hairy paws and two-inch leather belt couldn't solve. 'If you don't pass,' Dad warned Pieter, 'I'll *dônner* you until you're dead!'

They were prophetic words.

When Pieter got into bed that night, he had red stripes across his thighs and bum. By the next morning they had turned purple. Two days later, he got another thrashing when Dad walked into our room and caught him reading a Superman comic. He refused to eat that night which resulted in Dad dragging him off to the bedroom where he got another *klap*.

Although I didn't like Pieter, I felt sorry for him. Karel however, seemed to revel in the torture that was being inflicted on his younger brother.

'Did Pieter study?' Dad asked Karel every afternoon when he got home.

'Not much, Dad,' was his almost standard reply. As he went off to pour Dad a brandy and Coke, Dad would slide his belt off and tell me to leave the room. By then Pieter was already bawling.

A few Sundays later, on the eve of Pieter's final exams, Dad threw our bedroom door open and announced: 'Get ready, boys! We're going to church.'

Pieter said he felt sick. That was nothing new. Pieter was always sick, which resulted in him missing several weeks, even months, of school during the year. To demonstrate how unwell he was, he burst into a scratchy cough and sniffed fiercely.

Mom rushed into the bedroom and pressed her hand against his forehead.

'You'd better stay in bed,' she said. 'You've got a slight temperature.'

'Sissy,' Karel snarled. Dad sniggered and walked out of the bedroom.

It was the usual dreary service. Dominee Reyneke's monotonous voice put just about everyone to sleep. Karel had to elbow me out of my slumber and the only other thing that kept me awake was the sight of Elsa Reyneke's mane of brown curls a few benches in front of us. I have no idea what the service was about.

Dad was in a genial mood and bought a big tub of ice cream for lunch. He was one of those people who believed that whatever sins and misdemeanours he had committed during the week, he was absolved and everything was forgiven as long as he went to church on Sunday.

The first thing that struck me as I walked into the house was the smell of the roasting leg of lamb that Mom had put into the oven early that morning. As she rushed into the kitchen to check on the meat, I walked to our bedroom to put down my Bible and get out of my church suit.

Pieter was not in bed. That seemed to prove that the little halfwit wasn't sick and that he had lied to get out of going to church. If Dad knew that, he would be in mega shit. I walked back to the kitchen and asked Mom: 'Where's Pieter?'

'What do you mean?' There was a trace of anxiety in her voice.

'I dunno,' I said. 'He's not in his bed.'

Mom called him. There was no answer.

'Where's your Dad?' she asked me.

'Still outside.'

As she rushed outside to call her husband, she said to me: 'Well, look for Pieter. He has to be somewhere.'

I walked back to the bedroom. He still wasn't there. I turned around and walked across the passage into the bathroom. I could hear Mom and Dad walking into the house through the front door.

Pieter was in the bathroom. He was dangling from a rope tied to the shower head and around his neck. His eyes, wide open, stared at me. He was dressed only in his pyjama pants and his white body looked gaunt. His spindly legs drooped down to a few inches above the shower floor. Pieter had knobbly knees and big feet and they seemed to be more conspicuous than ever. A kitchen stool was standing alongside him.

Then my mind went blank. I vaguely remember Mom's cries as Karel and I were hustled off to our room. An ambulance siren ripped through the Sunday silence. We watched through the window as the ambulance men carried a stretcher out of the house. The tiny heap that was covered with a blanket must have been my brother.

Then the police came, then the dominee, then a doctor who gave me an injection, and then a host of other people.

I woke up late that night. Everything was quiet. At first I couldn't remember a thing. Then, as I stared at the ceiling, the image of Pieter hanging in the bathroom returned to me.

Since then, it has never left me.

In the days following Pieter's death, hundreds of people converged on our house. I was hardly aware of the aunties and uncles and nieces and nephews, teachers and pastors that hugged me and kissed me and patted my shoulder. The doctor had pumped me full of sedative to help me cope with the trauma. I felt as though I was floating on a cloud.

Only a few things stuck in my mind. One was that the word 'suicide' was never mentioned. I think everyone knew what had happened, but nobody mentioned it, as if they were pretending that Pieter had fallen victim to some strange illness. That was until the local newspaper broadcast the shame.

One morning, just before the funeral, Dad was on the front page under the headline: 'Son of top cop hangs himself'.

As we sat in church, Dominee Reyneke spun a delightful fairy tale about a beautiful and promising young life that had been tragically snuffed out by an evil demon. Like a candle in the wind, I remember him saying. But don't despair, he continued, because one day we will embrace Pietertjie again. He's awaiting our arrival where he sits at the throne of the Almighty Lord.

I listened to his sermon and thought: fucking hell, this dude is spinning us bullshit! Pieter was a tortured and haunted soul who had led a miserable existence. Just the other day in Sunday school the same Dominee Reyneke had warned us that taking your own life was the ultimate sin you could commit. So how on earth was Pieter going to get to heaven? And, let's be honest, if it was a demon who had tied that knot around my brother's neck, his name was Hendrik Goosen and he was sitting right there in church next to me. So how the hell was Dad going to get through the pearly gates to embrace his lost son? I think that was the day I lost faith in Jesus and turned my back on God and his so-called goodness and greatness and holiness.

I was one of the bearers of Pieter's coffin. I grasped the silver-coated handle and prepared to lift the coffin with all my strength, but was startled at how light it was. Was Pieter really inside, was my first thought? Maybe he'd already turned into dust. Was he that slight? I had forgotten how tiny my little brother was.

The dominee spoke more crap at the grave, and as the coffin was lowered into the hole, Mom collapsed. When I looked up at Dad I saw he was crying. It was the first and only time I had ever seen the great man sob. Whether it was out of shame, guilt or grief, or a combination of all three, I would never know. After we'd sprinkled rose petals on to the coffin and partly filled in the grave, the chapter on the wretched life of Pieter Wilhelm Goosen was tightly closed.

Dad regained his composure and Pieter's name was never mentioned again. It was almost as though he had never existed and had never been part of the family. At least that was as far as Hendrik Goosen was concerned.

Nothing was ever the same after Pieter died. Death had invaded our house and never left it again. We stopped living, stopped talking, stopped doing. Pieter's memory was everywhere and whatever we did, his ghost hovered over our heads. Although Dad pretended that it had never happened there was, for all practical purposes, still a white corpse dangling from a rope in the shower.

And Mom? Pieter's death slammed a crater the size of a soccer ball in her heart. It amputated her being and blew away her soul. Once a proud and upright woman, she was relegated to almost nothing. She turned grey overnight, started walking like a hunchback, and virtually stopped talking. She cleaned and maintained the house and fed and clothed us. And that was it. She never again warned Dad to stay away from The Leopard or to drink less. Mom was alive but she never lived again.

For years afterwards, I continued to be plagued by nightmares of a corpse hanging in the shower. Sometimes I was the one who had the rope around my neck. At other times it was Dad or Karel or Dominee Reyneke or someone I didn't know. Sometimes the corpse wriggled out of the knot and hurled itself at me. Many a night I woke and leapt from my bed in a layer of sweat.

I refused to use the shower. Every time I walked into the bathroom, I felt as though Pieter's eyes were boring into me. Even when I peed or sat down for a number two, I could feel his eyes on me. Dad wanted to sell the house, but Mom refused to move. She probably felt she couldn't leave her youngest son behind. In the end, Dad just shrugged his shoulders and headed for The Leopard where he buried his sorrows in Klippies and Coke and the gaping cavities of the station whores.

Four

I came face to face with Jakes Verster in a rugby scrum. Seconds later, I was led off the field with my face covered in blood. His head had ripped open my eyebrow. I could see it coming, but my hands and arms were stuck around the two props and I sort of dangled defencelessly in the air as Jakes grinned menacingly, dropped his head and rammed into me. The referee pressed his hankie against the wound, but the metallic taste of blood seeped into my mouth before it trickled down my chin and my neck and on to my rugby jersey.

A minute or so later, Mom had ordered me on to the backseat of the Toyota Cressida and as we sped towards the Krugersdorp General Hospital, she wanted to know: 'What happened, son?'

'It's their hooker,' I mumbled through the hankie and the blood. 'He just headed me for nothing.'

'Shame, my boy,' said Mom. 'Let's thank the Almighty Lord that it isn't worse.'

I was rushed into Emergency and told to lie down on an operating table. A few feet away, a nurse was preparing an injection. I clenched my sweaty hands and could feel the tears starting.

'It's going to be okay, son,' Mom said and drew her hand through my hair. I knew it was not going to be. An unfathomable amount of suffering, pain and distress were enveloped in that syringe. I burst into tears.

'Stop it, Gideon!' ordered Mom. 'You're not being murdered!'

I simply couldn't hold back. I was fourteen then. Today, I'm forty-two. A needle is still the most horrifying thing I know. I'm not scared of guns or knives or pain or goons or snakes. I've been fucked up every way possible and I've stared death in the eye. Nothing has ever scared me.

Many years later when I was arrested and interrogated by the cops, I told them to fuck off and refused to tell them a thing. But they could have wrung every last little detail from me if only they had known how petrified I am of needles. They wouldn't even have had to stick one into me. They could simply have brandished it in front of me and I would have told them everything.

Back to that rugby game. I was playing under 15B (yes, still second team, although there was also a third team) for Monument High and it was the annual sports day against neighbouring Randfontein High.

Let me tell you about Randfontein, only a few kilometres south of Krugersdorp. If we were Johannesburg's backwater, Randfontein was the backwater of the backwater. Any Krugersdorp *maplotter* would have been upper-crust in Randfontein. At least the Cortina Big Sixes in Krugersdorp revved and roared down the streets. In Randfontein they never got off their blocks and rusted away in filthy backyards. It was a known fact that there was a soup kitchen at Randfontein High and many kids went to school – even in winter – without shoes.

'I'm glad I'm not playing hooker tomorrow,' Karel had said at dinner table the previous night.

'Why not?' I wanted to know.

'Because they stink,' said Karel. 'Those people can't afford soap.'

I was amazed. 'Really?'

'Yes,' said Karel. 'They're like *houtkoppe*. They don't wash.'

'Oh, come on, Karel,' said Mom. 'It's not true.'

I arrived back at the field with twelve stitches in my eyebrow, a bandage around my head and my rugby jersey a bloody mess. I had refused to change into anything else. I liked my soiled gear, it gave me the image of a warrior who had emerged gloriously from battle – although, in my absence, Randfontein had wiped us by 21-9.

'We missed your hook foot,' the coach assured me. 'Randfontein took all the scrums.'

As I had hoped, my bandaged eye elevated me to brief celebrity status. My team mates flocked around me and I proudly removed the bandage to flaunt the neat row of stitches.

'*Jislaaik!*' said one. 'Is it sore?'

'Just a little,' I admitted.

'How did they put in the stitches?' asked another.

'With a needle,' I explained. 'They sewed me up!'

'*Jislaaik!* Did you cry?'

'No, man! I'm not a sissie!'

The interest in my wound withered after a while and my mates strolled away to watch the next rugby match. I also went to stand next to the field, watching Karel having a stormer of a game for the under 17A team. It was the beginning of the rugby season, and Dad had promised Karel a pellet gun if he could cement his place in the first team.

I was munching on a boerewors roll and sipping a Fanta when I felt a tap on my shoulder. I swung around. Staring me in the face was a stocky dark-haired boy wearing the black rugby jersey of Randfontein High. It was the hooker who had pulverised my eye. The first thought that sprang to mind was that he had sniffed me out to pulverise my other eye as well. I wanted to hit a line to Mom. But I knew I had to stand my ground. My mouth half-full,

I forced a feeble smile.

'Hi,' the boy said.

'Hi,' I responded.

'How's the eye?' he asked with a broad grin.

'It's okay,' I said. 'My mother took me to the hospital.'

Before he could respond, I added: 'My Dad's away; he's a policeman.' I thought it a good thing he should know that Dad was a lawman so his son was not to be fucked with.

'You know what?' he asked.

'What?'

'You've got one helluva hard head. Mine still hurts!' And he cracked up laughing. It was only then that I saw the boy standing next to him. While the hooker looked kind of normal, his mate was decidedly odd-looking. They were the same height, but the other boy, dressed in a dirty T-shirt and short pants, was much skinnier. What struck me was his head. It was a peculiar shape. I don't quite know how to describe it, but it resembled an egg. And as he merrily hooted along with his friend, I also noticed that his head wobbled drunkenly on his thin neck.

When they had calmed down, the hooker stuck out his hand: 'I'm Jakes.'

I took it hesitantly and said: 'And I'm Gideon.'

'And this,' said the boy named Jakes, 'is my friend, Johnnie.'

Johnnie didn't offer me his hand, but burst out laughing. 'You're not the first one,' he chuckled, 'that Jakes sent to hospital. And certainly not the last!' His voice changed to a higher octave and he stretched his mouth wide open in delight. He had a tooth or two missing.

'What does he mean?' I asked Jakes.

'I play rough. Rough and hard,' he answered.

'No fucking way,' said Johnnie and put his arm around Jakes. 'Not rough – dirty!'

I held out the half-eaten boerewors roll. 'Want some?' I asked Jakes.

He grabbed it, broke it in two and gave half to Johnnie, who stuffed it in his mouth.

'And you?' I asked Johnnie. 'Do you also play rugby?'

With his cheeks bulging like cricket balls, he shook his head and pointed to his feet. Johnnie was wearing a pair of heavy black boots.

'His feet,' explained Jakes as he forced the bread and wors down his throat, 'are funny.'

'Like what?' I wanted to know.

'Crooked,' said Jakes while Johnnie nodded his head. 'He can't run very fast.'

'I was born like this,' added Johnnie.

'He's a cripple,' said Jakes.

'*Sjoe!*' was all I could get out as I stared at the boots.

Jakes broke the spell. 'Do you have any more Fanta?'

'No,' I said. 'It's finished.'

'Let's get more,' said Jakes.

'I don't have any money,' I told him.

'No problem.'

'What do you mean?' I asked.

Johnnie spoke. 'We take it.'

'From whom?'

'From the kaffir who sells it,' said Jakes and turned around. 'Follow us.'

We spotted a cold drink vendor with a Coke box. I stood back and watched the two friends perform in perfect unison. Johnnie hobbled up to the vendor while Jakes lurked at his back.

'Howzit!' Johnnie greeted the guy. 'How much for one?'

'Fifteen cents, *kleinbaas*,' he said.

'*Nee God*, man!' protested Johnnie. 'It's more expensive than at the café!'

'Same price, *kleinbaas*,' the vendor assured him.

'God, kaffir!' said Johnnie moving closer. 'You're trying to cheat me!'

'No, *kleinbaas*! Sorry, *kleinbaas*! I'm not cheating.'

As the argument ensued, and with the vendor's attention distracted, Jakes moved like lightning. In a flash he had ripped open the cool box, pulled out four Cokes and sped away. He left a trail of dust as he disappeared around a corner. While the vendor threw his arms in the air in desperation, Johnnie casually turned around and limped away.

We found Jakes sitting under a bluegum tree on the side of the rugby field. We plonked ourselves down next to him, shook hands and hurled the cold liquid down our throats. Stolen goods, I realised for the first time, are much sweeter and tastier than those acquired with legal tender.

'*Jissus*, but you were fast, hey?' I praised Jakes.

'You ain't see nothing yet,' he said. 'Pies, Cokes, cakes, Crunchies, Chocolate Logs, whatever.'

'Anything you want,' confirmed Johnnie. 'We can get it.'

Back on the field, the ref had blown his whistle for half-time. As the two teams stood in circles to hold indaba and suck out their oranges, I pointed at the Monument team and said: 'That oke with the number twelve jersey, he's my brother.'

'Both my brothers,' said Jakes, 'used to play Randfontein first team.'

'How many kids are you?' I asked him.

'I've got two brothers and a sister. I'm the youngest,' he said as he looked at Johnnie, chortled, and said: 'Ask Johnnie how many snot noses they are.'

Before I could speak, Johnnie said: 'Guess. If you get it right, I'll nick you another Coke.'

Randfonteiners were notorious for breeding like rabbits. I thought for a moment and said: 'Six.'

'I'll give you another chance,' Johnnie said. 'Guess again.'

'Nine.'

'Wrong again!' said Johnnie.

'Sixteen!' trumpeted Jakes.

'No way in hell!' I cried out. 'Impossible!'

'Sixteen brothers and sisters!' Johnnie assured me.

'And where do you fit in?' I asked Johnnie.

'Somewhere in the middle,' he said.

'Do you know all of them?'

'Not quite,' he said and laughed, his odd-shaped head bobbing about on his shoulders.

'Every other day there's a new one!'

'How does your father feed all of you?'

'He doesn't,' said Johnnie. 'That's why we do it ourselves.'

'*Sjoe*,' was all I could say.

'Yes,' said Johnnie, 'and there are now even more in the house.'

'How come?'

'Two of my sisters had babies and they're also living there.'

Jakes turned to me. 'And you? How many kids are you?'

I mused for a moment and said: 'We're just two. Me and my brother.'

As stillness descended over us, probably because there was nothing else to say, I added: 'We were three. I had another brother.'

'Where's he?' asked Jakes.

'Dead.'

'What happened to him?'

'He got sick,' I lied.

'Mine are all alive,' said Johnnie as he rested against the tree trunk and took a last swig of his Coke.

'You're very lucky,' I told him.

'I'm not so sure,' he said. 'There're a few too many.'

'Johnnie sleeps on the dirty washing,' Jakes chipped in.

I was amazed. 'Why?'

'The beds are full,' explained Johnnie.

'*Sjoe!*' I couldn't think what else to say.

'What did you get for your last birthday?' asked Johnnie.

'I dunno,' I said. 'A bicycle, I think.'

'It was my birthday last week,' said Johnnie. 'You know what I got?'

'What?'

'A bag of oranges!' he said and burst out laughing. 'Fucking oranges!'

'You're joking!'

'I swear!'

'And what happened to the oranges?'

'My brothers and sisters ate all of them. That same day!'

'Ask Johnnie what job his father does,' said Jakes.

I asked Johnnie.

'He used to be on the railways,' said Johnnie.

'Doing what?'

'Pumping up train wheels!' sniggered Johnnie.

'But trains have iron wheels!' I protested.

'Exactly!' exclaimed Jakes. 'That's why his dad has no fucking job!'

The two burst out laughing as if it was the funniest thing they'd ever heard. Jakes told me his father was a truck driver while his eldest brother had been in the slammer for a year. He had another year to go. He had tried to rob a petrol station and had bashed an attendant on the head with an iron pipe.

'That's nothing,' I announced. 'My father killed a *houtkop* some time ago.'

'No fucking way in hell!' said Jakes. He pulled himself into an upright position. 'Tell us more.'

I recounted the demise of the *houtkop* in the finest detail; of him lying on the pavement with his brains next to his skull; of Dad who had to go to court but was set free, and of his triumphant picture in the newspaper. Jakes and Johnnie were hanging on to my lips and every now and then uttered a '*Sjoe*' or a '*Jislaaik*'.

When I had finished my story, Johnnie said: 'My older brother was a recce in the army. His name is Willem.'

I knew that recces were highly trained and dangerous soldiers. Dad had told me that the army's reconnaissance units were the elite of the elite and instilled fear in the heart of any terrie.

'Is he not a recce any longer?'

'No.'

'Why not?' I wanted to know.

'He went *bossies*,' said Johnnie.

'What's *bossies*?'

'*Bos-befok*.'

'And what's that?'

'Someone who goes mad in the bush,' said Johnnie. 'Willem went off his rocker.'

'And then what?'

'The army told him to go home.'

'What does he do now?'

'Nothing. He just wants to beat you up,' explained Johnnie. 'He doesn't sleep at night. He walks around outside looking for someone to fuck up.'

It was clear that I had the edge on Jakes and Johnnie in virtually every aspect of life. We were richer and smarter than they could ever dream of being. I learned a valuable lesson: if you just lower your standards a bit, you can be king!

Jakes invited me to visit him the next Friday afternoon. I said I certainly would. As I strolled away from the rugby field, the smell of barbecued boerewors permeated the cool autumn air. Rugby day at Monument was always an important family affair. Around me, husbands huddled around glowing coals while their wives lounged on folding chairs, filling in *Huisgenoot*'s crossword puzzles or knitting a jersey for winter. Children were chasing one another over the wintry grass, yelling, screaming and crying all in one voice.

I had a new family: my riff-raff friends that crawled out of the dungeons of Randfontein and filled my life with joy and happiness. Those two – Jakes Verster and Johnnie Swart – became closer to me than anyone else. I grew to love them more than Dad, Mom, Karel or Jesus. On that day, in the shadow of bluegum trees next to a rugby field, I had given birth to my new brothers. With stolen bottles of Coke in our hands and a bloodied rugby jersey, a brotherhood was born. For the first time in many years I felt as though I belonged somewhere.

I told you earlier that Dad had always been vehemently opposed to any contact or friendships with *maplotters* or low class residents. So how was I going to nurture my newly forged alliance with Jakes and Johnnie without stirring him up?

Easy. Dad was no longer there.

A few months after Pieter's funeral, he announced one

evening at the dinner table: 'I'm going to the border.'

'Where?' enquired Mom.

'To the border,' he repeated. 'I'm going to South West.'

'To do what, Hendrik?'

'I'm going to Koevoet.'

'What's Koevoet?'

'It's a new police unit,' he explained. 'Counter-insurgency.'

'So what do they do?' Mom wanted to know.

'It's a special unit that's been set up to hunt Swapo,' he said.

'Wow, Dad!' hollered Karel. 'You're going to shoot terries?'

'It's not that easy, son,' said Dad, 'but yes, something like that.'

'*Sjoe*, Dad!' I said.

'Yes, I think it's an honour,' he said. 'An opportunity to do my bit.'

'And where in South West are you going?' asked Mom.

'I'm going to stay in Oshakati,' he said.

'And for how long are you going?' she asked.

'For three months,' he said. 'Then back for a few weeks. And then off again.'

Karel and I brimmed with excitement, while Mom bowed her head and stared into her plate. Imagine: my own father was going to the border to hunt down and shoot terrorists! Boys' dreams and fantasies are made of stuff like that. Dad rose a few notches in my estimation, once again redeeming himself.

I asked Dad a day or so later what he was going to do in that place called Oshakati. He explained to me that he was being sent to extract the truth out of terries that had been captured by Koevoet.

'They bring them to me, son,' he explained, 'and then I have to get the truth out of them.'

'Like what?'

'Where their friends are hiding, what their plans are, and so on,' he said. 'And then we turn them into our own soldiers.'

'And how do you do that?'

He sniggered and said: 'I talk very nicely to them.'

'And if they don't listen?'

'Then I *dônner* them!'

I have to admit that I was slightly disappointed that Dad wasn't actually tracking down and shooting terries. I envisaged him skulking behind a bush and pumping them full of hot lead. But then Dad was sort of bulky and South West was mostly desert which could have meant he would have difficulty finding cover. It might have rendered him a plum target for the enemy.

Patrolling the Operational Area was a precarious activity. Dad said terries could be lurking behind every bush and they often found refuge in the *lokasies* that seemed to be sprinkled across the area. Although terries had difficulty shooting straight, there were so many of them that an enemy bullet occasionally hit its target. And then there was a nasty device called a landmine that they buried in the roads. When a car or a truck drove over this saucer-like gadget, it blew the vehicle and its passengers into the air.

'That's really low!' I said when Dad told us about the landmines.

From time to time, Radio South Africa announced the passing away of a soldier in the Operational Area. I remember to this day the ominous *toot-toot-toot* signal that preceded the notification: 'Defence Headquarters in Pretoria announces the death of Corporal or Sergeant or Rifleman So-and-so.'

A peculiar thing happened shortly before Dad left. Mom became an Apostolic. It started with her refusing to attend our own church services because she was *gatvol* of people's prying, pitying gazes.

She announced one night at dinner: 'I'm joining the Apostolic Church.'

I thought Dad was going to choke on his beef stew. 'What the hell is this?' he thundered and threw his napkin on the floor. Oh God, I thought for a moment, now she's really plucking at the lion's testicles! I remembered the days when Dad's outbursts resulted in smacks and slaps with his family scrambling in all directions to escape his fury. But since Pieter had died, he had barely lifted his hand against Mom. She had learned to keep quiet and didn't oppose him in any way. Karel and I still got a *klap* every other day, but it seldom floored us or left marks.

'Yes, Hendrik,' Mom said calmly. 'I'm joining the Apostolic Church.'

Before Dad could say anything, Karel exclaimed: '*Apostolie stink na olie!*'

Mom shifted her eyes to Karel, lifted her chin and said: 'If you ever say that again, I will personally pull you over my lap and give you the hiding of your life!'

Karel looked down at his plate and fiddled with his food.

'Maria, why are you doing this?' Dad demanded to know.

'They don't judge me,' she said. 'They accept me for who I am.'

Dad shook his head and stuck a forkful of stew in his mouth. I suspected that his imminent departure for South West had dampened his ire and he simply didn't care any longer. I don't think he minded skipping church as he usually had a motherfucker of a hangover on Sunday mornings. He dreaded wriggling himself into his church suit that was getting shinier and smaller by the week. It was left to Karel and me to ride to Sunday school on our bicycles – which of course we didn't do. We lingered at the corner café for an hour or two and used our church money to buy chips and play pinball.

A few days after Mom's announcement, Dad was off. He gave Karel and me a hug, pecked Mom on the cheek and got into a police car that drove him to Waterkloof Air Base. He flew in a Hercules to the Operational Area, a strip of land across the width of South West Africa that had been set up to prevent the terrorists and communists from reaching the Republic where they intended to kill or subjugate us.

I can't say that I missed the big man. The house was quieter, but then there had in any case been a deadly hush over the place since the demise of my little brother. Mom spent her days with her nose in the Bible and in praise and prayer with the happy-clappies. It was clear that she had swallowed hook, line and sinker the drivel that the Apostolics were feeding her. If her face wasn't buried in her Bible, she was walking around humming religious songs. Karel and I were more or less left to our own devices.

Dad's absence and Mom's Jesus fixation gave me an opportunity to pursue my friendship with Jakes and Johnnie. In the years to come, the three of us shared everything. We were good and we were bad. We were sad and we were happy. We cried, we laughed, we drank, we ate, we played, we fought, we bled, we cheated, we stole, we hated, we killed, we loved, we fucked.

To this day, the thought of Jakes and Johnnie brings a smile to my face. It is late afternoon and I'm sitting cross-legged on my bed in The Bomb. There's a streak of light sneaking through the barred window up near the ceiling of my cell. It's incredible how significant something simple – like a ray of sunlight – becomes when you're locked away in a dungeon like this. The ray embraces me with warmth and assures me that I'm still part of the world out there. During the winter, as the sun tumbles towards the horizon and the days shrink, the light disappears. Then there are months of gloom and chill.

But as the earth warms up again and the jacarandas cover the city in a purple blanket, it reappears. Just a week or two ago, the ray emerged from its winter doze. At first, it loitered for only a few seconds before it ducked away behind the high prison walls. I now hungrily await its arrival every afternoon and its visits are growing longer and longer. By Christmas, it will light up my cell for ten or fifteen minutes.

I'm not sure why I'm mentioning the ray of sunlight and Jakes and Johnnie in the same breath. Maybe because both fill me with sadness and happiness at the same time, and an incredible longing for the days when our love tied us together and we breathed as one.

I'm not going to try and fool you. The three of us were hardly rays of light! Jakes and Johnnie were in many ways the embodiment of the human garbage that lurked in the poorer suburbs of the West Rand. They were the kind of people that

Dad had always warned me against. They had respect for no one and simply enjoyed being delinquents.

If they wanted something, they took it. They loved stealing and cheating and were always on the prowl for something to snitch. They scorned the police and rooted for the bad guys. They were happy to be villains.

Early on they had set their minds on making a living in what Jakes would later call the informal economy. They were destined to be crooks. They didn't regard stealing as a crime; it was business.

'You know what I want one day?' Johnnie once said.

'What?' I wanted to know.

'A big fridge stuffed with steak, salami and Coke. And definitely a Ford Capri,' he said with a smile on his face.

Before I could answer, he continued: 'But that's not all.'

'What else?'

He thought for a moment, and then said: 'And a washing machine!' He burst out laughing and added: 'I never want to see a dirty pair of fucking panties again in my life!'

'Depends on who'd worn them!' chirped Jakes, and said he desired a hotted-up Kawasaki 750, a swimming pool and a blonde tart with – as he put it – a behind like a racing horse.

'Why like a horse?' I asked Jakes, who in terms of the love business was light years ahead of us.

'Tight, man, tight,' he said. I didn't understand what he meant and kept my mouth shut in order not to sound stupid.

'Gideon, old mate,' they asked me, 'and what do you want to be?'

'Dunno,' I said. 'Maybe a policeman.'

'Fucking why?' asked Jakes.

'Dad says it's a good career.'

'What's so good about it?'

'You catch the baddies,' I said.

'So now what?' said Johnnie. 'You're gonna catch us?'

'Of course not,' I said. 'Maybe I'll go and shoot terries.'

'Just remember one thing,' said Jakes. 'They fucking shoot

back.'

'Oh yes,' added Johnnie, 'you won't see me and Jakes there.'

'No fucking way in hell,' confirmed Jakes.

I don't think the two of them ever contemplated earning anything in a legal way. They never intended keeping some shitty job at some shitty place and getting paid some shitty wage that would enable them to lead some shitty life in some shitty neighbourhood among shitty people. Neither Jakes nor Johnnie ever dreamt of being policemen or firemen or pilots or soldiers. All they wanted was to be rich. They wanted to have lots and lots of money. And you can't blame them. Johnnie had sixteen brothers and sisters. His shirts and pants were always frayed because they were passed down from brother to brother. By the time they got to him, they were worn to a frazzle. His only advantage was that his crooked feet required special shoes that fortunately didn't fit any of his siblings. That was all he had of his own. His existence was dire. Johnnie didn't just sleep on dirty laundry, but had to fight to get his share of dirty shirts and soiled underpants to rest his head on.

You tell me: what's the smell of poverty? Soup bones and cabbage. Right? You smell it everywhere in the scumbag suburbs of Krugersdorp and Randfontein. In Johnnie's house, a stone's throw from the railway line in Lower Randfontein, there was often no smell. They were so down and out that there weren't even bones or cabbage to cook.

His older brothers were in and out of prison, usually for petty stuff like stealing clothes or nicking a loaf of bread or a pound of polony. Two of his sisters were pregnant at the same time, probably for flogging their cherries for a pie and a Coke or a tube of lipstick. Johnnie's father sent him and his younger brothers to town to steal food for the family. He knew that if they got nabbed, they wouldn't land up in prison. The only problem was that it didn't help Johnnie to steal just one loaf of bread or three or four meat pies. He had to nick the whole fucking shop to feed them all!

Jakes was slightly better off. There were fewer mouths to

feed and his father had an on-off job while his mother baked koeksisters for the local home bazaar. Their yard was full of fucked-up trucks that his father wanted to fix in order to start his own transport business. Nothing ever came of it. His dad, like mine, was a drunk although he never fucked up his family.

Johnnie had fuck all and Jakes almost nothing. Neither was a rocket scientist and their future prospects in the job market were always going to be, to put it mildly, extremely limited. Johnnie left school at sixteen with standard seven and Jakes at the same age, also with standard seven. So what chance in hell did they have on the straight and narrow?

None. Absolute fucking zero.

Five

One afternoon, two or three months after I had met Johnnie and Jakes, I got on my bicycle and cycled the eight kilometres or so to the smallholding where the Verster family lived.

Jakes in turn had fetched Johnnie on his bicycle.

I hadn't been there five minutes when Johnnie said: 'I'm hungry.'

'And I feel like chocolate,' said Jakes.

'A hamburger and chips,' said Johnnie, smacking his lips.

'A Crunchie!' said Jakes.

'Your turn,' said Johnnie, looking at me. 'You have to feed us.'

I knew that if I wanted to cement my place in the trio I would have to prove my mettle.

We headed for a corner café in downtown Randfontein. Jakes

and Johnnie had already hit the shop several times. They said the Greek owner was as thick as gravy and the sweets counter was in exactly the right position. The plan was that I would enter the café and go up to the counter. Johnnie and Jakes would then walk in and distract the Greek by begging for something to eat. At some point Johnnie would create a distraction by bursting into tears and that would give me an opportunity to nick a few chocolate bars.

The café was empty when I entered, apart from the Greek behind the counter. He was leaning on his elbows, paging through a comic. I positioned myself at the counter with the chocolate bars piled high in front of me. Johnnie and Jakes were a few metres away, bewailing their hunger and need. The Greek shook his head and waved them out of his café. I pulled a Crunchie from the bottom of the pile and stuffed it into my pocket. It was as easy as pie. I stole another one. By then Johnnie was sobbing in earnest. I soon had three chocolate bars in my pocket, but instead of turning around and walking away, I was determined to increase the size of my booty. I slipped another into my pocket. And another. Number six was fatal. The whole pile of chocolates fell down on me!

The Greek was on to me like a flash. Sensing calamity, Jakes and Johnnie scrambled out of the café. I tried to follow them, but the guy grabbed me behind my neck and I was trapped in his vice-like hands.

'Let me go! Let me go!' I yelped.

'Little cunt!' he growled and threw me to the floor. I remember to this day the soiled lino floor covering – and the reek of grime as he shoved my face into it. Then he walked to the entrance of the café and shut the door. I was completely and utterly fucked.

'What's your name, huh?' he snarled.

'Gideon, sir,' I squeaked.

'I'm George,' he said, 'and you're in big shit.'

George was a porky fellow with a broad moustache. His hair was Brylcreemed to the back of his head and his face was covered in acne scars. He was an ugly, oily fuck and worthy of the label sea-kaffir, as we generally referred to Portuguese and Greek scum who emigrated to our country to open corner cafés and crook everyone out of their hard-earned money. Dad always said that these people were not just lower than the lowest of whites, but lazier and dirtier than any *houtkop*.

George stepped forward, grabbed my collar, pulled me to my feet and said: 'Come with me.' Chocolate bars lay strewn all over the floor as he ushered me into a tatty little office behind the counter.

'How many did you take?' he asked looking at my pockets, still bulging with the stolen goods.

'Five, sir,' I said in a small voice.

'Take them out,' he ordered.

I took them out one by one and put them on the table in front of me. 'I'm sorry, sir,' I said.

'Too late now,' snapped George. 'You're in big shit.'

'I'm sorry, sir,' I said again.

'There're two things we can do,' said George. 'One is that I take you to the police.'

A bolt of alarm darted through me. The police? That was too terrible to contemplate. What would Mom and Dad say? Think about the humiliation and the disgrace! My eyes filled with tears.

'You're a thief,' said George. 'You'll have to go to court and maybe to prison.'

Court? Prison? The places where Dad hauled *houtkoppe* and criminals to be punished?

'Please, sir,' I begged, 'don't do that.'

'The other possibility,' George said as he stood menacingly over me, 'is that I punish you myself.'

I scrutinised his greasy face. He licked his fleshy lips with his purple tongue, exposing broken yellow teeth.

'Choose,' he said. 'And be quick. I have to open the shop again.'

I knew I had no option. 'How, sir?' I asked.

'I'll give you a hiding myself,' George said.

I made up my mind. I was accustomed to being *bliksemmed*

and it was by far the least damaging option. 'That's fine, sir,' I said.

Without saying another word, George grabbed a pen, scribbled a few words on a piece of paper, shoved it in front of me and said: 'Sign your name here.'

I could hardly read his messy handwriting, but it said something like: 'I admit that I stole five Crunchies from Pappas Take Aways.'

'Why, sir?' I wanted to know.

'It's evidence,' he said, 'so that you don't do it again.'

I wrote my name underneath his scribble. He took the piece of paper, stuffed it in his back pocket and said: 'Take off your pants.'

I looked up at George. I never ever had to remove my pants for a hiding.

'Why, sir?'

'Fucking take them off!' he snarled. 'Now!'

I slipped out of my short trousers and stood in front of him in my white briefs. His eyes gleamed and he licked his lips again.

'Everything,' he ordered.

'But why, sir?'

George pulled the piece of paper from his back pocket, held it in front of me and said: 'Hey laaitie, do you fucking see this?'

'Yes, sir.' By now I was on the brink of tears.

'This,' he snapped as he moved closer towards me, 'is an admission of guilt.'

His face was only inches from mine and I could smell his breath. It stank of foul fish. His fingernails were black with ingrained dirt and dandruff clung to his greasy hair. He pulled himself upright, took a step to his left and picked up the telephone.

'Shall I call the cops?'

'No, sir.'

'Then take them fucking off!'

I slipped my briefs off and stood naked in front of George. I knew something wasn't right. I covered my penis with my hands.

'Bend over!' ordered George.

I turned around and put my hands on the table.

'Lower!'

I bent lower. George pelted his hand down on my bum. It was more painful than I had expected. 'Ouch!' I screamed. I jumped up and looked around at his ugly face.

'Down, you little fuck!' he shrieked.

I bent over again, waiting for the second blow. But it didn't come. Instead, I felt his fingers sneaking down my bum until they were cupping and fondling my balls. I froze. I'm not sure what went through my mind, but I knew that what George was doing was horribly wrong and sinful. I tried to jump up, but he held me down on the table with his other hand. His fingers had by then crept up to my penis.

'What tiny little thing is this?' he said and laughed.

'Stop it!' I shouted. 'Please stop it!'

'You little fuck!' said George, sounding out of breath. 'I'll show you what I do to thieves!'

He took his hand away from my private parts and I could hear him fiddling behind me. Then he lifted his other hand off my neck and swung me around. Facing me was the ugliest thing I'd ever seen. Its purple head was standing in the air like an angry cobra and George was rubbing it up and down. I'd obviously seen many penises before, but none as big as his or in this state of excitement.

'Look what you're doing to me!' he said, rubbing even harder.

He grabbed my hand. 'You do it!' he said. I snatched my hand away but he grabbed it again and yanked it towards that ghastly thing. He pressed my hand against it and ordered: 'You do it! You do it!'

I wondered if it was possible to snap it off, but it looked and felt far too thick and strong. Before I could think what to do next, George roared like a wounded lion. His face was wrung in an expression of ecstasy and his hand squeezed mine even more tightly around his member. The next moment sticky, sickly white stuff spurted out. Some of it ran down my hand and splashed on to the floor. I felt scared and nauseous.

'Look what you've done, you little shit!' said George. He released my hand and shook the gooey stuff off his glistening thing. He stuffed it back in his pants. He gave me a dirty towel to wipe my hand. Then, as quickly as I could, I pulled my pants back on. What now, I wondered?

'Get out of here, you little thief!' ordered George as we stepped out of his office. I made a dash for the front door. 'Not so fast!' he ordered. He was holding the note he had scribbled in one hand and the chocolate bars I had nicked in the other. 'See this,' he said waving the note in the air. 'If you tell anyone what happened, this goes to the police.'

He pushed the chocolates into my hand. 'Take these,' he said.

I stuffed the bars into my pockets and scrambled out of the café. A hundred or so metres away Jakes and Johnnie were waiting for me. Jakes walked towards me.

'What happened?' he asked.

'Nothing,' I said and walked past him. I stopped where Johnnie was sitting on a wall, took the chocolates out of my pocket, dropped them in his lap and said: 'These are for you.'

'Fucking hell!' he said. His face was a picture of delight. 'How on earth did you manage that?'

'The Greek gave them to me,' I said.

'No way in hell!' said Jakes.

'I swear.'

'Why would he give you chocolates when he caught you stealing?' Jakes wanted to know. By then Johnnie had already ripped one open and was stuffing it into his mouth.

'Beautiful,' he mumbled.

I wanted to get as far away from the café as possible. 'I want to go home,' I said.

'No way!' said Johnnie. 'Aren't we going to grab a burger and chips from Uncle Harry's?'

Uncle Harry's was the local roadhouse where Johnnie and Jakes were notorious for grabbing food off the trays as it was being delivered to the cars. They were such a menace that whenever Uncle Harry spotted them lurking around his establishment he would send a waiter out to them with a packet of chips.

'No, I want to go home,' I said. I felt sick. That purple thing was milling around in my head.

'What did the Greek do?' asked Jakes as we cycled back to the smallholding, Johnnie sitting on the rack at the back of his bicycle.

'Nothing,' I said.

'Oh come on! He must have done something!'

I said nothing until we were back at the smallholding and had closed Jakes' bedroom door behind us. Johnnie was devouring the last of the Crunchies when I said: 'He touched me.'

'Who touched you?' asked Jakes.

'That horrible fucking Greek.' I said. I had to get it out of me.

'Touched you where?'

'My penis. He fucking touched my penis!'

Jakes heaved himself into an upright position. 'No fucking way!'

Johnnie dropped his half-eaten chocolate bar on the bed. '*Jissus God!*'

'And he forced me to touch him as well,' I went on.

'No!' said Jakes.

The two listened in silence as I recalled my ordeal in the smallest detail. Every now and then, Jakes muttered 'No way!' or 'Fucking hell!'

Johnnie shook his head and said: '*Nee, Jissus!*'

'I swear,' I said. 'It happened just like that.'

Jakes was quiet for a few moments, and then he said: 'He's a fucking moffie! We can't leave a thing like this.'

Johnnie nodded his head in agreement. 'No, we can't. Definitely not.'

'We must fuck him up,' said Jakes.

'We can't,' I said. 'He's big and he's got that note.'

'Forget the note,' said Jakes. 'He's in far bigger shit than you.'

'What now?' asked Johnnie.

'We must get more muscle,' said Jakes, getting up and leaving the room. A few minutes later, he returned with a thin, wiry guy of about eighteen or so. It was Barney, the second of the three brothers. He was wearing blue overalls and there was a streak of grease across his cheek. He had been tinkering with one of the broken-down trucks parked on the smallholding. Jakes had told me that Barney used to be an appie mechanic at the Tarlton race track outside Krugersdorp where he was honing his craft on dragster racing cars. Unfortunately, one of them blew an engine on blast-off and Barney was accused of shoddy workmanship. He was unceremoniously sacked. Since then, he had been loafing around on the smallholding.

Jakes told Barney how the Greek had assaulted me. He shook his head, looked at Jakes, and said: 'What do we do?'

'Fuck him up,' said Jakes.

'You're right,' said Barney. 'Let's get more guys and scrum him good.'

'We must get Willem,' said Johnnie. 'He'll fuck the Greek silly.'

'Who's Willem?' I wanted to know.

'He's my recce brother that I told you about,' he said.

'Isn't he sort of mad?'

'Very,' said Johnnie. 'That's why we need him.'

Minutes later, we piled into Barney's hotted-up Ford Escort and roared off in the direction of the old railway station. Johnnie's father used to be a loadmaster but was retrenched when the railways closed down the line and the station. All that remained of days gone by was a derelict building, complete with a white clock above the entrance, a pair of rusted passenger carriages, an overgrown track, and a row of corrugated iron houses.

Johnnie and his army of siblings lived in one of those houses. It was the first time I had been there. I was shocked to see the tumbledown state of the dwelling. Pinkish paint was peeling off the corrugated iron and several windows were broken and covered with cardboard. An array of broken bicycles, toys and vehicle spare parts was strewn across the uncut, weed-infested lawn.

A handful of children were cavorting on the lawn but paid little attention to us as we got out of the car. Oom Buks and Tannie Lena Swart were sitting on the stoep on a pair of old car seats. They were listening to Esmé and Jan's magazine programme which was broadcast every weekday on Springbok Radio. My mother was an avid fan of Tannie Esmé and religiously took down her recipes.

'Afternoon, oom. Afternoon, tannie.' Barney greeted them.

Johnnie's father gave us a big smile, exposing toothless gums. He was wearing a pair of thick, black glasses and hadn't shaved for days. Tannie Lena hardly looked up. She seemed to be immersed in Tannie Esmé's ingredients.

'Where's Willem, pa?' asked Johnnie.

Oom Buks shrugged his shoulders. How on earth, I wondered, do you keep track of so many children? We walked into the house. The cardboard covering the windows prevented light from entering the living room and gave it a gloomy atmosphere. There were more car seats and one or two tattered chairs in the lounge. We walked through the house. A snot-nosed toddler sat screaming in the passage, but nobody paid any attention to him. There seemed to be only two bedrooms, one obviously for the parents. There were four or five unmade beds in the second room, every one of them occupied by a sleeping child. They were taking a nap before the older brothers and sisters claimed the beds for the night. We walked through the kitchen towards the back door. The place was filthy and clearly hadn't seen a mop or duster for many days.

Johnnie found Willem and two of his other brothers congregated around a car wreck in the backyard. *God Jissus*, I thought when I saw Willem. His appearance was truly frightening and he looked every bit the mad recce that he was. He had an unruly mop of curly brown hair, tattooed forearms and a nose that looked as though it had been broken in a dozen places. His eyes were dark and had a manic gleam.

'Hey man, Willem,' said Johnnie. 'Come listen here.'

'What?' asked Willem in a low, rasping voice.

Johnnie took his brother aside and spoke to him for a minute or two. They walked back towards us. Willem eyed me for a few seconds. 'So Johnnie says the Greek fucked with you?'

'Yes, he did,' I said.

'Let's go teach him a lesson,' said Willem. He turned around, walked back to the car wreck and returned with a wheel spanner in his hand.

'What's that for?' I asked Johnnie.

'It's for the Greek,' he said. 'You'll see.'

The five of us got into the Escort. Barney seemed to be as revved up as his yellow *spoedvark*, as he called his car. He donated a layer of rubber to the tar as he pulled off, wheels spinning. Minutes later, we screeched to a standstill a few metres from Pappas Take Aways.

Barney and Willem, the wheel spanner in his hand, got out of the Escort and walked towards the café. The plan was for the two of them to enter, get George on the floor, and then call us to finish him off. They loitered in front of the café, waiting for two customers to finish their business. Then they filed in and closed the door. In the meantime, the three of us got out of the car and moved closer to the entrance.

A few seconds later, Barney peered around the entrance and beckoned to us. As we walked through the door, he closed it behind us. I saw Willem before I even caught a glimpse of the Greek. His hair was on end, as though he'd had an electric shock, and his eyes glowed with a lunacy that would have paralysed anyone. I was glad we were on the same side.

'Come, come,' he said, waving me towards him with the spanner. I could have sworn it had blood on it. 'He's behind the counter.'

George was lying on the ground in a foetal position. A pudgy hand covered one side of his head while a thin stream of blood trickled through his fingers and spilled on to the soiled lino on the floor. He was holding his other hand in the air as if to shield himself from another blow. He was making small peculiar sounds.

'Is this him?' Willem asked, pointing the spanner at George.

'Yes, that's him,' I confirmed.

George, recognising my voice, lifted his head off the ground. He gazed at me for a moment or two before slumping back on to the floor.

'Sit up, you fucking cunt!' Willem ordered. When George didn't immediately respond, he raised his voice an octave or two. 'Fucking sit up!'

George struggled to a sitting position. He had a bewildered look on his face and was licking his lips continuously. Blood was now dripping down his cheek and on to his brown checked shirt. I looked at the Greek, bleeding like a decapitated chicken, and thought: what a beautiful fucking sight!

'Do you recognise him?' Willem asked the Greek, pointing at me.

George's eyes dropped for a moment before he lifted his head again. Our eyes met briefly. He nodded his head.

'Why did you do it?' Willem demanded to know.

George looked down at the floor. Willem stood closer, lifted the spanner in the air and asked again: 'Why the fuck did you do it?'

George, his head tilted back and his hands in the air, said: 'I'm sorry. I'm sorry.'

All five of us were now standing in a circle around the Greek. Willem was holding the spanner in the air while Barney was wringing his hands in anticipation. Johnnie was stamping his boots on the ground and Jakes was flexing his fists in front of him.

Barney spoke for the first time: 'You know what you are?'

George shook his head. Barney said: 'A fucking boy-fucker!'

'Yes,' Willem agreed, 'a boy-fucker!'

George shook his head.

'And you know what we do with boy-fuckers?' asked Willem, and without waiting for George to answer, he continued: 'We fucking cut it off!'

George opened his mouth as if to say something, but Willem grabbed his greasy mane, pulled back his head and said in his croaky voice: 'You will never fuck a boy again!'

'Please! No, please,' begged George. There were tears in his eyes.

'Kneel!' commanded Willem.

George obediently shifted on to his knees.

'Now fucking pray!'

George looked up at Willem, who lifted the spanner even higher.

'Pray, cunt!'

George closed his eyes, held his hands together and murmured something in a foreign language.

Willem held out the spanner to me. 'Take it,' he ordered. I took the spanner. 'Clobber him,' he said. 'As fucking hard as you can.'

I grasped the spanner tightly and raised it in the air with both hands. As George opened his eyes, I crashed it down on his head with all my strength. Clang! He tried to cover his head with his hands. I lifted the spanner again. Clang! And again. Clang!

I was a natural! A born head-basher! A skull-cracker! A pulveriser of bones! A slammer extraordinaire!

I'm not sure exactly where my blows landed, but George plummeted to the ground like a piece of shit in a long-drop. Blood oozed through his hair and dripped on to the floor. Satisfied with my craftsmanship, I stood back and watched a feeding frenzy descend on the Greek, who was howling and begging at the same time.

Jakes had grabbed the spanner from me and was bashing George's face and head. Willem was kicking him in the ribs while Barney kicked his back. Johnnie punted him with his strange boots wherever he could find an opening.

'That's enough!' Willem announced suddenly. Jakes and Barney stood back. Johnnie, however, continued his blitzkrieg, his boot smashing the Greek's face over and over again. By then it was a grisly bloody mess. His eyes were still partly open but he didn't have the strength even to try to block any of the blows. Jakes grabbed Johnnie around his waist and pulled him away.

'Let's go,' said Willem, 'before anyone sees us.'

'Wait!' said Johnnie. He grabbed a plastic bag from the counter, hobbled across to the sweets counter and started filling it with chips and chocolates.

'Hurry!' ordered Willem, but he grabbed a bag himself and rushed to the fridge where the Greek kept cheese, eggs, milk and polony. Barney headed for the tinned food shelf while Jakes joined Johnnie at the sweets counter. I collected a bag and stuffed it with packets of biscuits.

Johnnie moved to the till and banged on the keys, trying to open it. 'How the fuck does this work?' he asked, hitting it with his fist. 'Ask the fucking Greek!'

But George was unconscious. He looked very dead to me.

'Forget the fucking money!' said Willem. 'Let's go.'

'No fucking way in hell,' said Barney. 'Just wait.'

He had joined Johnnie at the till and the two of them were shaking it frantically, but its stout locks and latches refused to give way.

'Quick! Quick!' said Willem.

Barney picked the till up and slammed it down on the floor. It landed with crash, but remained intact.

'That's it!' barked Willem. 'Come!'

Barney picked the till up, stuck it under his arm, grabbed his bag of tinned food and said: 'Right. Let's go.'

As we opened the doors, Barney said: 'Walk slowly. And don't look guilty.'

Imagine trying not to look guilty! We'd just whacked a man so hard that he'd never be the same again, raided his shop and nicked his money machine. And we had to pretend we'd just been to Sunday school?

Willem, who in the meantime had also picked up two loaves of white bread, was the first to stroll nonchalantly out of the café. Johnnie followed, then Jakes and I. Barney, the till under his arm, was last.

'Do you think he's dead?' I asked as we drove away. Jakes, Johnnie and I were half-buried under the five bags of nosh in the back of the car while Willem was in front with the till on his lap.

'No way in hell,' said Willem. 'You'll have to blow his head away to kill that piece of shit.'

'What if he calls the police?' I wanted to know.

'He won't,' said Barney. 'He knows he fucked up.'

'Anyway,' said Willem, 'the police don't like these fucking sea-kaffirs. Won't help him to complain.'

A while later, the five of us sat in a circle in a shed in Jakes' backyard. Johnnie had a chocolate bar in one hand, a Romany Cream in the other and a bottle of Old Brown Sherry in front of him. 'Beautiful,' he said as he sank his teeth into the chocolate. He took a swig from the bottle and passed it to Jakes, who was sitting cross-legged with a packet of biscuits in his hand.

'God bless sea-kaffirs,' he mumbled as he stuffed a biscuit into his mouth and washed it down with sherry. He handed the bottle to me. My head whirled and my throat burnt as I sucked the sweet liquid into my mouth.

Willem and Barney were swigging away on glasses of rum and Coke. Their initial exuberance was slightly dampened because the Greek's money machine had yielded less than they were hoping for. As soon as we got back to the smallholding, they took the till to the workshop, bashed it open with an axe, and then watched in dismay as a handful of notes fluttered from its drawer. There was only a small pile of silver and bronze coins.

'Hardly enough,' lamented Willem, 'for a bottle of Red Heart and a decent fuck at The Leopard.'

But I felt exceptionally cheerful and content. I realised that this was where I belonged. Being with Jakes and Johnnie and the rest of their clan meant that I was somebody in a world where I'd been nobody before. The incident with the Greek had been horrible and I didn't want to think about it ever again, but then, thanks to my new friends, it had been rectified in a most satisfactory manner. I felt fuck all for the Greek writhing around on the floor and had taken great pleasure in bashing his head with the spanner and watching his ugly face being modified by our shoes and fists. As for the till and sweets and chocolates and polony and other goodies we had taken, I was quickly learning that this was a kind of fringe benefit that went with this sort of mission.

I had learned a valuable lesson that afternoon and it became our motto: The pain of one is the pain of all. If you come from a neighbourhood full of nothings like Jakes and Johnnie, you're fuck all on you own. Everybody pisses on you. It's like the fingers on your hand, I thought in a moment of intellectual inspiration. What can you do with only one finger? Almost fuck all. You can scratch your balls or stick it in someone's eye or rake your tart's salad. But that's it. Now fold your fingers into a fist. God, you can do something with that! You can take what you want or hold a gun against someone's head or bust somebody's balls if he pisses you off.

That's why what happened that afternoon was so significant. I realised that if Jakes, Johnnie and I stuck together, we could be one helluva fucking lethal fist!

'How much money do we have?' asked Barney.

'About eighty bucks,' said Willem.

'That's enough,' said Barney.

'You sure?'

'Yeah,' said Barney. 'We can get a room and two whores. It's enough for all of us.'

'Let's go fuck!' said Johnnie brandishing the bottle of sherry in the air.

I wasn't sure what was going on. The idea of whores petrified me, and what was this about two sluts for the five of us? But I would soon learn that if you have nothing, sharing becomes second nature. You might have just a little but your buddy's hands are empty. So what do you do? You give him some of yours. Fluff was no exception.

'Hey guys,' said Jakes, 'Gideon has never done it before.'

'What do you mean?' asked Willem.

'He's never fucked,' said Jakes. 'Ask him.'

Willem looked at me and said: 'You must be fucking joking!'

I didn't know what to say and just shook my head. I should have been home a long time ago, but I was part of the group and didn't want to break the bond. I was a bit pissed and I have to admit the idea of seeing a naked woman, and maybe feeling female flesh, roused me.

'*Jirre, boet!*' said Willem.

'Come,' said Barney getting to his feet. 'Let's go fuck.'

Six

I wanted to run when I saw the two tarts. One was as old as my mother and her tits drooped almost all the way down to her flabby belly. The other, who was called Amber, was much younger but somewhat deformed by what seemed to have been a boob job that had gone wrong. I shut my eyes for a moment or two and thought, God please, this is a bad dream. Get me out of here!

When I told Jakes afterwards, he laughed and said: 'What! You wanted to run away from a nice fuck?'

When I opened my eyes again, granny was parked in front of Barney, balancing her buxom frame on a pair of high heels and swaying her hips from side to side. Her name was Bonny and she had her hands in her hair while her drooping mammaries wobbled slowly from bow to stern. Her thighs were covered with unsightly dimples and hollows. She was still wearing her panties and I decided then and there that I didn't want to see the pudding that was concealed under the shred of red cloth.

I think one of the reasons why I didn't want to look at Bonny's love box was that I suspected that she was the one who had had her tongue in Dad's mouth on the night that his family interrupted his antics at The Leopard. Those pouting red lips, the dimpled thighs, the black liner that slithered around her eyes and those droopy tits looked all too familiar.

When I later asked Jakes why Barney had chosen such a decrepit old tart, he said: 'Barney likes 'em old.'

'Why?' I wanted to know.

'Dunno,' he said, 'but Barney says they know how to fuck.'

'In what way?'

'He says they're desperate. They suck like a Hoover.'

A few feet away from me, Willem was fondling the younger woman's breasts. My eyes were impaled on those tits for quite some time. To start with, one was bigger than the other. The smaller tit's nipple pointed straight ahead, as I presumed it was meant to. It was, in fact, a rather perky and attractive boob. The problem was with the second tit. It wasn't just significantly larger than the other, but its nipple was skew.

'A coolie doctor pasted them skew,' explained Jakes when I asked him about her odd knockers.

'*Jissie!*'

'Yes,' he said. 'She wanted to make them bigger, but something went wrong.'

'No way!' I said.

'Yes,' said Jakes. 'That's why she's working the station. It's because of those tits.'

'*Jislaaik!*'

'Everybody calls her *Skewetiet*,' said Jakes. 'It's a pity about them 'cause there's nothing wrong with her *platanna*! She says she's going for another op, and then she'll hit the beat in Commissioner Street.'

For quite some time before this episode at The Leopard I had mused about who was going to bag my virginity and what it was going to be like. There were several chicks at Monument High who stirred my fancy, but I was too shy to woo any of them and would, quite frankly, not have known what to do if any of them had made eyes at me.

I had discovered the marvel of *draadtrek* and engaged in this delicious activity a few times a day. Whenever I got a chance, I sneaked my favourite *Scope* from Karel's drawer (his collection had grown considerably) and opened the magazine at the centrefold where 'Sinful Cindy' was lounging on her back. The foxy bombshell was wearing a teeny-weeny yellow bikini and her red lips, like her legs, were slightly parted. I knew every detail on that page, although my eyes were usually fixed on her bountiful boobs – one could see the shape of her nipples poking through the cloth – or her enticing and perfectly rounded *Volksie*-bonnet that gave just the slightest hint of what lurked down there. I wasn't sure what to call a girl's secret place, although Jakes and Johnnie had an assortment of names that ranged from *slymslote* to *genotgrotte*.

On the next page, Cindy's bikini top had fallen away and all that was between her luscious nipples and my admiring gaze was a pair of silver stars. At that time it was regarded as indecent for a broad to show off her assets. According to the caption, Cindy was twenty years old, loved horse riding and swimming and her dream man was a body-builder who knew how to satisfy his woman. I had often fantasised about Cindy brushing her nipples over my face before forcing me on my back and performing obscene acts with me. I knew absolutely zero about sex. My parents had a cold, affectionless relationship and no one had ever spoken to me about the birds and the bees, apart from a warning against masturbation from Dad who said it would sap our energy and make us frail and feeble.

This instruction from Dad was usually issued on the eve of a rugby match. Mom would tuck Karel and me into bed, say goodnight and, as she left, Dad would peer around the door and say: 'You boys must sleep well tonight. Tomorrow is a big day.'

'Yes, Dad. Goodnight, Dad.'

'And remember, hands above the sheets,' he would conclude. 'Otherwise you'll be too weak to play.'

That was it! And now with Dad away on the border fighting the terries, even that most meagre of advice was on hold.

In contrast with my sexual naivety, Jakes seemed to be a fuck freak and highly skilled in matters of love. He boasted that he first did it with his cousin when he was in standard five – that's twelve or thirteen years old – and since then had never looked back.

'It's easy, *boet*,' he said. 'Things just happen by themselves.'

I had no doubt that Jakes knew what he was talking about. He knew too much about the mechanics of screwing to have made it up. Anyway, it was well known that people in Randfontein started much earlier than others and had lower morals than we Krugersdorpers.

'What's the definition of a Randfontein virgin?' Jakes once asked me.

'Dunno,' I said. 'What?'

'The ugliest girl in grade one!' he said and cracked himself.

'Yes,' added Johnnie. 'Dogs start at one, cows at two, horses at three and Randfonteiners at four.'

Jakes was one thing, Johnnie another. He babbled away as though he was the heart-throb of the West Rand. I didn't believe a word he said. Not only was he a down-and-out and unsightly little fuck, but he was a cripple. I looked at Johnnie and thought: what a poor visual! I couldn't imagine him *pomping* away, boots and all!

I managed to avoid looking at Barney and the granny, apart from once when I glanced over my shoulder and saw to my horror that his head had disappeared between her plump thighs. I shut my eyes and swung my head back towards Amber. I had by then decided that, the coolie's blunder aside, she was rather pretty.

I had never in my wildest dreams imagined that a tart like Amber would bag my virginity. As I said, I had often wondered what kind of fluff would initiate me into the world of sex, but if you had told me that it would be a station whore at The Leopard,

I would have told you to go fuck your hand.

And here I was about to do battle with Amber's twisted tits. By then Willem was ripping her clothes off. He struggled to get rid of her white jeans, but once he had her on her back, he peeled them off like a banana skin. She was not wearing panties.

My eyes were fixed on the dark bush between her legs, but before I could properly appraise its splendour and mystery, Willem had dragged her off the bed and pushed her to her knees. He ripped his penis out and stuffed it in her mouth. I had heard of a blow job and both Jakes and Johnnie had at various times claimed to have been sucked bone dry, but it was the first time I had witnessed the act. Amber looked as though she was about to choke, but Willem was in the throes of delight and kept going.

'*Sluk daai mik!*' Johnnie spurred on his brother. He passed the bottle of Old Brown Sherry to me and, trembling with anxiety and expectation, I took long, deep gulps.

Willem concluded his business with Amber in a most sloppy manner. She stumbled to her feet, wiped her face with a towel and headed straight for me.

I had absolutely no control over what happened next. I had never wanted my sexual initiation to be like this and I shouted No! No! No! a thousand times in my head. I tried to cover my wickets and protested mildly at Amber's attention, but the next moment she had unzipped my fly and was fiddling with my penis which suddenly assumed a life of its own.

The whole thing couldn't have lasted more than a minute or so and I don't remember much more than the cheap perfume which enveloped me. She lowered herself on to me, pressed her lips against mine and stuck her tongue in my mouth. I thought for a moment I was going to choke and wanted to spit it out, but the next moment I clenched my fists, arched my back and erupted like a volcano. I thought it would never stop, but by the time I had regained my composure, Amber had already lifted herself off me and was moving on to Jakes.

A commotion had erupted on the bed next to me. Johnnie was shrieking at the top of his voice. 'Leave it alone! Leave it fucking alone!'

The granny had taken hold of one of Johnnie's boots and was trying to pull it off. 'Come on lovey,' she said. 'Take these ugly things off.'

'No, no, no!' said Johnnie kicking his feet in the air.

She finally receded, shook her head and diverted her attention to his pants. She fiddled with his belt and pulled them down. I wanted to look away, but for a moment or two my eyes were riveted. Johnnie might not have been graced with brains, beauty or straight feet but, my God, was he mightily endowed! It took even the hooker by surprise.

'*Sjoe, seun*, where did you get this from?' she said delightedly as she plonked her flaccid frame on top of him.

After we had all had an innings with the broads – Johnnie and Barney nailed Amber as well, although Jakes and Willem point-blank refused a second round with the geriatric – it was pitch dark outside. I had completely lost track of time. I usually went home at around five. It was hours later and my stomach started churning with anxiety.

The rest of the gang seemed in no hurry. Barney and Willem were engaged in a squabble with the whores who demanded a bonus for the amount of service they had provided.

'You owe me,' said Amber, 'because I did all five of you.'

'You were pretty *kak*,' snapped Willem.

'What's more,' said Bonny, pointing at Johnnie, 'that boy is hung like a horse. He hurt me.'

'Stop complaining, granny,' said Barney. 'You never had it so hard and good.'

'Cheers!' trumpeted Johnnie as he finished off the bottle of Old Brown Sherry.

'And you were not supposed,' said Amber, glaring at Willem, 'to shoot in my face.'

'Tried to cream your tits,' laughed Willem, 'but obviously I missed.'

The whores threatened to call their pimps, whereupon Barney and Willem vowed to disfigure them so badly that they'd never again be able to attract clients. They finally left with a few extra rand, swearing never to do business with us again.

It was too late for me to cycle home. We loaded my bicycle into the Escort and Barney drove me to Krugersdorp. I tried to conjure up excuses that I could present to Mom. Maybe I could say my bicycle had broken down. But she'd counter by wanting to know why I hadn't phoned. If I then explained that my friends didn't have a phone, she'd want to know who they were and how come they didn't have a phone. My head was swirling as I got out of the car and walked towards the front door. I dreaded facing her.

But it wasn't Mom who confronted me.

It was Dad.

As I opened the door and walked into the lounge, I saw the big man sitting in his Lazyboy. He was wearing camouflage uniform and army boots. After being away for months, he was back on leave – and it had to be the very day that I arrived home long after dark, pissed and reeking of whore's perfume. My mouth fell open and I froze. I could feel his bloodshot eyes piercing me. Sitting on the couch alongside him was Mom, a bunch of tissues clutched in her hand. She was weeping.

'I thought you were dead,' she whimpered, pressing the tissues against her face. 'We've already phoned the hospital and the mortuary.'

For several seconds after that, none of us said a word.

'Hey, Dad,' I managed to utter in a feeble voice.

'Where have you been?' he asked coldly.

'Nowhere,' I said. My mind had hit a blank and the story I intended to spin Mom was lost in a haze of panic and intoxication.

'Come here,' he commanded.

I stepped forward.

'Closer,' he said.

I shuffled forward until I was an arm's length from him, swaying unsteadily on my feet.

'What's wrong with you?' he demanded.

'Nothing,' I said.

'Are you drunk?' Dad rose to his feet. I thought for a moment that he looked mighty imposing in battledress, despite the fact that he had ballooned considerably while he had been in the Operational Area.

'No,' I said.

'You are!' he thundered. 'You are fucking drunk! I can see it.'

'No.'

'Fucking yes!' he thundered.

'No.'

Dad came closer to me so that his stomach was almost touching my chest. He bent forward and for a moment I thought he was going to kiss me. He pushed his nose against my neck.

'You're drunk and you smell like a fucking whore,' he said. He was obviously an expert on the subject. I took a step back. I didn't want to be too close to him.

I guess you know what was in store for me. So did Mom. She got to her feet and pleaded: 'Stay calm, Hendrik. It's okay … please.'

Dad swung around and shoved his finger in Mom's face. 'Shut up, Maria! I'll fucking deal with this.'

She fell back on to the couch. I'll never understand how she could do that. Was she going to allow a rabid fucking beast to kill another of her children?

Dad grabbed the front of my shirt. 'You fucking little shit!' he spat, almost lifting me off the ground. I felt a thin spray of spit exploding against my cheek. My shirt collar cut into the back of my neck. I gazed into his eyes, by then blazing with homicidal fury. Blobs of drool and foam gathered at the corners of his mouth and he smelled of brandy. The delicate veins on his cheeks ruptured into fine red networks that in turn swirled around hundreds of tiny blackheads. A clump of clotted, black hair squirmed out of each nostril.

What an ugly motherfuck, I thought.

After months of an uneasy ceasefire, carnage was about to burst forth. I was convinced that he was going to kill me and decided I had nothing to lose. I grabbed his hefty paw, which was still grasping my shirt, with both hands and I bit it as hard as I could.

The big man shrieked like a little boy. This encouraged me to chomp even harder, to the point where my teeth tore his flesh. I tasted blood and clenched my jaws even tighter. He grabbed my hair with his free hand and tore my teeth off his ruptured skin. I was vaguely aware of orbiting in space before plunging down on to the floor. His weight crashed down on me. I recalled one, maybe two, even three blows. Then, mercifully, everything went black.

Seven

I don't know how long I stared at the white ceiling before it dawned on me that I was in hospital. The first image that swam into my consciousness was that of George the Greek kneeling in front of me, the spanner crashing down on his head ... then Amber's splendid white contours and her sweet perfume ... Johnnie with his pants down and the granny's roly-poly body ... Barney's tattooed forearms, a berserk Jakes punting the Greek ... and Dad's maniacal eyes with those sooty hairs sprouting like vines out of his gaping nostrils.

My eyes moved from the ceiling to the side of the bed. A nurse in crisp white cotton was standing next to me. She pressed her thumb to my wrist.

'He's coming to,' she whispered. 'He's going to be okay.'

My eyes shifted to the other side of the bed. Mom stared at

me through puffy red eyes. In her hand was a crumpled bunch of pink and blue tissues. She bowed her head and said: 'Praise you, almighty Lord.'

And then I saw him. He was standing at the door with his arms folded, his legs apart. He was still wearing his camouflage uniform and army boots and I could see the three stars on each shoulder from where I was lying in bed. His shirt was tight around his waist and his *boep* looked like one of Mom's stuffed couch cushions. I detected a sneer on his face.

I wanted to jump up and tell the nurse all about him, but I couldn't lift my body. My head was pounding and my shoulder felt as though it had been ripped from my torso.

'Steady now, son,' the nurse said. I flopped back against the pillows.

'Oh, Gideon, I'm so glad you're all right,' said Mom, sniffing and mumbling: 'I thank you, God.'

Dad stepped forward. I shut my eyes tightly but could hear the plastic soles of his boots squeaking like a tiny bird on the tiled floor. I felt his hand on my forearm. I unlocked my eyes briefly and looked at the hand that was only a few inches from my face. The fleecy layer of black hair across its surface was covered with a large plaster. It was where I had bitten him. Good, I thought, I hope it gets infected.

'Gideon ...' said Dad. 'Son, listen to me. I still want to know where you were last night.'

Fuck you, I thought, sealed my eyelids and pretended not to hear him.

That was the day when I shut my eyes and ears to him. Adoration and respect were replaced by contempt and revulsion. Whatever had happened in the past – Pieter's death, the thrashings, the drinking, the whores – Dad had always been my father and was to a great extent the man of the hour. He had played rugby for Transvaal, he fucked up bad guys and hunted terries on the border. That was no longer enough.

Dad was a cunt. Finish *en klaar*.

He had dispatched me to hospital with concussion, cracked

ribs, a dislocated shoulder and a miscellany of bruises. No questions were ever asked – he was after all fucking Big-Gun-Police-Hero Captain Goosen of the counter-insurgency unit and he was virtually untouchable. Any social worker who stumbled across the Goosen household and scratched at the layer of 'normality' would have soiled her knickers and scrambled for the front door. Among his accomplishments could be counted his youngest son, who had danglingly departed from hell on earth, his middle son who was on his back in hospital, and his wife who had been pummelled into God's lair.

Mom and Dad hardly spoke to each other during his leave and I certainly never witnessed any tenderness between them. In any case, Mom was immersed in her choir activities. Since she'd discovered her passport to heaven with the happy-clappies, she had also joined the church choir.

'Now I know where Pieter got his talent from,' she once said. It was the only reference to my little brother she had made in months.

That left Karel, who you haven't heard about for some time. As we grew older, Karel went his way and I went mine and there wasn't much of a brotherly rapport. I knew he drank a lot, but he was still my brother.

Unfortunately I was not the only one who suspected that he was drowning his worries in a bottle. I was home from hospital and recovering in bed when Mom had one of her tearful outbursts. She had found two empty half-jacks of Smirnoff under Karel's bed. She sobbed the whole day, probably more in anticipation of the fate of her firstborn at the hands of his father than the vision of Karel hurling vodka down his throat. Anyway, when Dad came home from an extended boozing and whoring session at The Leopard, her eyes were still puffy and red and it took him only a few minutes to wring the truth from her.

Karel didn't land up in hospital, but his injuries were in many ways worse than mine. He was out of school for more than a week to give his black eye an opportunity to get back to normal and for his split lip to mend.

Ironically, at that time my brother and I were closer than we had been in years. We stayed in bed in the mornings listening to live radio commentary on the cricket Test matches between the Springboks and a rebel team from the West Indies. By the time the tour ended Dad was off again for another stint in the Operational Area.

A few days before his departure for South West, Dad was awarded a police medal for bravery. Mom returned from the hairdresser with a stiffened beehive and wore a new purple outfit. How ironic, I thought. Dad was being honoured by the commissioner while his two sons were on their backs in bed, recovering from the aftermath of one of his vicious attacks. Dad slipped into our room that afternoon holding the bronze coin with the blue ribbon in the air. 'It's for my contribution to combating terrorism,' he announced proudly.

Karel and I hardly glanced at it and continued listening to Charles Fortune describing a barrage of bumpers bowled by Clive Rice. Looking dejected, Dad shrugged his shoulders, turned around and walked out of the room.

I never did tell Dad what happened on that Friday afternoon. Even after I came home from hospital, he would lower his bulging torso over my bed, lick his fleshy lips and say ominously: 'Gideon, I'm still waiting for an answer.'

I had a standard response: to press my lips together and shut my eyes. I'm sure Dad suspected that his offspring had tasted the produce on the other side of the fence – especially after Jakes and Johnnie appeared unexpectedly at our house.

After I'd failed to show up in Randfontein two Fridays in a row, the two of them rocked up at our front door early on a Saturday morning. I was in bed and heard the familiar roar of the hotted-up Ford, but never dreamt that it could be Barney pulling up outside our house. I heard a knock.

Mom opened. 'Morning, boys,' she said. 'Can I help you?'

'Morning, tannie.'

I sat up in my bed. It was Jakes' voice!

'We are looking for Gideon, tannie.'

I stumbled to my feet and searched for my gown. 'He's here but he's still sick in bed,' Mom said.

I shuffled out of the room and headed for the front door.

Dad got there first. 'Yes, boys,' I heard him say. 'And who are you?'

I didn't hear their reply, but by the time I got to the entrance, his bulky frame was filling the doorway. Mom was standing behind him.

'And where do you come from?' he asked. The Escort was still idling in the street.

'Randfontein, oom,' said Jakes.

'Uh-huh,' said Dad. 'And how do you know Gideon?'

'Through rugby, oom,' answered Johnnie.

'And tell me, boys,' Dad continued, 'the other Friday when Gideon came home so late, were you with him?'

Neither of them replied. After a few seconds, Dad repeated his question, but this time in a far more menacing tone: 'I'll ask again: were you with him?'

'Yes, oom,' answered Jakes.

'We were together that day, oom,' confirmed Johnnie.

'And where the hell,' bellowed Dad, 'were you?'

There was a deadly silence. Dad took a step forward. Jakes and Johnnie must have been in retreat by then. 'I'm going to ask just one more time,' he blasted. 'Where on fucking earth were you?'

Jakes and Johnnie told me afterwards that they realised that a bag full of shit in the person of Captain Hendrik Goosen was about to explode over them. Dad must have presented a scary picture. He had just woken up, was dressed in a vest and short pants and had a motherfucker of a hangover – courtesy of a farewell party at The Leopard.

A fracas ensued. Dad lunged at them but Jakes and Johnnie were obviously a few paces ahead and both reached the safety of the Escort and piled into the car.

'If I ever see you near my house again,' thundered Dad as Barney threw the Escort into first, 'I'll wring your fucking necks!'

He staggered back into the house like a wounded bull, stopping when he saw me standing in the entrance hall. He glared at me and said: 'So are these your new friends?'

I said nothing. 'Are these your fucking friends?' he bellowed.

'Yes, Dad.'

'Were you with them the other day?'

'Yes, Dad.'

'And where the fuck were you?'

In a moment of utter defiance, I turned around and walked back to my room.

'Gideon!' fired Dad. 'I'm fucking talking to you!'

I kept walking. Dad hurled an assortment of threats after me – among them a promise to wring my neck as well – as I walked to my room and got into bed. As I pulled the blanket over my head, I heard something break. I later discovered it was Mom's Chinese vase that stood on a glass table under the mirror in the hall. I had no idea whether he smashed it on her head or threw it on the ground and, to be honest, I didn't fucking care.

Moments later, Dad stormed into our bedroom and ripped the blankets off me. I steeled myself against the blows that I presumed were about to rain down on me. They didn't. Instead, he continued to spew fire. 'Look at me!' he shouted. I opened my eyes and stared into his blotched, unshaven face.

'If you ever, but ever, see those Randfontein dregs again,' he hissed, 'I'll smash you to a fucking pulp.'

I said nothing. 'Do you fucking hear me?'

I realised that the snake was poised to strike. 'Yes, Dad,' I mumbled. He turned around and left. A day or two later, he was on his way to South West. I secretly longed for his plane to blow up in mid-air or for a Swapo-guided RPG to explode in his arse.

At the time I was in standard seven and about fifteen years old but this was essentially where my road with Dad ended. He was on service in the Operational Area for several years to come. Although I had to shake his hand from time to time and smile at his feeble jokes and nod my head at his bloodthirsty border stories – and I have to admit I thoroughly enjoyed some of them – I vowed to undermine him whenever I could and to have as little as possible to do with him. But I suppose by then the damage had been done.

Although I shudder at the thought that I might be a chip off the old block, I often ponder about the similarities between me and my father. On the surface, we're miles apart. My father was celebrated as a hero and a man who stood for law and order, an astute disciplinarian and a patriot, a father and a husband.

In contrast, I will one day be deposited in a hole in the ground as one of the most odious villains this country has ever spawned. If the death penalty hadn't been abolished, they would have tied a rope around my neck and strung me from a pole.

Dad's shenanigans were hidden from prying eyes. Whether it was his family or detainees that he had fucked up, there was always someone – Mom, us, the system – to pull a blanket over his appalling acts. But it didn't happen in my case. The media and the courts picked my bones clean and laid bare each and every miserable chapter of my depraved life.

During my trial the media speculated about how it was possible that an upright, decorated, God-fearing policeman could have spawned such a disgusting miscreant. Some smart-arsed chick from *Huisgenoot* tracked my mother down and bamboozled her into opening her heart to the magazine. Under the headline 'The tearful anguish of police parents', my mother was photographed sitting at the Lowry organ in the lounge with a photo album on her lap. It was here, in her private corner of the house, claimed the magazine, that she found solace by playing her killer son's favourite tunes. Sometimes Colonel Goosen would join her as she played songs such as 'The Green Berets' or 'Morning has Broken'. They'd look at that photograph of me standing on the beach in Margate with an ice cream in my hand and agonise about a once promising life that had gone horribly wrong. Mom rambled on … I was a gentle and endearing child who shied away from violence and conflict. She blamed my degeneration on mixing with the wrong friends.

She told them the story of how Karel and I had one day cut open two hamsters. At the time Karel still wanted to be a doctor and needed to hone his skills. He stole chloroform from his science class and got hold of a scalpel and two hamsters. Karel wanted to perform a heart transplant.

I prepared the operating theatre in the garage using one of Mom's fluffy white towels, a pair of her white church gloves and some kitchen utensils. Karel knocked out both animals with the chloroform, flipped them on their backs and made incisions across their chests. As the red blood stained their white pelts, my head spun and my stomach turned. When one of the animals started kicking in the air and opened its eyes, I decided I had had enough. I picked the hamster up, scurried into the house and presented the blood-soaked animal, by then in the throes of death, to Mom.

Sweet story, isn't it? It was, until she phoned Dad and asked him what we should do with the dead animals. What Mom didn't tell *Huisgenoot* was that when Dad marched into the house that night, he took off his belt and vowed to teach Karel and me a lesson we'd never forget. I don't know about Karel, but I didn't learn the lesson.

The last time I saw Dad was during my trial. Every morning I was shackled in leg and hand irons and transported from Pretoria Central to the court cells. Towards the end of the trial, as I stepped up to the bench where the accused sat, I turned around to acknowledge the presence of Mom, who had been there every day. She was not alone. Sitting next to her was a doddery old man in a grey suit. I hadn't seen Dad for years and his frail condition shocked me. He'd become thin and decrepit. I knew that he had taken early retirement on the grounds of ill health. He left the force a colonel. At tea break, Mom and Dad walked over to me. Without a word, he stretched out his hand, which I took. Even his grip, once so firm, was flabby.

'Good day, Gideon,' he said. 'It's been a long time, son. How are you doing?'

'Good day, Dad,' I replied. 'No, I'm fine. Hanging in and

hoping for the best.'

'How does the case look, son?'

'Bad,' I said. 'I'm going down.'

'Is it true?' he asked.

'Is what true?'

'The evidence against you,' he said. 'Is it all true?'

I looked him squarely in the eyes and for a moment I detected a glimmer of sadness or pain or regret or something like that.

'Most of it,' I said and looked down at the irons around my ankles.

That was the extent of our conversation. The next day the newspapers had front page pictures of Dad, supported by Mom, shuffling towards the court. 'Goosen's policeman father in court,' said the headlines. He didn't come again until the day of sentencing when, dressed in a grey suit and assisted by Mom, he limped into court leaning on a walking stick.

Sentencing was mercifully short, but devastatingly harsh. The judge peered at me over his reading glasses and paused for a highly charged moment. Then he proclaimed: 'Gideon Johannes Goosen, you are sentenced to three life sentences and thirty-five years' imprisonment. The sentences are to run concurrently.'

As I was about to be escorted down to the cells to start my life in hell, the policemen paused to give me a few seconds to bid farewell to my family. Mom threw her arms around my neck. She smelled of the same sweet-smelling powder I had known as a child. I could feel her tears wetting my left cheek and dripping on to my shirt. When I broke free, I stared into Dad's eyes.

'*Sterkte, seun,*' he said and put his hand on my shoulder.

As I was about to begin my journey down the steps, Dad did a most peculiar thing. He shoved something into my hand and whispered: 'Take this, son.' I looked down. It was a tightly folded hundred rand note. I stared at it, looked up at him and for a moment I thought I recognised a flicker of that same pompous smirk that had haunted me as a child.

What the fuck was this? Payout for what he had done to me? Blood money for the manner in which he had brought up his children; one dead, one in prison and the other lying somewhere in a gutter? I opened my hand, dropped the note next to my feet and continued on my way. I never saw him again.

About four months later, Mom told me during a visit: 'Bad news, Gideon. Dad's got cancer.'

I looked at her through the glass barricade and said matter-of-factly: 'I'm sorry.'

'It's his liver,' she said. 'The doctors say he doesn't have long.'

'I'm sorry.'

'He wants to see you before it's too late.'

'About what?'

'I don't know,' she said. 'I think he wants to say goodbye.'

I didn't answer her. She added: 'And maybe he wants to say he's sorry.'

'For what?'

'I don't know, Gideon. There are things eating away at him and he wants to set them right.'

I looked at the vulnerable woman sitting in front of me and for a moment her frailty punched a hole in my heart. I wanted to wrap her in my arms, hold her head against my chest and pour warmth and love into her soul. Her hands were bony and knobbly and blue veins branched like gutters across their surfaces. The corners of her eyes were deeply etched and even a blanket of powder couldn't conceal the creases on her face. Mom was not even sixty but she was an old, broken woman. Imagine her life. Her boys were fucked up and her husband, after decades of dragging her down and wearing her out, ultimately received his sentence as well. And as fate justly ruled, it was bound to be a horrid parting from the world.

In spite of my feelings for Mom, I simply couldn't envisage any reconciliation with Dad. Cancer or no cancer, I never wanted to see him again. I may have been incarcerated in a yellow-brick dungeon and I may have been the most degraded human being on the face of the earth, but I still had a choice: to lay eyes on Hendrik Goosen and grant him absolution, or to turn my back on the dying man and send him to hell.

'I'm sorry, Mom,' I said. 'I don't want to see him.'

Tears welled in her eyes. 'Why not?'

'I just don't want to see him,' I repeated.

'Why do you hate him so much?'

'I don't hate him,' I lied. 'I just don't want to see him again.'

'Oh, Gideon,' she whimpered, a tear rolling down her cheek. 'What's happened to my little ice cream boy on the beach in Margate?'

'Oh, Mom, please.'

'Do you know how cute you were?'

'Oh, Mom, come on!'

'And now you're turning your back on your own blood.'

'Mom ...'

'You know this is going to be very hard for him?'

'I'm sorry, but that's how it is.'

'Do you know, Gideon,' she said, 'that you're helping to dig his grave?'

I looked at her hunched body for a few seconds, then I stood up and asked a warder to take me back to The Bomb.

Dad died a month later. A social worker from Correctional Services brought me the news and asked me if I wanted to phone or write to my mother or send a message or even flowers for the funeral. I declined the invitation. Dad was dumped into a grave in Krugersdorp cemetery with none of his sons present.

Some time later, Mom brought me photographs of his grave and his Bible. I didn't want to hurt her and took them without a word. That night, I sat in my cell and looked at the photos. The last pic was of Dad's gravestone. Engraved on it were the words:

Hier lê 'n seun van die veld
'n Man in murg en been 'n held
Hy's met God's genade gebore
Maar is ons nie langer beskore

Loosely translated, it would read something like:

Here lies a man of the veld
A man a hero in heart and soul
He was born with God's grace
But now he's been taken away

I looked at the photograph for a long, long time and felt more forlorn than ever. Throughout my life I had wanted a father who would nourish me with those values every human being cherishes: decency, honesty, respect, integrity. My God, how difficult could it have been in the good old days of apartheid when each and every whitey was born with a silver spoon in his mouth? It was pretty hard to fuck up. Yet Dad flunked with flying colours.

I still think about my father and I have no doubt that I have many unresolved issues about him. Shortly after my incarceration, a prison psychologist summoned me for a session of what she called psychoanalysis. She was blonde with a pouting mouth, slim hands and fingers, rounded calves and a pair of knockout knockers – her nipples poked through the layers of Correctional Services uniform – so I agreed to a series of tests. She showed only a few millimetres of cleavage but that was enough to keep me focused and to answer her questions.

She concluded that I was suffering from a host of ugly things, like having a severe father complex, and that I harboured loads of suppressed anger. She wanted to conduct further tests but announced one day that she had fallen pregnant and might not be able to fit me into her schedule in future. I lost interest and never pursued further psychological testing.

In the end, I bade my father farewell with all the resentment and hatred I had nursed for many years. I often look at that family picture on my table and try to remember him as nothing but a father who in his simplicity and stupidity, and in his frequent bouts of intoxication, thought he was doing his best for us.

I've run from Hendrik Goosen my whole life, but have never managed to elude him. He lurked like a spectral demon in my shadow and the harder and faster I sprinted, the more and more I came to resemble my old man. My father and I seem to have possessed the same uncanny ability to destroy our worlds and those of the ones we loved.

Ultimately, Dad and I, we're just the same. We're two peas in a pod. We wrecked and ravaged everyone and everything around us. And what did we end up with?

Sweet fucking zero. Nothing but squandered lives of guilt and regret.

Eight

Gielie was the unloveliest fuck I've ever cast my eyes upon. I could easily spend a page or two elaborating on his repulsive features. He was a kind of 'Randfontein Special', in the same way we would brand an abandoned, tick-infested, mangy dog a 'pavement special'.

I'm going to give it a go. Gielie's head, to start with, was a freakish shape. It was elongated from front to back. If you checked him from the side, his head sort of kept going at the back. You'll remember that I also described Johnnie's head as being a peculiar shape. This was obviously a Randfontein phenomenon that might have had something to do with the poisonous gases and atmospheric pressure in the mines, or the fact that in many cases mommies and daddies and husbands and wives were also nieces and nephews. The town was nothing but one big happy family.

What added to the anomaly that was Gielie was that he bordered on obesity. Picture him: an elongated head with puffy cheeks and an almost double chin. His lips would have shamed a set of Firestones at the Tarlton drag-racing track. To round it off, his teeth were uneven and yellow and his skin looked as though it was on the verge of a septic explosion. Every time I looked at Gielie, I failed to understand why it was necessary to conduct medical experiments on dogs when Randfontein was a vast, untapped laboratory.

Gielie's physique belied his reputation as a lethal, iron-fisted fighter. He was deceptively fast and packed a devastating punch. If that didn't land his opponent on his back, he was prepared to butt head, to elbow, bite and kick.

If I mention his surname, you'll immediately recognise him as a former South African boxing champion. Yes, Gielie Geldenhuys. In later years as he rose through the boxing ranks and flattened and battered into submission one adversary after the other, he acquired the nickname of Big Baby. When he bagged the South African heavyweight title by pelting Gerrie Coetzee into oblivion and afterwards burst into a torrent of tears, he was rechristened Cry Baby. That changed again when he lost a world title elimination fight and broke the jaw of a journalist who referred to him as lazy, obese and a disgrace to the sport. He was retagged Bad Baby.

The Geldenhuys family – six boys – were debt collectors. Oom Japie Geldenhuys was as skinny as a reed but had a ferocious reputation as a collector who could wring anything from anybody. He used his sons as hitmen and at the time I met Gielie – he had just turned sixteen – he was already ramming down doors and breaking bones on behalf of his father. They were the mafia of Randfontein.

Gielie became the fourth member of our gang. Although he was a year older than us, at some stage he was in the same class at school as Jakes and Johnnie. When I met him the two had overtaken him and were respectively two and one standards ahead of him. Believe me, it required extreme stupidity to trail in the academic footsteps of Johnnie Swart, yet he towered like a rocket scientist over Gielie who had failed just about every standard he had ever attempted. But I suppose when you could unleash mayhem like he could, brains and an education were unimportant. Gielie's map in life was predetermined by his looks, his physique and his strength. He was always going to be an unsightly bone-breaker of some kind.

The Geldenhuys family lived on a smallholding not far from Jakes. It was an all-male household. Gielie's mother had absconded with the sheriff of the court many years earlier and his father never remarried. Despite the absence of a woman, the house was always spotlessly clean and tidy. They were certainly not as poverty-stricken as the Swart household, but Randfontein didn't afford as many opportunities for debt collecting as other places. It was mostly hi-fis and, sometimes, fridges and stoves that they had to recover. I think I've already mentioned that powerful hi-fis were the ultimate status symbol on the West Rand and people would cheat and lie to acquire one on hire purchase. Shops that sold the stuff didn't bother to hit those who had fallen into arrears with letters of demand or shit like that. They simply called in the Geldenhuys clan to smash down the front door, dish out a few *klappe* and repossess the item. They roamed the streets of Randfontein in their battered Ford F100 pickup and acquired a fearsome reputation.

Many of their assignments were not in Randfontein itself, but in the surrounding townships. Those were the years when blacks started acquiring wealth because they didn't pay taxes, and they started buying luxury items such as fridges and hi-fis. Gielie loved going into the township. While Oom Japie demanded restraint in the white areas, his band of terrorists had carte blanche in the *lokasies*. It was also much safer to do debt collecting in the townships because the police mostly ignored complaints from blacks.

Gielie's fist was often cut and bruised in the aftermath of such forays. He would hold his hand in the air and boast: 'A *houtkop's* tooth. But at least I still have my hand. His teeth are no more.'

The problem was apparently that as soon as blacks realised that they were getting into arrears with their payments and were in danger of losing their prized possessions, they would hide them in surrounding houses or shacks. Gielie said it sometimes took a lot of persuasion to convince a debtor to give up his hi-fi or fridge.

'And how do you do that?' I asked him.

He grimaced. 'By asking him very nicely where it is.'

'And if he doesn't tell you?'

'Then I bash my head against his!' Gielie said, lowering his head to reveal a number of tiny blemishes. His hair was shaved in a crew cut and wasn't more than a few millimetres long.

'But I thought they had very hard heads?'

'Nothing, *boet*,' said Gielie tapping his knuckles against his skull (believe me, it sounded hollow), 'is harder than this head.'

It was true. Gielie seemed to have an armour-plated skull. His head was a relatively big target and throughout his boxing career some of the hardest hitters in world boxing pelted him mercilessly on his pate. By going for the top, they might have achieved some brain damage – if there was anything to injure – but they never managed to floor him. In fact, when Gielie saw a punch coming, he often dropped his head to take the blow on his skull in almost the same manner as other fighters shielded themselves with their gloves. His weak point had always been his pulpy body and his corner was often forced to throw in the towel after a barrage of blows to his stomach and ribs.

The advent of Gielie gave us the opportunity to explore a new pursuit: kaffir-bashing. I know you are shaking your head and clicking your tongue in disgust. I'm also ashamed of it today but hey, man, back then it was sort of normal. Remember that we're talking about the late seventies and early eighties when it was illegal for a white man to *pomp* a non-white girl and makeshift magistrates could sentence black men to a hiding with a cane if they weren't carrying their passes. It wasn't just Randfontein and Krugersdorp who were engaged in kaffir-bashing, it was the

117

whole fucking country.

I can't say that I hated *houtkoppe*. It wasn't necessary to despise them; they knew their place, the streets of our suburbs were quiet and safe and they brought the gold to the surface in our mines. They were probably regarded more as a useful nuisance than anything else.

But Dad knew better. I was still a young boy when he warned that a sinister force was stirring up anti-white emotions in the townships. Communism posed a threat to whites and extreme measures were needed to counter this extreme threat. He was shown to be one hundred per cent right when communist agitators were found to be behind the 1976 Soweto uprising.

Dad might have been a cunt, but I quoted him liberally and he gave me insights into matters that others relished when I passed them on. The fact that he was doing duty in South West enhanced his reputation. During one of his visits from the Operational Area, which thankfully lasted only two weeks and passed uneventfully, he produced a pile of photographs.

The first few showed Dad in the police camp at Oshakati having a bash with his friends. The cops, glasses of police coffee in their hands, hugged one another, held their R1 rifles in the air and looked plastered. Dad and his friends were celebrating a victory over Swapo.

The other photographs were of the operation itself and some were truly gruesome. In the first few, Dad in his camouflage uniform was sitting on top of a Casspir armoured vehicle and questioning a suspect in an Owambo village. And then there were photographs of Dad holding his R1 in the air and posing triumphantly with his boot on the shot-up bloody corpse of a Swapo terrie.

'Did you shoot him, Dad?' I asked excitedly.

Dad was always secretive about his activities. 'There was a skirmish in which I participated,' he said. 'They came second.'

There were several more photographs of the dead terrie, some were close-ups that showed that part of his forehead had been blown away. There were other photographs showing several dead terries strapped across the wheel fenders of police or army armoured vehicles.

'*Sjoe*, Dad!' I exclaimed. 'Why do you drive around with them like that?'

'It's an old trick, son,' he said. 'We drive through villages so that the PBs can see it. Brings home the message that we're not taking any shit.' PB was an abbreviation for *Plaaslike Bevolking*, or local population, which was how the army and police referred to local inhabitants.

Of course, it wasn't long before I had snitched the pics and was brandishing them in front of the gang. Johnnie showed them to Willem who said: '*Ja*, that's how it is. If you don't stop 'em there, they'll come down south to kill us.'

It was Jakes who first came up with the idea. He said: 'We can't let that happen. We also have to do our bit.'

'What do you mean?' I asked.

'We can't sit around and wait for it to happen,' he said. 'We must teach 'em a lesson.'

'Like what?' I wanted to know.

'Like fucking them up,' said Jakes.

'But how?'

'I dunno. But we must let them know we're not taking their shit.'

Willem chimed in. 'Ask Oom Japie if you can come with us to the *lokasie*. Lots of fucking up is going on there.'

The following Friday we climbed on to the back of the truck and headed towards the Randfontein township. Gielie and two of his brothers had to repossess a hi-fi from a guy somewhere in the township. He'd ignored several calls requesting payment and had been warned that debt collectors were on his tail.

We must have resembled the oafs in 'Deliverance', that American movie classic about a group of city-slickers who go on a hunting expedition and get ambushed by barbaric inbred hillbillies. We stood in a row on the back of the truck. Willem, a red bandanna around his head, was clutching a baseball bat in one hand and wearing a knuckle-duster on the other. Gielie's two brothers, one armed with a shotgun, sat in the front. As we drove, we bellowed abuse at blacks walking in the streets.

'Fucking kaffir,' yelled Jakes. 'You're going to *kak!*'

'I'm going to trash you today!' Gielie shouted as we drove past an elderly black woman in a maid's uniform. He almost fell off the truck as he loosened his grip on the bar to raise his fists in the air.

I was the only one not standing up. I was sitting on the deck at the back, gaping at the antics of my friends. I had felt apprehensive about this operation from the outset and had no particular desire to fuck up a *houtkop*. But even if I wanted to I couldn't pull out. As a member of the gang I had to go with the flow.

It was the first time that I had ever been in a township. I was amazed to see row upon row of matchbox houses, like files of red-brick soldiers. Many boasted neat little gardens or even vegetable patches and scores of people were hanging around in the streets, laughing, talking and going about their daily chores. I don't know what I had expected. I knew that many blacks lived in houses but maybe I thought there would still be Zulus in skins dancing around straw huts and drinking kaffir beer from clay pots. And maybe a communist on every street corner, but I wasn't sure what they looked like. Instead it all seemed terribly normal.

That was until we roared past in the F100. People stopped, stared, and grabbed their children's hands. They jumped on to the pavements or scurried back into their yards. Some just stared in bewilderment. Whites were a rare sight in a township, and a bunch of screaming hooligans on the back of a truck must have been alarming.

'Yoohoo! Fucking kaffirs!' screamed Jakes and Gielie, waving their fists in the air.

We stopped in front of a tidy, white-painted house, substantially bigger than the standard box-like dwelling. A battered old Chevvy was parked on the pavement.

'Aha,' said Willem as we piled off the truck. 'The kaffir wants to be white but he's shy about paying. We'll teach him a lesson.'

Gielie strode up to the front door like a battering ram. Willem was right behind him with the bat in his hand. Gielie's brother, the shotgun held menacingly in front of him, was a step further back. The rest of us were behind him. Gielie hammered on the door with his fist and shouted: 'We're from Geldenhuys and Sons Debt Collectors and we want your hi-fi. Open up!' He waited a second or two and then hammered again: 'Fucking open up!'

We didn't hear a sound. Would you have opened your door for a bunch of marauding hooligans? No fucking way in hell! After Gielie had repeated his demand a number of times, he turned around and said: 'Looks like they're not here.'

Then, out of the corner of my eye, I saw something at the window. The curtains were closed but I was sure I had seen a movement. I thought for a moment that I must be mistaken, but then I saw it again. There was someone in the house!

'They're here! They're here!' I shrieked at the top of my voice. Everyone looked at me. 'I saw someone! At the window. They're inside!'

'Gielie,' said Willem, 'go fetch the pole.'

Gielie went back to the truck. He returned with a thick, wooden pole that he carried in both hands. 'Now you're going to see some sport,' he said as he to signalled Jakes, Johnnie and me to help him. We grabbed the heavy pole, held it out in front of us, stood back, and then stormed forward and rammed it into the wooden door. The door splintered, but didn't give way completely. At that moment, cries and screams escaped from the living room.

'Quick, quick!' urged Willem. 'They're going to get away.'

At our second attempt, the door shattered into pieces and we burst into the house. Women wailed and a child screamed. The curtains were closed and I couldn't immediately make out how many people were in the room. One or two were running out of the room towards the back of the house, obviously to try to escape through the kitchen door, but that exit was already blocked by Gielie's brother with the shotgun.

Someone threw the curtains open, just in time for me to see a figure diving behind a couch. Another was spreadeagled on the carpet. Two young women were sitting on the floor, holding on to one another. The inside of the house was rather smart. It was certainly vastly superior to Johnnie's or Gielie's or Jakes' homes, but then I was sure everything had either been stolen or acquired on hire purchase and never paid for.

Willem, recce that he was, swept through the house. He found a teenage girl with a small baby in one of the bedrooms.

'They're breeding like rabbits,' he said as he pushed the girl into the lounge.

'Please, boss, please,' she whimpered.

'*God, meid*,' barked Willem, 'shut up!'

In the meantime, Gielie had crawled on top of the couch and was extricating the bloke – literally by the neck – from his hiding place. He hauled him over the couch and dumped him on the carpet. He had a frenzied look in his eyes, a look I would grow accustomed to in years to come. It was usually reserved for that moment in the boxing ring when he catapulted his one hundred and forty kilos on to an opponent and smashed him into dreamland. The same thing was about to be unleashed on our hapless victims. Gielie reminded me of Dad in those moments when his cheeks bulged like a toad, his face became blood red and he was about to swing back his hairy paw to clobber his wife and sons.

I'm not going to bore you with every little detail of the blitzkrieg that was about to erupt; suffice to say that in a crude way it was Gielie at his very best. It started with a blast from the shotgun behind me. I nearly threw myself on to the floor. When I swung around, Gielie's brother was standing there with a wide grin on his face and the smoking gun in his hand. He'd shot a hole the size of a soccer ball through the ceiling. The *houtkoppe* must have thought that they were about to kick the bucket because they were screaming, pleading and wailing at the same time.

'Come, guys, come!' Willem said. 'We have to be out before the cops come!'

'Where's the fucking hi-fi!' Gielie thundered, glaring at the guy lying in front of him on the floor.

When he didn't answer immediately, Gielie swooped down on him with the fury of a wounded predator. Two short jabs and a head butt. That was all it took and the guy was out cold.

The second *houtkop*, who was also spread out on the floor, took one look at his buddy and decided that, come hell or high water, he was not staying. He was up in a flash and dived for the door.

Problem was that I was standing in front of the door. I can count my tackles on the rugby field on one hand – and there will be fingers over. This had to count as my best. I launched myself at him, grabbed him around the thighs and held on for dear life. He plummeted to the ground like a bag of mealies.

The moment he hit the ground, Jakes and Johnnie descended on him like a pack of wild dogs. He was trying to squirm free but Johnnie punted him with his big black boots. By then Jakes was also on him. I leapt to my feet and kicked him as hard as I could in the face. He babbled inaudibly as blood poured from his nose. He covered his face with his hands and at the same time mumbled something I didn't understand. I kicked him again and again.

One of the women swiftly revealed the whereabouts of the hi-fi – it was hidden in a shed in the backyard. One of Gielie's brothers took her by the arm and a minute or so later they returned with the machine.

As Gielie got to his feet and Jakes, Johnnie and I stepped back to inspect our handiwork, Willem turned towards the women and said: 'Come on, pay up! We didn't come here for nothing.'

'Come, come, come,' said Gielie. 'Pay up!'

The women scrambled around the room and produced two notes and a handful of coins. One of them held the money out to Willem, who looked at it with a sneer and said: 'Is this all you can come up with?'

'Yes, boss.'

'It's not enough,' said Willem. But he took the money and

stuffed it into his pocket.

'Sorry, boss.'

'Fuck that,' said Willem. He looked at Gielie. 'Let's fuck off.'

Both the men on the floor were in pretty bad shape. One was out cold, courtesy of Gielie's wrath. His face was a bloody mess. The second dude was lying on his stomach with his head a few inches above the floor. He spat out a gob of blood and a broken tooth.

A small crowd had gathered on the pavement but scattered in every direction when they saw us. We raced off with screeching tyres and war cries. On the way out of the township, Johnnie asked Willem: 'How much did you get?'

'Not much,' he said.

'Enough for a Klippies?'

'Yes.'

'And a fuck?'

'No ways.'

I have to admit that I was slightly disappointed. I'd been fantasising about Amber and her dark bush ever since she'd popped my cherry. I heard later that she'd married an old guy who had promised to pay for her to have her tits fixed. I was not making any progress with girls at school, although I had played *stinkvingertjie* with one of Johnnie's older sisters one Friday afternoon behind the shed in the backyard. I had to scramble for safety when she started fiddling with my belt. I had no desire to breed with a Swart. My love life still consisted primarily of *Scope* and my own hand.

We accompanied Geldenhuys and Sons Debt Collectors several more times on trips into the townships, and similar incidents – with similar results – repeated themselves over and again. I was becoming increasingly vicious and took great delight in smashing my fist into a black face. I discovered that I packed a mean punch and although I'd never match up to Gielie, I was on a par with Jakes. Johnnie still held the trophy when it came to kicking, his heavy boots saw to that. I relished the control that I exercised over our hapless victims; it made me feel big and powerful.

We twice extorted enough money for carnal excursions to The Leopard. The first time Willem got hold of a slightly frazzled-looking and clearly desperate tart who offered us a strip-and-screw package. By the time she'd flaked off her flimsy dress and flaunted her hindquarters inches from my face, I had already shot my load. The second time we spotted a succulent piece of meat standing some distance away from the others. Willem stopped and beckoned her closer.

'Good day, oom,' she said. She appeared a bit neglected, but looked clean and eager.

'Climb in, girl,' said Willem.

She looked at the back of the truck, counted us and asked: 'All of you, oom?'

'Count me out,' said Gielie. 'I don't do whores.'

I felt a prickle in my pants as we walked into the room. But it was not to be. When my turn came, it simply wouldn't move. The floozie squeezed and twisted my dick but there was zero reaction. She shrugged her shoulders and moved on to Jakes, who lived up to his reputation. It was a devastating blow to my self-esteem and for a while I stayed away from The Leopard.

Our Friday afternoon junkets consisted of three activities: kaffir-bashing, gang fighting and hunting. In between, we nicked sweets, chips, clothes and groceries. Gielie didn't participate in our shoplifting expeditions because he said he wasn't a bandit. We used Johnnie as our kind of front man. Whenever he got busted, shopkeepers took one look at his tattered clothes and crippled feet and told him to go. The manager of OK Bazaars once nabbed Johnnie in the act. He loaded him into his car, took him home and handed him over to Oom Buks who shrugged his shoulders, told his son in a lame voice not to do it again, and waved the supermarket man goodbye.

Our excursions into the townships came to an abrupt halt when the cops rocked up at the Geldenhuys smallholding and arrested Oom Japie and two of his sons for assault and malicious damage to property. The investigation fell apart when Gielie and his brothers visited the complainants and threatened to remove them permanently from society. For a while at least, the townships were no-go areas.

The hunting thing started with one or other town council declaring the vlei between Krugersdorp and Randfontein a nature reserve and breeding sanctuary for migrating birds. It was also supposed to be a tourist attraction and a picnic spot for families. But it wasn't long before the place deteriorated into a seedy hideout where ducktails banged their underage floozies in their hotted-up cars and low-class scum drank themselves into oblivion.

Willem came up with the idea of hunting guineafowl. Armed with the shotgun, we set off to stalk them. There wasn't a fowl in sight but it wasn't long before blood lust overwhelmed us. We started shooting at anything that blinked its eyes or moved – tinktinkies, bokmakieries, vinks, swallows, doves, rabbits, mice, whatever.

The vlei became a regular Friday afternoon hunting ground. We had no respect for any living thing. I discovered that I was a pretty mean shot. Admittedly, it is hard to miss with a shotgun, but I bagged more dead things than anyone else. I just loved holding the shotgun and pressing it into my shoulder. And when I pressed the trigger, it was as though the shooting-iron came alive: the smoke and thunder bellowing from its barrel, and an enormous kick into my body. I decided that I loved guns.

It wasn't long before we'd seriously reduced the animal population of the vlei and what was left moved off to safer fields. But by then we were engaged in fighting other Randfontein gangs. Gang fighting was a regular and acceptable pastime in that part of the world and most boys belonged to a gang. Ours was called The Dirty Harries – after the Clint Eastwood action movies.

We invaded a derelict railway house at the end of the station lane, pasted a 'No Entry' sign at the front door and hid stolen provisions like tinned food and biscuits under the floor. We cut our thumbs with razors (I had to fight back the tears) and pressed them against one another's, we stole red caps from Pep Stores and concluded the bonding rite with a group wank (Jakes shot the furthest, followed by Johnnie, me and Gielie, who managed only a few drops).

Willem was too old to be an active member of the gang, but with his extensive battle experience he was *veggeneraal* of The Dirty Harries. He lurked in the background with a knife and a chain – just in case anything went wrong. Not that he had to intervene too often. We looked like an unimposing bunch of push-overs. There was obese Gielie, crippled Johnnie, wispy me and sort-of-okay Jakes. But we made up for our appearance with a 'shock and awe' strategy.

Our battle plan involved Johnnie and Jakes wildly storming into action with heads, fists and boots. Jakes often sported Willem's knuckleduster and he more than once smashed teeth out and punctured skulls. What Johnnie lacked in speed and mobility, he made up for with fury and ferocity. Once the two had cut a swathe through enemy lines, Gielie – his head thrust forward like a battering ram – pounced with the devastation of a battle tank. I followed in his wake as the supreme finisher.

As Gielie pummelled our adversaries to the ground, I trampled, punted and clobbered what remained of them. Being at the back enabled me to stay clear of the firing line and I emerged from most brawls virtually unscathed. We soon acquired a daunting reputation and other gangs were hesitant to take us on.

The remainder of my sixteenth year passed uneventfully, although our friendship was threatened by two incidents. Just before our final exams, Jakes fell head over heels in love. He started skipping our Friday afternoon junkets, which seriously threatened our invincibility.

Jakes eventually introduced us to Sharon, the pigtailed, sixteen-year-old daughter of a gold miner. She was as thin as a reed, had knobbly knees and her titties were as flat as pancakes. But Jakes couldn't keep his eyes off her pimply freckled face and he clutched her skinny hand tightly.

'She's the one,' Jakes told us, a faraway expression on his face.

'*Nee God, man!*' said Johnnie. 'You look like a dog taking a shit!'

'She's my Barbie doll,' said Jakes.

'Is she still a virgin?' Johnnie wanted to know.

'She was,' said Jakes, 'but definitely not any longer.'

Jakes was bonking the shit out of Sharon and it was just a matter of time before she had a bun in the oven. Shortly before our final exams, he announced: 'Sharon's preggers!'

'*God, Jissus!*' bawled Gielie.

'What now?' I wanted to know.

'Going to marry her,' he said.

'Fuck no!' hollered Johnnie. 'You're mad!'

A week later, Jakes announced that he was leaving school. He had to find a job in order to provide for his future wife and child. Johnnie followed suit. He was almost certainly going to flunk standard seven for the second time, but it was an incident at home that accelerated his decision.

Johnnie was about to be elevated to bed-status when one of his pregnant sisters was kicked out by her boyfriend. She came home and snatched the vacant bed. Johnnie was pissed off and not prepared to continue dozing on dirty washing.

He told his mother the next morning: 'You see this face? Have a good look, 'cause you won't see it again.'

He stuffed a few rags into a plastic bag and moved into the empty maid's room on the Geldenhuys smallholding. He was going to pay for his board and lodging by assisting with debt collecting. Gielie languished at school for another few months, failed everything, and then – to everyone's relief – announced that he was flunking out to begin a career in professional boxing.

I passed standard eight by the skin of my teeth. Dad, back from South West for his summer vacation, growled and rumbled and threatened to demolish me if I didn't get my academic act together. We spent our summer holiday in the same beach flat in Margate. I spent most of my holiday indoors because I was too embarrassed to show my skinny white body on the beach. My face was a pimply mess and I stumbled over my words as soon as I got anywhere near fluff. I lusted after the lithe, tanned flesh of the girl in the flat next door but never had the courage to approach her. I uttered a sheepish 'Hi' whenever I saw her but eventually she wandered off with a surfer boy who had a Tarzan-like chest and thighs. I really missed my friends and longed to go home.

Jakes had to postpone his wedding when, a month or two into the new year, the military police arrived on the Versters' doorstep. Jakes had just turned seventeen and had failed to report for his compulsory army service. He subsequently escaped twice, was apprehended each time and locked up in detention barracks.

When he finally tied the knot, it was in the Randfontein magistrate's court in the presence of three military policemen. Jakes looked rather moronic in his army regalia while Sharon paraded her preggy condition in a pink crimplene miniskirt and white stilettos. Her mousy hair had been transformed into a mane of bouncy peroxided curls and her pouting mouth was coated with glossy cherry-coloured lipstick. A set of fiery red, artificial nails was pasted over her bitten fingertips.

Gielie and I bunked school for the day and plonked ourselves down in the row behind the lovebirds' families. Johnnie hobbled into the courtroom long after the ceremony started. I hadn't seen him for months and since then he had undergone a transformation. Half his face was hidden by a set of sun goggles, his hair was bound in a ponytail and a thick, gold chain adorned his neck. He was dressed in yellow bell-bottoms and a leather jacket.

The couple muttered silly vows and exchanged tinny-looking rings and were pronounced man and wife. Jakes and Sharon had an hour to celebrate their marriage before he had to go back to his cell in the military barracks at Voortrekkerhoogte. There was tea and cake at the smallholding.

I walked out of the courtroom with Johnnie because he had a new Suzuki 250cc that he wanted to show me. He wasn't going to the reception and just before he left, he slipped a half-jack of Smirnoff out of his pocket and ripped the lid off. As he hurled the burning liquid down his throat, I pointed at the bike and asked him: 'And where do you get all of this?'

'Proceeds,' he said passing the bottle to me.

'Proceeds of what?'

'Of wheeling and dealing.'

'With what?'

'Whatever,' Johnnie said, snickering. I took a deep gulp of vodka that took my breath away. Johnnie started the Suzuki and wheelied away.

I spoke briefly to Jakes at his reception. 'What's it with Johnnie?' I asked him.

'Our *gabba* Johnnie,' he said and chuckled, 'is busy with things that you don't want to know about.'

'How come?'

'The man's on a mission. He's making shekels.'

'Doing what?'

'Do you still wanna be a flatfoot?'

'I think so,' I said, 'but I'm not sure.'

'Then I can't tell you,' he said. He burst out laughing and walked away. I stuffed a few koeksisters in my mouth, got on my bicycle and pedalled the ten kilometres or so back to Krugersdorp. That was the last time I saw any of my mates while I was still in school.

By the time I wrote my matric exams my friends were nothing more than pleasant memories. I once stumbled across Jakes' brother Barney in Krugersdorp and he told me that Johnnie had been involved in a botched robbery at a petrol station and that the police were looking for him. I just shook my head and thought that it was maybe better that our ways had parted.

I wouldn't see Johnnie for more than two years. When I laid eyes on him again, he was huddled in a corner of the holding cells of the Brixton Murder and Robbery Unit.

Johnnie was up for murder.

Nine

Gloom has descended on my cell. Maybe it's because the onset of autumn has banished the light and warmth of summer. Like a terminal patient slowly departing this world, my ray of sun became shorter and weaker until finally it was gone. The jacaranda trees across Pretoria will have been the first to fall victim to the onset of winter. The chill gnaws at their leaves like a hungry hyena until they are nothing but skeletons of branches and twigs.

I haven't written about my fucked-up life for months. When my darling angel Debbie suggested for the first time that I put my wretched life down on paper and unbosom myself to her, she said it would be a journey of discovery for her and the road to healing for me.

'*Kak*, man!' I tuned her. 'You just get off on gory stuff!'

She turned her green eyes on me. 'Gideon,' she said, 'you

don't talk to me like that!'

'Sorry, man, Debbie,' I said. 'It's just that I don't want to think about all the things I've done.'

'You have to.'

'Why?'

'You have to repent,' she said, 'so that you can cleanse yourself.'

'All the Omo in the world won't wash away the *kak* in my life,' I responded. 'Never mind a few sentences on paper.'

'I don't want to hear about that,' she said firmly. She removed her hand from mine and her body stiffened. 'I can't continue with this relationship,' she said, 'unless you tell me every little detail of what happened in the past.'

'It's not a pretty picture,' I said.

'It doesn't matter, sweetheart,' she said, clasping my hand again. 'That's your old life. This is your new life. But I need to know where you come from.'

I turned my head and looked at her. Her frosty gaze had thawed and our eyes met. I leaned forward and pressed my lips against hers. They were soft and delicate and tasted like green apples. I pulled my mouth back and glanced around me to see if there was any warder checking us out. A few metres away, a shitty-coloured jailer had his back to me and was sipping on a Coke and stuffing a pie into his mouth. Across the square on the other side of the visitors' section a small group of jailers were standing around a bird. It seemed as though they were *kakking* him out and they couldn't give a fuck about what was happening on our side of the visitors' square.

It's highly irregular for a bird to tongue-kiss his chick but I wanted more. I grabbed Debbie around her neck and pulled her into me. Her mouth opened and our tongues entwined. It was as though I was sucking her soul and her warmth and her love into my mouth. I could feel it filling my empty body.

Just a week ago I had written to her: 'I have come to the point where I can feel myself sliding unstoppably towards a big, dark hole ... into the abyss. You have saved me. You have become my anchor and my lifeline. I need you like a desert flower waiting for those first raindrops to fall. You have become my life.'

It was true. Debbie had become a bright and shining light in the dark and lonely world that I was living in. She was my fountain of life and, quite frankly, my only possible ticket out of this hellhole. I'd already accepted – at least as far as Pastor van Heerden was concerned – the merciless fucking God Almighty Lord Jesus Christ as my personal saviour. That counts points. I also reckon that should I one day try my luck for early parole and can convince the board that I've got a loving and caring wife and a Little House on the Prairie waiting for me, it might just boost my chances three or fourfold. Above all, however, I love Debbie. Her gentleness and warmth have captivated me. I haven't been cared for like this since I was a laaitie. Maybe she reminds me of my mother before she was fucked up and broken by my father. I wanted Debbie to stay.

As she tore her mouth from mine, she whispered in my ear: 'And tell me, sweetie, has the flag been hoisted?'

The thing about the flag was our code word for a hard-on. I brushed her ear lobe with my tongue and quipped: 'The *oranje-blanje-blou* is flying at full mast!'

She twittered like a tiny bird who'd just gulped down a juicy worm. It was true: I had a *moer* of a boner!

'Touch me there,' I urged her.

'*Nee, jislaaik!*' she said and pulled away from me. Her cheeks were pink.

I often wonder what it would be like to bang Debbie. No, bang is the wrong word. I don't want to slap-bang-thank-you-mam fuck her. I want to wrap her in my arms and gently make love to her. I want to smell her breath and taste her skin and hear her gasp in my ear.

I haven't screwed for fourteen fucking years. That's more than five thousand days! Before I went to prison, I just took them: whores, broads, sluts, addicts, strippers, stiletto scrubbers, blondes, brunettes, redheads – tarts of any of creed, breed and colour. There were even a few chocolate ones and some with slitty eyes. I don't want to toot my own horn but, believe me, my love-tool seldom had a restful night.

When I saw Debbie for the first time, she didn't stir a thing. Who on earth wants to shag an auntie who reminds you of your beloved mother? After all, she was rather big-boned and a bit heavily padded around the waist. After three children her tits were sagging and I've always preferred them peppy and pert. My yearning for her flesh came only later, probably brought on by keeping my cock in my pants for so many years. I've contemplated paying a jailer to smuggle Debbie into prison for an hour of love. It's been done many times before. Wives, whores and girlfriends; they've all been here. The jailer would usually smuggle the popsy into the rooms near the entrance of the prison where lawyers consult with their clients. The bird just *pomps* her on the table.

There was a time when the jailers even smuggled the skirts into the sickbay so that birds could bed their broads properly. We called the place The Knockshop. Then a bank robber's wife got pregnant six months after he'd come in. When the dude elatedly announced he was going to be a father, the birds scoffed and tuned him that his turtle-dove was grazing in greener fields.

The baby was born and we lined up at The Three Ships to see pics of the bambino. The robber had peculiar features. He looked like some kind of rodent. He had sharp, ragged teeth that you felt he might sink into you at any moment. His head was snout-like – a bit like Johnnie's or Gielie's – and his eyes gave the impression that his mother had been inseminated by a Chinaman. The baby looked exactly like him!

When the tot visited the first time, I just shook my head about the startling resemblance between father and child. That wasn't the end of it. A few months later, the missus had another bun in the oven. And once more the baby looked like a rodent.

The shit started when the broad left dad for another bloke. She sued for maintenance (the cops had never got hold of his booty) and told the court that she had been fertilised inside The Bomb. Needless to say, the newspapers had a field day when they got hold of the story. That was the end of The Knockshop and since then lovebirds have been restricted to using the lawyer's consulting rooms.

Debbie might still have been persuaded for a session of copulation in The Knockshop, but there was no way she was going to allow me to spreadeagle her on a table in a bare little room with a warder a few metres away. It seemed degrading even to me. Problem is that a man feels that a broad will never be his until he's banged her good and hard. I'll simply have to wait. That's how much I love Debbie.

And that's why I've decided to write this shit. I'm not sure what I intend doing with all of this because I don't want Debbie to read everything I've written. Even she'll be shocked. It's a harrowing exercise and it evokes memories of things I'd long ago buried in the rubbish heap in my head. All kinds of fanged serpents creep out and disgorge their venom in my bowels.

Writing about my life eats away at me and tears at my flesh. Especially when I have to tell you about my elder brother. One would think that not much more could go wrong after Pieter hanged himself in the shower and Dad had ripped his family apart. But it did, and in the person of Karel.

Karel wanted to be a doctor, but his school marks were simply not good enough. He'd almost failed maths and was average in science and biology. When he finished school he had no option but to report for national service in the armed forces as all young white men were legally obliged to do – and then they say we had it easy under apartheid!

Karel worked his way into the medics – he'd always vowed one day to wear a white coat and hang a stethoscope around his neck – and was sent to the border in South West. His first letters indicated that he was somewhere in Owamboland in the northern parts of the country not far from the border with Angola. The area was a haven for Swapo, those cowardly black halfwits who claimed that they were fighting for the independence of South West but were nothing but puppets in the hands of the communists.

It was clear that my brother was in the thick of things. People often think about medics in the same vein as cooks or clerks – namby-pambies who are ducking the bullets and bombs. Not Karel. Dad told us during one of his visits from Oshakati that Karel was in the front line with the recces and the parabats and the infantrymen. He was saving lives. He was also being catapulted into a gaping void.

This left only Mom and me at home. I remember my last year or so in school as rather gloomy. Mom had a despondent aura about her and a morbid atmosphere had descended on the house. She served dinner every night at precisely seven-fifteen, after the news and prayers on the Afrikaans service of Radio South Africa. She edged closer to the transistor every time the bone-chilling *toot-toot-toot* signalled the announcement of another national serviceman who had pegged in South West or Angola. In the meantime, I had been elevated to Dad's seat at the dinner table. I was the head of the house.

Karel arrived unannounced on our doorstep one Friday afternoon. There was a knock on the door, I opened it, and there stood my *ouboet*. He was dressed in brown army uniform, had a reddish beret on his head and clutched a sports bag in his hand. He was so skinny that I almost didn't recognise him. He stretched out his hand and said: 'Afternoon, *boet*.' We shook hands briefly and then he walked past me into the house. There were two white stripes on his upper arm. Karel had been promoted to the rank of corporal.

When Mom saw her firstborn, she yelped his name, rushed forward and flung her arms around him. She began to sob uncontrollably. He stood with a sheepish expression on his face, patted her shoulder and then wriggled himself free of her frantic embrace.

'I'm fine, Mom,' he mumbled. 'Don't worry, I'm okay.'

Mom went to the kitchen, scratched around in the fridge and threw an enormous steak into a pan. Half an hour later, we sat down for dinner. Karel looked at the pile of food on his plate, took a bite or two, scratched around with his fork and announced that he wasn't hungry.

'You must eat, son,' said Mom. 'Look at you. Don't they give you any food up there?'

'This is enough for an army, Mom,' he said. 'And I'm not hungry.'

We ate in almost complete silence. I tried to get a conversation going by asking him: 'And how's it up there?'

'Okay,' he said.

'And where have you been?'

'All over.'

'Have you seen lots of action?'

'Here and there,' was his non-committal answer.

'And the terries?' I asked him.

He looked at me. 'What about them?'

'Well, have you seen any?'

'Some,' he said.

That was just about the sum of our conversation. He excused himself, saying he was tired, and went to his room. And that was where he stayed for his week of bush leave. His door stayed shut and he ate nothing. He refused to go to Aunt Magdalena for Sunday lunch, didn't feel like movies, and wouldn't go to church.

'Sorry, but I'm tired,' was his standard answer.

Mom bawled her eyes out and although she didn't say anything, she sensed that her eldest was unwell.

Karel left as quietly as he had come. I didn't see him again until after I had qualified as a police constable.

'I'm not sending more cannon fodder for the terrorists on the border,' Mom said when I'd passed matric (by the skin of my teeth) and had to contemplate my future. 'One is enough. Listen to your father and join the police.'

School leavers could gyppo the army either by joining the police or going to university, although the latter then had to do national service on completion of their studies. Going to a place of higher learning wasn't even an option for me and I had little choice but to report for service at the Police College in Pretoria.

What a perfect way to start a life of crime: join the men in blue!

It's long been known that a policeman is more likely to commit a felony than an ordinary citizen and that the force is the definitive university of crime. I eventually graduated with distinctions in gangsterism, cheating and assault.

It didn't start that way. I was more astonished than anyone else when I was the best student of my intake. I loved shooting and fortunately had had a reasonable amount of preparation before I entered the force. I was brilliant at self-defence, courtesy of our gang fights and kaffir-bashing in Randfontein and Krugersdorp. I found the marching and the lectures boring, except those by Colonel Neelsie du Plooy, a legendary security policeman who had fucked up more communists and agitators than anyone cared to remember.

The colonel was a highly strung character and had to leave active service as a result of a heart attack. His lectures at the college were a sort of retirement job but he had lost none of his passion or his aversion to Mother Russia and her surrogates on Africa's most southern shores. By the time Neelsie got to people like Joe Slovo and Chris Hani and Oliver Tambo, he was balancing on the tips of his toes, his voice was rising, his fists were clenched and spit was flying in every direction. As a result the first row of seats in the lecture room was usually empty.

I entered college towards the middle eighties when the ANC and their communist buddies had embarked on a campaign to make the townships ungovernable. It confirmed what Dad had told us a decade earlier: there was a Marxist onslaught directed at the country and black agitators would not rest until they had subjugated the whites as their slaves and servants.

I wanted to become a security policeman. They were generally regarded as the elite of the force, they didn't wear uniform and were treated with far more respect than ordinary cops. The road to the Security Branch was paved for me. Colonel du Plooy knew Dad and I discovered that my old man, cunt that he may have been, was respected and revered in the force. He had, after all, made mincemeat of the political detainees brought to him for interrogation. I know about only the one Sipho who had dived through the window (how stupid to make yourself airborne when your hands are shackled behind your back and there's a slab of concrete awaiting you on the other side) but there must have been many more who broke their necks after slipping on soap in the showers or tumbling down a flight of stairs.

I had all the makings of an exemplary security policeman. I was (although I didn't realise it then) a rather depraved character who had a grudge against the world and was filled with buckets of suppressed rage. I had no respect for anything or anyone and would happily have fucked up whoever crossed my path. The Security Branch seemed like the kind of place where I could live out all my diabolical fantasies. I was eighteen and had outgrown my childhood shoes. I was an able-bodied, healthy and fit young man of six feet two who weighed two hundred pounds.

Dad was immensely proud when I was awarded the medal for the best student of my intake. He flew all the way from Oshakati in South West to attend my passing-out parade. He wore full uniform while Mom tarted herself up in a pink, multilayered dress with an even pinker hat and matching lipstick.

Afterwards, Dad shook my hand warmly. 'Constable Goosen,' he crowed as he put his arm around my shoulder, 'I'm so proud of you, my son.'

I nodded, turned around and embraced Mom, who held me tightly and said softly: 'And look at my little ice cream boy today.'

'Oh Mom,' I said and gently pushed her away. 'Where's Karel?' My brother had completed his stint in the army and was staying with a friend in Berea while contemplating his future. I hardly ever saw him.

'He's sick,' she said.

'What's wrong?' I wanted to know.

'He's just sick,' she repeated.

I left it at that. The next morning over breakfast, dad spilled the beans. 'Karel's a bloody drug addict,' he said. 'He's in re-hab.'

I was wearing my blue uniform and about to report for my

first day of duty at the Brixton police station in Johannesburg's western suburbs. I looked up at Dad and shrugged my shoulders. I wasn't surprised. I knew something was wrong. Mom had lately been sobbing incessantly and I'd wondered about Dad's sudden trips to the Republic.

'Where is he?' I asked him.

'In Phoenix House in Melville,' he said. 'I booked him in three days ago.'

I visited Karel late that same afternoon. The place resembled a Christian concentration camp. Pinned to a wall was a poster of the 'Serenity Prayer'. It read: 'God, grant me the serenity to accept the things I cannot change, courage to change the things I can, and the wisdom to know the difference.'

They probably reckoned that if you chose God as your drug of choice you wouldn't need anything else. I didn't know a lot about drugs then, but I have always thought that God and Jesus and the Bible are as horribly and destructively addictive as rocks or smack or Colombian caviar.

'He's been through bad withdrawal, but he's better now,' said the sister who showed me to his room. It had a bed and a table and a chair and a wardrobe. Everything was white. Karel was lying on the bed with his arms around a pillow. He was facing the wall and didn't move. The nurse closed the door behind me.

'Karel?' I said. He didn't move. I repeated his name, this time a little louder. I called his name a third time. He eventually lifted his head and turned slowly towards me. A bolt shot through my guts and into my heart. I was looking at a skeletal face with sunken eyes. In the space of two or three years the Monument High first team rugby centre had turned into a bag of skin and bones.

He mumbled my name and fell back on his pillow. I sat staring at him until the nurse brought me a cup of tea and a cocktail of pills for Karel. She helped him to sit upright and he gulped it down without saying a word. The nurse left. Karel looked at me and spoke for the first time.

'Lekker fucked-up, hey?' he said. I nodded my head.

'Where's the old man?' he wanted to know.

'Going back to South West tomorrow afternoon,' I said.

'Thank fucking God,' he said. 'And Mom?'

'Dunno,' I said. 'Praying and crying. What else?'

Karel sniggered.

'What happened?' I asked him.

Maybe I shouldn't have been so inquisitive. Maybe it was all still too raw. But he nonetheless started talking.

It was a mass grave with mangled body parts and shot-up corpses of men, women and children that had propelled my brother on to the highway to cuckoo-land. It all happened at a Swapo terrorist base somewhere deep inside Angola. The army attacked the base and platoons of parabats were dropped over the town. When they hit the ground, the place was swarming not only with terrorists, but also with women and children. It was an old trick of the terrorists to hide behind skirts and nappies. Our boys had to smoke the terrs from their hideouts but unfortunately masses of civvies pegged as well. It's a reality of war and I don't think the top brass minded too much, but the medics had to clean up the mess.

Karel said it was a horrible business. 'There's no difference between a fucked-up whitey and a fucked-up darkie,' he said. 'Their blood's the same red.'

The medics were confronted by scores of wounded. Their first priority was to save their own, and then to tend to the enemy. They did what they could but were overwhelmed by the sheer number of gunshot wounds, bayonet gashes and bomb and mortar injuries. They had no choice but to leave the most seriously wounded to die. The dead were chucked into a massive hole in the ground. It was somewhere in that pit, in that heap of flesh and pulp, that a baby screamed.

Karel cried when he told me this, clutching his head in his hands. The troops didn't know what to do and milled about the grave. Should they leave it? What would another one matter? The baby's crying persisted, and then someone saw it half-buried underneath its dead mother.

'Get it,' an officer ordered Karel.

'Did you?' I asked him.

'I had to,' he said. 'I climbed in.'

'And then?'

'I pulled it out.'

I didn't say a word. Karel continued: 'You know what I'll never forget?'

'What?'

'The feeling of human pulp under my feet.'

That night, Karel said, he injected himself with a stiff dose of morphine, usually carried by medics to treat shock and pain among wounded troops. Several other medics were already addicted.

'It helped me to forget,' he said, 'and that's how I got through the army.'

Karel was hooked and completed the rest of his army stint on a euphoric high. Back in civvy-street, he had to find alternative supplies. Heroin and cocaine had arrived on our shores but there were probably only a handful of dealers in the city. Dagga and Mandrax were readily available but Karel needed something much stronger.

It wasn't long, though, before the needles arrived – and with them a prescription drug that users referred to as 'pinks'. Its pharmaceutical name was Welconal, a morphine-based schedule seven drug that cancer patients popped to soothe extreme pain. Addicts crushed the pill, dissolved it in water in a teaspoon over an open flame and shot it into their veins.

The quest for pinks led to a spate of pharmacy burglaries where the brightly coloured tablets were kept under lock and key. It wasn't long before Karel, craving a fix, smashed a pharmacy window with a brick. Problem was that the place was wired to an alarm and the cops found him trying to prise open the safe. He was locked up for a few days before the station commander phoned Dad who jumped on to the first plane back to the Republic.

The old man arranged bail and as Karel left court, Dad took him by the collar, shoved him into the car and dropped him at a rehab centre. I was in college and blissfully unaware of what Karel was up to. Dad ordered Mom to shut up about Karel's problems in order not to disrupt my training.

He absconded within days, wangled a few pinks from a dealer, couldn't pay for them and got into a bar brawl. He landed in *tjoekie* again. This time Dad said he had had enough of Karel and told his copper friends to fuck him good.

He spent two months behind bars.

Nothing changed. On his release, he returned to the streets. A few days before my passing-out parade, he found his girlfriend in their Hillbrow flat with a needle dangling from her arm. It looked as though she'd stopped breathing. Bewildered and confused, he stumbled around Hillbrow for half an hour before calling an ambulance. By then the chick had sustained brain damage.

Karel spent the night in Joubert Park before turning himself in at the Hillbrow cop station the next morning. He was sobbing like a baby. He didn't have any drugs on him and there wasn't much the cops could do except call Dad, who had in the meantime arrived for my passing-out parade. He fetched Karel who said that this time he wanted to be clean. Dad booked him into rehab again.

For an almost an hour, Karel rambled on, taking me through the battlefields of South West and Angola and into that mass grave and on to the streets of Johannesburg. He'd been on a narcotic binge and had smoked, snorted, swallowed and spiked whatever he could get his hands on.

At some point, the nurse opened the door and put a plate of boiled meat and peas on the table. She told me that I had to leave. I sat for another five or ten minutes before getting up. I looked at my *ouboet* slumped in a heap on the bed. The drugs had chomped any trace of fat from his body. His shoulder bones and vertebrae protruded like studs through his stretched skin. I bent over and put my arms around him.

'Get better. Just get better,' I mumbled.

He put his arms around me and he hugged me and I hugged him and I tried to pass the warmth and strength of my body on to him. He broke down and I felt his body shaking and my arm getting wet as tears gushed from his eyes. Although we'd never been close, he was my *ouboet*. We were created from the same flesh and born from the same womb and the same blood pumped through our veins.

We finally broke away from each other and as he wiped the tears from his eyes, he said: 'This is a pretty *kak* place. Will you come again soon?'

'Of course I will.'

'And will you bring Mom?'

'Sure.'

'But I don't want Dad to come. I'm tired of being *kakked* out.'

'He's leaving tomorrow.'

'Keep him away,' he said.

I promised to visit again in two or three days' time. 'You must eat your food,' I said as I closed the door.

Tears rolled down my cheeks as I drove back to Krugersdorp. I think I understood what had happened to Karel. There was a technicolour movie playing over and over in his head and it was driving him bonkers. And it wasn't 'The Sound of Music'. It was something like 'Apocalypse Now' or 'Platoon'.

There was more to the pinks or Mandrax or acid or whatever shit he was popping or smoking or spiking into his body. He was feeding and soothing his fucked-up mind.

I arrived home just in time for dinner. Dad was pissed out of his skull and was stumbling around in the lounge with a glass of Klippies and Coke. When he eventually joined Mom and me for dinner, he slammed his half-full glass on the table, looked at me and asked: 'And so, Constable Goosen, when are you joining the Security Branch?'

On the spur of the moment I decided that I would not give him what he wanted. I looked him squarely in the eyes and said: 'I no longer want to be a security cop.'

He let out an almighty burp, took a gulp of his drink and thundered: 'And why on bloody earth not?'

'I've decided to join the detectives or the drug squad,' I said. I thought for a moment the old fart was going to choke.

'Oh no, you're not!' he bellowed and his face turned red. Mom had her eyes fixed on her plate of lasagne, pretending to be unaware of the looming showdown.

'Oh yes, I am,' I countered.

Dad was about to rise to his feet. 'No son of mine will join that lot,' he said.

'And why not?' I asked calmly.

'They're losers and drunkards,' he said as he finally got up and wobbled out of the dining room to fill up his glass. As he disappeared out the door he said: 'I've got one loser son and that's enough.'

Mom had not said a word. I put my hand on hers and said: 'I saw Karel this afternoon.'

She looked up at me. Her eyes were damp. 'How is he?'

'He's not good,' I said. 'Why don't you visit him?'

'Your father said I shouldn't,' she said. 'Will you take me to see Karel?'

Before I could answer, Dad thundered: 'And what's that about Karel and me?'

His frame filled the doorway as he glared at Mom and me. I waited for him to plonk down in his seat and then told him that I had been to see Karel. He didn't say a word, just looked blankly at me.

'He's sick, Dad,' I said. 'He needs our help.'

His gaze changed to one of stupefaction, he raised his eyebrows and threw back his head. '*Kak*, man,' he bawled. 'Karel's a fucking junkie! A pot-head!'

I kept my calm. 'It's more than that, Dad. He's sick.'

'Sick? What fucking sick? Huh?'

'It's the border, Dad. Karel saw things.'

'Like what?' He was swaying to and fro on his chair.

'Like mass graves in Angola,' I said.

'And what do you fucking know about mass graves?'

The conversation was futile and I wanted it to end. Dad was never going to grasp the severity of Karel's condition. Post-traumatic stress or the so-called Vietnam syndrome was not yet accepted as a legitimate mental condition.

Nevertheless I ploughed on. 'Karel was in Angola. He said there was a mass grave and he had to get into it.'

'So what?'

'It's haunting him, Dad. He can't forget.'

'Humph!' he exclaimed and slammed his fist on the table. 'So now he breaks into pharmacies and sticks needles into his arm? *Kak* excuse!'

I stared at the malva pudding in front of me. Dad's blood pressure had by then skyrocketed and the Klippies was discharging like gunpowder into his veins. He slammed his fist on the table again, this time so hard that the dishes clattered.

'I've never heard such fucking bullshit in my life!' he said. He pushed back his chair and staggered to his feet. 'Karel's nothing but a miserable fucking criminal! My own son!'

He waddled out of the dining room towards the lounge. I looked at him and thought he resembled an overfed Christmas turkey that was about to burst open. I prayed he would get on to his plane to South West as soon as possible. And when it was high in the air, I wanted a Swapo missile to explode in its rear. I wanted it to tumble slowly earthwards and when it hit the ground, I wanted Dad to shatter into a million little pieces.

He wasn't finished though. A moment later his bald head and balloon of a torso appeared in the doorway. 'And you,' he blasted, pointing his finger at me, 'the next time I see you, you will be a fucking security policeman! Do you understand me?'

'Yes, Dad,' I said not looking at him. An aeroplane crash would be too merciful. I wanted him to perish slowly and painfully. It was about the only one of my wishes that has ever been fulfilled.

'Don't you disappoint me as well,' he said and disappeared.

Mom spoke for the first time. 'You must listen to your father, Gideon. He knows best.'

I turned my eyes to her, then I got up and walked to my room. I was on duty the next day and didn't speak to Dad again before he got on to the plane.

Mom and I never got to see Karel. He walked out of rehab two days later and was back on the streets.

Ten

Police work bored me out of my skull. I was assigned to the Brixton police station in the western suburbs of Johannesburg where I was mostly on charge office duty. I did little more than fill in accident reports, certify documents, take down statements and listen to endless complaints. The real action took place in two rooms at the back of the police station where detectives brought in killers and robbers for interrogation.

Those windowless rooms were nothing but square cubicles with dirty walls, a table, a few chairs and a bright light dangling from the ceiling – just like the movies. They were generally known as the *pynkamers* because lots of trials and tribulations awaited those who refused to cooperate or confess. They were apparently soundproofed in order to stifle the screams of the detainees, but I cannot vouch for that.

The Brixton Murder and Robbery Unit was among the most feared in the country and had an almost perfect conviction rate. Every young policeman in Johannesburg would have given his left testicle to be part of the unit.

Major Pietman Pretorius was the commander of the Brixton Murder and Robbery Unit and he was a legend throughout the country. He'd probably nailed more bad guys than the rest of the unit put together and his regular court appearances and unflinching testimony had elevated him to celebrity status. Pietman was so revered – and more than likely feared, too – that his reputation gave birth to a television drama series based on famous cases that he had solved. Of course it didn't show the way in which he extracted his information and confessions.

Major Pietman had an array of torture equipment in a steel cupboard in his office. Most famous of these was *Saartjie*, a *slinger-foon* from a bygone era. Remember the days when you had to turn the handle on the telephone to be connected to an exchange where a nosy auntie would put you through to the number you wanted? That was *Saartjie*. Connected to the phone box was a set of batteries and two wires with clips that could be attached to the detainee's fingertips, nipples, testicles, ears, or whatever. The turning of the handle sent a *moer* of an electric current through the detainee and it usually took only a few turns for the dude to sing like a fucking canary.

And then there was *Buksie*, nothing more than a piece of car tyre tube that was pulled over the suspect's head with the intention of suffocating him. This torture technique probably dates back to the invention of rubber, but it took a reasonable amount of skill to implement it. The trick was to release the tube the moment you felt the guy was knocking on the pearly gates. A moment too long and he might lose consciousness or even die.

There were several other torture techniques: hitting the soles of the feet of suspects with police batons, pushing their heads into buckets of water until they were half-drowned or, in really difficult cases, forcing broomsticks up their asses. Each detective had his preferred method of extracting a confession.

As Winston Churchill or Jan Smuts or some other fucking grand dude would have said: 'The moment maketh the man.'

I've heard of detectives hoisting a dude up a tree and making a fire under him in order to get him to sing. The cherry on the top belonged to the Northern Transvaal Security Branch which was based in Pretoria. I didn't know about it at the time, but years later at the Truth Commission it emerged that their preferred tool of interrogation was a generator. A fucking generator! Can you imagine? They didn't just stun their captives into confessing but turned them into fucking ash!

Late one night, a team of Brixton Murder and Robbery detectives brought in a *houtkop* who they suspected had raped a white auntie on a West Rand plot. He screamed like a stuck pig when they pulled him out of the van and escorted him to an interrogation room. But he maintained that he was innocent and refused to confess. He was a hard nut to crack so it turned out to be a long night.

As the first light of day cast its elongated shadows over the city, one of the detectives trudged into the charge office and ordered me to go find coffee and breakfast. I drove to Fontana in Hillbrow, a famous all-night takeaway joint slap-bang in the middle of the suburb of sin, where I joined the queue of hookers, pimps, drug pushers, clubbers, insomniacs and ambulance men.

Back at the station, I knocked softly on the door of the interrogation room. It swung open and I was hit by a wall of tepid, putrid air. I thought I was going to vomit. It was a pungent cocktail of stale breath, testosterone, sweat, fear, cigarette smoke, booze and the detainee's wet pants. It was the odour of torture and inquisition, a bouquet that carries almost pheremonal qualities for the professional tormentor. It was something I soon grew accustomed to.

There were six or seven policemen in the room, both white and black. Two cops were standing next to the detainee who was naked and cuffed. They'd obviously stripped him in order to attach *Saartjie*'s electric wires to his balls and nipples. He still

149

wouldn't talk. One of the cops, a short, thickset man with a florid sweaty face, had *Buksie* in his hand.

'Speak, kaffir, speak!' the cop thundered menacingly and took up a position behind the chair. He reminded me of Dad, who no doubt was a distinguished tuber himself.

The detainee shook his head. The cop tugged *Buksie* over his head, pulling it with all his strength. For a moment, the room fell silent except for the gurgles that escaped from under the tube.

'You can put it down there, son,' said a lanky policeman with thinning hair and ears like satellite dishes. He pointed to a table in the corner of the room. He was none other than the great Pietman Pretorius himself.

I put the tray down and walked towards the door. The cop had just released the tube and the detainee was gasping for air. The second cop stood closer and said: 'And now, kaffir, what do you say?'

The man murmured something inaudible. 'Ah, so you like it,' the cop bellowed. 'You want more?'

Without saying a word, he gave the dude an almighty *klap*. His head snapped back before falling on to his chest. He remained silent. Belting a detainee took know-how because the trick was not to rupture his skin. A suspect with a cut lip or a blue eye in court was a dead giveaway. It was relatively safe to clobber a *houtkop* on the head because his dark skin didn't show bruises so easily.

'It's okay, son,' said Major Pretorius as he took a bite of his toasted bacon and egg sandwich, 'you can go now.'

An hour later, the detectives were still working on the rapist. They had to be finished with him by eight because that was when the day staff and civilians reported for duty. *Buksie* and *Saartjie* had failed to break him and the detectives lacked the evidence to take him to court to charge him with rape. By refusing to cooperate, the dude had signed his own death warrant.

That night a black policeman rushed into the charge office, shouting that we should come to the cells at the back of the station. The detainee was hanging from a sheet bound around his neck and attached to the bars in front of the little window in his cell. An empty toilet bucket was alongside him. The scene evoked memories of my own little brother's demise, but I had to put it behind me and get on with an important task. I was instructed to compile the suicide docket.

'Son, you know what's expected of you, don't you?' Major Pretorius asked as I sat down in his office to take his statement.

I nodded. 'Yes, Major, I know.' Everything had been carefully orchestrated to make it appear like suicide. I don't know to this day if it was suicide induced by continuous torture or whether one of the major's men whacked him in his cell. It wasn't important. The cunt had refused to confess and the cops couldn't allow a rapist to be back on the streets.

Those were the days when a confession extracted in detention was enough to put a suspect away for a long, long time. Ensuring a conviction was as easy as beating or torturing the dude until he signed a statement. I often had to sit in on interrogations and take down confessions, mostly dictated by the detectives. By then the suspect was worn out by hours of torment or days without sleep and was slumped in his chair barely able to move, let alone speak.

It happened more than once that a suspect could only speak a kaffir language or couldn't read or write but was confronted in court by a perfectly composed statement in Afrikaans. Didn't matter: his fate was sealed as long as a cop testified that he'd made the confession of his own free will and it contained his signature.

Accused upon accused testified in court that they had been beaten and tortured into confessing, but judge upon judge and magistrate upon magistrate shook their heads and rejected their evidence as mere fabrication. Who would not believe the God-fearing, incorruptible Major Pretorius and his hand-picked team of upright lawmen?

Pietman's squad was, to put it mildly, a rough bunch. They each had a nickname. Second-in-command was Lieutenant Slang van Wyk, who acquired his name courtesy of his snake-like eyes. Chappies (the name of a cheap bubblegum) Horn was a puny little man with boyish looks; Duiwel Jansen was the most vicious interrogator of them all; Baksteen Botha had survived an attack from a murderer who had bashed his head with a brick, and Vleis McDonald was a pot-bellied cop with the strength of a beast. They wore civilian clothes, worked day and night, carried pistols on their hips, drove V8s, drank like fishes, swore like sailors, permanently removed hooligans and hoodlums from society, and indulged in *groeps-woepse* with hookers, although most of them had a missus and offspring at home.

Brixton Murder and Robbery cops had almost the same status as security policemen. They were admired by their peers, almost elevated above the law. Cops like Slang and Duiwel and Baksteen and Vleis were not unlike Dad, though they might not have buggered their own flesh and blood. They were all pretty depraved characters who could just as well have been henchmen in a gang of outlaws. Difference was that they hid behind the law and regarded themselves as upright citizens.

And yet I wanted nothing more than to be one of them and to be part of Pietman's team. After several years of being out in the cold, I longed for the warmth and camaraderie of a group. I wanted to belong somewhere. I was nineteen years old and still living with my mother, whose car I had to borrow to drive to work. I had hardly any friends and the only pussy I'd ever sampled was that of the hooker at The Leopard.

When I had a weekend off I sat at home watching Mom waste away. I applied to join Murder and Robbery, although I was far too young and would probably have had to do uniform work for a year or two. My application was turned down and I continued with uniform police duties. My partner on the beat was a scrawny guy with watery blue eyes and fleshy pink lips. Gallie van der Walt had been at the back of the queue when brains were handed out and the few cells his Maker had allocated him had in the meantime perished of alcohol poisoning.

Gallie was infamous for having lost his service pistol when he effected a rare arrest. A drunken hobo was caught shoplifting in a supermarket. When Gallie arrived, the guy went bananas and threatened to stab him with a broken bottle. Gallie was not one to be intimidated and pulled his pistol. The tramp stuck his arms in the air and apologised profusely but was nonetheless ushered to the van. As Gallie opened the back door to push the hobo in, he put his pistol on the roof. And that's where he left it. A police disciplinary hearing found him guilty of negligence and although he couldn't be demoted, he stayed a constable for a very long time.

We drove up and down the city streets looking for action. Gallie had an obsession with homosexuals, telling me that an uncle had fiddled with him when he was a little boy. 'Let's go look for poofters,' he'd say and we would head off in the direction of Hillbrow. Johannesburg's flatland was a plumber's paradise and there were several places where men congregated for suck-offs.

Gallie would shriek with delight when we pounced on a car parked in a shadowy corner of Joubert Park or the Doornfontein station. He was less thrilled if it was occupied by a guy making out with a prossie although we'd still beat the dude up. When it was two poofters, it was sheer pleasure. When one was black, it was even better. They were completely at our mercy.

Our approach was simple. We gave the dudes a choice: we take you in and charge you with public indecency or we punish you ourselves. To scare them good and proper, we added things like soliciting and indecent assault. If it was a mixed race couple, we could further terrify them with the Immorality Act. Some cried and begged and offered us money (which we took). Most couldn't afford to be charged because the missus was waiting at home with a plate of food in the warming drawer. By the time we had opened the back of the van, they would agree that we should dispense the punishment ourselves.

I was happy to pummel them with my fists and when they went down I booted them good and hard. Gallie had other ideas. He took off his belt, ordered them to bend over and walloped them as hard as he could. When, once or twice, he told them to take their pants off, I told him to go look for real pussy. We usually left the homos in a pretty bad state. If they were black, they were half dead.

My first year in the police force passed pretty uneventfully. I made a few arrests although I didn't have the opportunity to fire my gun. I pulled it a few times to hold up thieves, but that was it. My dockets were up to date and I had a clean record. I wasn't a spectacular cop but I reckoned I had a reasonably good future in the force.

I often thought about Gielie, Johnnie and Jakes. Jakes had long been released from national service after spending almost his entire two years in detention barracks. When he got out the Verster family moved to Port Elizabeth where Jakes trained as a panel beater in a family member's scrapyard. I had accepted that Gielie was destined for boxing greatness and that I might never see Johnnie again. He'd chosen crime and I was a lawman, so we didn't have much in common.

How wrong I was.

I was sitting in the charge office a few days before Christmas entering into the general register the names of suspects that had been brought in during the day. There were about twenty-five guys in the holding cells and their suspected crimes ranged from murder to rape to robbery to house-breaking to domestic violence to pissing in public. It was a tedious chore, and one I resented, and I was doing it without really thinking or registering the names.

19.12.85 – Barend Jacobus Swart – Age 25 – Murder and Robbery
19.12.85 – Johnnie Frederik Swart – Age 20 – Murder and Robbery

I was about to go on to the next name when I stopped and stared at what I'd just written. Swart? Johnnie Swart? Johnnie had a brother by the name of Barend.

I jumped up and rushed to the holding cells at the back of the station and asked the black cop to open for me.

'Why?' he wanted to know.

'*God Jissus!*' I exploded. 'Just open. I have to ID a prisoner.'

The first cell was full of blacks. I moved to the second cell and peeked through the window in the door. It was late afternoon and streaks of light lit up its bleak grey interior. There were eight or ten prisoners in the cell. Two were huddled close together in a corner. It was my old *gabba* Johnnie and his brother Barend.

I didn't have access to the cells so I didn't call out to him. I rushed back to the charge office, my heart pounding. The only other information on the charge sheet was that the investigating officer was Pietman Pretorius himself. It must have been a big case for the major to have been involved. At that time murder carried the death penalty and the state didn't hesitate to implement it.

I thought about Johnnie all night. Although I hadn't seen him for two or three years, I still thought of him as a dear friend. I couldn't picture Johnnie with the hangman's noose around his neck and his crooked feet dangling in the air. Would they allow him to wear his heavy black boots? Somehow I had to help him.

Although I didn't know Barend well, I remembered him as a soft-spoken guy with cauliflower ears. He was a mean rugby lock and years of going down in the centre of the scrum had wreaked havoc with his listening devices. The two were probably up for interrogation the next day or the day after. They must have been brought in late in the afternoon because their names were at the bottom of the list.

I was at work by six the next morning to await the arrival of Pretorius. The major was known for getting to the office at the crack of dawn to work through the pile of dockets that was always on his desk. By late morning, he was on the road hunting down criminals. He'd start interrogations late in the afternoon or early evening when the civvies had gone home. Minutes after he'd walked into his office, I knocked on the door. He called out that I should enter. His office smelled of stale cigarette smoke and coffee. The major was sitting behind his desk, almost perfectly framed by the piles of dockets either side of him. In front of him was an array of photographs of what appeared to be a bloody murder scene. His reading glasses were balanced on his nose and he looked over them at me. His Brylcreemed hair was combed with a lick crossing from one ear to the other.

'Yes, son?' he said. 'And what can I do for you?' His voice rasped like a rusty lock, probably because he chain-smoked.

'I want to talk to you about the Swart case, Major,' I said, but before I could add anything he passed one of the photographs to me. It showed a young blonde woman lying on her back with her mouth half-open and her eyes gaping wide.

'That's their work,' he said shoving another picture in my direction. It was a wider shot of the same woman. There was a hole in her chest and a pool of blood on the floor.

'They shot her in the heart,' he said, adding: 'They're seriously demented bastards.'

He went on to tell me that Barend and Johnnie Swart and two other as yet unidentified robbers had stormed into a building society in Roodepoort. They were wearing black balaclavas and were armed to the teeth. They held up the staff, ordered them to lie on the floor and demanded cash. As they were about to leave, the blonde cashier pushed the alarm button.

One of the gunmen swung around, pointed a shotgun at her chest and pulled the trigger. A black security guard charged the shooter, but Barend shot him at point blank range. Half his face was blown away and he was in a critical condition in Soweto's Baragwanath hospital.

The two unknown robbers rushed out to get the car started. Barend and Johnnie, overcome by greed, wasted valuable time attempting to stuff more money into their bags. They were jolted into action by the siren of an approaching police car.

But when they got outside, the other two were already speeding away, leaving them to fend for themselves. Two police cars screeched to a halt in front of the building. Barend fired several shots at the cops, but Johnnie threw his gun on the ground and raised his arms. Barend realised that he was fucked and also stuck his hands in the air.

'We think the two that got away were also Swart brothers,' said Pretorius.

'There are many of them, Major,' I said.

'And what do you know about them?'

'I grew up with the Swart brothers, Major,' I said.

'You move in nice company, Goosen,' he said, a smirk on his face. 'So why did you want to see me?'

'Maybe I can help, Major.'

'And how do you think you can do that?'

'Maybe I can persuade Johnnie to cooperate before you interrogate him,' I said. 'I don't think he's such a bad guy.'

'Constable Goosen,' Pretorius said heavily, 'I don't think you have any idea how wicked these fuckers are. They'd kill for a tickey. I've wanted them for a long, long time.'

'But Johnnie didn't pull the trigger, did he?'

Pretorius laughed. 'Jesus Christ, son, didn't they teach you anything in college? Johnnie's complicit. It doesn't matter who fired those shots. They're in it together.'

'What's going to happen to him?'

'I've already ordered that the two of them be separated,' he said. 'We'll start with Barend. I want the other two and they must know where they're hiding.'

'Can I see Johnnie, Major?'

'No, you can't,' he said curtly. 'Not unless I say so.'

Barend was escorted to the interrogation room late that afternoon and teams of cops took turns at grilling him. I don't know what kind of third degree they did on him, but I imagine they phoned, tubed and clobbered him.

He refused to give up his brothers. Two cops hauled him back to the holding cells late that night.

The next morning at seven, Pietman, Slang and Baksteen took charge of Johnnie's interrogation. Less than an hour later, they rushed into the charge office to book out three Uzi machine guns. The major had a broad smile on his face. 'Your friend is singing like a canary,' he said. 'We're going to fetch the rest of them.'

Pretorius was sliding nine millimetre bullets into the Uzi's magazine when he looked at me and said: 'Son, you said Johnnie was your buddy, didn't you?'

'Yes, Major, I know him well.'

'Do you know where he lives?'

'I've been there many times, Major.'

'Johnnie says he thinks the others are hiding in a shed in the backyard. Do you know it?'

'Yes, Major.' I couldn't tell him that that was where we'd bashed open the Greek's money-box and hidden our loot over the years.

'Get yourself a gun, son. You're coming with us.'

I couldn't believe my ears. I pushed the register I was busy with aside and said: 'Yes, Major!'

'You can handle an R4, can't you?'

'I dig guns, Major,' I said. 'I got the highest marks for sharp shooting in college.'

'This is not cowboys and crooks, son,' he cautioned me.

A few minutes later, I was in the back seat of a Nissan Skyline with Pietman and Slang. The R4 was balanced on my lap and I had two magazines in my hand. I lovingly caressed the cold steel. My finger ached to pull the trigger.

'The other robbers were Willem and Fanie Swart,' Pretorius said. 'Do you know them?'

'Yes, Major,' I said. 'Willem's completely mad. He was a recce. They kicked him out when he went *bossies*.'

The major laughed. 'Don't worry, son. The Task Force will be there as well.'

Fucking hell, I thought. The Task Force! Those guys were trained in all aspects of urban warfare and were the police version of the recces. The Task Force was called in when there was major shit like terrorists holding hostages or a loony hijacking a plane. If they were going to be there, Pretorius was expecting big shit.

'Do you know Fanie?' Pretorius wanted to know.

'The last time I saw him he was a boy,' I said. 'He can't be older than sixteen or seventeen.'

'Johnnie said he's seventeen,' said Pretorius. 'Your buddy told us everything.'

It had taken exactly five minutes to break Johnnie. The major had tied his arms to a chair and a black cop started undoing his bootlaces. Johnnie begged them to leave his feet alone. By the time the cop had ripped the first boot off, Johnnie was weeping. He squirmed and twisted when the cop pulled his socks off but the next moment his feet were exposed.

'Have you ever seen those things?' Pretorius asked me.

'No, Major. He doesn't show them to anyone.'

'Nor would I if they were mine,' he said. 'They're only half human. The other half is pig, ostrich and crocodile.'

The cops had uncuffed Johnnie and ordered him to remove his clothes. Initially he had refused but after a few *klaps* he was in his briefs. Van Zyl prepared the bush telephone while Pretorius picked up a cattle prodder. He said to Johnnie: 'You choose, son. It's either the prodder up your arse or we fry your balls.'

Johnnie didn't say a word. He was probably determined not to give up the others, but by the time the cop had attached the wire to his nipple, he relented and whimpered in a tiny voice that he'd tell them whatever they wanted to know.

We met the Task Force at the old Randfontein train station, not far from Johnnie's house. There were about thirty men altogether, in battle garb and armed to the teeth. Pretorius took control and briefed the men. The Task Force cops would surround the property, approaching it from the back through the bluegum plantation. We would enter from the front.

Half an hour later, we drove up to the corrugated iron railway house. It was in a worse state of disrepair than I remembered. The pink walls were a faded rose colour, the grass was overgrown, weeds standing half a metre high, and an array of broken car parts, toys and furniture was strewn all over the property.

An army of kids was running around in the street; it seemed as though the Swart clan had grown considerably since the last time I'd visited the house. We got out with our guns in our hands and walked towards Oom Buks and Tannie Lena who were sitting on the stoep. It looked as though Oom Buks had gone blind since I'd last seen him.

'Afternoon, sir. Afternoon, madam,' said the major. 'I'm Major Pretorius from Brixton Murder and Robbery.'

'Who are these people?' Oom Buks wanted to know. I stood at the back of the group, hoping that nobody would recognise me.

'It's the police,' Tannie Lena said. 'They're troubling us again.'

'Tell them to go away,' he ordered.

'What do you want?' asked Tannie Lena.

'We're looking for Willem and Fanus Swart,' Pretorius said. 'They're wanted for murder.'

'They're not here,' said Tannie Lena. 'Anyway, they're good kids. Leave them alone.'

Oom Buks heaved himself up. 'Get off my property!' he shouted.

By then several Task Force members had stationed themselves at strategic places around the house. Others had surrounded the shed. The children had fallen silent and for a few moments the only sound was birds twittering in the trees at the back of the house.

'Why don't you fuck off and leave us alone?' spat a white-faced Tannie Lena. She pointed a crooked finger at Pretorius and said: 'You are fucking worse than kaffirs!'

Major Pretorius ignored her. He raised his voice and issued an order: 'Men, begin your search!'

Policemen pounced on the house from all directions. I was a metre behind Pretorius and holding the R4 in front of me. The policemen searched from room to room, in the process waking up startled brothers and sisters and nieces and nephews who scampered out to the stoep to find out what was going on. I heard Tannie Lena saying: 'Those fucking snake-shit scum are here again.'

Willem and Fanie weren't in the house. We moved across to the shed that had already been combed by members of the Task Force. They weren't there either. A police helicopter circled above us and roadblocks had been set up around the area to intercept them should they try to make a run for freedom.

'The fuckers aren't here!' spewed Pretorius clenching his fists. 'Maybe Johnnie lied. Tonight his balls will fry!'

Then it struck me. A chill ran along my spine. I took a deep breath and said: 'Major! I know where they might be!'

He swung around and looked at me. 'What're you saying, son?'

Our old gang house! They might be in the old gang house! I'd almost forgotten about it.

'There's an old house on the other side of the station, Major,' I panted. 'We often played there and Willem knows about it and …!'

Pretorius interrupted me. 'Show me, son!' He turned around and rushed back through the house. I was right behind him with two or three others following me.

We ran past startled onlookers who had gathered in the street to see what was going on. Some cheered us on. 'Catch the fuckers,' shouted a toothless woman with a baby on her hip.

I had caught up with Pretorius by the time the old gang house came into view. Slang and Chappies were a metre or so behind us. 'Keep your head low, son!' Pretorius gasped, not a second too soon. A shot rang out from the house. I swear I could hear the bullet whistling over our heads. A second and a third shot followed.

'Take cover!' ordered Pretorius flinging himself on the ground. It seemed as though the fire was coming from two different windows.

I'd heard many times how the uninitiated shit and piss in their pants when they face fire for the first time. Not me. I ducked for a second or two and then heaved myself up and launched a solo blitzkrieg on the house. A number of bullets whizzed past me.

'Stay fucking down!' shouted Pretorius as I hit the ground again.

I was lying behind a low wall a few metres from the corrugated iron structure. Raising my head cautiously I peered over it. I couldn't see the gunman but I knew he wouldn't be able to spot me either. More shots rang out behind me as the rest of the Task

Force approached the house. The fire from the window stopped. The shooter was probably reloading.

I seized the moment, got on to one knee, shoved the R4 into my shoulder and took aim at where I thought the gunman was standing. I squeezed the trigger and pumped one slug after the other into the house. I knew the 5.56 millimetre bullets would penetrate the corrugated iron.

'Fucking lie low, Goosen!' Major Pretorius barked behind me. I ignored the order, emptied my magazine, ripped it off and clipped on the second one. Although the shooter hadn't started shooting again, I continued firing. I could see my bullets piercing the sheet of corrugated iron. I emptied the second magazine and then fell flat on my stomach.

An eerie silence descended on us.

Pretorius shouted: 'Come out with your hands in the air!' He had repeated it only once when a lone figure appeared in the broken doorway. His hands were in the air. It took me a few seconds to recognise Willem Swart, who had grown a wild beard and looked like a caveman. Task Force cops swooped down on him, threw him to the ground, cuffed his hands behind his back and dragged him away. The rest of the cops slowly entered the house.

One of them emerged a few minutes later and spoke to the major. The rest of the team went into the house. I followed them. The 'No Entry' sign that we had pasted on the front door was still visible and the house looked as though it hadn't been touched since the days when we'd met there. I could see the silhouette of a man's body stretched out on his back in a corner of a bedroom. He was next to one of the windows from which the shots had been coming. Above him was an assortment of holes where my bullets had pock-marked the corrugated iron. The room faced west and sharp rays of sunlight pierced the sheets of perforated metal. He had a single bullet in his chest that had probably penetrated his heart. It was a *doodskoot*. Blood had spurted from the wound and painted the floor around him with streaks of red.

I went closer to look at the dead man. Except that it wasn't a man; the glassy eyes that stared into nowhere were those of a boy. It was Fanie Swart, Johnnie's *kleinboet*. The last time I'd seen him he was a bony teenager with buck teeth and freckles. He often came with us on our hunting expeditions to the vlei and nagged until he was also given a go with the shotgun. He said he wanted to be a big game hunter when he grew up. Instead, he became a robber, and ultimately he became the hunted.

I had no doubt that it was one of my bullets that had caused his instant demise. The major and his men were armed with Uzis and, although they spurted out a rain of bullets, they didn't have enough velocity or fire power to penetrate the corrugated iron. There was only a handful of Task Force members on the scene and they had been firing mainly at Willem on the other side of the house.

Major Pretorius shared my conclusion. He put his arm around me. 'It's okay, son,' he said. 'He fired and you fired back. There was nothing else you could do.' Slang and Chappies patted my shoulder and mumbled something about it being either them or us. I shook my head but remained gaping at the boy's body until I heard the siren of an approaching ambulance. I turned around, walked outside and then watched as they carried out the corpse, covered with a grey blanket, and loaded it into the vehicle. I don't know whether I was in a state of shock, but fortunately the major and his men didn't give me much time to think.

On our way back to the station, Slang turned to me and asked: 'First one, hey?'

'Yes, Lieutenant,' I said.

'Fuck the lieutenant stuff,' he said. 'Here at Murder and Robbery we tune one another by our first names.'

A warm glow surged through me. I was one of them! A member of the brotherhood! Pietman confirmed it when he said: '*Leeutande* for you, son.'

'What's that, Major?'

'Wait and see, but be prepared.'

An hour or so later, Brixton Murder and Robbery arrived at the Van Riebeeck Hotel in Ontdekkers Way in Roodepoort. The

Van Riebeeck was a sort of Roodepoort version of The Leopard. Its bar was known as Vegkop (another battlefield where the Boers fucked up the English) and had the same reputation as The Leopard's Bloedrivier. It was a close call between them as to where the most vomit and blood had been spilt, the most marriages had disintegrated, and which entertained the highest number of venereal microbes per square centimetre. The standard collection of panties and rugby jerseys adorned Vegkop's yellow walls and there were even signed posters of country singers Lance James and Barbara Ray.

A hush descended on the bar when we walked in. Pretorius strutted up to the barman and ordered in his raspy voice: 'The *Leeutande*, and make it quick. We're thirsty.'

The barman brought out a jar that was half full of some murky concoction. He unscrewed it, filled up a wine glass and gave it to Pretorius. He slammed it down in front of me. 'Swallow, son,' he ordered. 'In one gulp.'

The *leeutande* obviously referred to the cloves of garlic that were floating on top of the liquid. I took one look at the fuzzy potion and then threw the glassful to the back of my throat. I closed my eyes and swallowed. I felt my stomach rejecting what surely must have been poison to any human constitution and dispatching it upwards. As it reached my throat, I decided I was not going to vomit and gulped it down again. It stayed in my stomach but my body was ablaze.

Pretorius clapped his hands slowly. Slang and Chappies followed suit and then the whole bar joined in. I'd made it! The guys told me afterwards that there weren't many first-timers who could keep a glass of *Leeutande* down. It was apparently a concoction of whatever they could find: gin, vodka, tequila, rum, brandy, whisky, whatever. They poured it in the jar, threw a few bulbs of garlic on top and left it for days, or even weeks, to ferment. The result was bottled dynamite. Slang and Pietman and Chappies and the others each had a glass of *Leeutande* after which I had a second, maybe even a third.

'You did well today, son,' the major said, his hand on my

shoulder.

'You fucked him good,' said Chappies. 'He deserved nothing less.'

'Don't worry, hey?' said Slang. 'The country's average IQ has gone up today.'

By then I had decided it was okay. Hurling my high-velocity slugs through the corrugated iron at Fanie Swart was absolutely fine. What on earth did the little fuck think he was doing taking on Brixton Murder and Robbery and the Task Force in a shootout? Playing cowboys and crooks? Don't scratch the lion's testicles and then be surprised if the beast mauls you.

I can't remember much of the rest of the night. I vaguely recalled a stripper whose enormous knockers heaved up and down. At one stage she was on my lap sticking her tongue in my ear – or was I on hers and trying to thrust my tongue in her mouth? Then things went black. I later learned that Chappies took me home and dropped me on the stoep.

News of my feat of bravery spread like a veldfire through the station. Suddenly I wasn't just a pimply nobody with an apologetic attitude. I had had a hand in bringing down a vicious gang, in the process permanently removing one of the hoods from society. Never mind that he was only seventeen years old. He was a vile little cunt.

Willem Swart was questioned for hours upon hours by the cops without any success. The former recce was as hard as nails and refused to say a word. He was deprived of sleep for forty-eight hours, was kicked and punched and phoned and tubed and just about drowned in a bucket of water. Only two words left his lips: 'Fuck off!'

Johnnie cried like a little baby when he heard that the police had shot his *kleinboet*. He sat in his cell shaking his head. Then he asked the cops for a sheet of paper. He said he wanted to make a statement. He wrote two lines: 'I hereby want to say that I was told by the policemen to remove my shoes and clothes and that they were going to shock me. I told them things that were not true.' Johnnie wanted to see a lawyer and lay a charge of torture against the cops.

The cops badly needed Johnnie's testimony against Willem and Barend in order to link them to other crimes. Pretorius ordered that he be brought back to the interrogation room. Johnnie told them to go fuck themselves and this time volunteered to take his boots off. Pretorius threatened to throw them in a rubbish bin and send him to the cells without them. If you don't cooperate, you'll do life imprisonment with bare feet, the major told Johnnie. That's if you don't get the death penalty. Johnnie said he didn't care.

Pretorius called me in the next day. 'We're in shit, son,' he rasped. 'We've got Johnnie and we've got Barend and we've got Willem and they're going down for the building society murder. But we don't have evidence to link them to other shit. We need Johnnie to talk. You must help us.'

'How?' I asked him.

'We can't fuck him up too badly because he wants to see a lawyer. So you must go talk to him.'

'Does he know how his little brother died?'

'No, we haven't told him about you at all.'

An hour or so later, I walked into the holding cells. Johnnie was sitting with his back to me and didn't even look up when the steel door clattered open. I walked up to him, put my hand on his shoulder and said: 'Hey Johnnie, man.'

He swung around and lifted his head. Although he hadn't seen me for years, his face lit up and he beamed from ear to ear.

'God, Goosen!' he exclaimed. 'What the fuck are you doing here?'

He looked my blue uniform up and down and added: 'And now you're one of them, huh? Are you also going to fuck me up?'

'I've brought you a Fontana chicken,' I said, 'and a litre of Coke.'

'Fucking hell,' he said. 'How come they're allowing you to bring it in?'

'They say they're finished with you,' I said and pulled the roasted bird out of the bag and broke it in pieces. 'They say they've got you.'

'Got me how?' Johnnie said as he tore the flesh from the leg and stuffed it in his mouth. 'Fucking beautiful,' he said.

'Eat first,' I said, 'and then we'll talk about it.'

'Don't worry. Nothing can destroy my appetite after the pig shit they feed me in here,' he said as he demolished the thigh. 'Tell me now.'

I looked at Johnnie and said: 'They think you're going to get death.'

He almost choked as he licked the wish bone clean. 'What do you mean, death? For what?'

'For the robbery,' I said. 'A woman died and a *houtkop* is busy kicking the bucket in hospital. It doesn't look good.'

'I didn't fire those shots,' he said. 'Willem and Barend did.'

'Doesn't matter, Johnnie,' I said. 'It's called common purpose. You associated yourself with Willem's actions. You did nothing to stop him.'

Johnnie snorted as he plucked the white flesh from the breast bone. 'How the fuck was I supposed to stop him? Willem was behind the whole thing and he said there wasn't going to be any shooting.'

'If you're not going to cooperate with the state,' I said, 'they'll ask for the death penalty. And God knows what judge you'll get.'

His mouth full of chicken, Johnnie looked at me and asked: 'So what do I do?'

'You have to testify against them,' I said.

'My own brothers?'

'Yes, Johnnie,' I said. 'That's your only hope.'

I stood up to leave. 'Don't go now,' said Johnnie. 'Stay longer.'

'They said only ten minutes,' I said, adding: 'Do you know what you get to eat the night before you swing?'

He looked at me anxiously. 'What?'

'Roast chicken,' I said. I knocked on the door for the guard to open and I walked out. I have to admit that my last words to Johnnie were not of my own devising. It was Major Pretorius' brainchild to let Johnnie stew in his own juice.

I went back to see him the next afternoon, this time with a Steers cheese burger and chips and an ice-cold Castle beer.

'Fucking hell, Goosen,' Johnnie said as he munched his burger and washed it down with a long swig of beer.

'You're going to be charged tomorrow morning,' I told him. 'And then off to Jo'burg prison until your trial.'

'What are they charging me with?'

'Murder, attempted murder, robbery, and unlawful possession of arms and ammunition,' I said.

'*Jislaaik*,' he said. 'That's fucking heavy.'

'The death sentence is almost a sure thing,' I said. 'You have to save yourself.'

He was quiet for a moment or two, then he looked at me and asked: 'And if I testify again Willem and Barend, what then?'

Pretorius had briefed me carefully about this moment. 'You'll get a lesser sentence – maybe six or eight years or so. You can be out in four. Think about it.'

'How do I know they won't cheat me?' he wanted to know.

'The state prosecutor will come and see you personally. He'll make the deal.'

'It's my brothers, man,' he said. 'My own fucking brothers!'

'Willem left you behind and drove away,' I said.

'I would have done the same.'

'There's no way you can help him or Barend,' I said, 'but you can save yourself.'

Two days later, Pretorius called me in. 'Johnnie has turned state witness,' he said. A Lucky Strike was burning between his fingers. 'You've done the force proud, son.'

My chest swelled and I think I blushed. He put his cigarette down in an ashtray, got to his feet and stretched out his hand. I took it, resisting the urge to squeal as he crunched my fingers. 'This is just the beginning, son,' he said. 'And by the way, congratulations.'

'For what, Major?'

'On becoming a member of Brixton Murder and Robbery,' he said giving me a broad smile. 'Your transfer has been approved.'

Eleven

It's deep winter and an icy chill has invaded my two metre by two metre dungeon and crept into my bones. It's Saturday night and The Bomb is ominously quiet, almost tranquil. I'm sure across the passage in Auschwitz they're sucking millions of white Mandrax molecules into their lungs until they topple over into one another's laps and dribble and drool from their oral cavities.

Taliep is probably gobbling up another fresh cream cake that landed on his filthy plate courtesy of a hundred rand note and a friendly warder. That will earn the scumbag another tattoo that some goon will etch on his chest or forearm with a blunt needle which I hope is soiled with deadly micro-organisms that will further infest his emaciated body.

Other birds are probably hallucinating about lighting braaivleis fires at home and thrashing out the Blue Bulls-Western Province game with their buddies while the missus throws together a potato salad in the kitchen. Or treating a chick to pizza and a movie and plying her with Stein or sangria in the hope that it will untie her thighs and loosen her moral resolve.

My mind tonight is preoccupied with a pair of eyes that were cut from the depths of the Arctic Ocean. A cascade of silken red hair. An unblemished skin that tasted like cream. Fingers and toes as suckable as the sweetest desert dates. Cherry lips. Tiny breasts with purple blossoms at their tips. A bewitching and ravishing nymphet by the name of Sharné.

It's only exquisite beauty that can inspire me to such florid penmanship and when you read this, my dearest Debbie, you have to understand that it's time to tell you about my first love. For a short time it filled my heart with such craziness and fever that I thought it was going to burst. It's different from the love I have for you, which is mature and real and everlasting.

You know by now that I was born with this ineptitude as far as fluff was concerned. I just couldn't get it on with girls, couldn't even string together a few sentences of conversation. Throughout my schooldays I stared and lusted and fantasised but made zero headway on the love front. If it wasn't for Jakes and Johnnie who got *skewetiet* Amber to flop down on me, I would have remained a virgin until long after I finished school. I couldn't even get a girl to accompany me to the matric farewell dance. Every boy had to ask a female classmate to go with him. I couldn't scrape the courage together and as the day dawned, I was still without a partner. A teacher called a sort of emergency meeting of the partnerless matrics and paired them off for the big night. I was momentarily in the company of the obese and the grotesque and thought that I might land up with a girl who had lost her leg in a car accident. I didn't do much better and was paired with a boy-hating lesbian. Not that any right-minded male would ever have ventured into her butch pants.

Mom was far more enthusiastic about the farewell dance than I was because Dad had been her date for her matric dance and that was where they kissed for the first time. It was hardly a notion to inspire me. Mom insisted on teaching me how to two-step and hired me a dinner suit with a bow tie.

'Look at my little ice cream boy tonight,' she said as she sent me off in a taxi to collect the dyke. Clitty (that's what we called her at school) was wearing trousers and had raked her hair into a spiky confection. She didn't bother to wear make-up although she was badly in need of it, and she remarked that I looked like an undertaker.

When we got to the school hall, I excused myself, went to the cloakroom, took the half-jack of Red Heart from my inside pocket and poured the burning liquid down my throat. I spent most of the night being sick and on my knees in the toilet.

The girl thing had become an almost insurmountable problem and I was convinced that I was doomed for life to my (already overused) hand and horny daydreams.

I had a thing for a girl shortly after I graduated as a policeman. Her name was Maryna. She was a funky doll with short-cropped dark hair and dark, almost charcoal eyes. She wore baggy pants and leather sandals, listened to Dire Straits and Neil Diamond and didn't eat meat. She read André P Brink and Linda Goodman and loved to walk bareskinned in the rain (not that I ever saw her doing it). She also hated her job as a cashier at Volkskas Bank in Roodepoort.

One day I was drawing money from my savings account and as she pushed the cash towards me, she looked at me and said: 'You always stand in my queue. Is it just a coincidence or what?'

I blushed and she laughed. When I regained my composure, I muttered something silly like: 'Yes, it must be a fluke.' I turned around and stumbled out of the bank. When I got outside, I shut my eyes tightly and cursed myself for being so inadequate with girls.

But Maryna was right. Every time I walked into the bank, I headed straight for the line in front of her. I couldn't take my eyes off her angelic features and her elongated fingers as she counted out the notes. At night I tossed and turned as an epic of conquest, love and unquenchable lust played itself out in my head. She was the girl of my dreams and I wanted her so much that it hurt.

I was in the bank two days later and again standing in Maryna's line. She passed her pink tongue over her kissable lips, glanced up at me and said: 'Hi, you again!'

I'd prepared myself this time. 'Hi,' I said taking off my Ray-Bans. 'Yes, in your queue again. Doing it without thinking.'

'How come?'

For a moment my next sentence stuck in my throat. I swallowed once and then spewed it out exactly as I had practised it time and time again in front of the mirror: 'Because you're so beautiful.'

She stopped counting the money, looked up at me and said: 'Wow! Are you coming on to me?'

I wasn't prepared for this response and my mind went blank. I stuffed the money into my pocket and mumbled: 'Uh, no. Of course not. Bye-bye.'

When I got home, I hardly greeted Mom. I went straight to the bathroom and closed the door. I stared at myself in the mirror. I knew I wasn't that fucking dreadful-looking. My pimples were clearing up and I thought I looked sort of okay. I'd never ever been on a proper date because I just didn't have the guts to ask a girl out.

In my cupboard hung a pair of natty charcoal trousers, a red shirt and black shoes. It was my party or disco outfit. Problem was that I'd never worn it. In my fantasies I'd stepped into it a thousand times and my own version of 'Grease' spun around and around in my head. I was John Travolta and Maryna (the only reason I knew her name was because she wore a name tag) was Olivia Newton-John and we tangoed the night away until I swept her up in my arms and flung her down on a sandy beach and lost myself in her breasts, white like milk and soft as flour. Afterwards, I asked her to marry me. Of course she said yes.

I started spying on Maryna. I knew exactly what time she left work and I followed her to the flat where she lived. I worked out a battle plan according to which I coincidentally bumped into her one afternoon after work.

'Don't I know you from always standing in my queue?' she asked. I blushed and nodded my head.

'You're G J Goosen,' she said. 'What's the G for?'

'Gideon,' I said. 'And you?'

It was a silly question. She tapped the name tag on her breast. It was time to make my move. There was a Wimpy just across the road.

'You want to go for a quick coffee?'

'I don't drink coffee,' she said.

Oh fuck, I thought, I've blown it again. She offered a solution. 'There's a bar not far from here. Want to go for a drink?'

On the way to the pub she asked me in what police unit I worked.

'How do you know I'm a policeman?'

'Because you pay your salary cheque into your account every month, *domkop*!' Maryna laughed. 'And only policemen earn so little.'

We ended up drinking a whole bottle of Nederburg Stein. I'd never been a wine drinker but the yellowish liquid was sweet and fruity and I imagined that was how Maryna's mouth would taste.

When we left, she asked me if I wanted to go to the movies the next night. I nodded sheepishly. As I drove home, I clenched my fists and hollered at the top of my voice, telling myself that I was in love and that the girl of my dreams was about to be mine.

You know by now that it was not to be, although our first date went brilliantly. I grazed her leg with mine and halfway through the movie our hands touched. She clasped mine and held it for a few seconds before she leaned over and whispered in my ear: 'Why's your hand so wet? Are you nervous?'

We started seeing each other regularly. I took her to Café Italia in Roodepoort where we ate lasagne and pizza and drank more Stein and laughed and joked and playfully brushed against one another. When I dropped her at her flat she embraced me and kissed me briefly on my lips. Her lips were velvety and I could swear that her nipples were hard.

Two nights later, we sat in Ster Kinekor watching Brooke Shields flaunting her willowy, tanned frame in some romantic comedy. 'Isn't it just beautiful?' Maryna whispered in my ear and took my hand. 'True love.'

When we got to her flat, she opened the door, turned around, flung her arms around me and sucked me into her. We clung to each other and for at least a few moments it was just like the movies.

That was until she was naked and I was naked and she was panting and craving me and was wide open and begging me to fuck her. I craved her too, so badly that absolutely nothing fucking worked. That's the only explanation I have. I was like an Olympic sprinter who was so petrified of losing the big race that he couldn't propel his body out of the blocks. Or a rugby winger who spilled the ball with the goal line beckoning and only a few minutes left in the final and deciding test.

'Is something wrong with me?' she said as she bemoaned my limp piece of boerewors.

'Of course not,' I said as I put on my clothes. 'You're beautiful.'

When I got home, I had a colossal boner. Too fucking late now, I thought. I dreamt of her bare thighs and woke up with a morning glory and called Maryna and asked her out for supper. I was sure my ineptness was just a fluke and would be put right that same night. She said she was tired but finally relented and I took her to a bar where we got smashed on German honey liqueur. I fingered her under the table and we left with our tongues buried in each other's mouths.

Back at her flat, it happened again. This time Maryna gave droopy one look and concluded: 'Sorry, it's not working between us.'

Then she fell in love with a helicopter pilot by the name of Kobus. I sat for a whole night in front of her flat in Mom's orange Toyota and watched him leave at dawn the next morning. He was square-jawed and broad-chested and I could swear he had a smirk on his face because he'd probably fucked her silly and would do so again the following night.

I vented my shame and humiliation on a *houtkop* robber with Mick Jagger lips and a hard-arsed attitude. He was cuffed to a chair in the Brixton interrogation room and I wanted to turn the handle of the bush telephone so hard that his balls would fry and turn to charcoal. The silly fuck wouldn't say where he'd hidden the pistol and money he'd ripped in a hold-up at a business in Florida.

The black cop who had to attach the wires to his testicles (white cops never went near a *houtkop*'s private parts so black cops had to do it) couldn't get his act together and my patience was running low. I thought about the chopper pilot lying on top of my panting girlfriend while I sat outside in my car in the cold. Something snapped in me. I had no control over what happened next; it was as though a strange force took hold of me.

I pulled my fist back and hit the suspect as hard as I could on the side of his head. His head jerked back and for a moment I could see a look of stupefaction and pain on his face. I thumped him again, this time on his choppers. I could feel my knuckles crunching into his teeth. He mumbled something and spat a gob of blood on the floor. His lip had been ripped open and blood gushed on to his shirt.

'Fucking kaffir,' I yelled grabbing his hair as if to scalp him. I couldn't get a proper grip so I grabbed him by the front of his shirt instead and threw him and the chair to the ground. I kicked him in the stomach.

The next moment, Chappies Horn was on me. He flung his arms around me, pulled me away from the suspect and pinned me against the wall.

'Stop it, you crazy imbecile!' he hissed. 'What the fuck do you think you're doing?'

Later that afternoon I was standing to attention on the red carpet in Pietman Pretorius' office. He looked at me over his reading glasses and there was an iciness in his rusty voice.

'What's wrong with you, son?'

I decided that the best line of defence was honesty. 'My girlfriend broke up with me, Major,' I said. 'Something just snapped in me.'

'So now you go around and fuck people up?'

'I didn't mean to, Major. I'm sorry.'

'Tell that to Chappies. You have fucked up his case.'

'How come, Major?'

'You arse is on the line, Goosen,' he said, holding out a detainee complaint report. 'The suspect has laid a charge of assault against you. He has concussion, you've knocked out two of his teeth and he had to have twelve stitches above his eye.'

'I'm really sorry about this, Major.'

'So am I, son. This means we'll have to get affidavits from policemen stating that the suspect attacked you during interrogation and that you restrained him and defended yourself.'

'Thank you, Major.'

'We still don't know where he hid the money or the gun. And we can't interrogate him again.'

'Sorry, Major.'

Pretorius dismissed me but as I turned around and walked towards the door, he called out to me. I turned back to him. 'I hear you pack a mean punch, son.' I didn't answer. 'Keep your fists for when it matters.'

That was the end of Maryna and I hope the pilot gave her *sif*. I had to put the girl-thing on hold until I found an answer for my feeble performance. I was spending my weekends off at home with Mom and for the moment my hand remained my best friend. The highlight on a Saturday was visiting Johnnie in prison. I'd make my way to Johannesburg Prison with a Fontana chicken, chips and a litre of Coke (spiked with Red Heart).

After he'd agreed to turn state witness and testify against his brothers, Willem and Barend were moved to Pretoria Central, although they hadn't been told that *kleinboet* was about to turn on them and commit the ultimate deceit.

'Jakes was here this morning,' Johnnie said when I arrived

one Saturday. 'You've just missed him.'

'You're fucking joking!' I said. 'How's our *gabba*?'

'As strong as a fucking lion,' said Johnnie, 'and wheeling and dealing as always.'

The last time I'd seen Jakes was at the christening of Little Jakes and that was almost three years ago. Soon after he'd been discharged from the army I went to the smallholding to see him, but his father told me he had moved to Port Elizabeth. I thought I'd never see him again.

'Is he back?'

'With a fucking bang. He said panel beating wasn't for him. You know he can't do a day's honest work.'

'What's he doing now?'

'He says he's into diamonds. He's got some connection in Angola.'

The following afternoon, I drove to the Verster smallholding in Randfontein where Jakes and his family were squatting with his folks. When I stopped the car in front of the house, Jakes was rolling around on the lawn with Little Jakes. He was dressed entirely in black – black leather jacket, black-rimmed sunglasses and a thick leather belt with a metal buckle in the shape of a skull. He had a poodle-cut (short on top with long strands at the back) and was wearing a gold chain around his neck.

'Jesus Christ, Jakes,' I said when I got out, 'you look like the fucking godfather.'

He chuckled, embraced me and said: 'And I hear you're a cop.'

We chatted and joked and reminisced about the rugby match where he'd battered my eye open, the Greek boy-fucker who got the thrashing of his life, the gang fights at school, kaffir-bashing with Gielie, stealing sweets and groceries, and Dad chasing him and Johnnie across our lawn.

'Those were the best days and the worst days too,' Jakes said.

At some point his mother brought us cups of soup and buttered bread and Jakes opened a bottle of Klipdrift brandy that we drank neat out of teacups. Sharon was sitting a few metres away gaping at us but not making a sound. She'd grown into a rather comely piece of fluff since last I'd seen her. Brainwise, however, she was running on completely fucking zero.

It was clear that Jakes was a bit down and out and that was the reason why he was squatting with his parents.

'Johnnie says you've got a new scheme,' I said. 'Tell me about it.'

He looked at Sharon and said: 'Hey, doll, don't you think it's time to go and bath Little Jakes?'

She clicked her tongue and left the room. 'It's easy money, *bra*,' he said. 'Your hands don't get dirty and you don't have to fucking whack anybody.'

Jakes had a connection in the army who had a connection with the Unita rebel movement in Angola. The place was kind of fucked up but Unita were the good guys because they were fighting the communists. They controlled the diamond fields and Jakes' connection's connection could lay his hands on vast quantities of uncut stones. Problem was that the Unita guy obviously wanted hard cash for his contraband, but Jakes was convinced that there were vast profits to be made once the diamonds were on home soil. The long and short of it: Jakes needed dough but nobody was going to invest in such a risky scheme.

For the moment, Jakes was almost destitute. He had barely enough for the bambino's nappies and Purity or for Sharon's eyeliner and hairspray. I didn't have a cent to lend him. My meagre police salary was barely enough for a monthly tube of toothpaste or a can of Mum for Men. I could only dream about having my own car or apartment.

All this was about to change.

Our lives are sprinkled with extraordinary moments that reshape our destinies and govern our tomorrows. I was about to encounter such a moment, and it started when Johnnie summoned Jakes and me to prison shortly before his trial. He had phoned me during the week and said: 'I want to see the two of you together. It's very important.'

'Why?'

'Don't ask questions. Just be here.'

At around lunchtime the next Saturday, we wrote our names in the visitors' register at Johannesburg Prison where Johnnie Frederik Swart was now an awaiting trial prisoner. His trial was to commence in the Rand Supreme Court the following Wednesday.

'Howzit my *gabbas*?' Johnnie asked as he walked towards Jakes and me waiting for him in the visitors' section of the prison.

'No, cool, man,' Jakes said. He handed Johnnie a plastic bag with the usual Fontana chicken, chips and Coke (spiked with Red Heart).

'You scheme I'm doing the right thing?' Johnnie asked me. I assured him that he had no choice but to testify against Willem and Barend.

'Willem will kill me when he finds out,' he said.

'Willem is never going to get out,' I said.

'And what if he does?'

'He won't. Besides, he's probably going to swing.'

'My *boet*'s going to hang? Because of me?'

'No, Johnnie,' I tried to reassure him. 'He's fucked in any case.'

We had the same conversation week after week. Johnnie wasn't just almost certainly sending Willem to an early grave but he was turning his back on his old man and old lady and the rest of the almost two dozen or so siblings and other assorted relatives who squatted in the railway shack. Willem was the mainstay of the household and provided most of the money for food.

Johnnie was pretty fucked himself. He'd signed a sworn statement detailing the crimes committed by Willem and the rest of the gang. If he refused to testify, the state would simply throw the affidavit at him. Any judge would take one look and probably give him the rope.

'I'm alone after this,' said Johnnie.

'Oh no, you're not,' I assured him. 'We're here for you.'

Jakes nodded, adding: 'You're our *gabba*, Johnnie. We're brothers, us three.'

When Johnnie looked up, he had tears in his eyes and I had a lump in my throat. 'I know I'm going in for a long time,' he said, 'so there's something I want you guys to have. Something I want you to take.'

Jakes and I glanced at each other. As far as we knew, Johnnie had absolutely fucking zero.

He cleared his throat, leaned forward and said in a low voice: 'There's money.'

Neither of us said a word. Johnnie added: 'Lots and lots of it.'

Jakes was the first to speak. 'What fucking money? Where?'

Johnnie smiled wryly. 'You guys thought I had fuck all, hey? You're wrong.'

'Where does it come from?' I asked him.

He looked warily at me. 'You're a cop. Can I trust you?'

'Of course you can.'

'Willem and I pulled a hold-up two days before the building society fuck-up,' he said. 'We got seventy fucking thousand. All in twenties and fifties.'

Jakes' mouth fell open. I began having heart palpitations. I did some quick sums. It was eight times what I earned as a policeman in a whole fucking year! In those days seventy thousand rand was a fortune.

'Where is it?' I asked.

'Buried,' Johnnie said, and he folded his arms and leaned back. 'Buried very fucking deep and safe.'

'Why haven't you told the cops?' I asked him.

'Because Willem said we needed to put it away for a nest egg,' he said. 'Now it seems Willem is fucked and I'm sort of fucked. That's why I want you to have it.'

'To do what with?' I asked him.

'To enjoy life,' he replied.

It appeared that Willem had inside info on the monthly transportation of wage money from a bank in Krugersdorp to a gold mine near Carletonville. He got hold of a traffic cop's uniform and set up a roadblock between Krugersdorp and Carletonville. Barend, dressed in the uniform, stood in the middle of the road and raised his hand to stop the truck. Willem, Johnnie and Fanie were in a stolen Mercedes behind the truck and when it slowed down at the roadblock, they rammed into its rear. The truck went off the road and came to a standstill in the veld. There were two guards in the van, each armed with a revolver and a shotgun. In the confusion that followed, they never even managed to get their guns out of their holsters or to lift the shotguns. The Swart brothers got out of the battered car with guns blazing. The guards had to squeeze their bodies into the truck's leg space to avoid being hit. Willem shot away the lock at the back of the van with his shotgun.

'Two bags full of money,' said Johnnie gleefully. 'There was about seventy-three. We've used three.'

'On what?' asked Jakes.

'Food, clothes, booze, fucking. Things like that,' he said. 'The rest we buried.'

'How?' I asked him.

'In four plastic shopping bags. We sealed them with masking tape.'

'*Sjoe*,' said Jakes. 'And now you want us to have it?'

Johnnie said there were two conditions to giving us the money. The first was that Oom Buks and Tannie Lena had to be given ten thousand. 'For loss of income and loss of breadwinners and loss of sons,' he said.

The second was that we couldn't spend every last cent on ourselves because we had to keep some to look after him in prison. 'I want a roast chicken and a Klippies or Red Heart every now and then,' he said. 'And I don't want anybody to fuck me.'

'Deal,' said Jakes, licking his lips.

'It's absolutely a fucking deal,' I agreed.

Johnnie told us that the money was buried beneath an old beehive in the backyard of the gang house – the very place where one of my bullets had pierced his *kleinboet*'s chest.

'Are you sure about this, Johnnie?' asked Jakes.

'Well, I'm pretty fucked, am I not? You know where it is and there's nothing I can do to stop you.'

He stood up, stretched out his arms and said: 'Come gimme a hug, you two.'

As we crushed one another in a warm embrace, Johnnie said: 'Oh *ja*, one last thing, boys.'

'And that is?' I asked.

'I want a new suit for court next week,' he said. 'I always said I wanted to go down in a hail of bullets, but I can just as well go down in pure fucking wool!'

When we got outside, I looked at Jakes and asked: 'What now?'

He looked at me and said: 'Let's go and fucking get it!'

When we arrived at the railway house we immediately ran to the back. There was indeed an old beehive. We pushed it away. The soil looked as though it had recently been loosened. Jakes fell to his knees and started delving with his hands. I ran to the car and pulled the wheel spanner out of the boot and joined him. Soil flew in every direction. We must have looked like two Jack Russells digging for an elusive lamb bone. We tunnelled in silence for about five minutes.

'I can feel fucking something,' said Jakes, his cheeks bulging and his face red. 'There's fucking something here!'

He pulled out the first shopping bag and held it in his hand. 'Do you think this is it?' he asked me.

Without saying a word, I snatched the bag from him and tore open the plastic with the wheel spanner. A brown R20 note was clearly visible. Without saying a word, we returned to our digging and pulled the remaining three bags from the hole.

'Let's fuck off,' said Jakes. We threw the bags in my car boot.

'What now?' I wanted to know.

'I suppose we have to count it and discuss what to do,' he said.

'Let's go to The Leopard,' I said. 'Maybe we can get a room and count it there.'

'See you there,' he confirmed. As I turned around and walked towards my car, he said: 'No, wait! Fuck The Leopard. Let's go to The Landdrost.'

'What's that?'

'Five Stars,' he said. 'Very larney.'

'Isn't it very expensive?'

'I'm sure it is,' he said, 'but we can just about buy the fucking place if we want to.'

A doorman wearing white gloves and a red jacket with matching cap swung the polished copper-framed doors of The Landdrost open and we strolled on to the thick red carpet. Patrons peered over their afternoon gin and tonics at the two down-and-outs encroaching on their opulence and reminding them in a most unpleasant way that there was another, ugly world out there. Our treasure hunt had left us with soiled clothing and Jakes was carrying a black dustbin bag. It contained the four bags of money.

A guy dressed in a black suit and a bow tie was at the reception desk. He looked at us as though he'd smelled something unpleasant. 'Yes, gentlemen, can I help you?' he asked.

'We want a room,' said Jakes.

'Sir, I'll have to check if we have one available,' he said.

He disappeared for a minute or so, came back and said: 'Sorry, sir, we are fully booked.'

'Oh come on, Mister Penguin!' said Jakes. 'Don't you have anything at all?'

'Sorry, sir, but only the presidential suite is available.'

'That's exactly what we want!' said Jakes. 'We'll take it.'

'It's seven hundred rand a night, sir.'

'Do you want it in fucking tens or do you want it in fucking twenties?'

Mister Penguin excused himself again. 'Fuck, Jakes,' I said. 'Did you hear what it cost?'

'Johnnie wouldn't have it any other way,' he said.

The black-suited guy returned with another black-suited guy. By then Jakes was on his knees scratching around in the bag. He'd ripped open one of the shopping bags and was rooting out one fifty-rand note after the other.

'We'll not only require upfront payment for the room, sir,' said the second black-suited dude, 'but also a deposit for any additional costs incurred.'

'Like what?' I asked him.

'Like room service, for example,' he said.

Jakes got up off the white marble floor with a wad of notes in his hand.

'Yes, we want room service,' he said. 'You can send up a bottle of Red Heart right away. And tell me, Mister Penguin, do you provide a massage service in this dump?'

But even the flippant Jakes Verster was lost for words when yet another black-suited dude flung open the doors of the Cecil John Rhodes presidential suite. I can only describe it as a stately refuge of glimmering oak and silky-soft-satiny trappings. For the next fifteen minutes, we jumped trampoline on the king-size bed and scurried like ten-year-olds between the lounge and the bedroom and the marble bathroom and pushed every button and ripped open every door. Jakes shrieked with delight when he unveiled the mini-bar.

'Fucking hell, yes!' he said as he poured two whiskies. We had a glass in each hand, one with Red Heart and the other with Johnnie Walker.

We ripped the plastic bags open, threw the bundles of money on the king-size bed and started counting. There was exactly seventy thousand, minus the thousand we had paid to the hotel for the room and the deposit. Even if we subtracted the ten thousand for Oom Buks and Tannie Lena, there was still thirty thousand for each of us. It was more money than I'd ever thought I'd accumulate in my life.

'Well, *boet*,' said Jakes. 'It's time to celebrate. That's how Johnnie would want it.'

'I'm hungry,' I said scanning the room service menu. I didn't know what most of the dishes were.

'What's the most expensive chow on that thing?'

'Lobster and caviar.'

'Have you ever had them?'

'No, have you?'

'No, so let's get them.'

'And let's get champagne. French.'

'Have you had that before?'

'No, have you?'

'No, so let's get some.'

I stared at the three names on the menu. Dom Pérignon, Veuve Clicquot and Moët et Chandon.

'Jesus Christ, Jakes,' I said, 'I don't even know how to pronounce this.'

He grabbed the phone. 'A bottle of Dom,' he said, and ordered the lobster and the caviar as well.

Another black suit brought a trolley with an array of silver bowls and dishes. The lobster had been cut in half. Jakes looked at the carcass and asked: 'And how the fuck do you eat that gogga?'

'I've had prawns before,' I said. 'I think you eat only the tail.'

'You can't exactly feed an army on that, can you?'

'The caviar, gentlemen,' the waiter said and lifted a silver dish the size of a saucer. It contained a tiny heap of black, jelly-like little balls.

'You must be fucking joking,' said Jakes.

'Exactly as you ordered, sir.'

'Why thirty-fucking-five rand for that?'

'It's sturgeon fish roe from the Caspian Sea, sir.'

'Sis,' said Jakes. 'I don't eat shit. Take it back and bring us two man-size rumps with mushroom sauce and chips.'

As we plunged into our food, Jakes lifted his glass of champagne and said: 'You know what we're going to do after this?'

'What?'

'Get some bitches and pour this shit over their tits!'

'Fucking hell, Jakes!'

'And what's more,' he said, laughing, 'no fucking worn-out

station tarts.'

'Please God, no!'

He scanned the classifieds in *The Star* newspaper and dialled the number of an escort agency by the name of Playmates.

'Do you have a fresh young blonde who knows how to satisfy an honest gentleman's every need?' he wanted to know. He nodded his head and stuck his thumb in the air. 'And what about a dark-head?' He shook his head. 'No, twenty-five is too fucking old. A brunette?' He smiled and gave me a thumbs-up. 'What about a redhead? You say you have a redhead? Real or out of a bottle? No fuck, get her pretty ass over here as well. No, we want all-nighters. We'll send them home after we've had them for breakfast tomorrow morning.'

Jakes put the phone down, giggled and downed his glass of champagne.

'You've ordered three?' I said.

'One is for Johnnie,' he said. 'But seeing he's not here, we'll have to eat his pudding.'

A short while later, the phone rang. It was the concierge, announcing that we had guests.

'Send them up,' said Jakes, 'and another bottle of that Dom shit.'

There was a knock on the door. Jakes swung it open, chuckled with delight and said: 'Welcome, ladies!'

The brunette was the first to walk in. She was a snake-hipped bimbo with fair-sized knockers that bulged from her skimpy mini. I swallowed once or twice and fastened my eyes on her lithe frame until the blonde came into sight. She was a strutting fuck machine on high heels, not all that pretty but with a body that looked as though it had been assembled in a Ferrari factory. She smacked her pouting red lips, looked at me and said: 'Hi, sweetie!'

I couldn't get a word out, just nodded my head sheepishly. The butler, pushing a trolley with another bottle of Dom in a silver ice bucket, followed next.

And then, a few paces behind the him, the third prossie

floated in. Her fiery locks partly obscured her face but, unlike the other two bitches, she was wearing jeans and her breasts were small and pointy. She tossed back her hair and when she fixed her heavenly deep blue eyes on me, I could feel my heart beating in my throat. She was an angel; an alluring young turtle-dove who took my breath away. Her name was Sharné and she was the loveliest thing I'd ever seen.

Twelve

The trial of the Swart brothers got under way with the advocate for the three accused asking the court for permission to have his clients' leg irons removed. The prosecutor leapt to his feet, objecting and describing the brothers as extremely dangerous and a flight risk. The brothers were sitting in the dock with choir boy expressions on their faces. Johnnie was wearing his brand new cream-coloured suit, an orange shirt and a black tie. Willem and Barend were dressed in ill-fitting grey suits.

'Look at accused number three (that was Johnnie), your honour,' said the advocate, a hopeless down-and-out lawyer who had been appointed pro deo for all three of them. 'He can't even walk properly, never mind run away.'

Johnnie nodded his head. The advocate continued: 'And accused number one (that was Willem), your honour, has changed his ways and has found God.'

Willem nodded his head. 'And there is serious doubt about the mental capacity of accused number two (that was Barend), your honour,' said the advocate. 'I request that he be admitted to a psychiatric hospital for observation.'

Barend nodded his head. On the bench was a hoary judge who was of an age where his contemporaries, if they were not in retirement and enjoying their grand- and great-grandchildren, had long been six feet under. He gave the three accused one look, shook his head and said in a high-pitched voice: 'Application rejected! Get on with it!'

The families of the victims were baying for the blood of the Swart brothers and their trial attracted its fair share of publicity. Johnnie even made it to the front page of *Rapport* when the newspaper sneaked a picture of the three brothers in leg and hand irons being escorted from a prison van into the Rand Supreme Court. Back in Randfontein, the Swart clan were falling over one another to give interviews to newspapers and every week another toothless wonder had some insight into the mental state of the accused.

There was general consensus that Willem was a deranged outcast who had a hold over Barend and Johnnie. One of the family members discovered a stack of photographs dating back to Willem's days in the recces. In several of the pics he was surrounded by shot-up corpses of Swapo terrorists, but the cherry on top was one where he grimaces while cutting off the ears of a terrie. Of course *Rapport* had a field day and dubbed the killer *Wrede Willem*.

The prosecution had a devastating case against the three brothers and the death penalty hung over their heads. The hangman, a sneer on his face and a noose in his hand, was knocking on their door. As the state was about to conclude its case, the prosecutor announced that he had one more witness to call. It was just before lunch on a Friday afternoon and the judge was probably looking forward to a game of golf or a session of hanky-panky with his perky-titted court clerk.

'Is this really necessary?' he grunted from the bench.

'Unfortunately it is, your honour,' said the prosecutor. 'It will cast new light on the activities of this gang.'

'Get on with it then,' said the judge in a dour tone.

'The state calls accused number three.'

For a few seconds there was absolute silence in the courtroom. As Johnnie got up from the bench, I could hear the creaking of his boots and the clanging of the leg irons as he shuffled out of the dock and made his way slowly to the witness box. Willem, who was holding his head between his hands and resting his elbows on his knees, jerked upright. He looked totally bewildered. Even Barend, who had shown no emotion during the trial and gave the impression that he didn't understand the severity of the charges against him, lifted his eyebrows. There was a buzz at the back of the room as brothers and sisters and cousins deliberated the significance of this development.

'What's happening now?' Oom Buks asked his wife. He and Tannie Lena had been sitting just behind the dock every day since the hearing started.

'Silence in court!' ordered the judge.

'What's happening now?' Oom Buks repeated, stamping his walking stick on the wooden floor.

'I said, silence in court!' thundered the judge from the bench, his face as red as a tomato.

Johnnie took the witness stand, held his right hand in the air and mumbled: 'So help me, God.'

Then he condemned his two brothers to the gallows. If there was any doubt that Barend and Willem were at death's door, Johnnie secured their rendezvous with the hangman. He didn't blink as he recounted robbery after robbery and crime after crime – with the exception of course of the Randfontein wage heist. He had told me that state investigators had questioned him for hours about the hold-up, but he gave nothing away.

It was late when Johnnie concluded his evidence. By then the judge looked as though he'd stuck his fingers into an electric socket. His white hair was standing on end, his face was florid, and his expression was one of exasperation and exhaustion.

There was another silence as Johnnie hobbled back to the dock. He sat down on the edge of the bench, as far away from his brothers as possible. Barend stared straight ahead of him while Willem's manic eyes were glued to Johnnie's face.

Two weeks later, the three brothers were convicted of murder and robbery. There was very little they could offer by way of extenuating circumstances. Tannie Lena took the stand and in a torrent of tears told the judge about the dire poverty and hardship her sons had endured throughout their lives. The judge shook his head and said curtly: 'Doesn't mean you have to kill, Missus Swart. Anything else?'

The next morning, the court resumed for sentencing and the accused were led into the room in irons. The hand irons were taken off; the leg irons remained. I was sitting with Jakes and Gielie near the back of the courtroom. Johnnie glanced around, saw us and forced a feeble smile.

The judge stared at the accused, took a swig of water (I'm sure it was spiked) and cleared his throat. He said all three accused had shown complete disrespect for human life and in the case of Willem and Barend he couldn't find any extenuating circumstances. Their newly discovered faith in the Almighty and their show of remorse had come too late, he said, adding: 'Keep up the trust in God, sons, because it will come in handy in the days to come.'

He then sentenced them to die by hanging. For a moment there was a hush, followed by a single, heart-wrenching sob from Tannie Lena. It was a signal for the whole Swart clan to join in and pandemonium broke loose in the courtroom.

Oom Buks was on his feet, brandishing his walking stick in the air and hurling abuse at the judge. Others jumped on to the benches, stamping their feet and joining in the chorus that was lambasting the judge. Willem recovered from his initial paralysis at hearing his fate and stumbled to his feet, screaming at the top of his voice. Two cops grabbed him by the shoulders and pushed him back on to the bench.

Order was restored only after a number of the Swart family members had been forcibly evicted and the judge had threatened the rest with contempt of court. He turned to accused number three. 'And you, young man,' he said, 'also deserve to hang. You have shown no mercy and have associated yourself with the actions of the other two. You are no better than accused number one or two. Do you understand this?'

Johnnie nodded and swallowed once or twice. The judge continued: 'But this court has to take into account that you have turned state witness and chose to testify against the other accused. Therefore a sentence of death or life imprisonment would not be appropriate.'

There was another rumble in the courtroom before the judge sentenced him to ten years' imprisonment. Johnnie looked over his shoulder at us and stuck his thumb in the air. We shook his hand briefly before he was led down the stairs to commence his sentence in Krugersdorp Prison. Barend and Willem were transferred to death row in Pretoria Central.

I needed a makeover. I had looked at myself in the mirror and decided that I'd had enough of a mousy fringe that drooped over my eyes, crimplene shirts, Hushpuppy shoes and ill-fitting jeans that looked as though a turd had been trapped in the back. At a Roodepoort shopping centre, not far from the Volkskas branch where Maryna had once wooed me into her queue (I had since changed banks), was a unisex hairdresser called Tony's Hair Affair. An ammonia-like smell emanated from the premises and I had often wondered if Tony would be able to do anything with my lustreless hair.

When I eventually plucked up enough courage to venture into the salon, Tony recommended a perm to give my hair some body. I said that I was a police detective and that my hair had to be neat and relatively short. I couldn't pitch up at Brixton Murder and Robbery with a mane of curls. Major Pretorius would have choked in his *Leeutande*. Tony suggested we stick with a cut and a wave. However, he lightened it with a few blond streaks.

'What's happened to your hair?' Mom asked when she saw me.

'Do you like it?'

'Sort of,' she said, 'but how come you've gone blond?'

'Must be the sun,' I said and thought it was time to tell her that I was leaving home. She looked at me as though I'd bashed her on the head with an iron rod.

'But why, *boetie*?' she asked, tears welling in her eyes.

'There's a time to come and a time to go,' I said and put my arm around her shoulders.

'But will you be okay on your own?'

'Of course,' I said.

'But looked what happened to Karel ...'

'Don't worry,' I said. 'I'll come and see you often.'

A few days later, I moved into my bachelor's pad in Hillbrow, newly furnished with a king-size bed, a leather couch, fluffy carpet and a powerful stereo.

It was time for a new wardrobe. I marched into an Italian outfitters in Hillbrow, pulled the funkiest and most expensive Levi's and T-shirts from the shelves, got hold of a black leather jacket and rounded everything off with two gold chains. Not bad, I thought when I studied myself in the mirror. I dowsed myself in Christian Dior, vowing never to touch Old Spice again. It reminded me of my old man and therefore made me want to puke. Afterwards I popped into a music store and bought all Leonard Cohen's CDs. I rounded off my shopping spree with an espresso and a cognac at Café de Paris.

A few days later, I pulled out of Dan Perkins Motors with an almost new second-hand Alfa GTV. It was red with white leather seats and mags as wide as the nothingness between Gielie's or Johnnie's ears. It was several months since Johnnie's fortune had transformed my life. The pile of twenties and fifties – wrapped in a plastic bag and stashed under the sink – had shrunk considerably and was dwindling by the day. It didn't matter; I had acquired a beast of a machine that left most of its competitors with only the smell of rubber in its wake. I stopped at a café, bought a packet of Gauloises (not quite Italian but close enough) and lit one almost immediately (I didn't usually smoke but it went with the Levi's-Alfa-Dior package), opened the window, stuck out my elbow and raced into the sunset.

All I needed was a broad who would sink into the leather seat beside me.

I didn't have to wait long. A few hours later, I knocked on the door of a ninth-storey flat in Joubert Park. It opened, and before me stood the woman of my dreams. Sharné. She took my breath away. She was wearing high-heeled white boots, a matching white mini-skirt and a red blouse. I could see her pointy nipples poking through the thin material. Her red mane tumbled down her shoulders. Her mouth was red and pouting and the tip of her tongue was sticking out through her white teeth. Her Arctic eyes were mischievous and gorgeous.

Ever since I had purchased her body for a night of carnal pleasure at The Landdrost, she had filled my mind and dominated my fantasies. When she left in a taxi the next morning she had scribbled down her telephone number and said she would like to see me again. Since then we'd had several rendezvous, each time without any money changing hands.

When Sharné saw my new set of wheels, she stopped dead in her tracks, pushed her manicured hands against her face and squeaked like a little bird. 'No, no, no,' she whooped, 'I don't believe it!'

'Eat your heart out, baby,' I said as I opened the door for her. As Sharné got into the car, her white skirt crawled up her firm white thighs and I couldn't help but wonder if she was naked under the tiny piece of cloth. She didn't like to wear panties and that suited me just fine.

The V6 growled to life as I turned the ignition key. Sharné was bobbing up and down excitedly. As I lifted my foot from the clutch and stepped on the gas, the force of fine Italian engineering propelled the Alfa forward and pushed me back into my seat. I donated a layer of rubber to the city council as we roared away with spinning tyres. The needle of the rev counter was almost in the red before I threw it into second and screamed around a corner.

Minutes later, we were at the drive-in in the sky. Those years (it might still be there for all I know), there was a drive-in theatre on an old mine dump just south of the city centre. It was generally known as *Fok-kop* because it was nothing more than a bonking haunt for dudes and their birds. By the time the main feature started, the whole fucking place was a legion of rocking and bobbing cars.

The Alfa was a mean and hungry son of a bitch that could charm the most unyielding thighs apart, but it did have a shortcoming when it came to the love act. There was a gear lever between the two front seats and because it was a sport coupé there wasn't really a back seat. It couldn't compare with, say, a Merc or a Fairmont. Not only did those automobiles flaunt seats like featherbeds, but you could easily have a threesome on the back seat and spreadeagle both broads.

Well, that's unless you are Gideon Johannes Goosen and your doll is the most agile and nubile creature ever crafted. I don't want to boast, but Sharné and I hadn't even finished our burger and chips before we were gobbling each other up. I'd been thinking about initiating my Alfa in the love act all afternoon and I dare anyone to bang as hard and continuously and creatively as we did for the duration of the whole fucking movie – of which I never saw a single frame. Suffice to say that Sharné spent an awfully long time with her feet behind her ears and at some point she was hanging out of the front window which caused the clip-on tray with our half-eaten dinners to shatter to the ground.

The next day I sent her twenty-four red roses. Twenty-four hours later, I took her shopping at Sandton City where she bought more miniskirts and boots and a white leather jacket. She had expensive tastes, I realised as I counted out a pile of notes. That night, I took her to an exclusive French eatery called Chez Michel where I ordered a bottle of Dom and duck in orange sauce. She wanted a plate of oysters.

'Sis,' I said. 'They're raw.'

'Take a sip of champagne,' Sharné said as she dripped lemon juice on to the oysters, 'and slip one into your mouth.'

'Where did you learn about these things?' I asked her. Oysters weren't something one associated with a runaway from Nigel.

'I've been around, honey,' she said. 'Come on, take one.'

'Ugh,' I said as I sampled the creature. 'It's slimy and salty.'

'What does it remind you of?'

'Raw fish.'

'No man, *domkop*!' she said and laughed. 'Think again!'

'I can't.'

'Don't you think,' Sharné said as she seductively rubbed her leg against mine, 'that it tastes like a vulva?'

'A fucking what?'

'A vulva!'

Later, as I lay naked next to her, I ran my hands over her naked thighs and whispered into her ear: 'I love your little oyster.'

Sharné said nothing, just kissed my neck and brushed her tongue over my ear. She was soft and warm and almost weightless when I picked her up and put her on top of me. Her perfume was sweet and her tongue slid over mine as we shagged hard and deep and fervently. She rolled off me and snuggled up against my chest.

'I love the way you take me,' she said.

'I'm addicted to you,' I said.

'Why?' she whimpered in my ear.

'It's all the things I see in your eyes.'

'Like what?'

'I don't know how to describe it. It's like a crazy loveliness.'

She didn't say anything. What I said next just slipped out. I had no control over what tumbled out of my mouth. 'I love you,' I said. 'Very much.'

I felt her body stiffen. It was the wrong thing to say. I tried to slip my finger into her but she clamped her legs together. 'You can't say that,' she said, lifting herself and sitting upright on the bed. 'It's not part of the deal.'

A few minutes later, I screeched away from Joubert Park and

hurled my machine up the hill towards Hillbrow. I'd never loved anyone so much. I was angry and disappointed and dejected and tossed around all night on my newly acquired king-size bed. I wanted Sharné next to me.

I was on weekend duty. I sat in my dingy office brooding about Sharné. I loved and craved her desperately, yet she was as out of reach as the most distant star in the universe. Just thinking of Sharné burnt a hole in my soul and filled me with an unreasonable rage. I had an urge to bang her silly and shower her with love and simultaneously to beat her senseless and throttle the air out of her lungs. I'd rather kill her than not have her.

I had to get rid of the fury that was building up in me. Once again I took it out on a suspect. I strolled into the interrogation room where Baksteen and Chappies were trouncing a thin guy who was cuffed to a chair. Baksteen was about to pull *Buksie* over his face.

'What's up, Blondie (my new nickname at Brixton Murder and Robbery)?' Chappies wanted to know.

'You need help?' I asked Baksteen and took the tube from him. They had been out the whole night hunting down the suspect and they were probably as fucked as he was.

By then they'd fried the *houtkop*'s balls to crackling but the cunt still refused to tell them where he was hiding a bag of jewellery he had stolen from a shop in the Carlton Centre.

'I'll fuck the cunt up,' I said and turned to one of the black cops. 'Get me a bucket of water,' I ordered him.

The suspect stared wide-eyed at me and whimpered *kak* like 'Please, boss' and 'No, boss' and 'I don't know, boss', and whatever.

I had by then developed my own signature style of torture. It wasn't altogether original but I executed it with such devastating efficiency that I was soon called upon to dispense it whenever a suspect refused to cooperate. I simply combined tubing with drowning.

With all my strength I pulled *Buksie* over his face. I wanted to tube every fucking molecule of oxygen out of him. When I released the tube, I allowed him one gasp of air and then pushed his head as deeply as I could into the bucket of water. I felt him squirm and wriggle and I pulled him out only when Chappies grabbed my arm and said: '*Jissus God*, Blondie, that's enough!'

The suspect lay gurgling on the cement floor. I pulled him upright and repeated the exercise. All the time I felt my resentment growing and I would happily have erased the cunt from the face of the earth. When I jerked him out of the bucket and dropped him on the floor the second time, I pulled out my pistol.

'What are you doing?' asked Chappies.

I pushed my nine-mill into his choppers and cocked it. I was ready to spray his brains across the floor when he gurgled once or twice. When I pulled the barrel out of his mouth, he vomited like a sixteen-year-old who'd had his first Old Brown Sherry. Then he started to sing. Like a fucking canary.

Less than an hour later, Baksteen, Chappies and I were in a Skyline, speeding towards the township of Alexandra, a mish-mash of matchbox houses next to the Ben Schoeman Highway on the other side of Sandton. It was the first time I'd ever been there. Alexandra was a human garbage dump which should never have existed in the first place. It was a disorderly hotchpotch of dwellings and gravel roads with discarded rubbish on street corners.

We drove behind two police cars with four black cops who had to show us the way. They were armed with nine-mills while Baksteen had a shotgun. I was armed with an R4. Chappies had an Uzi which suited him just fine because he had the looks and physique of a fourteen-year-old schoolboy.

The dude in the *pynkamer* told us that he had hidden the jewellery in his girlfriend's room at the back of a house in Alex-andra. It had rained the night before and we tramped through pools of mud and water as we scrambled out of the cars and descended on the red-brick house with the corrugated iron shack at the back. Chappies, two black cops and I pounced on the shack while the others swooped on the house. My R4 was cocked and ready. We were a few metres away when the door was flung open and a young *houtkop* dashed out. He sped past the startled black policemen, who were leading the way, and ran right into me. His eyes were as wide as saucers; I remember them to this day. He was so fast that I didn't have time to stop him or lift my gun. When he was a metre or so from me, he executed a sidestep that would have shamed Springbok rugby centre Mannetjies Roux in his heyday and dashed towards freedom.

'Catch the bastard!' shouted Chappies.

I regained my composure, turned around and ran after him. He had several metres advantage, the R4 was heavy and I'd never been a sprinter. I came to a standstill in the dirt road and lifted my rifle. The suspect – if he was one – was fifteen metres ahead of me and was racing towards an intersection where he could have disappeared around the corner. It was a Saturday afternoon and the road was alive with people. I pushed the R4 into my shoulder, steadied the gun and hunted over my sight for the running man's back. I'd been taught in police college to wait for that moment when your target seems to be sucked into your sight. That's when you gently squeeze the trigger.

My finger was tightening around the trigger when Chappies yelled next to me: 'No, fuck, Blondie, you can't kill him!'

I knew it was dicey – to say the least – to shoot a fleeing man in the back. However, it was my duty to make an arrest. I dropped the barrel a centimetre or so and in that fleeting moment before he would have disappeared from sight, I pulled the trigger once, twice, three times. One of those shots swiped him off his feet and flung him to the ground.

By then a commotion had broken out in the street with shrieking people darting in every direction. I ran towards the figure in the road. It was moving, so at least it was still alive. The dude murmured softly and his face showed his agony. His leg was a mess. The bullet had smashed into his knee and it looked as though the kneecap had been blown away.

Chappies, Baksteen and one of the black cops arrived on the

scene. 'Get an ambulance,' Chappies ordered the black cop.

I turned around to walk back. 'Good shot, Blondie,' said Baksteen. I smiled and stuck my thumb in the air.

'I don't think he'll walk again,' I said.

Back at the shack, the other two black cops were standing next to a woman who was sitting on the bed. She had her hands in front of her face and she was crying her heart out.

'Tell her to shut the fuck up,' said Baksteen and took up a menacing position in front of her. She sniffed a few times and muttered something in a black language.

'She says it was her brother,' the cop said.

'Why the fuck did he run?' Baksteen demanded.

The black cop translated for the woman, who dropped her hands in front of her face. She mumbled something and started crying again.

'She says he got a fright,' said the cop. 'He knows nothing.'

'Tough shit,' said Baksteen, bending forwards. His face was only a few inches from her face. 'Where's that fucking bag? Huh?'

The black cop translated. The woman shook her head and looked down at her hands, tightly clasped on her lap.

'She says she doesn't know,' said the cop.

'Bullshit!' growled Baksteen. 'She's lying.' He turned to me, pointed at the woman and said: 'Shoot the fucking bitch.'

I raised my R4 and took a step closer. She lifted her head and looked at me. She was young, very young. No older than seventeen or eighteen. She wore a red head scarf and her eyes were big and black. There were no windows in the shack but a gleam of late afternoon sun shone through the door. It cast streaks of light on her face. Her skin was velvety black and her lips were lush and ripe. I thought for a moment that she was beautiful, but immediately chucked the notion. I stuck the barrel of my gun in her face.

'Talk, *meid*, talk!' I said. Of course I didn't intend to shoot her but I thought that it was an appropriate way to deal with a robber's bitch. After all, I was white and she was black and she had to understand that she couldn't fuck with me or any member of Brixton Murder and Robbery.

She stopped crying and looked me in the eyes. She had a brazen, almost cocky expression on her face. There were a few seconds of silence, broken only by a black cop scratching around in a cupboard and voices outside the shack.

'Fuck you,' she said slowly. I was dumbfounded. I looked at Baksteen, who seemed as perplexed as I was. I stepped a metre back, lifted the R4 and aimed it between her eyes. My finger was on the trigger. The bullet would have sliced through her brain like a hot knife through butter and pulverised the back of her head.

'Fuck you,' she said again, and repeated it a third time. 'Fuck you.'

Chappies sniggered behind me. 'She's fucking with you, Blondie,' he said. 'She's got fuck all respect for you.'

I wasn't sure what to do next. She wasn't intimidated by the R4 and had called my bluff. 'Fucking *meid*,' I mumbled. 'Who the fuck do you think you are?' An almost sardonic smile floated over her luscious lips. Her expression said: 'And so, what are you going to do next?'

I took my trigger hand off the gun and made it into a fist. I wanted to ram it into her face. It was the only response I could think of. She was saved from being smashed to pulp when one of the black cops pulled a small blue sports bag from under her bed and unzipped it. It contained the jewellery.

'What about her?' I asked as we were about to leave.

'We don't have a case,' Chappies said. 'How do we prove that she knew what was in the bag?'

I looked at her, sitting on the edge of the bed. She held her chin in the air, the brazen expression still in her eyes. She was looking straight at me and I swear there was a faint smile playing around the corners of her mouth. She was what we call in Afrikaans *dom-astrant* – rebellious, defiant and stubborn.

The bitch was going to pay for it.

'Cuff her,' I ordered a black policeman. 'I'll see her in the interrogation room.'

'What for?' Chappies wanted to know.

'She might be an accomplice,' I said. 'I'll find out.'

The policeman stepped forward, took a set of cuffs from his belt and clamped them round her wrists. The smirk disappeared from her face but her eyes, full of hatred and disgust, never left mine. The cop took her arm, pulled her up, and shoved her towards the door.

'Don't worry, honey,' I said as she walked past me. 'You'll enjoy it.'

The policeman opened the back door of the car and pushed her in.

As we pulled away behind the black cops, Chappies turned to me and asked: 'What's it with you, Blondie?'

'What do you mean?'

'You're stressed out, man,' he said. 'What's up?'

'It's that fucking woman,' I said. 'She's freaking me out.'

'The redhead?'

'Yes, Sharné.'

'She's hot.'

'Fucking boiling hot.'

'So what's the problem?'

I glanced at the puny man who had in the past months become a close friend. 'She's a prossie,' I said.

'Fucking what?' hollered Chappies and laughed nervously. 'You can't be serious!'

'She's an escort at Playmates,' I said.

'Classy place,' said Chappies. 'Nice broads.'

'She doesn't belong there,' I said.

'Place is owned by a Greek,' Chappies said. 'A slimy bastard.'

'Drives me mad to think she bangs a host of men every day.'

'You must get her out of there,' he said. 'In the end they all get fucked up.'

'What do you mean?'

'Those prossies are never the same again.'

'Why not?'

'He fucks them up,' he said. 'It's all drugs and threesomes.'

'So what do I do?'

Chappies looked at me. 'Do you really want to get her out of there?'

'Yes, of course I do.'

'It's not going to be easy. You might have to bust his balls.'

'I'll do it with a song in my heart.'

'I hope you know what you're talking about.'

'I'll kill him if I have to.'

Thirteen

My job was going down the drain. I was exhausted and regularly phoned in sick so that I could spy on Sharné and follow her around.

To aggravate matters, the guy I'd *klapped* on the side of the head during my shit with bank clerk Maryna had laid a charge of assault against me. He said I had burst his eardrum. I couldn't explain the injury away because a medical report confirmed the rupture. The docket was referred to the Attorney General for a decision on whether to prosecute. Somehow I had to make the problem go away.

One of the black cops at Brixton was nicknamed 'Spyker', Afrikaans for 'nail'. He had acquired this name because of his success at procreation – apparently his offspring were scattered across Soweto. But Spyker, a portly charcoal bloke with a shaved head, was much more than just a randy cop. He was a cruel and sadistic bastard who respected nothing and no one except his white police bosses at Brixton Murder and Robbery. Spyker was a lay pastor who hummed holy tunes as he pulverised detainees.

He wasn't just a skilled and enthusiastic torturer, but was also the chieftain of a small band of black policemen who relished doing the unit's dirty work. We often had cases where there wasn't enough evidence to successfully charge and prosecute a potentially dangerous suspect, despite the fact that he was clearly involved in the crime. It was not desirable that these dudes should be released because they would simply have robbed, raped and murdered again.

There were three ways of dealing with them. The first was to hang them in the cells and claim afterwards that they had committed suicide. Most of the 'suicides' at Brixton Murder and Robbery were Spyker's handiwork.

The second was to take the suspect for a crime scene inspection, shoot him dead, and declare afterwards that he had tried to escape. Spyker would happily bury bullets in their backs.

The third was to set the suspect free and get him to sign a release form. The minute the dude walked out of Brixton Murder and Robbery Spyker and his henchmen would pick him up in an unmarked car, take him to an open stretch of veld, execute him and leave his body to rot.

I had never worked closely with Spyker but he always greeted me with a wide smile on his rotund face and he told me that he admired my tube-and-drown torture technique. I promised Spyker a hefty reward if he could make my problem go away. The trouble was that the dude had been transferred from Brixton and was in the awaiting trial section of Johannesburg Prison.

'No problem,' Spyker assured me. 'What do you want me to do?'

'I don't care,' I said. 'As long he can never again say a fucking word.'

A few days later, the suspect was floating in a pool of blood in the prison bathroom. A homemade knife was sticking out of his back. It cost me three thousand bucks but the dead cannot squeal and the case against me was withdrawn. I thought that was the end of it – until I got a message to report to Pietman Pretorius as a matter of urgency.

He hardly looked up when I walked into his office. When he eventually lifted his eyes from the statement he was writing, they tore me apart.

'So, Goosen,' he said, an icy edge to his rusty voice, 'I heard he died.'

I cleared my throat and looked at him with a sheepish expression. 'Who're you talking about, Major?'

'Don't fuck with me, Goosen. You know who. The bank robber.'

'I heard he died in a gang fight, Major.'

'How convenient,' he sneered and continued scribbling something on the paper in front of him. 'Nevertheless, you fucked up very badly.'

'I know, Major.'

'It's not the first time.'

'I'm sorry, Major.'

He looked up from his desk and took off his glasses. 'Too late, Goosen,' he said. 'You're out of here.'

I felt as though I'd been hit by a sledgehammer. It took a few seconds to sink in. Out of here! Out of Brixton Murder and Robbery? I'd been fucking shafted! I gaped at Pretorius and suddenly realised that he was one of the ugliest fucks I'd ever seen. His ears stuck out of the sides of his head like saucers, his eyes were much too close together, his nose was a malignant growth in the middle of his face, and his mouth was nothing but two thin lines.

'Clear out your office, Goosen,' he continued. 'You're going to cut your hair, get back into uniform and report for charge office duty.'

I tried to say something but no sound came out of my mouth.

'You're a fucking cowboy,' Pretorius said. 'You've become a

danger to us as well as to yourself.'

I started begging as never before in my life. I told the major that a woman was messing with my mind, that my brother was a junkie, that my mother was alone at home, and that my father was the kind of police hero who would fuck me silly if he found out that I'd been shafted. As I blathered on tears began to roll down my cheeks. Between sniffs and sobs, I told him that this was the most devastating thing that had ever happened to me. Please let me stay, I pleaded. Please, please, please. Please, major, please.

Pretorius leaned back in his chair and put his hands behind his head. I wiped my tears with the back of my hand and looked at him. There was a wry grin on his face.

'That was quite a show, Goosen,' he said.

I felt embarrassed and stumbled to my feet. I'd blown it and wanted to get out of his office as quickly as possible. 'I'm sorry,' I mumbled, pushing the chair back.

'Sit down!' he ordered. I slumped back on to the chair. 'I'll tell you what we'll do, son. I'll give you one final chance.'

My face lit up. I could breathe again. I wanted to jump up and hug him. 'Thank you, Major, thank you.'

'Not so fast, son,' he said curtly. 'You'll do office duty, you won't go near the interrogation rooms and you won't go out on investigations.'

'Yes, Major.'

'And sort out your shit with the floozie.'

'Yes, Major.'

'And when the rats' nests are out of your head,' he continued, 'come and see me again.'

'Thank you, Major.'

'You're dismissed.'

'Yes, Major,' I said and I turned and walked out of his office.

Chappies was waiting for me. 'Look at you! You've been crying!'

'Oh bullshit!'

'What happened?'

'He fucked me up.'

'Are you still with us?'

'Only just.'

'What did he say?'

I told him what had happened. 'You have to do something with that piece of skirt,' he said. 'She's scrambling your brains.'

'I know, but I love her.'

'Then you have to get her out of there,' he said.

'Will you help me?'

'Sure I will.'

I'd tried in vain to talk to Sharné after that Friday night when she dismissed my declaration of love and I left her flat in a state of torment. She had refused to take my calls and every time I knocked on the door of the flat she shared with other call girls, a powder-nosed prossie opened and said that Sharné didn't want to see me.

I'd become obsessed with her. My whole fucking existence was dominated by her red hair and Arctic eyes and the perky cunt that had liberated me from sexual inadequacy and banished the Volkskas bank clerk to the rubbish heap.

It had been a horrible blow to my self-esteem when Maryna dumped me for the helicopter pilot, but much of my anger was directed at my own failure to get it up. With Sharné, however, it was different. I thought we were perfect. I thought I had conquered her love and that we were meant for each other. And then she told me that it didn't work for her. I was not allowed to love and cherish her. She was slight and delicate, yet I wasn't allowed to shield or nurture her.

Problem was that Sharné was a prostitute. And not just any working tart, but a sought-after, up-market bimbo who charged loaded horny men an arm and a leg to suck their dicks or sit on their faces or milk their loads. I don't know how many clients Sharné serviced each day but the mere thought of her fondling and petting other men's dicks drove me to thoughts of murder. She was making so much money that there wasn't space for me.

I sent her cards and red roses. I wrote her silly love letters:

'Your scent lingers in my sheets and your soft mouth caresses me in my sleep.' She didn't acknowledge any of them, although I'm sure she shared them with her whore friends. I began to resent her and decided that if I couldn't love her, I was going to hurt her.

I spent hours and nights following her; from her Joubert Park flat to the Playmates escort agency in Bree Street in downtown Johannesburg. It was a brightly lit establishment with a pair of flickering bunny ears above the door. I sat in my Alfa across the road and watched the Mercs and BMWs pulling up and the suit-clad customers striding through the security doors. I watched her walk out of Playmates with clients and climb into their cars with her skirt creeping up her thighs. She was whisked off to double-storey residences or luxury hotels in smart suburbs like Sandton and Rivonia.

And then I started following her to the same mansion in Houghton. She sometimes went by taxi while at other times she walked out of Playmates hand-in-hand with the same thickset, suit-clad dude who whisked her away in a black Merc. The guy spent a lot of time at Playmates and more often than not his car was parked in front of the brothel. Sharné began to spend most of her nights at the Houghton mansion, only going home early in the morning.

I once fell asleep in my car in front of the house. The sound of traffic and the early morning sun woke me. When I lifted my head and peeked out of the side window, I saw Sharné standing on the pavement on the other side of the road. She was staring at my car. She'd been there for another all-nighter and was waiting for a taxi to pick her up. She looked like shit and had obviously not closed a leg during the night. She gazed at me; I gazed back. As I opened the door to get out, she slowly shook her head and turned away. Then the taxi pulled up, she got in and drove away.

I did a check on the dude's car registration number. His name was Theo Papadakis. Chappies had been a vice cop before he was selected for Brixton Murder and Robbery. I asked him if he had ever heard of the man.

'Of course I know him,' said Chappies. 'He's a dirty fuck!'

'How come you know him?'

'He owns Playmates,' said Chappies. 'He's got several other joints and he's also into drugs.'

According to Chappies, the middle-aged Papadakis owned a number of seedy hotels and clubs in Hillbrow that were nothing more than fronts for drugs and prostitution. Teams of vice cops had been assigned to nab Papadakis, but what did the mobster do but make them associates! Every time the cops were on the verge of arresting him, his snitches warned him. Playmates was raided once or twice but Chappies said it was nothing more than the cops wanting a handout. A few lollies and the evidence disappeared.

It seemed as though virtually every vice cop in the city was in the pocket of some brothel boss or drug lord. Chappies was no exception. He lived way above his means. Somewhere along the line there was a polluted fountain watering his comfortable lifestyle. He drove a shiny BMW with ornate mags and a state-of-the-art music system and lived in a luxury flat in upmarket Killarney. But Papadakis wasn't his money-man. Chappies detested him. He wanted to fuck him long and hard and deep.

'You have to get Sharné out of there,' Chappies said. 'God knows what he's doing to her. I've heard horrible stories about him.'

'Like what?'

'He's a kinky fuck. He likes fucking jailbait and feeds them drugs and makes them do *groeps-woepse*.'

I became filled with rage and fury. Papadakis was Sharné's sugar daddy; she was his fuck doll. He kept her purse bulging and in return she tickled his *sif* dick and succumbed to his demented fantasies. He was probably hurting and humiliating her. I decided then and there that I was going to say a hard goodbye to him. It was the only way to get rid of the toxic brew in my head.

'How do we get Sharné out of there?'

Chappies suggested that we assemble a group of heavies and reduce the joint to rubble. 'Then you tell her to stop her shit and that she's yours.'

'Why're you doing this?' I asked him.

'I hate the fuck,' he said. After a few moments' silence he said: 'I've heard there's a fortune in a safe in his office. We can split it.'

'I don't want any.'

'Believe me, you're going to need it.'

'Why?'

'Because Sharné is an expensive chick.'

Chappies said we had to plan the operation so that it appeared to be a robbery. Brixton would do the crime investigation. He was a former vice cop and no doubt would be called on to assist. He'd bring Baksteen on to the case and from then on evidence would disappear, or else it would be planted to suggest that the raid was the work of a rival brothel boss.

We assembled a team. When we got together on the night of the raid, it was a congregation of the savage and the sadistic. Our leader was the angel-faced, diminutive Chappies. But don't be fooled – behind his puny facade was a rabid terrier. He was the kind of guy who pounced from behind and then got into the thick of things once his adversary was on the ground. Then he was a savage son of a bitch.

Baksteen was his henchman. His name said everything about him: he was as tough as a rock. Apparently the brick that gave birth to his name when it crashed down on his head had broken in two. According to Chappies – who was there – Baksteen plummeted to the ground, shook his head once or twice and then got up with blood gushing from an open wound. What happened to the brick-wielding suspect should probably not be repeated, but he went to meet his Maker in agony. Baksteen was born on a game farm. By the age of fifteen he'd shot his first lion and ten years later he'd dispatched more robbers and murderers to the heavenly kingdom than most security cops achieved in a lifetime.

Spyker formed the rearguard of our line-up. We'd kind of hit it off when he dealt with my assault case. And it was handy to have a dude like him on call when there might be offal that needed to be disposed of. Jakes heeded the call to arms, arriving on a brand new Kawasaki, with a baseball bat and a bottle of Red Heart rum. He had returned from South West Africa a few days earlier with a handful of uncut diamonds. He was in a buoyant mood, and talked incessantly about a future life of luxury. Sharon was about to go in for her first boob job.

Minutes before we left, there was a knock on my front door. When I opened it, I found it filled with human bulk. About half of it was fat. The rest was a combination of strength, brawn and power. It was the kind of muscle and mass capable of flattening a Portuguese castle or bashing a tunnel through Fort Knox.

You might guess who it was: Gielie Big Baby Geldenhuys! I could hardly get my arms around my old *gabba*'s waist as I stepped forward to hug him. When he hugged me back, throwing his trunk-like arms around me, he just about squashed every bit of oxygen out of me.

I had last seen Gielie about a year earlier when he had battered his way to the South African amateur heavyweight title. Shortly afterwards, he turned professional and his first seven fights all ended within two rounds. Two of his opponents had to be treated in hospital (one went temporarily blind) while the rest probably also suffered varying degrees of brain damage but were already too far gone to realise it. Gielie had taken a cut or two to his face and a few blows to his head but nothing that rattled him. He was a boxing sensation, his picture was in every newspaper, and he was shortly to fight in an elimination bout for the national heavyweight title.

He was even bigger than the last time I'd seen him. He was known to wolf down a whole chicken for lunch, together with six rolls, a pile of chips, two litres of Coke and a tub of ice cream. Dinner was a man-sized steak, a heap of potato salad, more Coke and several bowls of his favourite pudding, jelly and custard. Oom Japie Geldenhuys had been Gielie's trainer during his amateur days but since he'd turned pro, he had acquired a professional coach who had ordered him to shed kilos. So for the time being

Gielie was pushing weights in the gym and cutting down on the ice cream and chips. He had Diet Coke with his rum.

His downfall was a tender middle-aged auntie by the name of Sherry. She had had a fixation about Gielie since his first fight and when she read about his relentless dieting she decided that the boy needed motherly love. The road to a man's heart is through his stomach when your name is Gielie Geldenhuys. Sherry attended one of his public sparring bouts and when the young boxer left the gym (without his trainer) Sherry was waiting for him at his car with a Tupperware bowl of her celebrated mutton stew and half a chocolate cake wrapped in tin foil. The next day she was waiting for him with chicken pie and baked apricot pudding. Two weeks later they tied the knot in the Randfontein magistrate's court and Gielie moved into her Mayfair home.

I didn't even know that Gielie had got married until I read about it in *Rapport*. There was a picture of the boxer on page three. He was holding a woman four times smaller than him in the air. The headline read: 'Gielie pulled the carpet from under his Sherry's feet.'

Sherry was a little bit past her best so I don't think Gielie had ever banged her. She was more or less twice Gielie's age, a mother of many and grandmother of two. Anyway I don't think that sex was on Gielie's mind. Moreover, his physique created problems for successful copulation. I had seen Gielie naked when we forged our school gang with a group wank, and it was tiny. Maybe Sherry made love to him over the stove and he devoured her steak and pudding instead of her. Sherry was the mother figure that Gielie had never had and she nurtured and spoiled her Big Baby.

As a result of this liaison, Gielie ballooned even more and it wasn't long before his trainer threatened to put him on the street. Gielie called his bluff and told him to fuck off. The trainer realised that he was sitting on a pot of gold and relented. From then on it was generally accepted that Big Baby Geldenhuys was probably going to remain the world's heaviest heavyweight and that there was no way that he was going to float like a butterfly or sting like a bee. His recipe to get to the top was simple: to trot around the ring like a wounded buffalo, trap his opponent in a corner and pummel him senseless. Everyone knew that any fight that went beyond three or four rounds would spell disaster because Gielie would never be able to keep up with the pace and would hit the canvas without a glove being laid on him.

'I'll help you to break in,' said Gielie, 'but I'm not going to hit anybody.'

'Why not?' I wanted to know.

'Because I might just kill him.'

'Then just break the place down,' I said.

When you were about to blitz a brothel and intended to fuck up everyone and everything inside it, a human caterpillar like Gielie Geldenhuys was invaluable.

'That, my friend,' said Gielie, 'I'll do with pleasure.'

Papadakis thought he was untouchable and security at Playmates was rather lax; nothing more than a bouncer at the door and another one inside. The security doors were rather flimsy and wouldn't withstand Gielie's debt-collecting pole. Chappies said the most important thing was to get to Papadakis' bodyguard before he could pull his gun. He didn't want the operation to degenerate into a shootout. We also had to get to the telephones before anyone could call the police. There were no cellphones in those days and there was no closed-circuit television.

Chappies knew the layout of the place like the back of his hand. He provided balaclavas for us. Gielie was a celebrity so his face definitely had to be concealed, although his physique might give him away. I assured him that if there was a problem I'd provide him with an alibi. But the balaclavas didn't fit his head and in the end he settled for a XXL black stocking pulled over his face. He cut a frightening figure.

Playmates was a far cry from The Leopard in Krugersdorp. It was decked out with fluffy carpets, the chairs and couches were purple velvet and the walls were hung with framed posters of *Playboy* pin-ups with brooding eyes, puffed-up tits and a hint of pubic hair. Sharné entertained her customers in massage rooms, lavishly furnished with circular beds, under-floor heating, private showers and a television set showing non-stop porn videos. At the front of the club was a bar, a pole-dancing stage, a snooker den, two Jacuzzi parlours and the Spank Bank, a cell-like room where a whip-wielding dominatrix cuffed and tied up her masochistic clientele. Two wrought iron doors decorated with curling vines and bunches of grapes led to the Roman Room, an orgy lounge with its own bar and spa bath.

We chose a Monday night because most of the popular escorts had that day off to recuperate from their weekend antics. Our team had assembled by ten o'clock, and by eleven we were pissed and charged up. Baksteen, Chappies and Spyker carried pistols (just for the hold-up) and Gielie had the pole on the back of his pickup. Jakes had a knuckleduster and the baseball bat. The guys insisted that I didn't carry any weapons.

'You'll shoot someone,' Chappies said, 'or bash some poor fuck's head in.'

'That's exactly what I intend to do,' I said, flexing my fists. 'Let's fucking roll.'

It was a frosty winter's night and only four cars, including Papadakis' black Merc, were parked in front of the brothel. We parked Gielie's pickup, Chappies' Big Six and a taxi that Spyker had hired in Soweto across the road from the club. We had a blue police light that we planned to put on the roof of the taxi. If any customers arrived during the raid, they would see the light and most certainly not hang around.

Jakes, pretending to be just another customer, strolled past the guard and through the security doors. He didn't care about showing his face because nobody would recognise him, apart perhaps from the girls we'd bonked at the Landdrost Hotel. And that wasn't a problem because we'd booked in there under false names.

Jakes walked out half an hour later. 'It's going to be as easy as taking candy from a kid,' he said when he got to the cars. 'The bouncer is standing at the entrance and the bodyguard is hanging around the bar.'

'Where's Papadakis?'

'I didn't see him but he must be somewhere in there.'

Spyker took care of the security guard at the door. He simply walked up to him, pulled his pistol, stuck it in the guy's ribs and warned him to shut up. At the same time, we pulled our balaclavas over our faces. Baksteen and Gielie, the pole in their hands, rammed the door. It crashed and splintered into several pieces. A wave of hot air rolled over us as we stormed in.

The first obstacle we had to face was a blond bouncer whose upper arms bulged out of a black T-shirt stretched over his steroid-bloated chest like a surgical glove. He froze when he saw what was bearing down on him – Gielie in full flight! Big Baby, the pole in his hands, bellowed as he crashed into the hapless man. The dude flopped on to the floor like a dirty rag. Gielie continued his journey of destruction through the reception area, shattering another door before charging into a Jacuzzi parlour.

Baksteen had been assigned to disable the bodyguard, who was sitting at the bar sipping a drink. His undoing was the second or two it took him to move his Ray-Bans on to his Brylcreemed head. By the time he'd reached under his cream-coloured jacket to pull his gun, Baksteen's pistol was pointing at his heart.

I made a beeline for the front desk where the receptionist, a skanky worn-out slut, had the phone in her hand. I snatched the instrument from her, pulled the whole device from its socket and threw it against the wall behind her.

Mayhem erupted. Prossies screamed and the few startled customers groped around for their clothes. A naked, dripping dude scrambled out of the jacuzzi. Jakes was swinging the baseball bat in the air and warning everyone to shut up and stand still. Chappies, his pistol in his hand, was looking for Papadakis.

'Where the fuck is Papadakis?' I asked the receptionist, pushing my face into hers.

Her terror-filled eyes widened like saucers and although her mouth was wide open, she couldn't get a word out. She reeked of smoke and sweet perfume. 'Where the fuck is he?' I demanded.

She pointed to the Roman Room. I turned around and

charged at the doors. A half-naked floozie was sitting upright on the purple satin sheets covering the outsized, heart-shaped bed. A flimsy negligee was pushed up over her pointy breasts and she was frantically trying to wriggle into her miniskirt. A second slut was scrambling around trying to gather her clothes. A pink dildo and a tube of lubricant lay on the bed. A fat fuck stood a few metres away from the bed. It was Theo Papadakis. His yellow shirt was unbuttoned and a Mickey Mouse tie hung loosely around his neck. He was pulling up his pants and trying to hide his semi-erect cock.

The sight of him flipped my switch. I vaguely remember the girls screaming as I leaped across the bed. Papadakis had an amazed expression on his face – a face that I intended to reduce to pulp. I pounced on the poor fuck like a wounded predator and unleashed months of bottled-up fury. He slumped on to the floor. The two girls fled the room.

'You fucking whore-fucker!' I yelled, kicking and punching him with all my strength. My arms were working like the blades of a windmill. His head was big and his body was soft but he wasn't going down fast enough. I spotted a coat rack made of wrought iron. I grabbed it and smashed it into his face and his groin. Again and again. His face was a bloody mess when Chappies grabbed me.

'What the fuck do you think you're doing?' shouted Chappies as we wrestled together on the bed.

'Killing the fuck!' I yelled. In his effort to pin me down, Chappies had ripped the balaclava from my head.

'Fucking stop it!'

I broke loose from Chappies' grip, got up and picked up the coat rack again. I stepped forward, lifting it high in the air. Papadakis lifted his bloodied face from the floor and stared at me, his mouth gaping. He was trying to say something, probably to plead for mercy. I crashed the hanger into his face. I swear I could feel bones crunching. The next moment both Chappies and Jakes pounced on me and all three of us fell on top of Papadakis.

'You're fucking mad!' Jakes screamed as he got to his feet. 'Don't fucking kill him!'

Chappies knelt over Papadakis and looked as though he was trying to revive him. In the reception room behind us, I could hear glass, chairs, tables, and whatever else you find in a brothel being smashed to pieces. Gielie and his pole, no doubt.

'Is he dead?' I asked.

'Only half,' said Chappies, 'but he's in fucking bad shape.'

'Let's kill the bastard,' I said.

'Are you fucking joking?' said Chappies. 'Who's going to open the safe for us?'

'Not him,' I said. 'He's not going to wake up soon, and we have to get out of here.'

'So let's cut our losses and fucking go.'

'We can't,' I said. 'The fuck-head saw my face.'

Chappies stared at me. 'So what do we do?'

'Take him with us,' I said. 'Spyker and I will take care of him.'

'This wasn't supposed to happen!'

'So what's a little accident between friends?' I sneered and turned away.

'Put on your balaclava!' he shouted as I left the room.

I pulled it back over my face and walked into the reception area. The prossies and customers were huddled in petrified heaps on the couches next to the demolished bar. The bodyguard was tied up on the floor. A menacing-looking Baksteen was standing a few metres away with the baseball bat in one hand and his pistol in the other. Gielie was somewhere in the back of the brothel reducing everything around him to trash.

I called Spyker who was standing guard outside. The hired taxi, a white Cressida, had the blue light on its roof and was by then parked right outside Playmates. The security guard, cuffed and blindfolded, was sitting on the floor at the entrance.

Spyker and I threw Papadakis on the bed and wrapped him in one of the purple sheets. Blood trickled from a cut on his forehead and a gash under his eye. His mouth looked like a crushed ripe tomato. His pants were unbuttoned and his flaccid cock dangled in the air as we lifted him up. I didn't want to look at it but I couldn't seem to stop myself.

'He looks a bit dead, Nkosi,' said Spyker.

'He's not,' I said, 'but he will be soon.'

We carried Papadakis past our wide-eyed captives to the car. We dumped him in the boot and as we drove off, the rest of the team emerged from Playmates to make their getaway.

'Where're we taking him?' I asked Spyker.

'To the mine dump.'

We drove for a kilometre up an eerie and deserted Bree Street, past several more neon-lit escort agencies and the Rand International Hotel. We turned right into Twist Street.

'If I dare ask, Nkosi, what was his sin?' asked Spyker.

The streetlights were playing hide and seek on his shiny round face.

'He fucked my girlfriend,' I said.

Spyker shook his head and we drove on in silence. My stomach was tightening into a knot, my hands were damp and my breathing was laboured. I was about to bump off Theo Papadakis. In icy cold fucking blood. I'd already decided that I was going to thrust Spyker's pistol against his head, pull the trigger and propel grey matter out of his skull. I was in two minds, though. On the one hand I wanted him to be dead by the time we reached the mine shaft, but on the other I wanted him to be in the land of the living so that I could have the satisfaction of finishing him off and putting an end to my rage.

Papadakis was very much alive when Spyker opened the boot. He was whimpering and babbled something when I shone the flashlight in his face. One eye was wide open; the other was closed and clotted with blood. I couldn't make out what he was saying. Spyker and I lifted him out of the boot and carried him the thirty metres to the disused shaft. It was pitch dark and the only sounds were occasional murmurs from Papadakis, the scraping of our feet on the concrete surface and the faraway drone of traffic on the M1 highway.

We stopped and dropped Papadakis on the ground for Spyker to open a gate. A few metres further and we were next to the hole. The gaping pit was coal-black in the inky night.

'Let's throw him in,' said Spyker.

'Give me your gun.'

'It will make a noise, Nkosi.'

'Give me your fucking gun!'

There was a movement at my feet. I shone the flashlight in Papadakis' face. One hand was waving in the air and he was gurgling something through his punctured mouth. I took Spyker's pistol, cocked it and went down on one knee. He smelled of a mixture of sweat and expensive aftershave. The cunt was pumping adrenalin and releasing odours, like a buck about to be flattened by a charging lion.

'Please ... don't ... please,' he mumbled.

'Please what?' I said and cocked the pistol.

'Why?' he said. 'Why're you doing this?'

My finger was on the trigger and I lifted the barrel and pointed it at his head. I thought maybe the miserable cunt deserved to know why he was going to die.

'Sharné,' I said shining the light in his face.

He tried to sit upright but Spyker pushed him back with his boot.

He slumped to the ground. 'What about her?' he asked.

'You're fucking her up.'

He was quiet for a second or two. 'I love her,' he said. Then he added: 'We're getting married.'

I stumbled to my feet, dropped the flashlight and stood back. I didn't want his blood on my skin or clothes. For a moment the pistol felt as heavy as lead. I was aware of my own heavy breathing and cold air gushing into my mouth and lungs. I wanted to say something but I stumbled over my tongue.

'Sharné's pregnant,' he muttered, 'with our child.'

I pulled the trigger. The nine-millimetre jolted in my hand. Its bang reverberated between the empty corrugated iron buildings. It was a beautiful, almost comforting sound; a bang that had solved a problem by obliterating the vermin lying at my feet. I squeezed the trigger again, and again, and again.

By the time Spyker grabbed my arm, I had almost emptied the magazine into Theo Papadakis.

'Stop it, Nkosi!' he said, snatching the pistol from me. 'People will hear us!'

I froze as Spyker rolled the brothel boss into the black bottomless pit.

Then my knees felt weak and my hands began to shake.

Fourteen

Okay, now you know about my first actual murder, committed with malice aforethought. I'd participated in the demise of individuals before; some legal and others illegal. There was Johnnie's *kleinboet* and the shattered eardrum robber found with a knife in his back. I've fucked many detainees good and hard. I have also fucked others who were not detainees good and hard. But this was different. I whacked Theo Papadakis in the coldest of cold blood and with bloodthirsty intent.

The judge, the public and the media have branded me a savage; a thug who revelled in the agony of his hapless victims; the kind of villain who ripped out children's hearts and took pleasure in wringing a little bird's neck. But, you know what? I didn't ever set out to hurt anyone. I couldn't kill a hamster when I was a laaitie and I recoiled from violence and fainted when I saw a needle. I was mommy's fucking little ice cream boy! That's why I don't know how it happened, all this rage and all this bloodshed and fury. Many people have asked me this question and I've never been able to explain it. It's a riddle I'll take to my grave.

So please don't ask me ever again why I did it. And don't expect me to go into every last detail of every little killing. It's not just tedious, but it's dangerous to sit in prison and write about things that weren't on the prosecutor's charge sheet when he whipped my ass. Better to let sleeping dogs lie.

The prison psychologist (the one with the pert tits and shapely calves) had a lot to say about how I was brutalised by my father and the subsequent rage that permeated my mind. It's too late to mull over it now, and it's not going to get me out of this dungeon. Maybe, as my mother believes, my deviant behaviour was the result of having the wrong friends. Or maybe my genes are freaky. Or maybe it's all of the above. Maybe I'm a psychopath and should be strapped in a straitjacket and locked up in isolation in Weskoppies.

Truth is: I'm probably just a bad person. Some doctors seem to have been born with scalpels in their hands, songwriters with tunes in their heads, soccer players with balls at their feet, and Indian shopkeepers with their fingers in tills. So maybe I was born with murder in my heart. Maybe there's a chemical imbalance roaring in my skull. Maybe, maybe, maybe ...

Let's get one thing straight: it's not as though I whacked someone every day or every week or every month or even every fucking year. I've been asked how many bit the dust as a result of my handiwork. You know what? I'm not sure. I was convicted for three murders and I have to admit that there were several more. Others might have perished later of their injuries or wounds sustained as a result of my actions. All I know is that killing is a lot simpler than most people would imagine. And once you've bagged your first corpse, they just seem to fall from the tree.

I think it's unfair that I was sentenced to life over and over again. It wasn't as though I zapped Mother Teresa. I was a cunt who fucked up other cunts. I know that every life is supposed to have equal value and whether you whack Nelson Mandela or a hobo stretched out in his own filth on a street corner, the punishment should be the same. Of course that's utter drivel. The cunt in the red robe should have given me credit for having permanently removed some seriously demented individuals from society – hoods and hooligans who made many a life a misery. Do you think their departure left society worse off? I don't feel sorry for *klapping* most of them.

I know that South African law, or any other law for that matter, doesn't recognise blind rage as an extenuating circumstance for murder, but believe me it's the only way I can even begin to explain my irrational behaviour. When I rammed that coat rack into the Greek's face in Playmates, and later emptied a magazine into his body, I had no control over what I was doing. My arms and hands and fingers were on automatic and went through their paces without the participation of my brain. It was as though I needed his blood to release the fury raging in my skull. But it didn't work because it was as though the cunt had cloned by making my girlfriend pregnant. Not much changed for me.

Can you imagine, I complained to Chappies and Jakes, that Sharné is carrying the cunt's fucking bambino? For as long as she was schlepping that tumour inside her, I didn't want to see her.

'*Ja, siestog*,' said Chappies, 'and now the little bundle of joy will have to grow up without a daddy.'

'It's because of you,' said Jakes, 'that daddy is somewhere in a hole with a body that looks like Swiss cheese.'

After killing Papadakis, I was tormented by the most appalling nightmares for the first time since the passing away of my little brother. And it wasn't the Greek rotting in a pit somewhere that woke me in a pool of sweat. Or the nine-mill jerking in my hand as bullet after bullet perforated his marshmallow body. I had no scruples about his demise, apart from the fact that I had committed a murder that could have landed me behind bars for a very long time – which, of course, is what happened in the end.

It was the cockroach in Sharné's belly that woke me with

my fists clenched and my eyes searching the darkness for slimy red-eyed aliens with razor teeth and hawk-like claws. Pamela Anderson or Cameron Diaz or some other luscious Hollywood tart once played in a sci-fi movie about hordes of creepy-crawly bugs that descended on mother earth in space ships. On arrival, each laid thousands of soft-shelled eggs that hatched within minutes. Out wriggled gooey toddlers, famished and dependent on human flesh to flower into full-blooded freaks. Then they gobbled up just about the whole of New York. It was their pointy teeth and luminous eyes that haunted my dreams. This movie seemed to be playing over and over in my head.

I don't know how long Sharné had been preggers before I whacked the Greek. All I knew was that I couldn't see her while she was preggers. Of course I wanted to see her, but I didn't dare go near her. Somehow, I knew that she knew that I'd taken pappa out.

A day or two after the killing, Sharné went back to her parents in Nigel. I didn't speak to her for almost a year, although I never stopped thinking about her. When I was awake, she was lying in front of me, her pointy titties enticing me like the first ripe peaches in November. Her flawless slit, framed with a layer of curly red hair, smiled at me and invited me in. But when I was asleep her legs closed, her tits shrank and her smooth stomach parted like the Red Sea. And out crept the ghouls with their beaks stretched, their eyes aglow and their claws menacing me.

I drove to Nigel a couple of times to snoop on Sharné. I sat in a park across the road from the matchbox house with the battered Toyota parked in the driveway. The garden was bleak and unkempt. I once saw her walking past an open window and another time she opened the door and walked out on to the porch. She picked up a tray of empty cups and went inside again. I didn't get a good look at her until she walked out with a man, probably her father, got into the car and drove away. I wanted to follow them but my car was parked some distance away.

It was the only time I managed to get a good look at her. She was wearing a long brown dress and her hair was shorter and bound in a ponytail. I don't think she was wearing any make-up. She was just another Nigel chick, apart from the ulcer protruding from her lithe frame. I knew she'd decided to have the baby, give it up for adoption, and leave Nigel as soon as possible. She detested living there and she and her stepmother didn't see eye to eye. (Her own mother died when she was a toddler.) I was in touch with some of Sharné's former flatmates and they frequently updated me on her condition.

You might want to know how I managed to deal with the rage in my head. Well, I didn't, actually. Pietman Pretorius had banned me from both the interrogation room and investigations, although ironically I was called in to help with the Playmates case. Slang van Wyk headed the investigation and was assisted (as we had planned) by Chappies Horn and Baksteen Botha. I was scared that someone would recognise us, but Chappies assured me that this wouldn't happen. We had been masked, the brothel was dimly lit, and mayhem tends to disorientate witnesses.

It wasn't long before Chappies claimed that he had an informant (who of course didn't exist) who, he said, was feeding him the low-down on the raid. Chappies was a master of deceit and before long he had fed a beautifully concocted story to a slutty journo on a Sunday rag – and scored a shag in the process. According to the paper, the killing was part of a campaign by a Lebanese brothel boss to take over the Greek's girls and whore-houses.

A task team was assembled to investigate the Lebanese who also had his tentacles into drugs, guns and money laundering. Needless to say, Chappies was right in the heart of the team. By then he had formally registered his 'informant' and was drawing substantial amounts in cash as payment for the dude. At some point the commander of the task team wanted to meet Chappies' informant to try to persuade him to turn state witness against the Lebanese. He then 'disappeared'. According to Chappies, he had probably been kidnapped and murdered by the Middle-Eastern brothel boss. The story again found its way into the newspapers, Chappies bagged another night of carnal delight, and the Playmates investigation hit a brick wall.

Some of the money we had accumulated as a result of our underground operation we kept for ourselves. We decided that the rest should be blown on a motherfucker of an all-night party on the night Gielie Geldenhuys was fighting for the South African heavyweight boxing crown. The champion was the favourite to retain the title and promised in pre-fight interviews to knock Big Baby into oblivion.

We knew it was easier said than done and we organised a massive bash at the Van Riebeeck Hotel, complete with strippers, whores and *Leeutande*. Vegkop was packed with pissed Gielie supporters and when the bell rang for the first round, many pairs of befuddled eyes were fixed on the television set in the corner. A peroxide bimbo with buck teeth and pimples, but with a body that was assembled in the Ferrari factory, sat on my lap. She was one of the strippers we had hired for the night. Ten minutes earlier, she had been caressing the silver pole in the opposite corner of the bar. Every now and then my hand slipped under her skirt.

The champ made the bad mistake of targeting Gielie's head instead of softening up his body. Our man's head took a mega thumping. It would have flattened any other boxer but seemed to bounce off his skull like .22 bullets off the armour of a tank. For three rounds Gielie heaved and puffed his way around the ring without throwing any counter punches. His lip was split and his nose was a bloody mess. Vegkop went quiet and the commentators expected his trainer would have no choice but to throw in the towel in the next round.

When the bell went for the fourth round, it was as though someone had ignited a rocket in Gielie's arse. He descended like a whirlwind on the startled champ – who hardly had time to lift his gloves – and unleashed a barrage of blows to his head, face and body. One or two might have landed too low but it didn't matter because the champ went down. He got up but Gielie just steamrollered over him, his fists flying like windmills in every direction. One of those fists thwacked down on the champ's head and he was down on the canvas once more, and remained there for the next ten seconds.

While a joyous rumpus erupted in Vegkop, sixty kilometres away in the ring at Loftus Versfeld, Gielie burst into tears when the ref hoisted his fist in the air. Big Baby became Cry Baby. He thanked the Lord for giving him his strength and took the opportunity to challenge world champion Mike Tyson to a title fight at Loftus. Jakes, Chappies and I just stared at one another in amazement.

We had to wait while the new champion had his lip stitched and attended a special prayer service that Sherry had arranged. By the time Gielie strutted into Vegkop, it was way past midnight and everybody was plastered. I was worried that Gielie was getting drawn into a Jesus thing but Jakes assured me that there was nothing that booze and whores couldn't fix.

Gielie's ascendancy to the title had rendered him even uglier. His eye was blue, his lip was stitched and a glob of dry blood was still stuck on his nose. He swallowed his *Leeutande* amidst a great commotion, but moments later, his eyes stretched like saucers and I swear I heard his tummy rumble above the noise in the bar. He made a beeline for the toilets but erupted before he could get his bulky frame around the door. Didn't matter: Gielie was the champ.

It was another matter to find a whore who was willing to do him. We tried a young-looking but rather unsightly tart with big tits and offered her double her fee to blow the champ. No fucking way, she said, I'm not going near him. In the end we were stuck with an obviously desperate hooker who said she'd do it for a bonus but wasn't prepared to kiss him.

'No way am I touching a whore,' slurred Gielie. 'It's a sin and, what's more, I'm a married man.'

'You don't have to do anything because she'll do everything,' I said. 'Remember, you're the one who said we must lay on the chicks when you become champion.'

Gielie shrugged his shoulders and stumbled up the stairs to a room we had rented. The whore was back ten or fifteen minutes later shrugging her shoulders. Gielie came down a few minutes later mumbling something about being too drunk. Didn't matter: he was still the champ.

'Don't we have a credit?' Chappies asked the desperate hooker. She winked and nodded. I got hold of my Ferrari number and whisked her up the stairs to the room where Jakes was already nailing another Vegkop bitch. At that time I enjoyed banging whores deep and rough. I wanted to hurt them; hear them whimper and moan and beg me to go slower and be more gentle. I'm not even going to try to hide this because all the shit was blurted out at my trial. But I want you to know that it was the old Gideon Goosen doing that. I've cleaned up my act since then.

It's the new Gideon Goosen sitting in the black heart of Pretoria Central spewing out his guts. When I get out of here, I will never again pursue that sort of life. It had no meaning and led to nothing but misery and waste. I now have my beloved Debbie with whom I want to create a wholesome and meaningful future.

It was Christmas time. I've always hated the festive season because it has no meaning for me and it's synonymous with falsehood and lies. But the Christmas of 1988 is etched in my mind because so much was happening around that time. My life was filled with raucous friends and boisterous parties, but I was incredibly lonely and constantly brooding over Sharné, who by that time wasn't far from popping her monstrosity. I didn't want any other woman. I had a short fling with a typist at Brixton Murder and Robbery. I popped her cherry and unfortunately she then expected me to pay for the damage by pleading true love and asking me the eternal question. I quickly sent the heartbroken missy back to where she came from.

There was also a family fuck-up when *ouboet* Karel paid an unexpected visit to my mother and asked her for money. She phoned me in a state of hysteria. I rushed home and found him sitting in the living room with a blanket around his shoulders. Mom was fretting like a chicken without a head, her hands in the air. Between her outbreaks of tears, she was praying and pleading for strength.

The last time I had seen Karel was three or four years earlier when he was in rehab at Phoenix House in Melville. He was already a sorry bag of bones then but the skeleton sitting shaking in the living room sent shivers down my spine. It was the middle of the day in the middle of summer but he was icy cold. He looked gaunt and withered, his eyes sunk in deep dark sockets. When he spoke, I saw that his front teeth were decaying. I would learn only later that it was probably caused by crack pipes.

We greeted each other and that was about it. It would have been silly to have asked him how he was. Karel was a junkie and it was clear that every time he was shooting shit up his veins, he was also shooting life out of himself. But that was his choice.

As we sat staring at each other, I heard Mom on the phone to Dad in Oshakati. A minute or so later, she said he wanted to speak to me. I told her I didn't want to speak to him. She kept on insisting and when I refused again, she began crying. I took the phone from her.

'Arrest him!' Dad bellowed on the other side.

'For what?'

'Anything! Say that he threatened your mother!'

'He didn't threaten her.'

'Doesn't matter!' he continued. 'Keep him there. I can be back tomorrow.'

'And then?'

'Then I'll fucking sort him out!'

'By doing what?'

'I'll decide when I get there. Just keep him for me!'

By then Karel had stumbled to his feet. He was looking at me and shaking his head. Mom was sobbing uncontrollably and holding on to his arm.

I took the instrument away from my ear, thought for a moment what to do and then slammed it down. Moments later, it rang. It was obviously Dad so I pulled the phone from the wall plug.

I almost wrestled Karel from Mom's grip and loaded him in

my car. I kissed her on her forehead, hugged her and assured her that I would look after him.

'Where do you want to go?' I asked him as I pulled away.

'I need a fix,' he said. 'Very fucking urgently.'

'Where to?'

'Hillbrow,' he said, 'and then I want to go to Durban. I have friends there.'

Karel was on edge as we made the forty-minute journey to the concrete ghettos of Hillbrow and Berea. I stopped at a bank, drew a wad of cash and stuffed it in his hand. He directed me to the Chelsea Hotel in Hillbrow and told me to wait for him while he scored a fix. I sat in my car for an hour, maybe longer, and then ventured into the dive. It reeked of sweet perfume, beer and piss. Black whores with hanging tits and trunk-like thighs pouted their red lips at me. I turned around, walked out, got into my Alfa, and drove away.

I phoned Mom and told her that Karel had promised to find help and that he was okay. I have no idea what happened to him after that. It was the last time I saw my brother. I know he's alive and that he phones Mom from time to time, but for me that was the end of *ouboet*.

Mom called the next day and said that Dad had arrived home and would be staying until after Christmas, which was only a few days away. He wanted to see me urgently. I told her I was too busy. She said he was very upset and I had better make a plan to speak to him. I was not going to, I said. She started crying and I said goodbye.

She phoned again the day before Christmas to make sure that I would be coming home for lunch. She said she was roasting a turkey. I lied and said I was on duty. What about Boxing Day then, she wanted to know? I said I was still on duty. It was the first Christmas I had spent without my family.

Early on Christmas morning, Jakes and I went to Krugersdorp Prison with a picnic basket for Johnnie. I'd met a friendly warder the day before and paid him to smuggle a bottle of Klippies and a box of Kentucky into the prison for Johnnie. I had to keep his spirits high because, believe me, there's no bleaker day behind bars than the twenty-fifth of December. More birds slash their wrists or hang themselves on that day than on any other day of the year.

Johnnie, however, was in a buoyant mood, despite nursing a slight hangover. He had served a third of his sentence and would be considered for parole in the new year. He was convinced that he was going to get out.

'Is there anyone we can bribe?' asked Jakes.

'I'll find out,' said Johnnie, 'because I'm not parking in here for a single fucking day longer than I have to.'

Jakes wanted me to quit the cops as soon as Johnnie got out. He wanted us to go into business with him. He'd done two or three illicit diamond deals and was bagging some bucks, but now had a scheme that he called 'knocking'. It wasn't an altogether new concept, but in the years to come the three of us would give new meaning to this criminal enterprise.

Jakes' plan was to use illicit diamonds to lure potential buyers. As soon as a price had been fixed, a date and place would be arranged for the deal to be finalised. It would more often than not be a hotel room. Jakes would arrive with the diamonds and the buyers with the cash.

'Then we just take it,' said Jakes. 'As easy as that.'

'What do you mean?' I asked him.

'We take the bucks but we don't give them the stones.'

'And if they pump us full of lead?'

'We'll be faster,' said Jakes. 'We'll hold them up first.'

'That's fucking robbery!' I protested.

'They'd do it to us if only they'd thought of it first,' he said.

'And if they call the cops?'

'Who's going to complain?' he countered. 'You think they'll own up to a crooked diamond deal?'

I had to admit that it made sense. Johnnie was already rubbing his hands and stamping his feet. I liked the idea of thieves stealing from thieves but I first wanted to discuss it with Chappies, who always seemed to have the low-down on this sort of enterprise.

To be truthful, I wasn't sure that I wanted to be a policeman any longer. A month or so before Christmas, Brixton Murder and Robbery commander Pietman Pretorius had unexpectedly announced his resignation. He called us into his office and said that he was leaving the force in order to pursue business interests. Fucking hell, was everyone's first reaction, what does this *platpoot* know about making bucks?

'I've heard other rumours,' announced Chappies.

'Like what?'

'That they're setting up a special unit.'

'To do what?'

'Fight terrorism,' he said, and added: 'To fuck up the ANC.'

I had little interest in what was going on around me. I knew there was a state of emergency and that the army was in the townships but as far as I was concerned we were relentlessly fucking the commies and the ANC and the other troublemakers.

I was far more interested in the private enterprise Chappies and I were pursuing at the time – selling intelligence to the Lebanese brothel boss. He was a slimy son of a bitch but his pockets were deep and he wasn't shy about emptying them for the almost worthless pieces of paper that Chappies lifted and copied from the task team's files. It enabled me to booze, fuck whores and fill up the Alfa GTV.

Somewhere between Christmas and New Year, I received a phone call that would dramatically change the rest of my life. It was from Pietman Pretorius and he wanted to meet Chappies and me at Fontana in Hillbrow. The city's most cosmopolitan suburb was already showing signs of decay. *Anderskleuriges* were moving into the suburb and previously decent blocks of flats were reduced to slums overnight.

I almost didn't recognise the wiry Pietman. His hair was always Brylcreemed with a lick from one ear across to the other but he had let it grow much longer, which meant that it curled over his conspicuous ears. He was also sporting a beard and was wearing a pair of gold-rimmed Ray-Bans. I couldn't help but think that he resembled a middle-aged ducktail who had gone on a hunger strike.

'You look as though you're under cover, Major,' I said as we sat down and ordered coffee.

He said: 'Goosen, if you ever call me major again, I'll fuck you so hard you'll never be able to sit again.'

Pietman's hoarse, rusty voice could not be disguised, so who the fuck did he think he was bluffing?

'Goosen,' he asked me, 'have you learned to control your temper?'

'Yes, sir,' I said. 'I'm back on the beat.'

'Good,' he said. 'I want you guys to work for me.'

Chappies and I glanced at each other. He was the first to speak. 'Doing what, sir?'

'Starting a new enterprise for me.'

'And that is?'

Pietman looked at us and I could feel his steely grey eyes piercing me. He eventually announced: 'I want you guys to open a brothel for me.'

My mouth fell open while Chappies stared goggle-eyed at him. It took a few seconds for me to get my voice back. 'A what?' I asked him.

'A brothel,' he repeated. 'An escort agency, call it what you like. Here, in Hillbrow.'

I couldn't think of anything better to do than running a brothel. Imagine having a platoon of luscious broads at your mercy! It was like hiring an alcoholic to run a brewery. But something didn't add up. We all knew Pretorius was a prim and proper family man and an elder in the church. Why on earth would he want to venture into the whore business?

He told us that he had recently bought a hotel in Hillbrow and that he wanted to convert part of it into a brothel. '*Kêrels*,' he said, 'we'll make a fortune! And I can't think of anyone better than you two to make it work.'

I had already made up my mind, but we agreed to meet again early in the new year. As we drove off, Chappies turned to me and said: 'You see, I told you there was something cooking.'

'Like what?'

'Do you think a fuddy-duddy like Pietman would open a whorehouse? No fucking way in hell!'

'So what do you think it is?'

'It's all about this new undercover unit.'

Chappies, as usual, was right. At our next meeting, we told Pretorius that we had discussed his proposal and found the idea tempting. 'You guys must know,' he said, 'that this will also give you an opportunity to do something for *Volk en Vaderland*.'

Chappies kicked me under the table but neither of us said a word. 'What I'm telling you now is top secret and if either of you ever say a fucking word I will personally cut off your balls.'

We nodded. 'The hotel doesn't really belong to me,' he said, 'and nor will the brothel.'

We continued to nod our heads like dogs wagging their tails. 'It's all part of a top secret undercover operation,' he said. 'You'll be working for the state as covert operatives and I'll be your commander.'

My head was spinning and I wasn't sure that I was grasping all this James Bond shit. Could it be that I, Gideon Goosen, was on the verge of becoming a secret fucking agent? I could already see Jakes pissing himself and Johnnie kicking his black boots in the air. I had to say something. 'It sounds like heavy stuff.'

'What are we supposed to do?' asked Chappies.

'You'll be operating against elements of the ANC and the SACP,' he announced.

'Doing what?' Chappies persisted.

Pretorius leaned forward, forced his thin lips into a wry smile and said in a slow monotone: 'Fucking them until they cry!'

Chappies glanced at me and said: 'Sounds like fun to me.'

'Oh yes,' I echoed, 'to me too.'

'Are you boys in?' asked Pretorius.

'Yes, we are,' confirmed Chappies. I wasn't overenthusiastic about the Big Brother shit but was attracted by the freaky and kinky nature of whoredom. We agreed to submit our resignations and join his network. I hoped secretly that I would never have to do any undercover stuff.

'When do you want us to start?' asked Chappies.

'As soon as possible,' he said. 'The brothel must be up and running in a month's time.'

'Where do we find girls to staff it?' I wanted to know.

'That's your problem, Goosen,' he said and smiled. 'I've heard you're well acquainted with the Jo'burg vice world.'

Pretorius shook our hands, beamed from ear to ear and announced: 'Welcome to the CCB, kêrels.'

'And what's the CCB?' asked Chappies.

'The Civil Co-operation Bureau,' he said. 'From now on it's your mamma, your pappa, your girlfriend and your best friend.'

The next day we reported for a confidential briefing at Pietman's Trennery Hotel in Hillbrow. We were ushered to a suite on the seventh floor where Pretorius and two plain clothes dudes were waiting for us. To our surprise, Baksteen, Slang, Duiwel and Spyker were also there.

Proceedings kicked off with each of us taking an oath of secrecy. A steely-faced dude in a light-brown suit, who obviously usually sat in some air-conditioned office in Pretoria at a polished desk with a portrait of P W Botha behind his back, warned us that if we ever mentioned the CCB or divulged any information about its existence, we could expect to be incarcerated for a period of up to fifteen years. (It took me exactly a day to blurt it all out to Jakes.) We were working for the military, but neither our names nor our details would appear in their records. Some general would keep our files in his safe, but as far as everyone else was concerned, we were in the employ of Pietman Pretorius. We wouldn't be paid by the army, but out of the proceeds of the hotel and the brothel.

Then followed a lecture on that ugly gogga called the Total Onslaught and the ANC and its communist surrogates and their dastardly conspiracy to make the country ungovernable and force the white government to hand over power to the black rabble. An important instrument in the hands of these instigators, said the dude, was white liberals, many of whom were secretly working for and collaborating with the ANC.

The dude mentioned as an example a new leftie Afrikaans newspaper that was openly calling for the unbanning of the ANC, and a group of whiteys who were organising a campaign against conscription.

'Why don't you just prosecute them and lock them up?' asked Chappies. I was wondering the same thing.

'It gives them the publicity they want,' he said. 'They stand up in court and make political speeches and it's all over the newspapers.'

That's where we came in, he continued. We were specifically charged with acting against these white ANC lackeys. That was why our unit was so deeply under cover. It was one thing to blow up an ANC safe house in Lusaka or make a plan for an agitator in the townships; it was altogether another thing to target a white liberal.

There was silence as all this sank in. Chappies cleared his throat and spoke: 'And how are we supposed to act against these people?'

'That will depend entirely on the target,' the man said matter-of-factly. 'You might be tasked to throw sugar in his petrol tank or poison his dogs or break his potplants.'

Pretorius, who was sitting a metre away, chuckled sheepishly. Even the military dude, who had remained expressionless through-out this diatribe, forced a feeble grin on to his face. I glanced at Chappies. He seemed confused. I was sure we were thinking the same thing: did these cowboys honestly believe that they were going to throw a spanner in the commies' works by jamming engines or killing ferns?

Then he continued: 'But you might also be ordered to take much sterner action.' He looked at each of us in turn. 'Like per-manently removing an individual from society.'

I couldn't say I was shocked. In his earlier briefings Pretorius already indicated that we were going to fuck up the ANC. What was much more significant was that the scheme had provision for so-called 'production bonuses'.

'And what do we have to do to earn a bonus?' asked Chappies.

'That depends entirely on the target you eliminate.'

I know it must sound as though this weird shit could only have been hatched in a Frederick Forsyth novel or a Quentin Tarantino movie. But the existence and workings of the CCB is today a chapter in our history – otherwise nobody would have believed me.

I initially thought that Pietman's unit was the sum total of the CCB. Only later did I find out that there were units all over the place and that it bumped off dudes just about from Cape Town to Cairo.

My impression at the time was that they were cowboys who had nothing better to do than scheme up boy scout fantasies. But the more I thought about it, the more I realised that this was fucking hectic stuff. I'd never contemplated shit like this in my wildest daydreams. I was about to be introduced into a world even darker and more sinister than those of murder or robbery or gangsterism.

Fifteen

There's only one little bloodbath that I really regret, and that was whacking the good professor. I was led to believe that he was a member of the ANC's military wing and a threat to apartheid's longevity. I thought I was pulling the trigger for *Volk en Vaderland* and that the coarse-grain pellets from my shotgun were going to exterminate a despicable communist. But then it turned out that he was nothing more than a daydreaming leftie with idiotic but harmless fantasies about a country where everyone loved and multiplied with everyone else. He had zero fucking ties to Mother Russia or Umkhonto we Sizwe. It's not so much that I lament the unfortunate demise of an innocent man, but his whacking caused all hell to break loose and initiated an unprecedented manhunt for the killer. It took the bastards a couple of years but eventually they bagged me and buried me good and deep.

My downfall started when I became a licensed, accredited, officially sanctioned hitman. I knew these guys existed all over the world but I thought they were phantoms that lurked in shadowy lairs; death-defying characters who couldn't find T-shirts big enough to cover their muscle-bound chests, who strangled their victims with tissues, and blew up buildings with cans of air freshener. One would have expected a state assassin to be highly trained, toned to a tickey and motivated by patriotism.

The CCB was a dicey concept to start with. Then what did they do? They got the diciest characters to set it up. They assembled a bunch of barflies, torturers and hooligans, threw wads of shekels at them and put them in charge of fifteen hookers and a knock-shop. And what did they expect? That we were going to wipe the ANC from the face of the fucking earth?

Let's start at the top. Pietman Pretorius was a *platpoot* to the core; he was devoted to his blue uniform but he was not a fucking rocket scientist. His career was built on brute force and torture. I've no doubt he was committed to this cowboys-and-crooks shit and saw himself as a kind of an urban *grensvegter*, but he had no idea how to put a hit squad together. Guys like Duiwel and Slang were his clones, and they were not blessed upstairs either.

At the bottom of the heap were Chappies, Baksteen, Spyker and me. You've already seen what we were up to. We were no-good hooligans. Take me, Gideon Goosen, for example: a whore-loving and booze-guzzling skunk driven by nothing but pleasure and a longing for his former girlfriend. Whacking the ANC was the last thing on my mind. All I wanted was to pursue my perversions.

I didn't know it at the time, but when I look back at myself today, I realise that by then I had already made up my mind to be a hood. I suppose somewhere along the line, without registering it, I had gone the Johnnie and Jakes route. I didn't want to waste my life worrying about silly shit like bank overdrafts, house loans, creditors' letters, babies' nappies, school fees and a missus with a headache. Maybe I was doing everything and anything I could not to be like my father. I couldn't imagine settling down with a pathetic bag like my mother who lolled around in her slippers all day and picked up her husband's soiled underpants. Instead, I wanted to drink too much, flirt with strange women, throw money around, and play psycho if I felt like it. Doing crime became almost normal, although I didn't see it like that. To me, it was more like a profitable enterprise.

We decided that Chappies would be general manager of the brothel. Spyker was in charge of the cocktail lounge. Baksteen detested brothels (he was a Sunday school teacher) and opted to be the hotel maintenance manager. I wanted to be the brothel's head of operations because that would place me in the heart of whoredom. I wanted a bouquet of sleaze in my nostrils and a bevy of sluts at my beck and call. Of course my position also enabled me to hand-pick our workforce and Chappies and I vowed beforehand that we were not going to display a model in our showroom unless we'd personally test-driven her!

As the hotel renovations neared completion, we had to decide on a name. Pretorius for some reason pushed 'Winkles', Baksteen proposed 'Fillies' and Chappies wanted 'Room69'. From the outset I had nurtured only one name: 'Club Sharné'. Baksteen almost choked when I offered my suggestion, and Chappies started giggling like a teeny-bopper who'd found a dildo in her lunch box.

'Who's Sharné?' Pretorius wanted to know.

'Someone I once knew,' I said. 'But that's not why I like the name. It just sounds good.'

Chappies looked at me, shook his head and suggested a compromise. The gang bang parlour became Room69, the bar was Fillies and the restaurant Winkles. Club Sharné was born.

We had to postpone opening night for a week for two reasons. The first was that a team of blue-overalled dudes in a white van descended on Club Sharné to install an array of spy equipment throughout the place. Two of the cubicles were fitted out with surveillance cameras that were linked to a television set in Pretorius' hotel suite.

'Can you fucking believe it!' snorted Chappies. 'The kinky

cunt is going to watch the customers fuck!'

The second reason was that we had to give our head of security time to take up his position. We also thought it presented an appropriate opportunity to celebrate his homecoming. Pretorius just about had a stroke when I presented him with our choice.

'You mean the Johnnie Swart that we put away a few years ago?'

'That's him, sir.'

'Why on fucking earth this guy? We don't want a massacre in the brothel.'

'He's seen the error of his ways and he's found The Lord,' I waffled. 'And he really wants to do something for his country.'

'Do I look like a moffie, son?'

'Of course not.'

'Then don't tune me *kak*.'

'Please, sir,' I begged. 'I shot his little brother. I owe him.'

He looked at me pensively and then said: 'I'll tell you what, son. I'll appoint him on one condition.'

'And that is?'

'I want results by the end of this month.'

'Like what, sir?'

'I want a hit. There's a shitload of pressure on me.'

I'm not sure what spun through my head, probably something like: what the hell is murder between friends? I'll qualify for a bonus and they might just bestow a medal on me that I could shove up Dad's arse. 'You've got a deal.' I said.

Jakes and I waited for Johnnie in the Alfa outside Krugersdorp Prison. In the boot was his cream-coloured court suit, a small suit-case of clothes, a wad of money and a bottle of Red Heart rum. Johnnie had nowhere to go. Willem Swart had been executed about a year after the court case and although brother Barend's sentence had been commuted to life on the grounds of his mental instability, Johnnie was persona non grata at the Randfontein railway house. His family hadn't visited him once during his time in prison. So I had arranged for him to live in Pietman's hotel.

He walked through the prison gates with his arms in the air, holding them skywards until he reached the car. Then he hurled them around us.

'Where do you want to go?' I asked him as we drove away.

'You know where I wanna go, china?' he said.

'Where?'

'The Leopard. I wanna go to the fucking Leopard.'

I'm not going to go into all the seedy detail, but for the next two days Johnnie didn't leave The Leopard or, in fact, his room. There were never fewer than two hookers with him, and Nando's and Steers ran a non-stop delivery service to the joint. He spent much of his time naked on his back (with his socks on) with an array of tarts all over him. He mumbled 'fucking beautiful' over and over again.

A few days later, Club Sharné opened. Our ad in *The Star* newspaper promised a haven of erotic exploration and a place where you could live out your wildest orgasms. I won't say our establishment was in the same league as Playmates but the joint was steamy and sexy and the broads were saucy and hot. Unlike Playmates, it was unpretentious and, from the minute you walked through the doors, it was about one thing only: screwing your purse out!

Chappies, kinky rubbish that he was, had decided that the cubicles should be mirrored from floor to ceiling and that television sets should pump out non-stop hard-core porn from every nook and cranny. I thought this was over the top. I was concerned that all the shimmer would give customers a headache before they had their pants down or, in the worst case scenario, all that smut might cause them to shoot their loads before they'd emptied their wallets.

We had problems persuading Pretorius to sign the cheques. 'Why all these mirrors and television sets?' he wanted to know.

'People like to check themselves,' Chappies assured him. 'And the TVs will entice them to get on with it.'

Room69 was my brainchild and was more or less based on the Roman Room in Playmates. I commissioned a furniture manufacturer to build an enormous heart-shaped, rotating bed.

Pretorius shook his head and asked: 'Son, why on fucking earth do you need this?'

'Some freaks out there, sir,' I said, 'but they like spending money.'

'No ways, son,' he protested when I presented a plan for a snooker room and a small casino. 'People aren't here to play ball. And, besides, gambling is illegal.'

We started our joint with twelve white girls, including three Bulgarians, three Coloured, two Indian, and three Chinese girls. A few days later, Chappies suggested that we get some proper darkies.

'No reason why we shouldn't have chocolate mouse on the menu,' he said.

A few days after opening night, Pretorius called Chappies, Baksteen and me into his suite and pointed at a pile of files on a desk. 'Target files,' he explained. 'I want you to study them and present me with a plan of action.'

He divided the files among us. As we were about to leave, Pretorius said: 'Goosen, stay behind, son. I want to talk to you.' Chappies and Baksteen closed the door behind them.

Pretorius showed me to a chair and poured me half a glass of sweet red wine. 'It's port,' he said as he lifted his glass. 'I grew up on this farm. My *boetie* is farming it now but I'm going back when this is all finished.' He continued: 'I have high expectations of you, son. Don't disappoint me.'

'I won't, sir,' I promised. When he said nothing more, I swallowed the syrupy liquid and asked: 'May I go now?'

'Sure,' he said. 'Report back tomorrow. I need results.'

I studied the three files, all marked 'Top Priority', that night. I opened the first and stared into the face of a middle-aged man with a mop of unkempt greyish hair and a beard. He was wearing round, thin-rimmed glasses. He looked a bit of a *takhaar* and I thought he resembled Marx or Lenin or some other communist weirdo. He was the editor of the new anti-government Afrikaans newspaper called *Vrye Weekblad*. According to the intelligence report, his rag was a front for the ANC and was funded by leftist sympathisers. He didn't have a fixed home address but the report suggested that he could be targeted at the newspaper offices in Bree Street in Johannesburg. Or he could be infiltrated by a female who could set him up for elimination. The guy was a serious womaniser.

The second dude was a former army lieutenant and one of the leaders of the End Conscription Campaign, or ECC, an organisation that intimidated and brainwashed young men into not reporting for their national service. This campaign, said the report, emanated straight from the ANC high command and the organisation channelled funds through front companies to the ECC. In contrast with the ducktail, this dude was clean-shaven, and he also wore little round spectacles. What alarmed me was that the report said he was armed and well trained. I decided that I was the one who was going to do the shooting and therefore put the file aside.

When I opened the third file a handsome open face flashed a wide smile at me. The dude was a sociology professor at Wits University but instead of teaching his students how to be good citizens he was apparently involved in helping the ANC to smuggle weapons into South Africa and he also held so-called 'tea parties' for the families of political detainees. Can you imagine anything more silly?

His name was Paul Williams and he had various research projects in northern Natal. An army informant had spotted him meeting ANC dudes on the South African border with Mozam-bique – apparently to secure weapons. The report recommended that further intelligence was needed on his activities. It mentioned the Yeoville address where he lived.

Yeoville was alongside Hillbrow and was known as a leftie outpost where, in any of the bars, you could spot blacks necking whites and where the permanent reek of dagga filled the air. I jumped into my car and went to look for the professor's home. He lived in a small semi at the end of a quiet tree-lined cul-de-sac. I peered over the man-high wall. The lights were on in the house but the curtains were drawn. This promises to be a walk in the park, I thought.

We assembled in Pretorius' suite for a staff meeting the next day. I looked from one face to the next and thought, fucking hell, are we the sharp end of the state's fighting machine? Pretorius, who had swallowed hook, line and sinker his new mission as chief hitman, had mutated into a Ray-Banned, Brylcreemed spook. Slang was desperately trying to imitate his idol and had also turned into a ghost. Chappies and I were fine-tuning our gangster guises. The colour was black and the look was leather. No goon guise would be complete without gold chains and dagger and skull tattoos. I had to forgo the latter because I wasn't going to let anyone near me with a needle. My unwieldy poodle hairdo made up for it – centre parting, relatively short around the ears, with a rat's tail hanging down the back.

My mother got the fright of her life when I pitched up for an unexpected visit. 'What will your father say?' she said, ready to burst into tears. 'You look like a hippy.'

'I'm under cover, Mom.'

'Doing what?'

'Catching crooks,' I said.

'And what's your unit?'

'It's secret, Mom,' I said. 'I can't talk about it.'

She shook her head and spoke about Dad who would soon be returning permanently to the Republic. His unit was being closed down. The government had made some deal in South West, paving the way for elections to be held.

It was the monkey business in South West – or Namibia, as it later became – that was the first item on the agenda at our staff meeting. It turned out that Slang and Baksteen had been tasked to disrupt the elections and make sure that the Swapo terrorist organisation didn't get into power.

'And what did you decide?' asked Pretorius.

'Um, sir, we selected an individual for elimination,' Slang said, mentioning the name of a Swapo big gun. They had devised various other schemes, like blowing up the terrorist printing press, throwing cholera germs into the drinking water of villages that were sympathetic towards Swapo, putting sugar into petrol tanks, and throwing snakes into crowds at rallies.

'Well done, colleagues,' Pretorius said. 'Proceed with the operation.'

You think that was bizarre? Listen to this: Chappies and Spyker were tasked to devise a campaign against the Anglican Archbishop of Cape Town (a black guy who had long been a pain in apartheid's neck) and a Malay lawyer who was acting for ANC members who were in custody. The Archbishop – they referred to him as the Ayatollah – wasn't to be killed but the lawyer was. Spyker wanted to bewitch the Ayatollah by hanging an ape foetus in a bottle in his garden. Can you fucking imagine? Worst is, Pretorius fell for it.

'I suppose we don't always understand black witchcraft,' he said. 'What will the effect of this be?'

'Very, very bad luck,' said Spyker. 'He might even die of a terrible illness.'

'Proceed then,' said Pretorius. 'What about the lawyer guy?'

Chappies spelled out an even more elaborate plot. The dude had heart problems and had to take a pill or two every day. Chappies said he'd made contact with a Coloured gangster on the Cape Flats who would (obviously at a price) break into the dude's house and exchange his heart pills for poison pills which would induce a heart attack.

'Brilliant!' exclaimed Pretorius. 'Proceed. And you, Goosen, have you studied the targets?'

'Yes, sir, I have.'

'And who have you decided on?'

'The professor,' I said holding up his file.

'Why him?'

I couldn't tell Pretorius that the professor was a sitting duck, so I said: 'He's smuggling weapons for the ANC, so we need to make a plan about him.'

'You're sure about this?'

'That's what the report says, sir.'

Pretorius pondered for a moment and then asked: 'And how

do you plan to carry out the elimination?'

'Shoot him with a shotgun as he opens his gate to leave for work.'

'Sounds good, son. Proceed as soon as possible.'

As the meeting closed, Baksteen came up with the cherry on the top. What about stocking our brothel with black whores who were infected with Aids?

Chappies started giggling and I just about choked in my coffee.

'Shut up, Horn,' barked Pretorius and turned to Baksteen. 'Why hookers with Aids, Botha?'

'Well, I just think that any guy, but especially a white man, who sleeps with *meide* deserves to get the virus.'

Pretorius slowly shook his head. 'And where would you find these girls?'

Baksteen shifted forward on his chair. 'We get some *houtkoppe* with Aids and get them to hire whores. We put those whores in the brothel.'

'I like the idea,' said Pretorius, 'but it's not quite part of our brief.'

'In most cases *meid* fuckers are also supporters of the ANC,' countered Baksteen.

A fundamental problem with the plan was that some of Pretorius' own boys had developed a hearty appetite for liquorice candy and the three black girls at Club Sharné hardly closed a leg at night. Several CCB operatives had made the brothel and the adjacent bar their local watering hole. The Trennery Hotel had become the headquarters, or at least an important meeting place, for the organisation. Every other day, another Ray-Banned guy with a bad haircut trotted into the hotel for a meeting with Pretorius. Operatives from all over the place descended on the joint for operational briefings and to collect an array of guns and explosives from a specially built storeroom on the bottom level of the underground parking garage. Afterwards, they would pop into Club Sharné for a drink or a rendezvous with an exotic slut and often for both.

I watched these killers: they were nothing but gangsters. Don't be fooled: I was one of them. Each of us had that bluster, that bravado, of being untouchable. It wasn't quite as though we were defying enemy bullets or shared battle scars, but we were seduced by the lure of living on the edge and felt we were invincible. The excitement of the underworld propelled unusual amounts of testosterone through our systems which bubbled to the surface in the brothel where we wanted to shag anything and everything that moved. The ebony beauties were particularly popular and I don't think it would be untrue to say that the CCB operatives were their main clients. Maybe it was as though we were fucking the enemy. Club Sharné had six cubicles; two of which had cameras. We allocated the other cubicles to the operatives. I don't know if Pietman Pretorius knew what was going on in his brothel, but if he did, he probably perceived it to be some form of war therapy.

It was in the cocktail lounge of the brothel that I discovered the extent of the CCB's operations. The CCB had come into existence a year or more before Pretorius assembled his band of psychos. They operated mainly in the neighbouring states and, from what I could gather, they had caused major shit. Each and every one of these dudes had taken oaths of secrecy and was deeply underground, but once rum or brandy had raced through their veins and a hooker hand was rubbing the inside of their thighs, war stories just gushed out.

Fortunately for them, the vast majority of whores had long ago fucked their skulls empty and weren't doing what they did in order to fund their master's degrees in applied mathematics. They didn't care what the hand that had just caressed them had been up to outside the walls of their sanctuary as long as it continued to take the notes from its wallet.

These deeply covert operations were so widely known that some gave birth to nicknames for some of the operatives. One such dude was Sousie van den Berg, a stocky individual with a healthy paunch and a round ruddy face who was operative in Mozambique and Zimbabwe. He was one of the regular *meid* fuckers and if Baksteen ever got his ingenious plan together, Sousie would be a prime candidate to be whacked by the bug.

Sousie loved to trumpet his grisly triumphs to whoever would listen. He blustered about smuggling bottles of poisoned beer to the ANC in Maputo and delivering a booby-trapped television set to the head of the organisation in Harare. The dude wasn't home so his wife took possession of the gift and switched it on in the living room. She and her two kids were blown up.

'The lower part of her body,' he said, 'flew through the window and landed in the street! Can you fucking imagine?'

Sousie somehow believed that his blood and guts stories got the prossies charged up and he usually saved his most gruesome stories for when he had a girl on either side. His favourite operation was the one in which one of his operatives planted a car bomb in Maputo. A white ANC dude (who's now a famous judge) opened the door. The car exploded and he was blown to smithereens, except that he didn't die. He emerged from the carnage with a disfigured face and he lost an arm.

Sousie would smack his flabby lips and exclaim with glee: 'I made a *sousie* out of his arm!'

'How fucking revolting!' I responded when he first told me the story. I subsequently had to listen to it several times over.

'A lovely little blood sauce!' he exclaimed, chortling and slipping his hand under a prossie's skirt.

He once asked me: 'So, tell me, *boet*, have you *klapped* anyone yet?'

I shook my head. 'When then?' he wanted to know.

'Soon,' I said.

'And who is it?'

'You know I can't tell you.'

'Okay then,' he said, 'but tell me, are you going to bomb him or shoot him?'

'Shoot him,' I said.

'Beautiful! But, tell me, with what?'

'A shotgun,' I said.

'Excellent! So it will be at close range. I want to give you some advice.'

'What?'

'When you pull the trigger, look in his eyes.'

'Why?'

'So that you can see them go blank. It's a beautiful sight.'

The whacking of Professor Paul Williams became one of the most widely publicised killings ever. I'm still not sure why. Nobody knew who the dude was before it happened. Overnight the leftie professor and tea party host became an icon of the resistance and a symbol of the struggle against apartheid. That was the day, it seems, when I made the sun go dark and turned the moon to blood.

The surveillance we'd done on the professor's house had shown that he left for work every morning at around eight thirty. It was the perfect time to nail him.

It was a chilly winter's morning on the Transvaal highveld as Johnnie and I made our way to Yeoville in a car with false number plates. He'd volunteered to be the getaway driver. On my lap was a sawn-off double-barrel shotgun. Shortly after eight, we parked our car across the road from Williams' house. We uncapped our plastic cups of coffee and spiced them up with slugs of brandy.

'How do you feel?' asked Johnnie.

'I feel fuck all,' I said. 'I just wish the cunt would come out now.'

I don't remember that I was nervous or apprehensive. Killing wasn't new to me and you don't have to be Sylvester Stallone to whack a dude with a shotgun when he's not expecting it. And after all this was an officially sanctioned project, approved at the highest level and I was doing my job. I just wanted to get it over as quickly as possible.

The street was quiet and deserted. An old lady with a cocker spaniel on a lead wandered by but didn't even look at us. A few yellow leaves fluttered to the ground and a brilliant blue sky beckoned through skeletal branches. It was a perfect day for murder.

Just before eight-thirty, I got out of the car and turned my back to the professor's house. I was wearing a long woollen jacket under which the shotgun was concealed. My finger was on the cold trigger. My senses were razor sharp and I remember to this day the cold air flowing into my nose and the voice of Leonard Cohen groaning away on the tape in the car.

> But I know from your eyes
> And I know from your smile
> That tonight will be fine,
> Will be fine, will be fine, will be fine
> For a while.

'He's coming out!' said Johnnie, turning down the volume. I didn't dare look around as I wanted it to appear as though I was waiting for someone at the house closest to us.

'What's he doing?' I asked Johnnie.

'Saying goodbye to his bitch,' he said. A woman! I hadn't seen a woman at the house before. I glanced over my shoulder. Williams was standing at the gate hugging her. He was no more than fifteen metres from me and I could probably have whacked both of them with one shot. I looked away. I could hear him unlocking the gate.

'What now?' asked Johnnie.

'Tell me when he gets out of his car to close the gate again,' I said, 'but only if the woman has left.'

I heard Williams start his car and begin reversing it down the driveway. I cocked the gun and my finger tightened around the trigger. The car stopped.

'Okay, fucking go!' said Johnnie. 'Go, go, go!'

I turned around and walked straight towards his car. My eyes were fixed on the figure at the gate, fiddling with the lock. He had his back to me. From the corner of my eye I could see the woman walking back to the house. I erased her from my memory and settled my gaze on him. I was like an American F16 fighter pilot locking his sights on an enemy MiG-29.

I was no more than four or five metres from Williams when

he heard my footsteps behind him and swung around. He was dressed in a blue jacket, white shirt and khaki pants. His eyes were brown and bright and they were filled with astonishment. He opened his mouth to speak. I pulled the shotgun from under my coat and aimed it at his chest. I was virtually on top of him and in that fraction of a second before I squeezed the trigger, I saw his expression turn to horror. He knew that he was going to die. The shotgun jolted in my hands.

As if in slow motion, his feet lifted off the ground and he was flung against the gate, his arms spread out as though he was about to be crucified on the iron railings. Then he slowly slumped to the ground. There was a big red smudge on his white shirt. I knew he must have been dead before he even hit the ground.

I turned around and ran back to the car. My ears were ringing with the report of the gun and with the screaming of a woman. A dog started barking somewhere. Johnnie had opened the door for me and as I landed on the seat, he pulled away with screeching tyres. He threw the half-jack on to my lap. I unscrewed the bottle, threw my head back and flung the burning liquid down my throat. I looked out of the window at the bare branches rushing past and for a moment I thought I was going to be sick.

Then I turned the volume up again and closed my eyes. Leonard Cohen was still lamenting the departure of his beloved.

And I know from her eyes
And I know from her smile
That tonight will be fine,
Will be fine, will be fine, will be fine
For a while

Sixteen

I never thought that so many bucketfuls of shit would splatter in so many directions after the passing of the good professor. Paul Williams, until that winter morning a little-known academic, was suddenly the be-all and end-all of the ANC's communist crusade. His body hadn't even cooled before hysteria erupted throughout the country.

After Johnnie and I had parked the getaway car in the basement of Pietman's hotel and hidden the shotgun in my flat, we headed to the Wimpy for breakfast. As I was stuffing bacon and egg into my mouth, the news of the murder came through on Radio Five. Johnnie stopped munching and lifted his eyebrows. He looked at me.

'Do you think she saw you?' he wanted to know.

'Who? His girlfriend?'

'Yes.'

'I don't think so. She was too far away.'

'Here come years of fucking shit,' he said.

'Why do you say that?'

'I just know it,' he said. 'And I was the getaway driver. Can you imagine if they pick me up again? I'll fucking swing.'

'Don't stress, *boet*. Pietman and the might of the whole fucking state is behind us.'

An hour later, the Minister of Police, or Law and Order, or whatever they called the halfwit at the time, branded the killing a cowardly act, offered his condolences to the deceased's family, and vowed that his men in blue would not rest until they had hunted down the killer or killers. *Siestog*, I thought, for once the cops had zero to do with a hit, but the sweet words of the minister were pissed on by the commies and the radicals and the opposition parties and each and every leftie in the country. They were baying for his blood and saying that the murder carried the hallmark of yet another police hit.

In the next news bulletin, the police announced a reward of fifty thousand rand for information leading to the arrest of the killer and said that a special team had been set up to investigate the killing. Tributes to the professor flooded in. He was said to be a champion of human rights and a dedicated campaigner against the evils of apartheid. Well, I thought, that's exactly why the dude got whacked.

An hour later, Pietman sent for me. I knocked on his door and heard the familiar '*Kom binne!*' I swung the door open. I was used to seeing Pietman sitting behind his desk with his glasses on his nose and his face in a file. It was usually a few minutes before he would look up and pay any attention to whoever was there. It was his way of affirming his authority.

This time, however, he was on his feet as I entered his suite. He had a wide grin on his face. He walked around his desk and without saying a word he put his hands on my shoulders, looked into my eyes and hugged me like a long-lost son. I was a bit dumbstruck and wasn't sure what to do. Hug him back? Pat him on his Brylcreemed skull? For one horrible moment I thought he might smooch me! Who fucking knew what was going on in the guy's head? Then he pulled back. I thought his eyes were moist. It took a few moments before he said anything. 'Thank you, son,' he muttered. 'It was brilliant. Absolutely brilliant.'

He showed me to a chair and poured port into two glasses. He pushed one towards me, lifted his and said: 'To a well-executed and professional mission. I hope there will be many more.'

I spoke for the first time: 'It was easy, sir. Everything went according to plan.'

'It was a perfect hit,' he said and filled the glasses again. 'There were no witnesses, no evidence, nothing.'

'His girlfriend didn't see me?'

'No,' he said and smiled. 'When she heard the shot and turned around, you already had your back to her.'

I gave a sigh of relief, raised my glass and threw the liquid down my throat. Pietman stood up and walked towards a safe in the corner of the room. He slowly unlocked it, looked at me and smiled. I had an idea what it was: my production bonus. He took out two sizeable plastic bags, put them in front of me and said: 'For a job well done, son. You deserve every cent of it.'

I looked into one of the bags. It was stuffed with pink fifties. Must be thousands, I thought. Pietman satisfied my curiosity. 'It's sixty thousand, son,' he said. 'Forty for yourself and twenty for Johnnie Swart. He, too, did well.'

My mouth fell open. God Almighty, I thought, for forty grand I'd volunteer to whack any fuck! It must have been the easiest money I'd ever made. I never thought a hit could be as easy as a stroll in the park, and that I would discuss it afterwards as if it was just another day's work.

Pietman held out his hand. I took it and he put his other hand on top of mine. 'Son,' he said as he slowly and warmly shook my hand, 'you've done us proud. It's because of men like you that we're winning this war.'

Of course Pietman was talking pure, unadulterated drivel because nine months later Nelson Mandela and his cronies were out of *tjoekie*, the ANC was let loose and Piet's cats were running around like chickens without their heads. But, for then, my chest swelled with pride and warmth. Maybe Pietman was the father I never really had, I thought. I decided that I loved the hoary old fuck, despite all his grouchiness.

As you will soon see, this newborn son-father affinity lasted less than twenty-four hours and dissipated as quickly as it had sprouted.

Johnnie was waiting for me outside Pietman's office. I held the bags in the air.

'How much?' he wanted to know. I smiled but said nothing. 'How fucking much? he repeated.

'Twenty,' I said.

'For both of us?'

'No, just for you.'

'Jesus Christ!' he said. 'So when can we do it again?'

We were welcomed like heroes downstairs in the whore den. Sousie van den Berg and three or four other CCB dudes were in the bar and when we walked in they forced glasses of *Tiertrane* into our hands. This concoction was the CCB's equivalent of Brixton's *Leeutande* and was infinitely more potent. *Tiertrane* consisted of Stroh rum (eighty per cent alcohol!), peppermint liqueur, tequila and fruit that had matured in a sealed jar in the sun for two weeks. It got its name from the involuntary tears that welled in your eyes as it burnt itself down your throat and ignited in your guts.

Nobody mentioned the professor's name or asked for details, but I knew that everyone knew. Bagging your first hit in the CCB was a bit like scoring your maiden try in a Springbok rugby jersey, or popping your first cherry in matric. It guaranteed you entry into an exclusive club and elevated you to another level among your peers. There were in fact only two types of operatives: those who had done it, and those who aspired to do it. I had become a member of the organisation's inner circle.

Sousie patted me on the shoulder. 'So tell me, did you do as I told you?'

'What do you mean?'

'Look in his eyes,' he said.

'I don't know what you're fucking talking about.'

'Oh come on, big boy,' he said. 'You can tell me. Did you check him out?'

'No ways,' I said. 'It happened too fast.'

'Pity, man, pity,' he said. 'Remember next time.'

The Star newspaper that afternoon was full of the murder. 'IN COLD BLOOD', screamed the headline. Splashed across the front page was a photograph of two policemen standing around the pool of blood in front of the gate. The professor's girlfriend stood a metre or two away, pressing a bunch of tissues to her face. She had only seen the back of the gunman and described him as white and tall with darkish hair. Brilliant, I thought with a smirk on my face. That fitted at least a million men in the country.

There was another picture of her further down the page. She looked like a mouse with her short-cropped hair and make-up-less face.

'Siestog!' said Sousie. 'Where on earth will this cookie find another boyfriend?'

'No way in hell,' said Johnnie. 'That was her last chance.'

'The broad's a screamer,' I said. 'She screamed like a pig when I nailed him.'

Because it was about Volk en Vaderland and God Almighty delivering the enemy into the hands of his chosen people, one would have expected the aftermath of such an operation to be spent with heads bowed in prayer. Well, the only time these oafs got to their knees was in one of the cubicles, and their only interaction with God was when they pounded a prossie and murmured a little prayer that an ugly bug wouldn't nab them.

'You need some lipstick on your dipstick!' said Sousie waving at three hookers lining the bar to join us.

I want to tell you something that sounds warped and weird, but there's nothing to galvanise a boner like a good, old-fashioned whacking. It's almost an aphrodisiac. It's as though a little bloodshed injects an extra bit of lead in your pencil. It's a case of a homicide a day will keep Viagra at bay and it had become a tradition to ply an operative who'd returned from a mission with whores and booze.

On the other hand, though, it was astonishing to see how turned on those peroxide-blonde bimbos were by this macho display of brawn. The scrubbers loved the exhilaration of gangland. Maybe they thought that those cocked guns were just a hint of what was to come or that the guys had the stamina and endurance of marathon athletes. We all knew it wasn't true and bravado often merely compensated for what was seriously lacking down below.

I was no different from any of the others and for the remainder of that day of murder, I downed whatever was put down in front of me and showered an assortment of hookers with pink fifties.

Sousie, back from yet another excursion to a cubicle, came up to me and said: 'Come with me, I want to show you something.'

One of the Bulgarian broads was rubbing a pointy titty against me and I had zero interest in Sousie's disclosures. But he insisted, so in the end I kissed the whore on her neck, whispered an obscenity in her ear and followed Sousie through the hotel and down the escalator to the weapons store on the bottom floor of the parking garage. Baksteen was waiting at the iron gate.

'Goosen, you're not supposed to be here,' he said with a broad grin on his face.

'Oh come on, Botha,' said Sousie, 'he's one of us. Open up, *broer*.'

Baksteen unlocked the iron gate and then another steel door. The room smelled musty. He switched on a light. AKs, R4s, Uzis, shotguns, missile launchers and wooden crates of ammunition and hand grenades were stacked from floor to ceiling. There was enough hardware to invade the Soviet Union. Sousie walked towards a steel cupboard, unlocked it and opened one of the drawers. He pulled out a brown parcel and said: 'Isn't this the most beautiful gift you've seen in your whole fucking life?'

'What is it?' I asked.

'This is a sauce maker!' he quipped. His high-pitched cackle echoed through the garage.

It was a letter bomb, addressed to a white priest in Zimbabwe. The wrapper carried the emblem of the Anglican diocese in Cape Town. I'm still not sure why Sousie wanted to show me his bomb. Maybe it was to back up his reputation as the CCB's chief thug.

A month or so later the bomb exploded in the good father's hands. One was blown off and the other had to be amputated. Flying shrapnel scarred his face and he lost the sight in one eye. To this day he walks around with bionic hands.

It was time to sweet-talk Sharné into coming back to me. The morning after the professor's killing I was in a florist shop with a motherfucker of a hangover sending twenty-four red roses to Sharné. By then she had given up her baby for adoption and was working as a stripper at a rather seedy joint in Alberton to the east of Johannesburg. I had decided that it was time to make my move and try to win her back. I ordered roses to be delivered to her flat every morning for seven days.

My pager beeped. Pietman wanted to see me immediately. When I entered his office and saw the expression of thunder on his face, I stopped in my tracks. He didn't say a word as he pointed to a chair. Pietman wasn't alone. Sitting in another chair was the stony-faced military guy who had given us the lectures when we joined the CCB. He was wearing his light-brown suit again. He nodded at me but I ignored him.

Pietman threw a brown file on to his desk. It landed with a thud in front of me. I immediately recognised it as the file of Professor Paul Williams. Pietman spoke for the first time: 'Did you read that file, Goosen?'

Gone was the usual 'son'. The last time Pietman had called me by my surname was at Brixton when he had summoned me to kick me out of his unit. I knew this indicated that mega shit was about to descend on me. I started having heart palpitations.

'Yes, sir, I did,' I responded, looking at the file.

'Are you sure you did?'

'Yes, sir.'

'Well, Goosen,' he sneered, 'you obviously can't fucking read.'

'I can read, sir.'

'Then you've read like your fucking arse.'

I looked up at him. His eyes were full of rage and his pencil-thin lips were tightly compressed. I decided that it was best to shut up. I looked down at the file again. 'Open it on page six,' Pietman ordered. I opened the file at that page.

'Read paragraph forty-one,' he said.

I cleared my throat. I have never been a good reader and I stumbled over the first few words. 'The aforementioned information is based on the unsubstantiated observations of a single informant. It is necessary to gather further intelligence before a final decision is made on possible action against the subject.'

It hit me like a lorryload of bricks. In my eagerness to perform, I had ignored vital information about the professor. I remembered reading that paragraph but most likely thought that I wasn't going to let a rumour stand between me and a production bonus.

'I gave the file to you to study.'

'Yes, sir.'

'You reported that he was smuggling weapons.'

'Yes, sir.'

'You didn't tell me it was just hearsay.'

'No, sir.'

'In your stupidity you might have killed an innocent man,' said Pietman. I looked up at him and our eyes locked. So fucking what, I wanted to spit back at him. How many guiltless suckers have you sent to prison or to the gallows with confessions you'd tortured out of them? But I kept quiet. 'Do you fucking understand what you've done, Goosen?'

'Yes, sir.'

'You're a fucking imbecile.'

'Yes, sir.'

The guy in the suit cleared his throat and spoke for the first time. 'Mister Goosen, you have to understand that this elimination has put President Botha and his cabinet under tremendous pressure.'

I shifted my eyes to him. The word cunt was written across his clean-shaven baby face.

'This is a most unfortunate incident,' he continued.

I wanted to tell him that I couldn't care less about sloppy-lipped P W Botha and his wagging finger. Or the half-witted clowns he surrounded himself with. Or the CCB. Or Pietman. Or you, you fucking pansy.

'You've let me and the unit and the country down, Goosen,' said Pietman. I looked at him again. I had been a hero only twenty-four hours earlier. My fear was giving way to a furious anger. It was you, I thought, who wanted a body. I delivered a spectacular corpse and you were thrilled, and now you're behaving like a kid whose candy has been snatched from his mucky little paws.

'You've put the future of the whole unit in jeopardy,' he went on. 'You stupid fucking arsehole!'

The other dude's voice droned again. I was no longer listening. Pietman was also talking but I'd shut my ears to him as well. Fury was raging in my skull, my fists were clenched and my heart was pounding in my throat. I had been humiliated enough by Pietman Pretorius. I was ready to jump up and smash his face to a pulp. I'd killed or seriously damaged before in this kind of rage, and I had an urge to do it again.

I stumbled to my feet and leaned across the table. At that moment, Pietman reminded me of Dad. That same smirk. I wondered what I should do. Punch him on his lopsided nose or *klap* his dish-like ears? Throttle him? I could see confusion in his eyes.

'Sit down, Goosen,' growled Pietman. 'I'm not finished with you yet.'

'Fuck off,' I said. It bubbled out, unpremeditated. I was no longer in control of myself when I added: 'Ugly fucking cunt.'

Pietman's face was a picture of bewilderment and his lips parted slowly as though he wanted to say something but couldn't find the words. I knew I'd jerked the lion's testicles and that his fury was about to be unleashed on me. I turned around and marched to the door.

I glanced over my shoulder and hissed a final insult: 'Why don't you go fuck yourself?'

As my hand turned the doorknob, Pietman had regained his composure and was slowly lifting himself from his chair.

'Goosen!' he bawled. 'Fucking come back here!'

I ignored him, slammed the door and walked down the steps. I heard him opening it. His voice thundered through the building as he hurled a barrage of insults at me.

'Goosen, I'm going to fuck you up!'

I reached the ground floor and went into the brothel. There were no customers and Johnnie was lounging on a couch in the bar.

'Come!' I said. 'Fucking come!'

'What's going on?'

'Just come! I'll tell you later.'

As we drove away, my pager started beeping with messages from Pietman to return to the hotel. I switched the pager off and threw it out the window. I looked in my rear-view mirror and saw it bouncing on the black tarmac.

That was the sum of my involvement with the CCB. During my trial I was branded a state assassin who had annihilated just about every living being who had ever opposed apartheid. Nothing could be further from the truth.

There you have it: one miserable hit. And it was a mistake.

Johnnie and I drove to Rosebank to Club Jezebel, the up-market brothel that belonged to the Lebanese gangster that Chappies and I had been selling information to. I flopped down on a couch, ordered double tequilas with salt and lemon and told Johnnie what had happened in Pietman's suite. He shook his head, downed his tequila and ordered another.

That night there was a knock on my front door. It was Baksteen Botha, who had just returned with Slang van Wyk from their mission to South West to clobber Swapo and single-handedly prevent them from taking power. I was delighted to see my old china, although we were not as close as before. Baksteen had a Jesus fixation and was troubled by my flirtation with anything kinky.

'Why have you come to see me?' I asked him.

'Pietman sent me,' he said.

'I thought so,' I said. 'Tell him to fuck off.'

'He wants you to come back.'

Pietman had good reason to want me back. When you are in command of a death squad, you want it to function like one big, happy family. You don't cast your operatives out in the cold. A hungry man is an angry man and who knows what a disgruntled killer is capable of? He might just blow the lid off your whole enterprise.

'Pietman says you're dangerous and God knows what you'll do next.'

'Tell him to fuck off,' I repeated.

'He's like a mad cobra,' Baksteen said. 'He walks up and down his office talking to himself and screams and shouts at everyone.'

'I have no intention of going back.'

I uncorked a bottle of Klippies, poured two heavy slugs, added a little bit of Coke and passed one of the glasses to Baksteen. After a few swigs his throat was oiled and his mouth was loose.

'And so,' I asked, 'did you throw your snakes?'

'You won't believe what happened,' he said and laughed. 'We sent two goons to go and catch some. They got two puff adders and a cobra and put them in a box. When we opened the box to take them out, two were dead. I think they fought.'

They had to abandon their cholera plan when they discovered that the drinking water was treated with chlorine which would kill the cholera bacteria. Silly ideas like sugar in petrol tanks and blowing up printing presses remained exactly that in their empty skulls.

Slang and Baksteen waited for a week outside the Swapo leader's house before reading in the newspapers that he was overseas. They scanned the papers for an alternative hit and stumbled upon some white Swapo guy who had written some scholarly shit in one of the rags. They found his address in the telephone directory and Baksteen nabbed him in his driveway with an AK. The guy was nothing but a loudmouth rabble-rouser, revered more for his drunken parties and womanising than his political activism.

There was such uproar about his killing that the poor sod of a minister stood up in parliament and said that his men would never have shot him because he was a spy who had been feeding them valuable information. Can you imagine that the CCB might have whacked one of their own? Well, I suppose that's what's going to happen when you elevate lunatic torturers to executioners.

'What did Pietman say about all of this?' I asked.

'He stormed around his office like a madman and fired all of us,' Baksteen said. 'Then he reinstated us but we're grounded. We can't go anywhere.'

'And what happened to Chappies and his stuff in Cape Town?' I wanted to know.

'Chappies is in even bigger shit,' he said.

Spyker and Chappies had managed to climb over the archbishop's wall and hang the ape foetus in a bottle in a tree but a gardener found it the next morning and called the archbishop, who took one look at it and threw it away.

Chappies recruited the gangster who was going to swap the lawyer's heart pills with poison pills. A few days later, he reported that his mission had been accomplished and was paid fifteen thousand rand. Chappies and Spyker waited a week and when nothing happened, they picked the gangster up, drove him out of the city and took him to an open piece of veld where they beat him to a pulp. He admitted that he'd never swapped the pills. He was found the following morning on the side of the road with a neat incision across his throat.

'Fuck-up is,' said Baksteen, 'that Spyker bonked one of the gangster's popsies. He gave her his pager number and now the cops are on to him.'

'So now what?'

'Pietman is trying to fix it but the cops are smelling a rat,' he said.

Worst of all was that while Pietman and his band of loonies were carrying out their shenanigans, white South Africans were sleeping like babies because they thought their men in uniform were clobbering the communists and the terrorists. It could not have been further from the truth. With the CCB running things, victory was a sure thing for the terrs and the commies.

'You must be careful,' he said. 'That man's capable of anything.'

Two days later, Chappies arrived on my doorstep. He was dressed in black leather and the gold around his neck and arms probably outweighed his body mass. He had also dyed his hair black.

'Did Pietman send you?' I asked him.

'No, I'm not supposed to be here,' he said. 'We're not allowed to speak to you.'

'And why not?'

'He's planning something against you.'

'Like what?'

'I dunno,' he said. 'But Spyker says he overheard the guys speaking.'

'How come he heard it?'

'He works in the bar. He hears everything.'

'What's Pietman planning?'

'I'm not sure, but it seems like a hit.'

I leaned forward. 'A fucking what?'

'He wants your blood. He says you're a threat to the organisation.'

'So now he wants to kill me?'

'It seems like it.'

Although the CCB wasn't an organised criminal network in the mould of the Sicilian Mafia, it operated according to the same code of behaviour. Of course killing is unfortunate but it's an acceptable element of gangster life – even if it means whacking one of your own. Once an insider breaks the code and weakens the group's invincibility and threatens to split on his cronies, he's as good as dead. And that's exactly why Pietman wanted to whack me. I was out of line and a menace to his unit's survival.

'And who's supposed to kill me?'

'I'm not sure,' he said. 'Maybe Sousie.'

'Fucking Sousie!' I hollered. 'So Sousie is going to make a *sousie* out of me?'

'I'm not sure, but that's what I heard. Sousie or one of his men.'

It was a frightening prospect to be the hunted with Sousie the hunter. He was one of the more accomplished hitmen, quite James Bond-like compared with any of the Brixton band.

'What should I do?'

'Go see Pietman and apologise like you've never apologised before.'

'I'd rather die than do that.'

'Then your arse is on the line.'

'Can you get me a gun?' I asked him. I decided that if I was going down, it would be with guns blazing. Whoever was coming for me, I was going to shoot back. I still had the shotgun with which I'd nailed the professor, but it was hardly the kind of hardware you could strap to your waist when you ventured out into the street.

'I'll see what I can do,' Chappies said. He delivered a nine-millimetre pistol and two full magazines that same afternoon.

'Look after yourself,' he said. 'And don't use your phone. I think Pietman has it tapped.'

A deep depression overwhelmed me when I realised I was pretty much fucked. I'd abandoned my police career in order to take part in Pietman's moronic enterprise. I obviously had no future as a triggerman in the military. I had little education, a down-and-out family and crooked friends. I had two options. I could either become a bum or throw my lot in with my buddies. There was no need for reflection. I knew what my fate would be.

I felt completely alone. I went out to the local liquor store. It was a bleak winter day and dry leaves fluttered to the ground and fell in front of my feet. I stocked up on an assortment of booze, locked myself in my flat, pulled the phone from its socket and drowned my sorrows. I didn't bath or shave for the next few days.

There were several knocks on my door. Each time I jerked upright, grabbed the shotgun or pistol and waited for Pietman's assassin to break through the door. Once my unannounced visitor was gone, I slumped back on to my pillow, pressed a bottle to my lips and tried to forget my troubles.

I wished I was a kid again. I longed for the warmth and smell of my mother, my *ouboet*'s one-time lust for life, and the carefree days with Jakes and Johnnie. I wanted to be ten years old again when my *kleinboet* was still alive and Dad was a hero and I played 'Love is a Beautiful Song' for Linda. And to score the winning try for the first rugby team.

Scenes from my life flashed in front of me: Pietertjie dangling from the rope in the bathroom, Dad's hairy hand clobbering me into oblivion, an emaciated Karel curled up on his bed in rehab, Mom falling backwards and lying on the floor with a big blue bruise appearing on her cheek. I was not even twenty-four years old and my life was a mess. Mom's little ice cream boy had turned into a killer, an assassin, a torturer, a cheat, a thief, an alcoholic, a brothel keeper, an unemployed bum. A down-and-out fucking loser. I hurled more booze down my throat and fell into a deep sleep. I dreamt of demons with ropes around their necks and cockroaches with red faces and fluffy paws and butterflies with gooey tots in their bellies.

I woke up in a pool of sweat, reached for a bottle and thought of Sharné. I wasn't sure whether I had dreamt about her but I could smell her and feel her and hear her. I reached for my wallet and searched for the piece of paper on which one of the hookers in the brothel had scribbled her number. She lived somewhere in Hillbrow, for all I knew just around the corner from me. I plugged in the phone and dialled the number. The next moment, her voice was on the other side. It was the first time I had heard that sweet voice in a year.

After a few seconds I said: 'It's me.'

If she had put the phone down – as I expected she might – I am sure I would have picked up the nine-mill and blown my brains out. I looked at the silver gun on the bed and then her voice came back.

'The roses are beautiful,' she said.

'Which colour did you get today?'

'Yellow,' she said, 'but the pink ones are my favourite.'

'I was hoping that you'd like them.'

'Why do you sound so funny? You sound pissed.'

'I am,' I admitted. 'I'm pretty smashed.'

'Why?'

'It's a long story,' I said. 'Want to hear it?'

'Sure? When?'

My heart was beating faster. 'Now,' I said. 'I want to see you now.'

'Where?'

'Café de Paris,' I said. 'Give me an hour. I need to shower.'

'See you there,' she said and put the phone down.

I leapt in the air and yelled at the top of my voice. My pounding headache vanished and my future suddenly did not seem so bleak. I stuffed Leonard Cohen in the CD player and plunged into the stream of hot water.

An hour later, my Alfa screeched to a halt a few metres from the steps that led to the first-floor entrance to Café de Paris. As I got out of my car, I saw her standing halfway up the steps – an angel wearing a short clinging yellow dress with a blonde mane cascading down her back. Sharné had changed the colour of her hair but she was still the most beautiful woman alive.

I leapt out of the car and waved to her. She lifted her hand to return the greeting. I didn't hear the car stopping next to me. Sharné's hand was in the air and her mouth was partly open and then there was a loud bang. Everything turned into a slow motion movie. Her mouth stretched wide and she screamed. A hammer hit my chest. The first bang rang in my ears and then there was a second. Another hammer hit me, somewhere in my upper body. My wallet and sunglasses fell to the pavement. I pressed my hand against my chest. My shirt was wet. It was blood. My blood. My arms slumped to my sides and I could feel my legs giving way. I turned my head but I collapsed before I could see my executioner. I tried to open my eyes but everything was fuzzy. There were sounds, many sounds. Shrieks, tyres screaming, footsteps, people babbling. I realised that I had been shot more than once and that the pieces of metal that had ripped my flesh had ricocheted around my chest. I wondered whether my heart had been punctured and whether I was going to die. I didn't want to die. Please God, don't let me die. It was only then that the pain hit me. My body was flooded with it, the most excruciating pain I'd ever experienced.

I seemed to be slipping in and out of the world.

A soft hand touched my forehead. I forced my eyes open. Staring down at me was an angelic face with Arctic eyes. They were full of tears.

Then everything went black.

Seventeen

There's nothing like a nugget of hot lead and a few days in a coma to reignite the flame of love. When I opened my eyes, I looked into eyes hungry with desire. She was wearing red which made her hair and skin seem even more radiant. She put her hand on mine.

'Gideon?'

She was beautiful and magnificent and mysterious. She bent over me and I closed my eyes. Her velvety lips caressed my forehead before moving to my ear.

'You're going to be okay,' she whispered.

If the bullet in my ribcage was going to explode and my heart was going to stop beating and the blood in my arteries was going to clot and my skin was going to turn yellow before I turned from dust to dust, that would have been a perfect time for it to happen.

Her closeness satisfied me like a raindrop quenching the thirst of a desert flower. She murmured something else but I didn't hear it. With her fragrance around me, I slipped back into darkness.

I had been trolleyed into theatre where a team of doctors cut me open and removed one nine-millimetre slug from my torso and another from my shoulder. When I opened my eyes many hours later, Sharné was there. Only then did I become aware that there was a tube in my nose and a battery of machines around my bed.

I'm still not sure why she decided to stay. She usually arrived at around three in the afternoon and left again at eight at night. I knew she went to her stripper job and thought that she probably needed to sleep the whole of the next morning to recuperate. I thought she was just ripping her clothes off, but I later discovered that she was also whoring.

During the days that followed there were many people around my hospital bed. Jakes and Johnnie, always armed with a bottle of booze or a spiked Coke, came as often as Sharné. Gielie and Sherry brought me Tupperware dishes of chicken pie, lamb stew and chocolate pudding. Chappies sneaked in – he had been told he was not allowed to see me – and always left a *Penthouse* or *Playboy*. He said Pietman Pretorius was as surprised as he was when he heard I had been shot. I told him he was talking bullshit.

Mom came every second day with tears in her eyes, a hanky in her hand and a prayer on her lips. I didn't mind her coming, except when she brought Dad with her. He was back from South West and had just retired on medical grounds. I couldn't avoid the old fart and, to make matters worse, the shooting had elevated me to brief celebrity status – for all the wrong reasons.

A few days after the incident, Sharné waltzed into my room with the Sunday newspaper in her hand. I had come round from my surgery only the previous night and it was my first day out of intensive care. She held the paper in the air and opened it on page three. It felt as though another bullet was tunnelling its way into my body. My picture was splashed across the page under the headline: 'Brothel Boss Shot in Turf War'.

The photograph was several years old and had been taken at my passing-out parade. I looked bright-eyed, boyish and cheerful; a far cry from my poodle haircut and gangster gear, but it was nonetheless me.

'Oh fuck, no,' was all I could get out. I wanted to pull the sheets over my head and bury myself in my hospital bed. The first thing that went through my mind was Mom. This might just send her to an early grave.

Sharné read the article. It said that warfare had been raging in Johannesburg's gangland for more than a year and that it was thought that my shooting was linked to several other attacks on the city's brothels. So-called 'informed sources' revealed that the attack on me might have been committed by the same people who had ransacked Playmates and were suspected of being involved in the disappearance of its owner eighteen months earlier.

When Sharné got to the paragraphs about Playmates, she swallowed, stumbled over one or two words but then read on as though she'd never heard the name before.

'So what do you think of all of this?' she asked.

'It's bullshit!' I said. 'Who wrote it?'

She told me the name of the journalist. It was none other than Chappies' loose fuck who he used to plant false stories – and scored shags in return. I was sure that he was responsible for parading me as some big shot slut supremo. He's always denied that Pietman ordered him to do it, but I'm not so sure.

Some time later, Dad strode into my room. Mom followed a few metres behind. Her eyes were red and puffy; she had probably been crying and praying all day. Dad was as bloated as a hot-air balloon, his eyes bulging like a toad's. His skin was its usual florid colour. I don't know if the cancer cells were already nibbling at his liver, but he was uglier than ever and had lost none of his abrasiveness. He didn't greet any of my friends.

'And so?' he sneered. 'Now it's brothel boss Gideon Goosen. My own son!'

Jakes, Johnnie and Sharné retreated a metre or so. Mom

tugged at Dad's sleeve and said: 'Wait now, Hendrik. Let's get the facts first.'

'Is it true, Gideon? Is it bloody well true?'

I wanted to press my bell and summon a titanic nurse and ask her to chuck him out on his ass. I looked at him for a second or two and then I said: 'No, it's not true.'

'What is it then?' he demanded.

'The brothel is a front,' I said.

'For what?'

'A secret unit,' I said.

'What secret bloody unit? The police don't have brothels!'

I looked at his torso heaving up and down and his flabby titties swelling through his tight-fitting shirt. My chest was sore and I was tired. I shut my eyes for a moment, opened them again and looked into his muddy eyes.

'You know what?' I said. He lifted his eyebrows. 'It's top secret, and I can't tell you. So please leave me alone.'

I shut my eyes tightly so I didn't see his reaction, but Mom whimpered once or twice and I could hear Jakes sniggering.

'I'll *dônner* you right here!'

I opened my eyes. Dad's forefinger was pointing at Jakes. A layer of spit covered his purple lips. He looked down at me.

'And you,' he said as he dropped his finger, which came to rest only inches from my face, 'are a disgrace! An absolute bloody disgrace!'

Then he swaggered out the room with Mom following close behind. She was pressing a tissue against her face.

'Your dad is hectic, hey?' said Sharné.

'He's the ultimate fucking cunt,' I said.

'Mine too,' she said.

'Mine's a cunt too,' said Johnnie.

'Mine's not great either,' said Jakes.

'Why then,' I said, 'don't we start the Cunt-fuck Daddies Club?'

Everyone laughed. 'That calls for a celebration,' said Johnnie and pulled a half-jack from the pocket of his leather jacket.

'No, he can't,' said Sharné as she stroked my arm. 'He's still too sick.'

'Of course I can,' I said as I grabbed the half-jack and took a big gulp.

Mom was back the next day. 'Your father is devastated,' she said as she put her hand on mine. Her powdered skin hung loosely from her cheekbones and deep-etched lines covered her face.

'So what?' I said.

'He's very angry,' she said. 'He's talking about disinheriting you.'

I sniggered. 'So who is he going to leave his wealth to? The police fund for widows?'

Shortly after I regained consciousness, Brixton Murder and Robbery detectives descended on my room like hawks. Although I couldn't think straight, they threw a barrage of questions at me. I said I had no idea who wanted me dead and of course nothing ever came of the investigation.

At more or less the same time, Baksteen rocked up at my hospital bed and after talking shit for a few minutes, he cleared his throat and said: 'Pietman sent me.'

I didn't answer him. 'He's concerned that you might say something about the organisation and blow our cover.'

'So what does the cunt think I'm going to do?' I responded. 'Tell the cops about the CCB?' As an afterthought I added, 'And that I shot the professor?'

'He's worried that you'll give us away.'

'Is that why he tried to kill me?'

'He didn't do it.'

'Who the fuck did then?'

'I dunno,' he said. 'Maybe one of your whores had a jealous boyfriend.'

'*Kak*, man,' I said. 'But I want you to tell Pietman something.'

'What?'

'I'll keep my mouth shut,' I said, 'but he must pray that nothing happens to me.'

'Why?'

'I've made a statement to my lawyer and given him a copy of the Paul Williams file.'

'Why?'

'Because if anything happens to me, my lawyer will give it to the cops and Pietman's dirty arse will be blown into the fucking sky.'

Baksteen left a few minutes later, his tail between his legs. I would love to have been the cause of Pietman's slow and agonising demise. Something like a bullet through his stomach, another to pulverise his kneecap, and a third to puncture one of his nicotine-charred lungs. I wished him a prolonged deathbed.

But I knew it was not going to be. Pietman was surrounded by lethal hitmen of the likes of Sousie van den Berg and the Trennery Hotel was a fort-like military base. My revenge came from an unexpected source: a bespectacled and make-up-less leftie journalist with unkempt hair and the dirtiest mouth I'd ever heard.

One morning after breakfast, she walked into my hospital room. She was wearing a creased T-shirt, a pair of faded jeans and leather sandals. I've already told you she didn't wear make-up but her skin glowed and was the colour of peaches. Her mouth was wide and painted with a cherry-coloured lipstick, and her green eyes were clear, cool and hard to ignore. Her high cheekbones gave her a don't-fuck-with-me appearance while her mousy hair was pinned at the back of her head. A pair of round thin-rimmed glasses balanced on her nose. All of this should have warned me that she spelled trouble but I was so taken aback by her appearance that I just stared at her.

'Are you Gideon Goosen?' she asked but before I could answer, she plonked herself down on the chair next to my bed and crossed her legs like a man. Her ankles were covered with a layer of longish black hair. Jesus Christ, I thought, she's an *au natural*!

'And why do you want to know?' I asked her.

She leaned forward. 'Because I want to talk to you,' she

said.

'But I don't want to talk to you,' I responded. 'So leave me alone.'

'Don't be a stupid *poes!*'

I looked at her, probably with a shocked expression. *Poes* is one of the dirtiest words in the Afrikaans language, a close call behind *kaffir* for top honours in the obscenity stakes. It's a word one associates with the inmates of Auschwitz in The Bomb. I don't think I'd ever heard a white chick use the word, and certainly not with as much gusto as this toughie.

'Sis, man,' I said. 'Why do you swear like that?'

'Because you're behaving like a *poes*,' she said, holding out her hand. 'My name is Georgina du Toit.'

'And where did you get a funny name like that?'

'My grandmother was named Georgina,' she said. 'I think it's fucking cool.'

'And what do you want?'

'I'm from *Vrye Weekblad*,' she said. 'I'm a journalist.'

I looked at her and thought, oh fuck, her *takhaar* editor was one of the guys on Pietman's hit list. If I remembered correctly, the newspaper was allegedly funded by the ANC and full of leftist propaganda. What was she doing here?

'I don't want to talk to you,' I said. 'Go away.'

'Don't be so rude,' she said. 'Why don't you want to talk to me?'

'Because you're all fucking communists,' I said.

She threw her head back and laughed. 'Don't be a *poes!*' she hollered. 'You don't even know what a communist is!'

'What do you want?' I asked her.

'I'm doing a story about the brothel war,' she said. 'And I think you can help me.'

'With what?'

'Maybe you have an idea who's after your blood.'

'Listen, doll, keep your nose clean,' I said. 'You'll get nailed, too.'

'I'm not your fucking doll, okay?' she said. 'And, besides, I'm not scared.'

I watched Georgina's hands waving as she shot off her foul mouth. 'Will you help me?' she said, looking pleadingly at me.

A scheme was spawning itself in my head. Nobody would ever suspect that I was in cahoots with a bunch of hothead ANC puppets and communists. 'Come back tomorrow,' I said, 'and maybe we can talk.'

As she got up, stuffing her notebook and pen into an old leather bag and pulling her T-shirt straight, I remarked: 'And try to look less like a commie. One of my friends might spot you.'

'*Jou poes*, man,' she said as she slipped out the door.

A week or so later a photograph of Pietman Pretorius decorated the front page of *Vrye Weekblad* under the headline: '*Pietman en sy hoere*' ('Pietman and his whores').

Georgina had done a fantastic job. The story exposed the dramatic descent of South Africa's once most revered policeman into the filth and sleaze of whoredom, international trafficking and sexual exploitation. Much of it was true, although I had made up some of it.

The newspaper had managed to sneak a pic of the bearded, Ray-Banned and Brylcreemed Pietman creeping into Club Sharné with Slang van Wyk a few steps behind him. And then followed the story of the inner workings of his brothel.

It was alleged that Pietman was enslaving Bulgarian, Chinese and Mozambican women who were in the country illegally. Criminal syndicates had smuggled the hookers into South Africa and sold them to Pietman and his team of former Brixton Murder and Robbery policemen who had joined him in the business. Our men in blue, said the story, were lining up to have a go with these exotic sluts. They were especially fond of *groeps-woepse* in Room69 and orgies were so commonplace that the hookers referred to them as police dances. The bit about the syndicates wasn't true, but that the hookers were in the country without passports and were relentlessly fondling cop cocks was spot-on. Of course there was not a word about the fact that the brothel and hotel were fronts for a secret military unit.

Vrye Weekblad had a minute circulation but Georgina assured me that other papers would pick up on the story and would further shame and humiliate the former cop. She was right. *Rapport* and the *Sunday Times* had a field day. They hounded Pietman to such an extent that he and his whole family had to go underground. One of the papers speculated that sections of the brothel were fitted with spy equipment to enable him to blackmail customers.

The week after the story was published Pietman announced the closure of the brothel through his lawyer. He said he was unaware of any shenanigans taking place in his club. It was too late; by then the Dutch Reformed Church had stripped him of his elder status and there were reports that his wife had taken their children and gone back to her mother.

Chappies later told me that Pietman stomped around like a wounded bull when the story hit the streets. He was convinced that one of the hookers was responsible for his fall from grace. He threatened to kill Chappies for not exercising proper control over his sluts and for lack of security.

A team of Military Intelligence agents swooped on the Trennery Hotel and took control. Pietman and his family were evacuated to a military safe house and the rest of the operatives were told to go home and stay there until further notice. The local hookers were given a handful of cash and told to go fuck somewhere else while the foreigners were put on the first aeroplane back home. This was the beginning of the end for the CCB.

'How was that?' asked Georgina when she walked into my hospital room a few days later. I was propped up on a pile of pillows scouring the newspapers for the latest dirt on Pietman. She was again wearing a T-shirt, jeans and sandals but her hair was loose and freshly washed and it fluttered around her face. She smelled of flowers.

'Perfect,' I had to admit.

She pulled a half-jack of brandy from her handbag, unscrewed it and passed it to me. She pointed at the newspapers on my bed and said: 'You know what you call that?'

'What?'

'*'n Fokken poesklap!*'

I laughed so much that I thought the stitches in my chest would burst open. It's difficult to translate *poesklap* but it would be something like a 'cunt slap'. It's a word one would not use in polite company but it was part of Georgina's usual lingua franca.

We were still laughing and joking and emptying the half-jack when Sharné arrived. She was wearing a skimpy green dress and white high heels. She froze, stared at the woman sitting by my bed and then looked at me. Georgina got up, held out her hand and said: 'Hi, I'm Georgina.'

Sharné took it and said warily: 'And I'm Sharné.'

Georgina chuckled mischievously and said: '*O poes!* So are you the Sharné in Club Sharné?'

Sharné looked as though she had been given a *poesklap* herself, then she tittered and said: 'Uh, not really. It's just a coincidence.'

'*Moer* of a fucking coincidence,' said Georgina. She picked up her bag and winked at me. 'Behave yourself, *grootseun*. See you soon.'

A few seconds after she'd walked out, Sharné asked: 'And who on earth is that creepy-crawly?'

'A friend,' I said.

'And since when do you surround yourself with such nasty pieces of work?'

'She's just different.'

'Very different,' she said. 'Not your type.'

'Are you jealous?'

'Of her?' said Sharné as she kissed me. 'You must be joking, doll.'

I was discharged after two weeks in hospital. Sharné took one of my arms and Jakes the other, while Johnnie led the way and opened the car door for me. I was whisked away to Sharné's flat somewhere in the concrete ghetto of Hillbrow.

A short while later we were alone. I was lying on my back on her bed when she came and snuggled up next to me. She stroked the bandage wrapped around my chest and asked: 'Is it still sore?'

'Not when you touch it.'

'Shall I kiss it better?'

Without waiting for an answer, she kissed my neck. I put my arm around her and pulled her against me. Her mouth moved down my torso, leaving a shiny trace in its delicious wake. She teasingly stopped at my bellybutton, circled it with her tongue and continued her heavenly downward journey.

'You're going to be the cause of my early death,' I mumbled.

By the time she had pulled my pyjama pants down, I was so hard that I thought my cock was going to burst out of its skin. It was as though my whole body was encased in her mouth and I was floating on a lukewarm, silky-soft ocean. I remained in her mouth even after I had gushed my lust into her.

That was the beginning of our journey together. For four years, Sharné consumed and absorbed my life. Then she spat me out and gave me up and buried me for ever.

The first few miles of this junket were exhilarating and delicious and fulfilling but by the time it ended, she had become a scrawny slut who existed in a chemical cloud. Her eyes had turned foggy, her once honey-tasting cunt was rancid and her head had turned to pulp. In between the beginning and the end of our journey were days of bliss and days of anguish and days of playing and days of fucking and days of whacking and days of robbing and days of knocking and days of coking and days of smacking and days of rocking and days I can remember sweet fuck all about.

We never discussed her child or its father who I'd blasted full of holes. She probably knew, or suspected, that I had killed him, but she never said a word. Try to understand that there was very little that was good or wholesome in this relationship. It was built on everything that was wrong and rotten. The sex, up to a point, was deliciously dirty and kinky but that was just about it. She once told me, after a chemical inhalation fest, that she hated men. Her father had abused her for many years. I don't know all the seedy details, but she said he forced her to wank him off, night after night, for many years. By the time she left school at sixteen, she had already had a backstreet abortion. She never excelled at schoolwork or sport, but she sucked and fucked for the first team.

'If you hate men,' I asked her, 'why do you love sex so much?'

'I dunno,' she said. 'Maybe because I do it so well.'

We were two lost souls from different sides of town who for a while found solace in each other. I was naive to think that this was everlasting love, that we would grow old together and cement our devotion with a team of offspring. By the time Charmaine was kicking like a locust in her womb, love had turned to hate, adoration to resentment and hope to despair. We had worn each other out, and the hyenas in blue were closing in on me.

Georgina du Toit was a stark contrast to Sharné, and in a bizarre way she became the other woman in my life.

Every time I saw the leftie journalist, my head spun like a yo-yo. I think Georgina knew I was bewitched by her and she, in turn, played me like a soccer ball. I never told anyone about my commie friend and only saw her about once a month. We always met at the Yard o'Ale, a restaurant at Johannesburg's Market Theatre that was frequented by frazzled-looking lefties. Half of them wore round little glasses and the other half didn't wash and none of them knew how to dress. I stood out like a sore thumb. Georgina spent a lot of time at the Yard and seemed to know everyone there.

We always sat at the same table in a corner where she ordered two double brandies and Coke. She usually finished hers before I did and would then order steak and chips for me and a vegetarian platter for herself.

'Don't you eat meat?' I asked her.

'Only boerewors,' she said, then burst out laughing. She

added: 'But I prefer my *wors* to be on the *boer*!'

One day, towards the end of 1989, I met Georgina at the Yard. She looked like shit. Her hair was an unwashed mess and she looked as though she hadn't slept for days.

'Didn't close a leg last night, hey?' I quipped.

'*Jou poes, man!*' she said. 'Let's have a double brandy and then I'll feel better.'

As she waited for our order to arrive, she leaned forward, fixed her green eyes on me and said: 'I want to ask you something but you first have to promise that you won't tell anyone.'

'I promise,' I said. 'What do you want to know?'

'Swear,' she said.

'I absolutely fucking swear,' I said.

'Have you ever heard the name Vlakplaas?'

I jerked upright, grabbed my glass and poured the cold liquid down my throat. That was the moment I should have got up, kissed Georgina on her cheek – as I always did – and walked away. Instead, I looked into her green eyes and was, once again, held captive by their gaze.

Of course I'd heard of Vlakplaas. There was a lot of talk about this place among the CCB operatives, especially when the *Tiertrane* had kicked in, the war stories came out and a probing whore hand was creeping up a thigh. I wasn't really interested in Vlakplaas but I overheard many discussions in which we were compared with them.

Vlakplaas was the police equivalent of the CCB and operated from a farm outside Pretoria. It was supposed to be top secret but both Chappies and Sousie van den Berg were frequent visitors to the place so the secret was no more. The Vlakplaas policemen sounded like a rough bunch and they could drink even the CCB under the table. Chappies told us that they had their own *Tiertrane* concoction and that he and Sousie once went there for a drinking competition. They lost hands down. Both of them passed out.

Sousie was sure that the CCB had the potential to be a better death squad than Vlakplaas but maintained that our biggest problem was the fact that Pietman Pretorius was inexperienced in this kind of covert warfare. In comparison, he said, Vlakplaas had a commander who led from the front and was like a mad fucking dog when it came to hunting down and taking out the enemy. He mentioned his name but I couldn't remember it. I did, however, recall his nickname: Prime Evil.

'This guy,' said Sousie, 'makes Pietman look like a silly fucking Sunday school teacher. He's a mean son of a bitch. Wears these thick glasses but I've never seen anyone shoot like him.'

Sousie told us that one night he was drinking, braaiing and playing pool on the farm when some *houtkop* policeman walked up to Mister Prime Evil and told him that he had lost his service pistol somewhere in a township.

'You would not fucking believe what happened!' he said, rubbing his hands together. 'You will not fucking believe it!'

'What?' we chorused.

'He didn't say a word,' said Sousie, 'but he turned around, took his snooker stick and whacked the goon over his head!'

'No ways!'

'Broke the stick in two,' said Sousie, 'and then all fucking hell broke loose!'

'Like what?'

'The guys fucked the bloke there and then.'

'How?'

'Kicked him, hit him, punched him, crushed his balls,' he said. 'Dead as a fucking bird!'

'And then?'

'Rolled him up in a carpet and took him away.'

'What did they do with him?'

'I'm not sure,' he said, 'but they usually blow up the corpses with dynamite to get rid of them.'

'No fucking way!'

'Oh yes,' he said, 'and then the black cops have to scrape the pieces of flesh together with their bare hands.'

'Jesus Christ,' I said. 'They don't take shit, hey?'

'You have no fucking idea,' said Sousie. 'They've made many

sousies out of many okes.'

I waited for the waitress to deliver my next glass of brandy and took a deep gulp. Georgina frowned at me. 'Why aren't you saying anything?'

I should have told her I knew nothing because it was none of my business. But somehow I wanted to please her, impress her, keep her coming to me. And so I said: 'Yeah, I've heard of Vlakplaas.'

'What have you heard?'

'I'm not supposed to say anything,' I said.

'Please tell me,' she said and put her hand on mine and kind of fucked me with her eyes. I melted.

'It's a farm outside Pretoria,' I said. 'They fuck up people like you.'

'And Eugene de Kock,' she said, caressing my hand with her fingers, 'have you ever heard of him?'

I was in the palm of her hand. I could feel myself getting a hard-on. I leaned forward to kiss her but stopped inches from her face. Her mouth was wet and slightly open and her tongue slid over her lips.

'They tune him Prime Evil,' I said. 'He's a mean son of a bitch.'

Her breath was warm and sweet and she moved her face even closer to mine. 'Tell me what you know.'

'I can't,' I said.

'Please, I beg you,' she said. 'Please tell me.'

And so I did; every little detail that Sousie and Chappies had conveyed to me in the strictest confidence. Her face lingered inches from mine as though she was gobbling up and swallowing every word I uttered. When I was finished, she asked me: 'And how do you know all of this?'

'Because the guys talk,' I said. 'And I'm a good listener.'

'Do you think Vlakplaas killed Professor Paul Williams?'

I tried to keep my face expressionless, realising I had already shot my mouth off. But my mouth seemed to have a life of its own.

'No,' I said. 'Vlakplaas didn't kill the professor.'

'How do you know they didn't kill Williams?'

'I can't tell you,' I said, 'but I know they didn't kill him.'

'Who then?'

'I can't tell you, but it wasn't Vlakplaas.'

She loosened her grip on my hand and leaned back in her chair like a leech that had sucked its prey dry and was marvelling at its handiwork. I knew she was like a ferocious predator who would attack again and again until she had sunk her fangs into my neck. And like a zebra foal on wobbly legs, I was too weak to withstand her attacks.

When she left that afternoon, she pressed her lips against mine. They were wet and soft and sweet and although our mouths touched for only a second or two, I could taste her for a long time afterwards.

'Ciao, *grootseun*,' she said. 'See you soon.'

A few weeks later, the Vlakplaas story broke on *Vrye Weekblad*'s front page under the headline 'Bloedspoor van die SAP' ('Bloody trail of the SAP'). It seemed that the death squad commander who had preceded Eugene de Kock had turned against his own and spilled the beans.

By then, I was infatuated with Georgina and she occupied my mind all the time. She was a far cry from the slutty little tarts with nippy little tops, shaved little slits, painted little toes and firm little asses that kneeled obediently in front of me and decorated my bed. She had an off-beat, earthy loveliness and I thought that maybe she didn't need a layer of base, a brush of mascara, a bottle of dye or a razor blade. I fantasised about her voluptuous body, her cherry-coloured lips and her ravenous green eyes. I wanted to peel her clothes from her body and push my face between her thighs and smell her and taste her. I'm sure she was one of those chicks who preferred to be on top and do the fucking instead of just spreading and waiting to get fucked. You know what I mean?

Eighteen

I now have to tell you about those four years before I skidded on my ass into The Bomb. Problem is that my recollection of some of the events has dissipated into the chemical cloud that surrounded me. When I was finally hauled in front of that red-robed cunt in the Pretoria High Court witness after witness told of how I'd boasted that I'd permanently removed the good professor from society. I stared blank-eyed at them because I couldn't remember who I had told what or whether I had told anything to anybody or nothing to nobody.

'Why did you tell everyone you killed Paul Williams?' my advocate wanted to know. By then my profession of innocence had been peeled away and I stood bare-assed before the judge. I was going down the drain.

'I can't remember anything,' I said.

'How come?'

'Because I was goofed out of my fucking skull,' I told him.

So don't ask me to tell you everything because in many cases I can't remember anything and I've already told you that it can be detrimental to your well-being to admit to events that didn't make it on to the charge sheet.

The reason for my memory loss can be attributed to the thousands of tiny snowy peaks in which I'd buried my nose and the yellowish crystals that I'd stuffed into a thin glass pipe, lit with a flame and sucked into my lungs. They ignited tiny explosions in my brain which left me perpetually in a fuzzy chemical cloud.

You know what I'm talking about: in both cases the stuff is jetted across oceans and continents in the arses of human mules or in the false bottoms of suitcases. Once here, pitch-black brudders who'd left their overpopulated and fucked-up kwantry in pursuit of udder opportunities take possession of the bounty. In their shiny pointy shoes, with their knob-like rings and gold chains, and blessed with soapy slippery mouths, they dilute it with baby powder or cook it with baking soda and sell it on street corners in tightly wrapped pieces of supermarket plastic.

If you're an avid patron, Ike or Mike or Spike will come to you, probably in a BM with an 'I love Jesus' sticker on the back. Chances are good that the plastic nuggets will be hidden in a Bible on the front seat. Otherwise you'd have to venture to Johannesburg's flatlands where you'll find these two-legged hyenas lurking in the shadows of their girl slaves, hoary, wasted eighteen-year-old wretches who are fucked out of their eyeballs and prowl the streets for gonorrhoeic dicks to stuff into their warty cavities in return for hits of head candy.

Whichever way, once home or back in your favourite joint, you'll lay the white powder out on a CD cover or a public toilet seat, chop up the crystals with a credit card, roll up a hundred rand note and propel it up your nose. Somewhere in the recesses of your brain, shit happens, very nice, delicious fucking shit. You can call the powder what you like: coke, schnaaf, Colombian caviar, party powder, blow, Bolivian bon-bon, nose candy, hoover, ajax, whatever. To snort cocaine is to make a statement. It's like having live oysters and bubbly for sundowners. The kind of people who get coked also exercise in the Virgin Active Gym, drive home in Mini Coopers and BMW X5s and watch National Geographic on DSTV.

The crystals, yellow and grimy, are called crack or rock and are far more potent than coke because you inhale all the chemicals at once and therefore jet off to cloud cuckoo land on the wings of a Concorde. Although crack is often the drug of choice of junkies and whores and gangsters, and has a reputation for delivering devotees to a bottomless bottom that ends in a calamitous calamity, it delivers a chemical orgasm a thousand times stronger than the purest coke.

Whenever I brought a flame to the thin glass pipe, the crystals snapped and popped and promised another chemical blast-off, igniting gunpowder in my body, hurtling my heart into overdrive and reducing my head to pulp. It didn't matter that the glass pipe scorched my fingers. I couldn't wait for the poison to invade my lungs and penetrate my mind and make me spin and rave. Drugs have never been foreign to me. In a place like Krugersdorp, dagga was as common and accessible as station whores, cheap brandy and pub brawls, and at some stage in their lives everyone was on *zol*. I first encountered it when I was fourteen or fifteen when Jakes and Johnnie shared a *skyf* with their *ouboeties* in the shed at the back of the station house. I'd never even smoked cigarettes so when I took a long draw and attempted to force the smoke down my throat, I barked and coughed like a terminal emphysema patient and didn't try it again. Johnnie swore that dagga contributed to his legendary boners but I cannot vouch for that. Years later, bank clerk Maryna brewed me dagga tea with honey but I didn't like it and never used it again.

I got a *moer* of a fright when I saw my brother Karel in rehab but he was on shit like morphine and pinks and heroin; stuff I never touched. Cocaine seemed civilised and harmless and crack was a natural progression from that.

Let me tell you how it started. A few weeks after I left the hospital, Sharné suggested we take a holiday, just the two of us. We packed the Alfa and headed south past Bloemfontein and then east towards the Wild Coast. The brown expanse of the Karoo surrounded us and the road stretched like a black python in front of us. Heat waves fluttered like phantoms on the hot black tar.

'I'm tired,' I said.

'Do you want me to pep you up, sweetie?' Sharné asked.

'How? Are you going to give me a blow job?'

'You had one just before Bloem,' she said. 'Stop and I'll give you something else.'

When Sharné took out the white lump of plastic and un-wrapped it, I knew exactly what it was. I wasn't shocked or surprised. When you'd just whacked your third victim, had stared death in the face and were shortly to embark on a spate of robberies, a gram of coke was no more significant than a lollipop. I had my first line under the blue sweep of a Karoo sky that spanned from one horizon to the other.

She cut four lines, pressed the note in her nose and snorted two of them. She passed me the *Huisgenoot* and the rolled-up note. Princess Diana was on the front cover of the magazine, her perfect features disfigured by the two white strips that cut through her unblemished English skin.

I inhaled the powder and for a moment my nose was an in-ferno. The back of my throat tingled with a bitter, scratchy sensation; the 'drip' that cocaine users so cherish. I'm not sure what happened next, but it was as though the coke jump-started my brain and threw my mouth into motion.

As we pulled away, I started babbling, God knows about what but my larynx was like a long-distance athlete on an overdose of steroids. It refused to stop or get tired. We each had two more lines before we sped into Coffee Bay and booked into a hotel.

When we got to our room, I ripped Sharné's clothes from her body and flung her down on the bed. All I wanted to do was fuck. I wanted to fuck her, the television set standing in the corner of the room, the chairs and tables on the veranda, the rocks guarding the bay, the fishermen on the beach and the oil tanker on the horizon. That's how horny I was.

When I had her open, wet and panting, I looked down at myself. I was as soft as a baby. I pulled and wanked and she pulled and wanked. I had the dirtiest thoughts possible and she told me the dirtiest things I'd ever heard. There was still no movement. Not a stir. Nothing.

I was momentarily concerned that my earlier impotence had returned but Sharné assured me that cocaine was notorious for having this effect on some people, despite making them horny as hell. She had brought five grams of coke so it goes without saying that for the first few days of our holiday, we failed to engage in any significant amount of baby-making. My bodily functions returned to normal once our stash was depleted.

'How long have you been doing this shit?' I asked her.

'For some time,' she said. 'It helps me with the job.'

From then on we were cokeheads and I was frequently zoomed off my head. I didn't mind walking around with clenched jaws and a bitter drip because my mind was razor-sharp and my body surged with energy. The crack came later.

Sharné moved in with me and I found a job as security manager of a brothel in the posh suburb of Rosebank. Remember the slippery Lebanese brothel boss who bought information from Chappies and me? Well, he owed me big time for eliminating his competition and for keeping him a step ahead of the police investigation into his operations.

Club Jezebel had one of the best addresses in Johannesburg: Oxford Road in Rosebank. From the outside, it was just another double-storey mansion with high walls and state-of-the-art security. I don't think the neighbours ever knew what it was.

The place had Middle Eastern furnishings – Persian carpets, brass lanterns, hubbly-bubbly tobacco pipes, and burgundy satin sheets were draped across the ceilings to create a harem ambience. The chicks were something else. Not your average streetwalker or sleazy slut. Believe me, these tarts were prime meat. Each and every one was a beauty with a body that had been chiselled in the Ferrari factory. The Lebanese – his name was Alex – wanted his brothel bitches to be well groomed and well dressed. Not that they were always well behaved, though. After all, they were whores and there's not that much difference between a cheap dick and an expensive dick.

Club Jezebel wasn't the kind of joint where you could pop in for a drink and a hit-and-run. It was by appointment only and most of the clients were regulars. They wanted their meat fresh, tight and young. That meant that the hookers had to keep themselves in shape because the moment their tits began to sag or dimples appeared on their thighs, they were no longer popular.

Two of Alex's regulars were top police officers and they got special on-the-house treatment every time they walked through the door. The girls were told to shower them with adoration and to provide whatever service they required.

The reason for Alex's closeness to the cops was plain and simple: he was a criminal. And he wasn't just a small time thug like Jakes, Johnnie and me, but a gangster of formidable proportions. Chappies told me that prostitution was merely one of his illicit activities and that he had tentacles in gun running, drugs and money laundering. Some of these enterprises were based overseas and he spent a lot of time travelling.

Alex never made me a partner in any of his ventures but working for him had several advantages. The first, of course, was being surrounded by a bevy of beauties for whom boning was as everyday as brushing their teeth.

The second was that, as security manger, I was in charge of a small arsenal of guns that were locked away in a safe behind the bar. There were two pump-action shotguns, an Uzi machine gun and two nine-mills – all legal and licensed courtesy of one the brothel's police friends. I had a key to the gun safe and the hardware it contained came in handy when you were about to embark on a hold-up.

The third advantage was that cocaine was, after condoms, probably the most used commodity in Club Jezebel. It seemed to be everywhere and Alex, a coker himself, sold it cheaply in the brothel and didn't mind the girls dipping their noses into candy. It kept them skinny and made them work harder, faster and better. When I later became a ghetto scientist and manufactured my own crack, Alex sold me almost pure coke at cost.

I did only one job for the Lebanese. One of his high-up police buddies had decided to quit the force. Nelson Mandela had been released from prison, the ANC had been unbanned and the guy was convinced that his days in the force were numbered. But he needed to boost his career to ensure a last-minute promotion so that he could secure a better pension.

The guy was a security cop and he was convinced that an attempt on his life would do the trick. Alex called me into his office. He was a spindly little man with a bald head. Sharné, who worked as receptionist at the brothel, said he reminded her of a grasshopper. He was sitting behind an enormous oak desk that dwarfed him even further.

'Want to earn some bucks, Goosen?' he wanted to know.

'Sure, Mister Sarkis,' I said. 'What can I do for you?'

'I want you to do a favour for Brigadier Coetzee.'

'I'll do whatever I can to help.'

Two days later, at five o'clock in the morning, I slipped on to the brigadier's property in Florida, west of Johannesburg. In my hand was a black bag containing a limpet mine with a timing device. The brigadier himself had set the clock for ten past seven. His official car was parked in the driveway. I attached the mine underneath the car and left. It was as easy as pie.

That same afternoon, *The Star* carried a front-page picture of the devastation caused by the mine. All that remained of the brigadier's car was a crumpled piece of metal. There was a crater the size of a small swimming pool in his driveway and the garage door had been ripped off its hinges.

The brigadier said he had no doubt that this was the work of the armed wing of the PAC, and if it weren't for the fact that he had been delayed by a phone call, he would have left for work at seven as usual, and would have been blown up in the morning traffic. He said the PAC wanted him dead because he was investigating their armed activities, which had shown no signs of abating since their unbanning.

The brigadier was sure to get his promotion and I bagged a cool thirty thousand for planting the limpet. The money, said Jakes over a brandy and Coke in my flat that night, was exactly what we needed to pull our first knock – that and the guns in Club Jezebel's safe, of course. Johnnie agreed that it might be just the break we needed.

Jakes had never managed to get his diamond dealing enterprise in Angola off the ground and after South West became independent his contact had left the country. Jakes was spending a lot of time in the diamond fields of the Western Transvaal and had managed to bag a few small stones, but not nearly enough to provide him with the lifestyle he was aspiring to. It was time, said Jakes, to turn from smuggling to knocking.

The Verster family lived in a small house in Mayfair. Problem was that Sharon had rather expensive tastes. She had had a boob job a few years earlier. Her knockers were now so big that she developed back pain. She wanted to have a reduction and also wanted Jakes to sponsor a hip and tummy tuck at the same time. She was too thick to hold down a job and contribute to the family income.

Jakes' predicament was aggravated by an additional complication: he'd got another chick pregnant and she was demanding compensation to keep her mouth shut.

'How much does the bitch want?' I asked him.

'I need fifteen grand very soon,' said Jakes. 'Otherwise she'll split on me. Sharon will cut my balls off.'

After our getaway from Club Sharné, Johnnie had also fallen on hard times. His murder conviction meant he was pretty much unemployable, although from time to time he freelanced as a driver at Club Jezebel. I've explained that a knock was nothing but a robbery. In this particular case Jakes was planning to set up a group of illicit diamond dealers in some dusty dump in the Western Transvaal. They didn't have a prospecting licence and had a couple of uncut stones they wanted to sell. Jakes had told them that he was interested and so he needed enough money to buy at least one stone.

'Just to stir their greed and establish their trust in us,' he said. 'Then they'll bring out the big ones.'

'And then?' I wanted to know.

'Then we take them,' he said.

'As long as we don't have to shoot them,' said Johnnie.

'Will they be armed?' I asked.

'I'm sure they'll have a gun,' said Jakes, 'but ours are bigger and faster.'

'What if we get shot?'

'Then at least we die with our boots on,' said Johnnie.

'In a hail of fucking bullets,' said Jakes.

'I've always wanted to die in action,' said Johnnie.

'I don't want to fucking die at all,' I said.

I cut up a tiny heap of coke into six thin lines, rolled up a note and passed it to Jakes. The two of them had taken to nose candy as eagerly as I had. Only difference was that it had absolutely no effect on their sexual prowess.

'How much will we make?' I asked. Jakes knew a diamond dealer in Jo'burg who was willing to buy the uncut stones.

'Four hundred thousand,' said Jakes. 'Maybe even more.'

Problem was that we had to share our booty with a coloured diamond smuggler by the name of Charlie. He was a dirty sleaze-ball but he had approached Jakes with the low-down on the diggers. As a result, he wanted a twenty-five per cent cut for setting them up. He had been part of their smuggling operation and had convinced them that Jakes was reliable.

Jakes and Charlie drove to the Western Transvaal the next morning and came back that same night with a tiny, dull-looking stone not much bigger than a match head.

'You must be joking,' I said when I held it in the air. 'You want to tell me this is worth twenty thousand?'

'Even more,' said Jakes. 'Wait till you see the others.'

Two days later, as the sun rose over the eastern horizon, we got into the Lebanese's black BMW that Johnnie used to drive the hookers to their clients and headed west towards the dusty outpost of Wolmaransstad. We were armed with my sawn-off shotgun, the Uzi and two nine-mills.

It was a hellishly hot summer morning. The roadsides had been transformed into gardens of purple, pink and white cosmos flowers and fields of yellow sunflowers quivered in the slight breeze. I was sitting in the front seat with Johnnie who was driving, while Jakes and scumbag Charlie parked in the back. We passed around a bottle of tequila.

I knew nothing about Wolmaransstad, other than that it had long ago ceased to be the hub of the maize farming community it had once been. The discovery of diamonds had turned struggling farmers into instant millionaires and excavators had replaced tractors. The place wasn't much more than a main street lined with houses and shops, a hotel, grain silos that towered in the distance, a formidable Dutch Reformed Church that basked in the morning sun, and a statue of some Boer general on his horse.

'Looks like the fucking Wild West out here,' I said as we stopped in front of a bar by the name of Rugga Buggers. It had just opened its doors. It was one of those places where fading rugby jerseys and nylon G-strings flutter over the heads of bar-flies and where the smells of booze, vomit, piss and blood per-meate the air. It was just past nine but several regulars were already oiling their dusty throats. Can't say I blamed them; if I had to live in a dump like that I'd be perpetually pissed.

A hush descended over Rugga Buggers as we swaggered into the joint. The patrons, caressing their glasses of Klippies and Coke with rough hands that had sifted through many tonnes of gravel, looked warily at us. Our black leather jackets and poodle cuts were a dead giveaway; we were clearly out-of-town ruffians on some shady mission. Charlie was a coloured and in a place like Wolmaransstad a *hotnot* was not welcome.

'Four double brandies and Coke,' said Jakes to the barman, a burly, paunchy fellow wearing a tight-fitting Springbok rugby jersey. He had a shaved head and an enormous pair of cauliflower ears. He had clearly been a rugby player who had gone down in far too many scrums.

'I'm sorry but we don't serve people like him,' the barman said pointing his forefinger at Charlie. It was a few months after the unbanning of the ANC and in places like Wolmaransstad people remained convinced that the country was going the same way as the rest of Africa and that black hordes were going to invade their farms. I can't say I disagreed with them, but I just didn't care.

'Go wait in the car,' Jakes ordered Charlie and said to the barman: '*Bra*, I absolutely agree with you. Get yourself a dop as well.'

Shortly before ten we booked into two interleading rooms in the local hotel under false names. We cut a snowy peak into eight lines, propelled it through a crisp note into our lungs, and checked our guns. Johnnie and I were in one room, Jakes and Charlie in the other. Jakes assured us his plan was foolproof.

It turned out that it was. When the three diggers knocked on their door, Charlie alerted us by phone. Exactly two minutes later, Johnnie and I stormed into the room with balaclavas over our heads. He had the shotgun in his hands; I had the Uzi on my hip. Jakes pulled the pistol from under a pillow and pushed it against the head of one of the diggers. They were fucked.

Minutes later, the three diggers were lying tied up in the bathroom. One pleaded with Jakes to leave a stone or two behind because his family's survival depended on it but all he got for his trouble was a barrel in his ear and a smelly sock in his mouth.

We walked nonchalantly out of the hotel with a suitcase containing the guns and the metal box with the diamonds. We stopped briefly just outside Wolmaransstad to pep up our noses and open the metal box with a set of keys we had found on one of the diggers. Jakes' face lit up when he opened the box. He lifted out a stone the size of a fingernail and said: 'Fucking beautiful. Six, seven carats.'

The selling of the diamonds bagged just over three hundred thousand, much less than Jakes had expected. I thought it wasn't bad for a few hours' work but problem was that sleaze-ball Charlie demanded seventy-five thousand for his contribution to the knock. Jakes gave him fifteen thousand and told him to fuck off.

It was a serious mistake. Two days later, I was woken by a phone call. Sharon was on the other side, weeping hysterically. She was almost incoherent but between her sobs I managed to find out that the cops had picked up Jakes.

I rushed to their Mayfair home and found her waiting for me at the front door. Little Jakes, wide-eyed, was behind her. Her bottle-blonde mane was a mess and she was wearing only a skimpy dressing gown, probably with nothing underneath. She threw herself into my arms and for a few seconds I pressed her voluptuous frame against mine and stroked her back.

It appeared that an hour earlier a squad of cops had descended on their house, just about broken down the front door and burst in. Jakes tried to make a dash for the back door but ran into the arms of more policemen. The cops then raided the house.

'Did they find the money?' I asked.

'No,' she said and took me to the bathroom. She removed a wooden panel at the side of the bath. The money was hidden in plastic bags under the bath. I phoned Alex Sarkis.

'Sir,' I said. 'I need a lawyer who knows how to handle the cops. My friend is in shit.'

Charlie had ratted on Jakes. I still don't know if he was a police informant to begin with or whether he went to the cops and cut a deal with them. Long and short of it was that Jakes was in mega shit and the next morning he was taken to the Wolmaransstad magistrate's court and charged with robbery.

Jakes had never told Charlie who Johnnie and I were and he didn't know where we lived. However he'd seen our faces and could bring us down with Jakes. There was another problem: if the cops wired Jakes' balls or pulled a tube over his face, he might just tell them who his accomplices were.

'There's only one solution,' I said to Johnnie over a brandy and a line.

'And that is?'

'Charlie has to fucking die.'

He looked at me for a long time, shook his head and said: 'You sure of that?'

'Absolutely,' I said. 'He's a ratter.'

'And the diggers?' asked Johnnie. 'What do we do with them?'

The three diggers had been roped in by the cops and were queuing up to testify against Jakes. There were therefore four state witnesses against him. On the face of it, he was facing time. A long fucking time.

'We have to whack Charlie in such a way that it sends a message,' I said.

'Like what kind of message?'

'That if they give evidence against Jakes,' I said, 'they're going to die as well.'

'And if they don't listen?'

'Then we kill them all.'

'Jesus Christ,' said Johnnie, 'this is going to be a lovely little bloodbath.'

It took us three nights to hunt Charlie down. Elaborate witness protection programmes were not yet in place so the cops had probably just warned him to stay away from his usual drinking holes and whoring dumps. But with a pocket full of money, he simply couldn't resist the underbelly of the city's concrete ghettos and we spotted him in a smoky pool bar with a sad-assed, empty-eyed whore.

We sneaked into the bar, skulked at the back for an hour or two and watched Charlie lose a small fortune on a table before he walked out of the joint with the whore. When they got outside, he flung his arm around her waist and pressed her against him. As they shuffled past a strip of nightclubs, bars and brothels, streaks of red, blue and yellow danced over their bodies. When a dark patch gobbled them up, we were right behind them; the nine-mill was in my hand.

I pushed it into Charlie's ribs, put my arm around his neck and hissed in his ear: 'Do as I say or you'll die like a fucking fly!'

In the meantime, Johnnie got hold of the whore and told her: 'And you, love doll, you just fucking walk straight on.'

She glanced over her shoulder, nodded her head and did just that. With the pistol concealed in the pocket of my leather jacket, we escorted Charlie to the BM that was parked in a quiet spot less than a block away. We ordered him on to the back seat. I pressed the pistol against his heart while Johnnie tied his hands. He whimpered and begged while silver teardrops glistened in the corners of his eyes.

'Stop being a fucking cry baby!' I said and pushed the barrel even harder against his chest.

'I swear,' he murmured, 'that I won't say a word. Please. I won't say anything.'

Those were the last words he spoke before Johnnie shoved a cloth into his mouth. We drove through Hillbrow in silence. I thought about the Greek who, a year or two earlier, lay in my boot while Spyker and I drove through the city centre towards the worked-out mine dumps. I was in a sombre mood that night, and I could feel it descending on me again.

For a moment I felt sorry for Charlie. He was a miserable fuck who had probably grown up in one of those tumbledown coloured slums where he was sodomised by his father and ignored by his mother. His face was covered in scars, his lips were cracked and his eyes were dull. He had probably never had a chance in life, and he was about to meet his Maker in a sordid and excruciating manner.

'Stop here,' said Johnnie.

'Why?'

'I need a line,' he said.

'Make it a fat one,' I said.

The coke took care of my anxiety, kind of deadened any feelings of compassion for Charlie, and ignited a tingle in my fingers.

'Okay,' I said to Johnnie. 'Let's get rid of the fuck.'

Charlie moaned and moments after I'd pulled away, Johnnie exclaimed at the top of his voice: 'The cunt is pissing in his pants!'

I could smell it. In the Lebanese's limousine! On the very

leather seats that had been so lovingly polished by a miscellany of shaved, moist, perky little cunts! Whatever chance Charlie had of redemption, he'd just pissed on it!

I stopped the car, got out and opened the back door. We were in a dark deserted back street, far away from where the Brow's action was pumping away in its seedy bowels. It was, I thought, the perfect place for murder. I pulled Charlie out of the car, pushed the nine-mill in his back and jerked him towards an alley-way. I heard Johnnie opening the boot of the car. He was taking out the murder weapon.

A few metres into the alley, we stopped. It was almost dead quiet except for Johnnie's footsteps behind us and the squalling love song of a cat a block or so away. I swung Charlie around. As I did so, Johnnie pounced on him. In his hands was Little Jakes' baseball bat that we had fetched earlier that afternoon. The bat whooshed through the air and thudded down on Charlie. Crash, splinter, crack! Johnnie had missed his head and was pulverising his shoulder instead. Can you fucking believe it? Missing a target as big as a head!

I grabbed the bat from him and swung it as hard as I could. It came down right on top of Charlie's head. Thump! And again, crack! I remember those two sounds to this day. I felt a speck of something wet exploding against my cheek. It must have been his blood. I wiped it off. Charlie tumbled to the ground. It was dark in the alley so I clobbered him two or three more times just to make absolutely sure. I have to say I prefer to shoot someone because this was a messy affair.

Remember the scene in the movie 'The Untouchables' where Robert de Niro, who played Al Capone, leapt up at a meeting of the bosses and bashed one of his rivals to pieces with a baseball bat? Blood and brains everywhere? Well, that's more or less what happens when you bang someone hard enough with a bat. When I was growing up, we had a pomegranate tree in our yard. My brother Karel and I pretended that the fruit was the head of a terrorist or a *houtkop* and thrashed it to pieces with a cricket bat. I never thought then that one day I really would pulverise a head.

'Do you think he's dead?' asked Johnnie.

'As dead as anyone can fucking be,' I said and told him we should get out fast. Johnnie knelt down to try to feel for Charlie's pulse but I pulled him away and we drove off.

The whacking of Charlie is one of the reasons why I'm in The Bomb. I don't think it's right. He was a useless son of a bitch and a good for nothing gangster. Anyway, that crack-headed bimbo that he dragged with him out of the joint identified me in a line-up. I don't know to this day how they found her but I would cheerfully have whacked the bitch as well. By then, however, I was locked up and she was somewhere in witness protection. I was fucked.

An hour or two after we whacked Charlie I called one of the diggers from Jakes' home. By then we'd cleaned the baseball bat, burnt our clothes and washed any traces of murder from our faces and bodies. The phone rang for about a minute before a male voice crackled on the other side. It was one of the diggers.

'I'm Jakes' friend,' I said. 'I took your diamonds.'

He didn't answer. I continued: 'Jakes is in shit. And now I hear you want to fuck him even further.'

Still silence. 'I want you to think about this very carefully.'

'Why?' croaked the voice.

'Because if you don't keep your fucking mouth shut,' I continued, 'you'll join Charlie.'

'Where?'

'He's fucked,' I said. 'He's just died.'

There was no response.

I said: 'I want you to listen very carefully.'

'Yes?' said the voice.

'If you say a thing,' I said, 'you're dead.'

'Yes?'

'If you keep your mouth shut, you'll not only live,' I continued. 'You'll even get some of your money back.'

'Like how much?'

'A hundred thousand,' I said. 'I'll give you a hundred thousand.'

Johnnie just about choked on his rum while Sharon flapped her hands in the air. Jesus Christ, cookie, I thought, I'm trying to save your hubby's fucking ass!

'When will I get it?' asked the digger.

'I'll leave Johannesburg now,' I said. 'You'll have it before tomorrow morning.'

'Are you fucking mad?' Johnnie said when I put the phone down. 'Why are you giving our money away?'

'Think about it, dickhead,' I responded. 'We've shut Charlie up, the diggers are happy, Jakes is going to be okay and we've got almost two hundred thousand left.'

'It's enough for my tummy tuck,' squeaked Sharon and smiled sweetly at me, 'and maybe a new lounge suite.'

'Makes sense,' said Johnnie. 'A lot of sense.'

'Don't any of you know anything about diplomacy?' I asked.

We arrived in Wolmaransstad as high as kites and babbling at the same time. I phoned the diggers from a tickey-box at the twenty-four-hour garage. They were obviously shit scared to meet us and told me to leave the money at the Dutch Reformed Church.

'You must be joking,' I said.

'In front of the big doors is a red chest labelled Prayer Box,' I was told. 'Put it in there and leave.'

When I told Johnnie what we had to do with the money, he looked at me and said: 'You must be fucking joking!'

'Come on, Johnnie,' I said, 'time for you to go to church.'

'Let's wait for them and kill them.'

I laughed, untied the piece of plastic and sprinkled a tiny heap of coke on to a CD cover. For the next few seconds, the only sound was the chop-chop of my bank card. A few minutes later, we stuffed the money into the prayer box until it was full. The rest we left in a plastic bag on the steps.

So that is the story of our first little knock and our first little murder. It wasn't altogether a great robbery because I had to whack an accomplice, Jakes was parked in the slammer for more than a month and we lost half our loot. Important thing is that we pulled it off; we somehow pulled it off.

A quarter of the money was spent paying the lawyer to get Jakes out on bail. I'm not even going to try to tell you about the debauched bash we had when he strolled out of prison, except to say that Sharon and Sharné were not present and that we spent most of the evening competing with one another to determine who could make the longest line on a girl's tit.

At Jakes' next court appearance, the state prosecutor informed the magistrate that the case against the accused would have to be dropped due to a lack of evidence. Jakes was standing in the dock with an angelic expression on his face.

'I thought we had four witnesses against the accused,' growled the magistrate.

'We did, your honour,' said the prosecutor, 'but unfortunately the most important witness passed away.'

'And the others?'

'They can no longer place the accused on the scene, your honour.'

'And why not?'

'It's a case of loss of memory and mistaken identity, your honour.'

'Oh rubbish,' barked the robed cunt, his eyes boring into Jakes. 'Well, I have no option but to order that the charges against you be withdrawn.'

A month after Jakes' release, we pulled our next diamond knock, this time in a place called Taung in the Northern Cape. It went as smooth as cream and we bagged almost half a million. That was followed by a lovely little stick-up in Kimberley. As easy as pie. More than half a million. Dewetsdorp in the Karoo. A couple of hundred thousand. Klerksdorp. Only a quarter of a million. No need to worry. Makwassie in the Western Transvaal. Six hundred thousand. All of this without a single shot being fired. This exemplary record was broken in a heist in Pretoria when one of the poor fucks, clutching the bag of diamonds, tried to make a getaway. Johnnie shot a hole in the ceiling with the shotgun and stopped him dead in his tracks. Another eight hundred thousand.

There was so much money that the hole behind the bath in Jakes' house was getting full. I hid several bags behind the geyser in my flat while Johnnie buried them in his back garden.

I arrived at a BMW dealer with a suitcase full of money, pointed at a black 325i and started counting the notes. Jakes bought himself a Honda Blackbird and a dainty MG for Sharon. She also got her tuck and reduction. Johnnie got himself a Ford Mustang and persuaded one of the hookers at Club Jezebel to give up her profession and move in with him.

Candice was a petite brunette with big brown eyes and an enormous set of knockers. She was known at the brothel as 'Miss Dominatrix' and most clients booked her when they craved some perverted shit. She once clobbered the police brigadier so hard that he had to seek medical attention. Johnnie said she was doing things to him that he never knew existed and for the first few months he walked around with a permanent smirk on his face. Only problem was that he had to pay Candice what she would have earned at the brothel.

Sharné had in the meantime become Sharon's New Best Friend and demanded that she be allowed to spend her share. I got her a nifty little Lancia and then she decided that she also wanted a boob job. Her tits were a lovely handful and I told her I wasn't paying for it. So she simply dipped into one of the bags and Sharon escorted her to the plastic surgeon. When she came out, I couldn't help thinking that the two of them looked like twins. With her brand new D-cups, she announced that she wanted to strip again. Just for recreation, she said. I shrugged my shoulders and cut another line. By that time I was walking around with a perpetual sniff and dipped my nose in candy the moment I opened my eyes in the morning. It wasn't doing my love life any good.

We spent a fortune on cocaine but there were no worries that the money would run out. We simply did more knocks. Another in Pretoria, one more in the Western Transvaal and a stick-up in Lesotho. We're talking hundreds and hundreds of thousands. It would have been enough for other people to retire on. Not us. Our gold chains got heavier and the broads had every plastic job they fancied. Sharon had her bum trimmed and Sharné had a nose job. We bought three chic townhouses next to one another in Sandton.

Johnnie married his Candice in a white suit in the magistrate's court and then the rented Rolls proceeded to the Sandton Sun for a lavish reception. Everything was white and pink, from the champagne to the smoked salmon to the strawberry mousse to the wedding cake. His best men – Jakes, Gielie and me – wore white suits with pink ties.

In the meantime Gielie had made a bid for the world heavy-weight title but some black Yankee Popeye clobbered him into oblivion in the third round. His boxing licence was under review. As a result he wasn't working out and was rapidly putting on weight. Some nasty newspaper rechristened him – from Cry Baby to Bye Baby – and his boxing future looked bleak.

The newly-weds went on some silly cruise on a ship called *The Melody* but were back after five days. Johnnie was seasick (actually he ran out of cocaine) and they abandoned the vessel at the first port.

I don't remember everything that was happening around me at the time, but gangster life was intoxicating and irresistible. It's difficult to describe the feeling. It's that jungle culture, the lion syndrome, the Tarzan tag; the invincibility, the lure of living on the edge; having not just one woman but a whole brothel on your tail; the shooting irons, the fast cars and the endless supply of cocaine.

Jakes, Johnnie and I were closer than family because we shared battle scars, defied fate, and escaped justice.

The nooks and crannies of my townhouse were overflowing with money. Other people dig up their gardens to plant ferns and lilies; I did it to bury another bag of money.

And drugs? Well, I knew I was taking too much but then I was always in control, wasn't I? Who says crime doesn't pay, drugs and booze are bad, or the wrong friends land you in shit?

Nineteen

Her mouth was red and enticing and her green eyes seemed to draw me into her soul. It was the first time I'd seen her in a dress. I couldn't help but notice her round, well-toned calves and sturdy yet elegant ankles.

'You look pretty,' I said. 'You should wear a dress more often.'

'I'll wear my mini next time,' she said. *'En dan sal ek mooi sit vir jou.'*

We laughed and she leaned forward, put her hand on mine and kissed me on the cheek. Then she sat back, looked at me and said: 'And so, what do you think about everything that's happening in the country?'

Although I was in a perpetual chemical haze, I remember the time well. It was the early nineties and shit was splattering in every direction. The ANC was fucking up the government and the government was fucking up the ANC and somewhere between them were Inkatha's impis with spears and guns, PAC dudes attacking whites in churches and bars, and white scum with swastikas and hunting rifles. And then, lurking under all the shit, there was a sinister group that became known as the Third Force. These guys were members of the good old apartheid forces who refused to hand over power to the communists and were engaged in secret, underground operations directed against the ANC. It was a confusing situation. There was Colonel Prime Evil's police shooting party at Vlakplaas, a death squad in Military Intelligence, and the CCB. Pietman's circus was disbanded after Georgina blasted him in her rag, but as far as I could gather other CCB units were still roaming the land and causing major shit.

I know all this because my good friend Chappies was one of those covert military operatives and I have to tell you that if it hadn't been for Pietman burning my ass, I would have been right in there with them. I didn't see Chappies too often because he was far too busy delivering AKs and hand grenades to Zulu hostels around Johannesburg.

But when we did sit down for a rum and Coke, he was as forthcoming as always with classified information. He boasted that he personally ferried weapons to Inkatha leaders and that their impis used his hardware to attack ANC strongholds around Johannesburg. Women and children were killed in these assaults, but Chappies merely remarked that this was a tragic reality of warfare.

In turn, I passed all this information on to Georgina in order to keep her interested in me. Week after week, her commie newspaper screamed 'foul' on its front page with yet another revelation about the Third Force. Poor F W de Klerk had so much shit coming down on him that he had no option but to appoint a commission of clever people to investigate both the police and the military.

Then an incredible thing happened. In a dog-eat-dog scenario, the police hit back and some star-studded general called a press conference and said that it was unfair to blame the police for every hit or massacre when in fact it was another organisation that was responsible for the mayhem: the CCB. He mentioned Pietman Pretorius by name and said that the police had good reason to believe that CCB thugs were responsible for the assassination of Professor Paul Williams, among other murders.

The exposure of the CCB hit the country like a nuclear bomb. Pietman had hardly recovered from his previous ordeal when a pack of journalists descended on his smallholding outside Pretoria, demanding to know who had pulled the trigger of the gun that wiped the good professor from the face of the earth. He kicked them off his property but later huffed and puffed his way through a radio interview saying that the CCB didn't target innocent civilians and therefore Williams was never a CCB project. He added that rogue elements within the organisation could have nailed him, but he had no idea who it might have been. He no longer worked for the organisation and his unit had been dissolved.

I had heart palpitations when I saw the reports. Jakes ran in one direction to cut me a line and Johnnie scrambled in the other direction to fix me a crack hit. I sucked so hard on the pipe that a hazy chemical cloud ballooned around my head and invaded the room. My brain cells jumped and jolted and jiggled and jived because I knew then that, come hell or high water, the truth was going to come out.

Georgina called minutes later and said she wanted to see me. She was calling from a telephone booth in Rosebank because she was afraid that the cops might be tapping the newspaper's phones. Jakes and I were about to leave for Bloemhof in the Western Transvaal to set up a family of farmer-diggers for an enormous knock but I immediately postponed that. Whenever Georgina wanted me, I jumped. I would have done anything to see her.

We agreed to meet at a coffee shop in the Rosebank Mall. When I swaggered in, she was already there, waiting for me with a smile that revealed her even white teeth. Her green dress was the same colour as her eyes and her hair fluttered loosely over her shoulders.

'And so, Gideon,' she said, 'you were a member of the CCB?'

I couldn't deny it because it was rather obvious. I'd given her the low-down on Pietman and she knew that I had worked for him. And now that he'd been named as commander of the CCB I was at her mercy.

'And so?' I asked. 'Are you going to blast me in your leftie rag?'

'Of course not,' she said with a frown. 'Do you think I'm a fucking *poes*?'

'So now what?' I asked her.

'Tell me what you know and I'll protect you with my life.'

For the next hour, I recounted most of what I knew about the CCB. I told her about Baksteen's operation in South West when they whacked the white Swapo leader and plotted to throw snakes into crowds and cholera germs into the drinking water. And remember the ape foetus that was found at the archbishop's home in Cape Town? That was the CCB. And then there was a guy called Sousie who pulverised the arm of some white ANC guy in Maputo and blew off the hands of a priest in Harare.

'And your *takhaar* editor,' I said, 'was also on a hit list.'

'No ways!' she howled. 'You should have shot the *poes*!'

I told her that his file had been given to me to assess for a possible hit. I don't know why I told her because I was implicating myself in the unit's operations and that was a sure way to get my ass in the slammer. Maybe I wanted her to know that I had been in the thick of things and wanted to be sure that she would come back for more.

'Do you know who shot Paul Williams?'

'I know nothing about that guy,' I said. 'Absolutely zero.'

'*Jissus!*' she said. 'Don't be a *poes*!'

Georgina moved her hand slowly towards mine and for a moment we touched. Her skin was cool. She was the ultimate cock-teaser, I thought. Just a hint of her skin, just a whiff of her smell, just a promise of her touch.

'I've never heard of the poor fuck,' I said swallowing my

brandy. I needed another pipe very fucking soon. But I was incapacitated because her fingers were sliding over mine and not even the lure of a hit of crack would make me move.

'Come on,' she said, 'you know you can trust me.'

By then her hand was covering mine. I could feel the words of a confession creeping up my throat and hovering at the back of my mouth. Should I or shouldn't I? I closed my eyes for a moment, swallowed hard and then jumped up.

'I have to go and fetch something from my car,' I said. 'I'll be back soon.'

I ripped a tobacco bag out of the cubbyhole. Inside was a thin glass pipe with a piece of steel wool at one end. I untied a plastic parcel, took out a dirty yellow rock and dropped it into the pipe. I brought a white flame to its tip. The sound was like music to my ears. Snap! Crackle! Pop! The crystal was dissolving into liquid and producing a vapour that lingered like cool mint in my lungs making my mind swim and spin and float and flow. By the time I got back to the table, I felt simultaneously calm and crazy.

'How come,' she continued where she had left off, 'you know everything about the CCB but not a thing about Paul Williams?'

'Maybe they didn't kill him,' I said. 'It could have been Vlakplaas.'

'*Ag poes, man*,' she said. 'We know who Vlakplaas killed. Williams wasn't on their list.'

'I really don't know,' I said.

'Did you shoot him?'

I gazed into her green eyes and for a moment it felt as though they were burning a hole through my facade and delving into my innermost secrets. It seemed futile to try to keep anything from her.

'Of course not,' I mumbled.

'One day you're going to tell your Georgina everything,' she said as she took my hand and folded it in hers. 'You know you can trust me.'

As Georgina's Bohemian allure enveloped my mind, I became

less and less enchanted with Sharné's trashy persona. She woke up after lunch, dived into nose candy and stomped around in a tracksuit until it was time to go to Club Jezebel where she was still the receptionist and an occasional stripper. She would wriggle her skinny frame into a skimpy little dress and go off for the night.

She came home in the early hours of the morning and sometimes she reeked of brothel: scented oil rubbed on her body, perfume, sweat and booze. I was sure she was bonking other men. In fact, that's what she told Sharon who told Jakes who told me. The only thing I don't know is whether it was for money or for free. I just shrugged my shoulders and snorted another line.

You've gathered by now that I'd added crack to my daily dose of cocaine. I had heard that it kicked like a mule and intended to try it sooner or later. Then Sharné produced it one day. She untied the little parcel, stuffed the crystals into a syringe, lit it, drew long and hard and then passed it to me. Within a minute I was floating and flowing in a hazy wonderland. When I sobered up I decided that I needed more. I suppose we were both hooked. I introduced Jakes and Johnnie to the magic crystals and soon we were all going around in a chemical mist.

Sharné was in a psychedelic stupor when she told me she was preggers; that there was a new life growing inside her. I told her to get rid of it. The grasshopper in her tummy, already three months old, might not even have been mine. She threw a tantrum from hell and said I was no better than her father and then, weeping copiously, she begged me to allow her to keep the child.

'You can breed if you want to,' I snapped, 'but I'm not going to play happy daddy.'

How was it possible, I wondered, that my infatuation with her could so quickly change to boredom and resentment? I'm not sure how it happened; maybe it was the baby thing. Our love life had seriously deteriorated over the previous year – courtesy of coke – and I no longer craved her. I'd fallen out of love and the last thing I wanted was a screaming bambino with her trailer trash, whorish genes.

There wasn't much time to ponder Sharné's fall from grace because Jakes, Johnnie and I were setting up our first multimillion rand knock in Bloemhof, about seventy kilometres on the other side of Wolmaransstad. It was as godforsaken and unsightly as any other Western Transvaal town except that there was a big dam nearby so at least there was water, a precious commodity in that part of the world.

Jakes had stumbled upon the deal in the watering holes of these towns where the talk was of two brothers who were eager to get rid of a whole box full of uncut stones. We hadn't bagged a million in a single knock yet but this one promised not just one million, but several times that. After this one, said Jakes, we were going to retire.

'The talk is that these diamonds are valued at nine to ten million,' he said. 'I'm sure we can get five, six million.'

'Sounds beautiful,' said Johnnie. 'Just beautiful.'

Koos and Chris de Wet were bald, pot-bellied, khaki-clad twins who had inherited several maize farms, but the great drought of the early eighties had forced them off their tractors and on to diamond machinery that was now scattered across their vast tracts of land. They claimed that they were direct descendants of the great General Christiaan de Wet who had routed the English during the Second Boer War. One was named after him, the other after the equally illustrious General Koos de la Rey.

I don't know if true blue Boer blood was pumping through their veins. Frankly, this sort of claim did not impress me. But it meant that we had to spend an awful amount of time listening to stories about the greatness and godliness of the Boer people. I'm still not sure why God settled on them as his chosen people, except that they could fight like demons, pray like priests and breed like starving Ethiopians.

More important was that Koos and Chris had safely locked away in a vault in First National Bank in Bloemhof a metal box stuffed with the most precious diamonds that they had dug out over the previous ten years. This was their pension and their insurance against the ANC's expected land grab that would drive whites off their mealie farms to make space for hordes of darkies who would plunder what they could and then run the farms into the ground.

Jakes had the low-down on the fortune: eight hundred and twenty-nine uncut stones comprising two thousand, four hundred and one carats – more diamonds than a man could hold in his cupped hands. Among them were a twelve-carat rare yellow and an eleven-carat blue stone that was the shape of Africa. I had no real appreciation for the merits of this collection, but it made Jakes short of breath. He said the very thought of it made his blood bubble like champagne.

'I'm going to put that blue one on Sharon's finger,' he vowed.

'And I want that yellow one for a tongue stud for Candice,' said Johnnie.

'She won't be able to close her mouth, you imbecile,' I countered.

'I don't want her to,' said Johnnie and burst out laughing. 'Can you imagine the BJs?'

We exchanged our leather and chains for chinos and khaki and both Jakes and I had haircuts. The De Wet brothers were determined to get rid of the diamonds before the election of a new government. Their reasoning was that a black victory at the polls would be followed not just by an invasion of white farms, but by the seizure of valuable assets like diamonds. The last thing they wanted was to see their yellow stone dangling around Missus Mandela's neck or the blue one beautifying Missus Tambo. At the time the diamond market had hit rock bottom because, among other reasons, so many South Africans were trying to sell their stones. If the twins had approached a registered diamond dealer, they would probably have got only sixty to seventy per cent of what the collection was worth.

Jakes introduced himself as an agent for an Israeli diamond magnate who bought quality stones throughout the world. I was the Israeli's bodyguard. We hadn't produced Johnnie yet because he was too seedy looking, and anyway we wanted to use him later as our surprise hitman.

A great deal of our time was spent gaining the twins' confidence, which meant listening to tedious political discussions in the bar of the local hotel. Both brothers were God-fearing church elders and members of the Afrikaner-Weerstandsbeweging, although they were losing faith in the organisation because it had been promising a white homeland for Afrikaners for a long time and so far nothing was forthcoming.

'What we need,' said Koos, 'are more organisations like the CCB. I support them one hundred per cent.'

I had just come back from a coke break in the toilet and my head was zooming and my mouth was in overdrive. I decided it was my turn to contribute to the negotiations, which were progressing at a snail's pace. If I had to spend much more time in the company of Koos and Chris, I would slash my wrists.

'I know all about the CCB,' I said. 'I was a member.' The twins looked as though they were getting a blow job under the table.

'No way!' said Chris. 'You must be joking!'

'God is my witness,' I said. 'I was one of their operatives.'

'I can confirm that,' said Jakes. 'I was in there with him.'

'I am blessed,' I said, 'that I was able to contribute to the struggle against communism.'

'But what is all this stuff,' Koos said, 'about the prostitutes and whorehouses and things?'

'Don't believe everything you read,' I said. 'That, my friend, was just a front. God is my witness that we didn't go near those *meide*. Wouldn't have touched them with a pair of tongs.'

'So what did you do for the CCB?' asked Chris.

'Have you ever heard of Paul Williams?' I asked.

They looked at each other and then Chris asked: 'Wasn't he some communist professor or agitator who was shot dead?'

'That's him,' I said. 'He smuggled guns for the ANC.'

'How can white people do things like that?' Koos wanted to know. 'He deserved what he got.'

'Absolutely,' I said. 'Nailed him right in front of his gate.'

'Only one bullet,' said Jakes. 'And that was that.'

'Well, I have to congratulate you guys,' said Chris. 'It's good to do business with fellow Christians and patriots.'

We raised our glasses to one another. For the next half hour, I elaborated on my work with the CCB and its role in bloodying the nose of the enemy. The twins were especially fascinated by Sousie van den Berg making *sousies* out of ANC body parts, and by the time we left, they were eating out of our hands and eager to do business with us.

The next morning, they took Jakes to the bank, retrieved the metal box from the vault and showed him the stones and the valuation documents. A few hours later, Jakes got out his diamond scale and bought a flawless white diamond for a hundred thousand. This, he bullshitted, was being couriered that same night to Israel as proof to the buyer that the stones would be an excellent investment.

A week later, we met the twins again. The Israeli, Jakes fibbed, had been bowled over by the quality of the sample stone and was on his way to South Africa. He was offering eight and a half million for the whole lot. Koos and Chris said they wanted five hundred thousand more.

There had recently been a Zulu massacre somewhere in the Vaal Triangle and I mentioned this to press home the fact that the political situation was highly volatile and that intelligence sources had confided in me that the *verraaier* and *kafferboetie* F W de Klerk might *hensop* to the ANC at any moment. The dreaded red flag might be flying over Pretoria sooner rather than later, I said. The twins finally agreed to the price.

Only problem was that we needed an Israeli businessman. Chappies might not have had a curved nose, but everything else about him mirrored Mister Fox. We offered him five hundred thousand to portray diamond tycoon Isaac Solomon. He accepted without hesitation. I doubt whether the twins had ever seen or heard an Israeli before so we invented an accent, bought Chappies a grey woollen suit, printed false business cards and booked him into the Sandton Sun.

The next day, Koos and Chris drove from Bloemhof to Johannesburg to meet Mister Solomon at his hotel to discuss the terms and conditions of the transaction. They fell hook, line and sinker for his story and it was agreed that the deal would take place in two days' time in a motel outside the town on the banks of the Bloemhof Dam.

Two days later, the four of us left for the Western Transvaal in two BMs. In the boot was a suitcase stuffed with money. Early that morning, we had dug up plastic bags of money from our back gardens. There was just under two million.

The agreement was that the respective parties would be booked into their motel rooms by twelve noon. A few minutes later, Jakes and I would take the suitcase with the one and a half million to their room. We would return with the yellow diamond, which was worth exactly that. The twins would count the money and we would inspect the stone. If both parties were happy with the first deal, we would proceed with the second and the blue diamond would be exchanged for another suitcase of money, and so on, and so on, until they had their eight and a half million and we had our eight hundred and twenty-nine stones. Well, that was the idea.

We planned to pull our stick-up after the first deal because obviously we didn't have eight and a half million. We intended returning to Johannesburg with all the stones *and* our money. We doubted whether the twins would go to the cops because it was illegal to sell uncut diamonds to unregistered buyers. If they dared, we would offer them a million to withdraw the charge. If they didn't comply, we might be forced to offer them a very painful end.

We were armed with an AK-47 (courtesy of Chappies who kept one back when he delivered an arsenal to a hostel in Alexandra), my sawn-off shotgun and two nine-mills. We knew the twins would be armed because they carried pistols on their hips as a matter of course, and I was sure they had even deadlier hardware in their gun safe.

We were in our motel room long before the agreed time to

check our guns, stuff our noses, fill our lungs and down a bottle of tequila to settle our nerves. There was a tense atmosphere in the room. It seemed almost too easy.

'Oh please, God,' said Johnnie as he threw another tequila to the back of his throat, 'don't let me have to shoot them. This time I'll get the fucking rope.'

'There is no more rope, *domkop*,' I tuned him. 'They don't hang criminals any more.'

At twelve, Koos and Chris de Wet's bakkie drove up to the motel. We had booked rooms at the back of the motel to ensure maximum privacy. It was a Monday morning and the place was deserted. We peeked through the window. The twins sat in their vehicle for a few minutes and then Chris got out. He had an R4 semi-automatic gun in his hand. It was army issue so he must have been a member of the Citizen Force or something.

'Jesus Christ,' said Jakes. 'Do you see that?'

'Fucking hell!' I said. 'He'll mow us down!'

'I think we can do it,' said Johnnie. 'We're four against two.'

'Count me out,' said Chappies. 'You've hired me to be the Israeli. I'm not a hired gun.'

'Well, we also have a machine gun,' said Johnnie, 'and my finger is itching.'

'You don't even know how it fucking works,' I countered. I felt that I should be carrying the AK because of my police experience, but Johnnie insisted that it fitted his hand like a glove.

'It's easy,' he said. 'Chappies showed me.'

Koos got out of the bakkie with a hunting rifle in one hand and a leather bag in the other. We guessed the diamonds must be in the bag. He glanced around him and then the two of them walked to their bungalow. It was clear that the twins were not easily going to part with their life savings.

'We must call it off,' I said. 'These guys are fucking hectic.'

'No way,' said Jakes. 'We've worked too hard for this. We have to do it.'

Half an hour later, Jakes and I walked across to the twins' bungalow. We knocked on the door and Chris opened almost immediately. He was holding the machine gun rather menacingly in front of him. He waved us in. Koos was sitting on the bed with the hunting rifle next to him. Both had pistols on their hips.

Chris opened the case and looked at the piles of money. He nodded his head. Koos scratched around in the leather bag and pulled out an envelope. He took out the diamond, handed it to Jakes and said: 'Twelve carats rare yellow. It's all yours.'

Jakes took it and said: 'See you in an hour.'

When we got back to our bungalow, I said: 'Boys, we have to think this over. There's going to be a bloodbath today.'

'No way,' said Jakes. 'They don't suspect anything. They're just a bit jittery, that's all.'

Fifteen minutes later, after several lines, three crack pipes (Chappies didn't smoke the shit) and shots of tequila, we put our plan into action. Chappies called the twins' bungalow and said it was 'Mister Solomon' speaking.

'Mister de Wet,' he said in his exotic accent, 'there's something wrong with your diamond. My scale tells me it is only eleven carats and not twelve as you maintain.'

There was an exchange of words and then he said: 'Well, I suggest you bring your scale to our room so that we sort this out. Otherwise we cannot proceed.'

We held our breaths. Were the twins going to fall for it? We wanted to split them up and take them down one by one. If they had more than one brain cell between the two of them, they would have stayed in their room and called the transaction off.

A minute or so later, there was a knock on our door. Johnnie was hiding in the bathroom with the AK. Jakes opened the door. It was Koos and he had their diamond scale in his hand. Chris was obviously guarding the diamonds with the machine gun.

Our diamond scale was standing on a table against the wall. Koos invited Mister Solomon to put the diamond on the scale. The next moment Johnnie was standing in the bathroom door, the AK on his hip. He looked truly terrifying as he hissed: 'Put your fucking hands in the air!'

Jakes and I pulled our pistols and Chappies grabbed the

sawn-off shotgun from under a cushion. As Koos stuck his hands in the air, I saw something in his hand – a grey matchbox-like device with a red button. It was a panic button! He was alerting his twin brother or a security company, or whatever. As it fell to the ground, Jakes and I looked at each other. 'Fucking cunt!' he bellowed. 'Come, we don't have time to waste!'

Jakes told Koos to get down on the floor and said to Chappies: 'Keep an eye on him or shoot him or whatever!'

Johnnie led the way with the AK on his hip. Jakes followed with a pistol in his hand and I brought up the rear with another nine-mill. I wasn't sure what we were going to do, but it seemed to me that a shoot-out was imminent and that it would make the Wild West seem like a child's game. Our heads were zooming with crack and coke and we were greedy and demented.

As we crept out of our door and moved towards the twins' bungalow, Chris came prowling around the corner, the R4 held combat-style in one hand, the leather bag in the other. Can you fucking imagine? I don't know who got the bigger fright but Jakes dived to the ground. I hit the dust a fraction of a second later and just in time. Two or three bullets whistled over our heads. I was sure Johnnie had been hit. The two of them were hardly ten metres apart and how do you miss at that distance?

Well, Chris obviously did, because his burst of fire was followed by the deafening crack of machine gun fire and the smell of gunpowder filled my nose. I looked up. Johnnie was standing like some Rambo with his feet a metre apart and the AK on his hip. Chris had had his chance and now it was Johnnie's turn, and he didn't believe in taking any prisoners.

He was firing on full automatic. Doef-doef-doef-doef ...! All thirty or so high velocity bullets in the magazine spewed out of the AK in a matter of seconds and pierced the wall above Chris' head. By then Chris was lying spreadeagled in the Western Transvaal dust with his arms over his head, cement and dust showering down on him. Johnnie's magazine was empty. He looked around at me, pulled the trigger once or twice with no response, threw the gun aside and dived for cover. I realised that if Chris got hold of his R4 he would massacre us. The gun was lying a metre or so from him, the leather bag a metre further away. I got to one knee, lifted my pistol and fired several shots over his head. I'm sure I could have hit him but the last thing we wanted was a corpse on our hands.

'Put your hands in the air!' I screamed.

All of a sudden, Jakes' bulky frame was in my pistol's sight. I'd been about to pull the trigger and my finger froze at the very last moment. The sight of the leather bag on the ground must have been too much for him. Jakes was getting heavy around the waist and had never been known for his nimble-footedness, but he scampered like a rabbit across the dust, raked up the leather bag with one hand and made a beeline for the BM. I stopped firing.

It took Chris a few seconds to realise that his diamonds had taken flight. He wasn't a lightweight either but was up in a second. He bent down to gather his R4. I lifted my pistol and screamed: 'Fucking stop and put your hands in the air!'

Chris looked at me and for a second or two our eyes locked. I think he knew that if he had gone for his gun, I would have had no option but to pump a bullet into him. He stood frozen for a moment and then turned around and made a dash for the bakkie. By then Jakes had reached the car and I heard the door slam. He roared away in a cloud of dust.

'Stand still or I'll shoot you!' I screamed but Chris ignored me and kept running. He reached his bakkie and was after Jakes in an even bigger dust cloud.

By then Johnnie had scrambled to his feet. 'You should have shot the fucking bastard!' he screamed.

'Shut the fuck up and let's get the hell out of here,' I said. 'The police will be here in minutes.'

Back in our bungalow, an ashen-faced Chappies had the shotgun levelled on Koos where he was lying on the ground with his hands behind his head. I heaved him to his feet with my pistol in his back, lifted the revolver from the holster on his side and shoved him into the bathroom. I locked the door.

'Come-come-come!' I said to Chappies. 'Let's get out of here!'

I had no idea which direction Jakes had taken, but we'd agreed beforehand to avoid the national road and drive back to Johannesburg via Welkom in the Free State. So that was the route we took. Although there was no sign of him, I was convinced that the BMW would have outsprinted the bakkie and that Jakes would be waiting for us in Johannesburg with the diamonds.

We arrived home long after dark. The BMW wasn't there. Sharon was already in her skimpy dressing gown. When we asked her if she'd heard anything from Jakes, she just burst into tears and flung herself at me. As I stroked the back of her head, she whimpered: 'I've always known that it was going to end like this.'

'Don't worry, sweetheart,' I said. 'There's nothing to worry about. Jakes will be here soon.'

Johnnie, Chappies and I stayed the night. When Jakes wasn't back by daybreak, we knew that something terrible had gone down. Sharon wanted us to go to the cops but what were we supposed to tell them? That our buddy had gone missing after trying to pull a robbery?

By that evening, we had to face the grim reality that Jakes had been killed by Chris de Wet and left somewhere in the veld to rot. Sharon said she was going to the cops the next morning and was going to tell them everything.

Then the phone rang. It was a sergeant at the Klerksdorp police station. A cold shiver ran down my spine. The cop asked to speak to Missus Verster so I handed her the phone. She listened to what he had to say with tears streaming down her cheeks. She put the phone down and ran to me. It was probably ten minutes before she could speak.

'My Jakes,' she babbled, 'is in hospital ... he's very badly injured.'

At least he was still alive! He was conscious and had given the hospital staff Sharon's name and telephone number. The hospital had asked the police to contact her.

At six the next morning we left for Klerksdorp. We found Jakes in intensive care, lying like a bandaged mummy with his foot in the air, an oxygen mask over his face and needles and tubes in his arm. Sharon, of course, collapsed in my arms in tears.

The doctor told us that virtually every bone in his body had been broken. A broken rib had penetrated a lung, he had suffered serious concussion and his jawbone had been broken. They were still considering whether to operate on the perforated lung but, otherwise, his condition was serious but stable. He'd regained consciousness the previous night but was under heavy sedation for pain.

'How did he get here?' I asked the doctor.

'Somebody dumped him at the Bloemhof hospital,' he said. 'They stabilised him and sent him here.'

'Did they bring any of his possessions?' I wanted to know. 'Like a brown leather bag?'

'Not a thing,' he said. 'But speak to the police. They're investigating the case.'

Detective sergeant Bellingham, tubby and bespectacled and dressed in a grey safari suit, was sitting behind a pile of dockets in a crummy little nook at the back of the station. He was clearly not the brightest spark in the force and had probably been overlooked for promotion several times. There was no reason why one of those dockets shouldn't go missing. He probably earned a pittance and had three children to feed.

'When I see you with all those dockets,' I said to him, 'I miss the good old days.'

'How's that?' he asked.

'I was in the force myself,' I said. 'Brixton Murder and Robbery.'

An expression of admiration flooded his face. 'Well, it's an honour to meet you,' he said. 'Did you work with Pietman Pretorius?'

'I was his right-hand man,' I said. 'I must say, he knew how to get a confession out of a suspect.'

'I would like to hear all about it,' he said. 'Can I get you some coffee?'

He opened a file on his desk and stared at its contents for a few seconds. He shook his head and said: 'There are several things that don't make sense. Do you know what your husband was doing in Bloemhof?' he asked Sharon.

I had coached her beforehand to say 'no' to virtually every question and to play the dumb blonde and naive wife – which wouldn't be difficult for her. She shook her head.

'And did he drive a black BMW?'

'No, detective,' she said and smiled sweetly.

Bellingham told us that he was trying to establish whether there was a link between what had happened to Jakes and a shoot-out at a motel outside Bloemhof the same day. When the cops arrived at the motel, they found a local farmer trying to break out of a bathroom that someone had locked him into. In the bungalow next door, money was strewn all over the bed and the floor.

'What did this guy say?' I asked, an innocent expression on my face.

'He refuses to cooperate or to lay a charge,' said Bellingham. 'We questioned him but all he said was that he wanted his lawyer.'

The next morning, a farmer had reported an abandoned BMW parked next to the road just outside Schweizer-Reneke.

'It looked as though the tyre had been shot out,' Bellingham said. 'The car had false number plates and we're still trying to find out in whose name it was registered.'

'And what does all of this have to do with Jakes?' I asked.

'We're trying to determine if all these incidents are linked,' he said, shrugging his shoulders. 'Something just doesn't make sense.'

The last thing I wanted was for Bellingham to link Jakes to the motel or the BMW. Two days later, I offered him the position of head of security at Club Jezebel. I was no longer enthralled with the brothel and persuaded Mister Sarkis that I had the perfect replacement for my position.

'A brothel?' Bellingham said over a Castle at the local Spur. 'What do I tell my wife and kids?'

'Tell them it's a cabaret club or dance studio or disco or something,' I said. 'Tell me, how much do you earn?'

'I take home about three every month,' he said.

'You'll earn at least four times that,' I said. 'And I'll give you twenty-five thousand for relocation costs.'

'And what's it like working at a place like that?'

'Those chicks, my friend, love a real man with a really big gun,' I said. 'But you'll have to get rid of those safari suits, hey?'

Late that night, after many shots of tequila, I asked Sergeant Bellingham to stop his investigation and get rid of the Jakes and Chris file.

He peered at me over his glasses that had slid down to the tip of his nose and slurred: 'And why, if I may ask?'

'Because Jakes is a very good friend of Mister Sarkis and he's not going to like this,' I said. 'Might just cost you your new job.'

'In that case, my friend,' he said, 'I think it's a very good idea that the file gets wings.'

It was almost two days before Jakes was in any state to tell us what happened. Knocks and stick-ups are hazardous enterprises so before we'd pulled the knock we'd spoken at length about what we would do if the police busted us at the motel or intercepted us during our getaway.

But it wasn't the police who nipped our enterprise in the bud. What we didn't envisage was an encounter with hooligans on horses, bikes and in bakkies, who brandished hunting rifles and flew red flags decorated with warped swastikas, and vowed that they were prepared to die for their ideal of a *Boerestaat*.

I'm talking about the AWB's military wing – the *Ystergarde*. I knew little about them, but I recalled seeing pictures of their scuba unit at some rally in the Western Transvaal. They also had an air force unit – a single crop-spraying plane – and a medical corps of geriatrics.

What the *Ystergarde* lacked in resources and grey matter they made up for in manpower: an army of jittery, *paraat* and well-armed members based in the Western Transvaal, who manned their two-way radios in constant anticipation of terrorist assaults on their farms.

When Chris de Wet got into his bakkie to give chase to Jakes and his diamonds, he got on to his two-way radio and activated just about every *Ystergarde* cell in the area. His comrades in arms abandoned their tractors, their stables and their diamond diggings, jumped into their black uniforms, grabbed their guns and piled on to their horses and into their bakkies and rode out to intercept the intruder.

Jakes told us that when he had raced away from the motel he had taken the road to Schweizer-Reneke, convinced that his three-litre German machine would easily outsprint the bakkie. He soon lost sight of the vehicle in his rear-view mirror, and was just beginning to relax and work out a route back to Johannesburg when he was confronted by two bakkies parked in the middle of the road and three men in black waving him down with a red flag. At first he thought they were farmers driving their cattle to auction who wanted to warn oncoming traffic, but then he saw the guns in their hands. The first thing that entered his head was that it was some police unit or the Citizen Force. He managed to negotiate his way around their bakkies without losing too much time or speed.

Ten kilometres further on, with the town now distant, there was another *Ystergarde* blockade. This time there were three bakkies, a man on a horse and a whole platoon dressed in black. Jakes realised he wasn't going to get through. As he approached them he slowed down, saw a dirt road on his left and turned on to it. He probably had no other option but it was nonetheless a fatal mistake because he was now on an equal footing with the *Ystergarde* who took off after him in their bakkies.

He couldn't see his hunters in the cloud of dust behind him, but the next moment the car swerved and skidded and rocketed off the road. That must have been when the tyre was shot out. The car bumped through the veld and burst through a fence. Jakes said he kept his foot on the gas and gained a further few metres before it jerked to a halt.

'I was out in a flash,' said Jakes.

'And the diamonds?' I wanted to know.

'Had them in my hands,' he said.

'What did you do?'

'I ran.'

'Where to?'

'I dunno,' he said. 'I just ran.'

By the time Jakes was hurling his well-fed frame through the grass and bushes, the bakkies had skidded to a standstill and the *Ystergarde* were in hot pursuit. Chris de Wet was a few kilometres behind but his mates had radioed him and he was rushing towards the scene. Jakes knew he had no chance in hell of outrunning his pursuers. It wasn't that they were so fast – their *boepe* were a serious handicap – but they had the advantage of numbers and were probably expecting reinforcements.

'What happened then?'

'I got into a hole.'

'What hole?'

'An animal hole or something.'

'And the diamonds?'

'In the hole with me.'

Jakes managed to wriggle his frame into a hole, pulled a branch over his head and stayed put. The *Ystergarde* scoured the area around him. I don't know how long Jakes sat in his hole but the sun was heading towards the horizon when the dog unit arrived. Ten or twenty minutes later, he was hauled out of his hole – his pistol in one hand, the leather bag in the other – and held at gunpoint.

'Chris wanted to shoot me,' he said.

'Why didn't he?'

'The others stopped him,' he said.

'And then?'

'Then they just fucked me up,' he said. 'At some point I passed out.'

'And the diamonds?'

'Chris must have taken them,' he said, 'including the yellow one in my pocket.'

We'd lost our loot and most of our money and Jakes was on his back and wrapped in bandages. That was our last knock. When Jakes limped out of hospital two weeks later, Sharon had already packed up the house. His uncle in Port Elizabeth had died and he had inherited his scrapyard business. He had to choose between us and his wife and kid.

'This is it,' he said. 'If I stay, I'm going to die. And I don't want my laaitie to grow up without a father.'

'I understand,' I said. 'I would have done the same.'

Jakes departed from my life as abruptly as he had entered and starred in it. There was no farewell party, no reminiscences of our years together, no pledge that we would be there for each other in the years to come. Jakes had chosen life, a future and his family. When he said goodbye, he threw his arms around me and hugged me to him. His eyes were wet and neither of us could speak. He was saying goodbye; really goodbye. Goodbye for ever. I saw Jakes only once again: when he stepped into the witness box to testify against me.

When he roared away on his Honda Blackbird to join Sharon and Little Jakes who were already in Port Elizabeth, Johnnie turned to me and said: 'You know what? I wish he'd died in that knock. At least he'd have gone in a hail of bullets.'

Twenty

I was killing myself. The beast in my gut was hurling me towards destruction. I was free-wheeling down a highway at death-defying speed and I knew that ahead of me there was a series of hairpin bends that were impossible to navigate.

It was too late to slam on the brakes. I didn't want to think about the fact that at the age of twenty-seven I was a multiple killer, had pulled about ten robberies and was a crack addict. And I was one of the most wanted criminals in the country for having taken aim at anti-apartheid South Africa's most beloved white son.

I was fucked. As fucked as Paul Williams when he swung around at his gate and saw me bearing down on him with a shot-gun. Or as fucked as the Greek brothel boss when I hauled him out of the boot of my car and dragged him towards that black hole. Or creepy Charlie when we shoved him into a dark alleyway and pounced on him with a baseball bat.

There wasn't time to clean up or sober up or choose life. My joy ride to hell was almost over and it was too late to change course. Life offered no pleasure, no accomplishment, no meaning. There were no more good times, no fun, no joy.

I hadn't been out of my townhouse for some time. All I was concerned about was a hit to clear my mind, steady my hands and numb me out. Only then did the night retreat, the dreams fade, the ghosts hide and the sun shine.

The townhouse had become my cradle of misery. It was dirty, messy and unkempt. Fresh sheets, brushed teeth and a clean body are a waste of time for an addict. At times it seemed that the place was a narcotic tomb where we would die and rot; alone, wasted and forgotten.

I no longer saw anyone, not even my mother. I often thought about her with anguish and despair. I hadn't seen her for months. I didn't care about Dad because he was – in Georgina's words – a *poes* from hell. The last time I saw Mom she told me he had been ill. If the old fart were suddenly to kick the bucket, I didn't know how she would get hold of me. Mom was the dearest person in my heart, but to all intents and purposes her little ice cream boy had vanished from the face of the earth. The thought of her wrinkled, powdered face and her sad, wintry blue eyes pounded a hole in my heart.

In the meantime, a life was growing in Sharné. As her tummy ballooned like a cancerous ulcer, she spent her days in bed lamenting her disfigured body and the loss of her career as a stripper. She suffered from acute depression and threatened to do something to damage herself. Her antidepressants didn't help and the only things that alleviated her angst were crack and coke.

'You're going to kill that baby,' I said.

'I don't care,' she said. 'I don't fucking care.'

When her waters broke early one morning, I told her to hang on. I stuffed a pipe, drew poison into my lungs, loaded her in the car and dropped her at the hospital. While Sharné howled and pushed her bundle of joy into the world, I was smacked out in my townhouse. I picked her up two days later. She was clutching the baby girl in her arms and I looked at the shrivelled little face with its tightly shut eyes. I had expected a deformed monstrosity because the only nourishment it had received from its mother for the nine months it spent in her womb was the residue from crack and coke. Against all expectations, it had ten fingers and ten toes.

Sharné wanted to name the baby Charmaine after her mother. I said I didn't care. I never held or cuddled her or attempted to change a nappy or soothe her to sleep. Yet I sometimes looked at her shiny Arctic pools that stared at me as though she wanted to say something. I felt a pang of pity but I didn't know what to do with the child. It had a permanent snot nose, screamed like a stuck pig and was generally neglected. I wanted to load her in my car and take her to Mom and ask her to look after her until Sharné had sobered up – which she promised to do every day. But I didn't want Mom to see the state I was in, so I did nothing.

My money was running out. I'd dug up the last bag in the garden. I regarded myself as in a kind of junkie limbo until I'd decided on my future. Jakes' departure for the Eastern Cape had stopped our knocking ventures in their tracks and we weren't sure how to revive them. Problem was our expensive habits. I suppose I could have sold the townhouse but, thank you very much, I enjoyed parking in the northern suburbs.

'Why don't we just rob a fucking bank and get it over with?' I asked Johnnie.

'No ways,' he said. 'I've been there. Too risky.'

It was Sharné who came up with the brainwave of manufacturing not just our own crack, but turning into entrepreneurs by supplying an ever-growing demand. It was her brightest moment in all the years I'd known her.

I paid a Nigee brudder a few grand in return for a demo. It was as easy as cooking an egg. Two parts coke, one part baking soda, mix in water, boil slowly. The foam that forms is crack. It's dried and cut up into small nuggets to make delicious, heady smack.

We invested our last forty grand in two hundred grams of coke and, a day or two later, we were cooking. My townhouse became a backstreet factory with Sharné doing most of the manufacturing. An ammonia-like reek permeated the air. I was in charge of production and Johnnie of distribution. He was setting up a network of smooth-mouthed runners and dealers in and around Hillbrow.

Sharné might not have been a rocket scientist but she was a fucking ace backstreet scientist and her crack kicked like a mule. Although we dipped heavily into our produce and therefore our profits, there was still enough left to ensure a steady trickle of money. We were up and running again.

Virtually the only time I'd venture out of the townhouse was to meet Georgina. I'd try to sober up, shave, bath and splash some Christian Dior on my face. Her phone calls drove Sharné mad. She was convinced that I was having an affair with some sleazy slut.

'You don't want to fuck me any more,' she whined. 'So now you've found a new girlfriend.'

'Look at you,' I said. 'Do you blame me?'

She was emaciated. Her once lithe and magnificent frame had shrivelled into a bag of bones. Her mouth, once sweet as honey, tasted like smoke and chemicals and her unblemished skin had become spotty and sandpapery. Her halo of locks had turned into dull, droopy hair. She'd become a sad-assed, wasted tart who was slowly rotting away. She was, however, a bloody good cook.

'I'll get myself a boyfriend,' she said. 'Don't think I can't.'

'Eat your heart out, honey,' I said as I slammed the door behind me. I could easily have removed her from my life and dumped her somewhere in the Brow where she could scrounge the streets for a hit. But that was easier said than done. There were complications. The first was that Sharné was, as I've said, a narco bleu cook of note. And what would I have done with Charmaine? There was no way I could have looked after the child myself.

Most important, though, was that Sharné knew far too much about my criminal enterprises. Pillow talk and coke confessions seriously impacted on my future freedom and survival. I'd told her virtually everything I'd done. Paul Williams, Charlie, the knocks, the whole lot.

The biggest mistake I'd made was the night, just after the Bloemhof debacle, when I decided to get rid of the AK and the shotgun and loaded them into the boot of my car. Sharné, about to pop the child, had come with me in order to pick up a bag of cocaine from Mister Sarkis at Club Jezebel.

I took a detour and stopped at the Westdene dam. When I was sure that nobody was around, I opened the boot and chucked the two guns into the dam. When I got back into the car, Sharné asked me: 'And what was that all about?'

'Getting rid of evidence,' I said. 'We're finished with that.'

'What did you throw in?'

'The AK and the shotgun,' I said. 'Won't need it any longer.'

'The one that you killed that bloke with?'

'Who're you talking about? Paul Williams?'

'Yeah, I think that's his name.'

'Yeah,' I said, 'that's the shotgun.'

Georgina knew I was on drugs. I was as thin as a reed, my eyes had retreated into their sockets and my head bobbed around on my shoulders. I preferred not to look at myself in the mirror.

'What're you on?' she asked.

'Dagga,' I said. 'I make a zol every now and then.'

'*Ag poes, man!*' she retorted. 'I smoke dope and I don't look like a corpse.'

'You don't want to know,' I said.

'Are you on heroin?' she asked.

'No,' I said. 'I don't touch that shit. It fucked up my *ouboet*.'

'What then?' she persisted. 'Cocaine?'

'Crack,' I told her.

'Won't that shit kill you?'

'Probably,' I said, 'but what a fucking way to go!'

She shook her head, took my hand and said: 'Why on earth are you trying to kill yourself?'

Her voice was soft and I swore I could detect anguish in her eyes. I stared at her without saying a word and then, without knowing why, I told her that I had become a father.

'It must be a beautiful baby,' she said.

'I don't know if I'm really the father,' I said, adding that Sharné had become a complete and utter hophead and was probably unfit to be a mother.

'Let's go and get her,' she said.

'Go and get who?'

'The baby,' she said. 'We can't leave it like that.'

I shook my head and ordered another brandy and Coke. At the time, I believed that Georgina cared about me, harboured a soft spot for me. Today, I know otherwise. She was a bounty hunter; a hungry predator on the prowl for that opening, that moment of weakness that would enable her to pounce on me and sever my aorta and leave me to bleed to death. The only thing she cared about was finding out who had killed Paul Williams so she could bag another scoop.

'You have to trust your Georgina and tell her everything,' she said.

'And why do I have to do that?'

'Because that's your only way out,' she said. 'Otherwise you'll land up with your arse in prison.'

The end of apartheid had created new impetus to bring to book the killers of anti-apartheid activists and communists. On the one hand the ANC was intent on revenge, and on the other the whiteys who made it into the new government were trying to emphasise their loyalty to their new bosses. Vlakplaas killer Eugene 'Prime Evil' de Kock was the first assassin to go down when he was arrested just after the election and charged with more than two hundred crimes. Then the search was on for the killer of Paul Williams.

It was as though Georgina had smelled blood and was setting me up for the kill. I was suddenly seeing her almost every day. She was soft, lovely and enticing. Her long slender fingers offered me warmth and her cherry-coloured mouth brought me solace. She had enticed me into her web and her irresistibility was working on me like truth serum.

It was somewhere in the winter of 1994 and Sharné and I were smoking more than ever before. I'd forgotten to pay the bills and the water and electricity had been cut off. A winter chill seeped into every corner of the house and penetrated every bone in my body. Sharné was standing over a gas flame in the kitchen cooking crack. It was the only warmth in the house. Charmaine was lying wrapped in a blanket on the kitchen table, staring at us with wide eyes. She was sick and coughing her feeble lungs out.

'Please go and pay the bill,' Sharné beseeched me. 'We're going to freeze to death.'

'I'll do it tomorrow,' I said. 'It's too late now.'

'No, now,' she said. 'Please go now.'

'I don't have money,' I responded. 'So shut up and cook.'

'Now,' she yapped. 'Now, now, now!'

She started crying. I sucked on my pipe. She pulled at my shirt. I tried to walk away. She grabbed me around my waist. I was shaking and my heart was racing and my mind was turning to soup. She banged her fists on my back. The crack was like a viper that injected toxins into my veins and ignited TNT in my body.

My fists assumed a life of their own. I did what my father did; exactly that for which I hated him so much. My memory is garbled but I swung around and rammed my fist into her face. She fell and I continued to hit her. I also smashed my boot into her body. Her bawls and screams turned to whimpers and groans. I grabbed her hair and heaved her, screaming, to her feet. She spat in my face. I threw her back on to the floor. Her cries rang in my ears as I stormed out of the house.

I remember sitting in my car shivering like a wet dog. And it wasn't because I was cold or smacked out. I was scared. I knew that I was killing myself and that I would eventually put Sharné out of her misery too. I had to stop.

Stop. Stop. Stop.

Not now, I thought, and lit another pipe and, with my heartbeat in overdrive, I raced into the night.

I phoned Georgina and half an hour later, she flung her arms around me and held me against her body. Her nipples brushed mine, her breath tickled my neck and her hair smelled like spring blossoms.

'I hit her,' I said. 'I've fucking hit her.'

'Who?' asked Georgina.

'Sharné,' I said. 'I hit her with my fist.'

'Tell me what happened,' she said. 'Tell me everything.'

I was goofed out of my skull, delirious, and my mind was working on and on and over and over. I can't remember what I said but I ranted, raved and babbled. I vaguely remember that at some point I started sobering up and asked her to come with me to my car where I torched another pipe. It was cold and the windows were closed and the car turned into a chemical cocoon.

She asked me again about Paul Williams.

That was when the dam wall broke.

I'm not sure at what time I got home but Sharné was stomping around with a purple bruise on her cheek and her eyes were red and swollen. I took her in my arms and told her how sorry I was for hitting her. She pushed me away, said she hated me and was going to take the baby and go back to her family. Of course she never did. I made her a pipe so she stayed.

I tried to phone Georgina the next day. My heart was beating in my throat because I knew I had spilled my guts and told her about Paul Williams. I wasn't sure what I'd told her but we had been in the car for a long time and my mouth was racing at the speed of light. She didn't answer her phone. I called her incessantly, and must have left twenty messages. The next day I called again and left more messages. She didn't return any of them, for the first time ever.

I had a sinking feeling that I had buried myself.

Two days later, I left home early in the morning heading for the corner café. I pulled up when I saw the *Vrye Weekblad* poster pasted against the window.

It was just four words; four words that felt as though they were propelling every remnant of life out of my body.

'I KILLED PAUL WILLIAMS.'

I stumbled into the café with my head down, grabbed the newspaper and paid for it with trembling hands.

On the front page was a photograph of Georgina and me sitting in the Yard o'Ale. The pic must have been taken surreptitiously during one of our earlier meetings. She'd been plotting this for a long, long time.

'*On Wednesday night,*' said the article, '*former CCB operative Gideon Goosen admitted that he had pulled the trigger that killed anti-apartheid activist and Wits University professor Paul Williams on the first of May 1989. The assassination of Williams was an official CCB project that was approved at the highest level.*'

I stared at the newspaper. Every detail of the killing was in the story. The second paragraph read: '*Goosen, a former police detective, said the Wits academic flew like a bird through the sky when the shotgun pellets entered his body while his girlfriend screamed like a stuck pig in the background. The CCB celebrated the success of the operation with copious amounts of alcohol and black prostitutes.*'

I drove home, made myself coffee, lit a pipe and sat in the lounge with my head in my hands. At some point I pushed Leonard Cohen into the CD player but I was in no mood for his lamentations and switched it off again. I felt utterly forsaken. This was the end of my freedom, the end of my life, the end of Georgina. I had no future, no hope, no escape.

I didn't hear Sharné stumbling into the living room. She picked up the newspaper, studied it for a while and then burst out howling: 'That's the slut you fucked! And now she's fucked you!'

'I've never fucked her,' I retorted. 'I swear I've never touched her.'

'You're a liar!' she shrieked. 'You *have* fucked her!'

I got to my feet. Remember that blind rage I've told you about? When my fists and my fingers go through their paces without the participation of my brain? Well, I felt it again. I moved towards her with fury in my eyes and murder in my hands. She saw me coming and darted for the front door. Thank God she made it, otherwise I might have throttled the life out of her. Minutes later, she returned with Johnnie, who lived just two townhouses away. I had fallen back into the chair and didn't even look at him. I heard the crackle of the newspaper in his hand.

'Why did you tell her?' Johnnie demanded. 'Why on fucking earth did you do it?'

'I dunno,' I said. 'I was fucked.'

'And now we're all fucking fucked!'

'I didn't tell her your name,' I said. That was the only omission in the story: the name of the man who had driven the getaway car. I assumed that even in my confusion, I'd not told Georgina that Johnnie had been in the car with me.

'That's means fuck all!' screamed Johnnie. 'They're going to find out and take me down with you!'

'Just listen to this!' raved Sharné, pointing at the second story at the bottom of the page. The headline said: '*Conversations with an apartheid assassin*'.

It detailed our more than three years of meeting and how Georgina had managed to extract from me every secret of the CCB.

'You've been fucking conned,' she continued, 'by this fucking tart!'

'What does it say?' asked Johnnie.

Sharné read: '*Gideon Goosen is on the surface the open-faced son of a police colonel but underneath this facade lurks a repugnant and cruel gangster who has confessed his partici-pation in a criminal spree that included murder, robbery, prostitution, drug dealing and political assassination for the apartheid regime.*'

'Jesus Christ!' bawled Johnnie. 'I'm finished with you, Gideon, fucking finished!'

'Wait, wait, wait!' said Sharné. 'Listen to this.'

'*When I saw him on Wednesday night, he was clutching between his thumb and forefinger a glass syringe stuffed with crack. Back home in the affluent suburb of Sandton, his prostitute girlfriend was cooking crack over a flame in his kitchen while his newborn baby was lying neglected somewhere in the house.*'

Johnnie stormed out of the townhouse. The newspaper shook in Sharné's hand.

'So what do you suggest I do?' she wanted to know.

'Do when?' I asked and lifted my head.

'When you're in prison,' she said. 'We have a baby, you know.'

'No,' I said '*You* have a baby.'

I waited for four days for them to come. Four days in which I didn't sleep. Fuck that, I thought, where I'm going there's plenty time to doze. Four days during which I didn't wash either. Fuck that too, I thought, I'm going to have enough time for that as well. I didn't eat simply because I wasn't hungry.

Instead, I focused my attention on that activity which was going to be difficult to sustain where I was bound to end up. I fired up my torch and converted dirty yellow crack into a delicious venomous poison that permeated the cells in my lungs and catapulted my head into overdrive.

I smoked and smoked. The crack and sizzle of coke and bi-carb filled the silent nights. Solids turned to vapour. My heart thudded and bumped in my ribcage. My head zoomed and spun at speeds I'd never imagined. On and on, and over and over, it worked.

The baby cried somewhere upstairs. I didn't want to hear it because I didn't want to be reminded that it probably hadn't had a clean nappy for days. Her mother was somewhere up there as well but was also fucked out of her skull. The child didn't stop crying so I pushed Leonard Cohen into the CD player.

Another pipe, another flame. Its shadows danced against the walls. I smoked until I got nauseous. I tried to puke but there was nothing in my stomach to regurgitate. My heart threatened to burst out of its cage. I might overdose, I thought. I opened the door and walked into the garden. I stumbled up and down the tiny patch of lawn. Keep moving, keep moving. It felt as though the muscles in my face were hopping in every direction.

By the time the cops came we had cleaned up the house, got rid of the cooking equipment and just about scorched our fingers and lips as we smoked the remaining crack as feverishly as was humanly possible. I was remarkably calm and collected. What else was I supposed to be? I had overnight become one of the most recognisable faces in the country. I was in every newspaper and on every television news bulletin. The country was baying for my blood. There was no possibility of a getaway.

They arrived with a force big enough to invade a neighbouring state. First, I heard a helicopter hovering overhead, and then there were ferocious bangs on the door. Charmaine started crying and Sharné huddled in a corner.

I opened the door. I don't know whether they had expected me to come out with guns blazing but the barrels of semi-automatic weapons were pointed at my heart. They were wearing bullet-proof vests and had grim expressions on their faces. I shrugged my shoulders, tried to force a smile and said: 'I'm not armed. I'm ready to go.'

I was cuffed, read my rights, pushed into a police car and driven off in a convoy of flickering blue lights. It was winter and the air was dry and the sky was a pale waxen blue. I marvelled at the buildings, the trees and the houses flashing past us as though it was the very first time – or the very last – that I would see them.

Around me, the country had changed. An election had taken place – in which I played no part – and the ANC and Nelson Mandela had come to power. As far as I could gather, everything was still more or less intact and working as before. I didn't believe it would stay that way.

I don't know what I'd expected at Brixton Murder and Robbery; probably to be marched into the interrogation room, cuffed to the chair and confronted by electrical wires and a black car tyre tube. The policemen were the same but the attitude had changed. Everybody was courteous; ominously courteous. I discovered that I had constitutional rights.

'I want to make a phone call,' I said.

I didn't call for a lawyer. I didn't call Sharné either. Or Johnnie, for that matter. I called Mom. She answered after the first ring. She'd obviously read the newspapers and had probably been praying non-stop since then. Her voice was soft and fragile.

'Where are you?'

'At Brixton, Mom,' I said. 'They've taken me in.'

She cried. Fucking hell, I thought, everybody around me seemed to be bawling their eyes out. I was the one who was in shit and I wasn't prepared to shed a single fucking tear. Not for myself and not for anybody else.

'Do you have a lawyer?' she asked.

'I don't need one,' I said, 'but there's something I want you to do, Mom.'

'What can I do you for you, son?'

'You became a grandmother,' I said, 'a few months ago.'

She sniffed. I could hear Dad's voice growling in the background.

'Mom,' I said, 'please listen!'

'Yes, Gideon?'

'The child is called Charmaine. She's with her mother but she's a crack addict and you must go get her.'

She interrupted me. 'Is that the same drug the newspapers said you're on?'

'Yes, Mom. It's very bad stuff. Charmaine will die if you don't go get her. Please fetch her and look after her.'

I didn't know where Sharné was. For all I knew she had been taken in for questioning. I gave Mom the address and put the phone down.

After my fingerprints and photograph had been taken, I was marched off to the very interrogation room where I'd clobbered and tubed a string of detainees. The stuffy little room had the same grimy walls and continued to emit the sweating, pissing and boozing odour of torture and inquisition. But this was the new South Africa – thank God – and the rules of interrogation had changed.

A black-suited, clean-shaven man with grey-blue eyes and immaculately manicured hands took a seat opposite me and introduced himself as a state advocate. Before he spoke, I said: 'There're two things I want you to know. The first is that I'm a crack addict and that I'm going to suffer from withdrawal very shortly.'

The advocate lifted his eyebrows and said: 'And so what do you want us to do about it?'

'There're two options,' I said. 'You can either get me a doctor or a pipe. The choice is yours.'

'You're in no position to make any demands, Mister Goosen.'

'Oh fuck you,' I said, and when he pressed his lips together and didn't respond, I continued: 'The second thing is that I don't intend to say a fucking word. Not to you or any other cunt on your side of the table.'

By then, I could feel that ravenous beast knocking on the door, demanding his hourly fix. The state advocate ignored me and asked me whether I had shot Paul Williams. So I ignored him and transported my mind to the taste of roasted maple syrup at the back of my throat that would dispatch waves of pleasure through my body and down my arms and legs. I seriously needed a crack fuck.

The advocate was getting pissed-off. Some high-ranking policeman was getting in on the action and pointing a skew fore-finger at me. I smiled and waved at them. Only one thing could make me talk: a pipe. Otherwise, they were trying to shoot a dead dog.

Back in my cell, I clasped my arms around myself and curled up into a little ball. And then it took hold of me: aching, nausea, sweat, chills, headaches, craving. Imagine the worst hangover you've ever experienced and multiply that by a hundred. Just a tiny little pipe, every cell in my body promised me, and the excruciating pain would dissipate. I was too tired to stay awake but too ill to sleep.

I'm not sure how long I lay on my bed but at some point a platoon of cops fetched and cuffed me. They drove me to Johannesburg Prison near Soweto and threw me into a single cell. A doctor came to see me. He gave me pills that were supposed to combat withdrawal but they made me sick and I puked pieces of my stomach out. He came again the next day and gave me an injection. I later realised that I was their prize prisoner and they were tarting me up for my keenly awaited court appearance. It was a bit like a farmer grooming his thoroughbred bull for the agricultural show.

The steel door of my cell swung open and when I lifted my head, I saw a guy in a grey crimplene suit and a yellow Disney tie strolling into my cell. A slick of greasy hair was combed across his head. He said he had been appointed as my advocate and wanted to talk to me. I told him to fuck off and slumped back on to my bed.

'I've been appointed by your father,' he said. 'I'm Rassie Roelofse.'

'Jesus Christ,' I said, 'my old man is really making sure that I'm going down.'

He sat down on the bed next to me. 'We'd better talk, Mister Goosen, because you're due to appear in court tomorrow.'

'So fucking what?'

'You'll be officially charged with the murder of Paul Williams.'

'I didn't do it.'

'As far as I know, the journalist Georgina du Toit has sworn an affidavit about what you told her.'

'I was on crack,' I said, 'and as far as I can remember, I only did it to score a fuck.'

'And did you?'

'Of course, yes,' I said. 'Fucked her silly.'

The next morning, a warder brought me a dark suit, a white shirt, a blue tie and a bag of toiletries. He said my mother had delivered them the previous day. When I put the suit on, it hung on me like a mealie bag. The last time Mom had seen me, I was fit and healthy. I shaved and looked at myself in the mirror. My eyes were wide and wild, my cheekbones poked through my skin and my complexion was a sickly, ashen colour.

I was taken to the holding cells underneath the Johannesburg magistrate's court. The cell door opened and my advocate walked in. Behind him was Mom. A bolt darted through my heart and I turned my face to the wall. When I looked around, she was standing in front of me. She was wearing purple, her grey hair was neatly coiffed, her eyes were sombre and a question mark was etched on her powdered forehead.

Neither of us said anything but I could see the tears in her eyes. Then she stepped forward, put her hands on each side of my face and kissed me on my forehead.

'Don't worry about anything, my son,' she said. 'I love you and I will stand by you.'

'Thanks, Mom.'

'Did you do it, son?' she wanted to know. 'Is all of this true?'

'No,' I said and dropped my eyes. How do you tell your mother you're a killer, a robber, a drug dealer? I looked up at her again and asked: 'And Charmaine, Mom, did you get her?'

'Don't worry, son,' she said. 'She's safe with us.'

'For how long?'

'We've applied for temporary custody,' she said. 'It seems Sharné doesn't want her.'

Only later did I learn that when Mom and Dad arrived at the townhouse, Sharné was literally scrounging around on the floor searching for a crumb of rock. Charmaine was upstairs in her cot. Her little body was shivering and she was wet and dirty. They told Sharné they were taking the baby and when she protested, Dad stuffed five hundred rand in her hand. The police found her smacked out the next day, took her in for questioning and persuaded her to turn state witness. She was whisked off to rehab.

Mom left me a Tupperware dish with sliced leg of lamb and my childhood favourites, *boerboontjies* and *strooppampoen*. I ate it slowly, savouring the delicious taste of my youth. Strength seeped back into my body.

When I was finished, Rassie Roelofse passed me a newspaper and said: 'I've got bad news for you. Look at this.'

On the front page was a colour picture of police divers in a dam. There was a second picture of a policeman with an AK in one hand and a shotgun in the other. 'WILLIAMS MURDER WEAPON FOUND', announced the headline.

'Fucking hell,' I said and looked up at Roelofse. 'What does this mean?'

'Your girlfriend has turned,' he said. 'She told them where you'd thrown the guns.'

'She's a crackhead,' I said. 'You can't believe a word she says.'

'They're investigating at least thirty other charges against you,' he said. 'From murder to robbery.'

'I've been set up,' I insisted.

The courtroom was packed. As I stepped into the dock, an excited buzz fluttered through the room and dozens of pairs of eyes settled on me. This was what a monster looked like; a man who had made a pact with the devil and lived by the sword. The side benches were lined with journalists. Georgina was not among them. The only person I recognised was Mom in the front bench and Paul Williams' girlfriend a few metres away. I tried not to look at her.

'How do you plead to the charge of murder, Mister Goosen?' the red-robed cunt wanted to know.

'Not guilty,' I said, loud and clear.

The state prosecutor informed the magistrate that a host of other charges against me were being investigated and that the case would have to be referred to the Supreme Court. I knew I was fucked but I still don't know why I professed my innocence. Maybe the crack and coke had fried my brain and rendered me mentally defective.

As I languished in my cell in Johannesburg Prison, the newspapers reported progress with the investigation. Most alarming was that informed sources were quoted as saying that CCB members who had been questioned denied that the murder was sanctioned by Pietman Pretorius. They claimed I had done it in order to make money. The police said they expected to arrest the driver of the getaway vehicle soon.

I phoned Jakes in Port Elizabeth. He just about choked when he heard my voice and said: 'Why the fuck are you calling me? I know nothing about any of this.'

'I'm looking for Johnnie,' I said.

'I dunno where he is,' he snarled and added: 'And don't call here again.'

'I think you know where he is,' I said. 'If you do, tell him to come and visit me. I have a plan to get him out of this.'

Two days later, Johnnie's spare frame limped into the prison. He had attempted to change his appearance by cutting his hair, growing a beard and wearing sunglasses.

'Howzit,' he said sullenly. 'Why do you want to see me?'

'To help you,' I said. 'I don't want to see you in prison with me.'

'You should have thought about that before you got cosy with that newspaper bitch.'

'I never thought she'd do it.'

'It's because you were thinking with your *kleinkoppie*,' he said. 'Did you at least bang the bitch?'

'Not even close,' I admitted.

'So how do you propose we get my ass out of this shit?'

'You have to turn state witness,' I said, 'and testify against me.'

'And then?'

'You'll get indemnity,' I said. 'You'll be free to go.'

'I'm not a traitor,' he said. 'You're still my *bra*.'

'I'm not your *bra*,' I said. 'Not any longer.'

'Why not?'

'I want to tell you something,' I said. 'Something you don't know.'

'Like what?'

346

'Do you remember Christmas of 1985?' I asked him. 'You were in prison and I was a cop at Brixton.'

'Sure,' he said. 'What about it?'

'That's when Fanus was shot dead.' I said. 'Your *kleinboet.*'

'Sure I remember. How can I ever fucking forget?'

'He was your favourite *boet*, wasn't he?'

'Sure.'

'Didn't you share the dirty washing?' I said, smiling.

'Oh fuck, Gideon, what's this all about?'

'I shot him,' I whispered. 'With an R4. Right through his fucking chest.'

Johnnie's mouth fell open revealing two gold teeth. A frown appeared on his forehead and he waved his puffy hands in the air. 'Huh!' he shouted. 'What the fuck?'

'I led the police to the old station house,' I said, 'and then I blasted your *boet.*'

'It can't be,' he muttered. 'It can't be.'

'Oh yes, it's true,' I continued. 'And it felt fucking good.'

He swept his hand over his head. 'It can't be true.'

'I was a hero,' I said. 'I'd do it again if I had the chance.'

He leaned forward and asked: 'And why have you never told me?'

'Because I'm not your *bra*,' I said as I got up. 'So get yourself a lawyer and cut a deal with the cops.'

Eight months later, one of the most eagerly awaited trials in the history of the country got under way when I stepped into the dock in my dark suit and blue tie. I had languished in the awaiting trial section of Johannesburg Prison for eight months. I felt completely alone. My only visitors were Mom and Dad. My friends had not just deserted me – they were lining up to testify against me. Jakes, Johnnie, Gielie, Chappies, Spyker and Baksteen were all on the witness list. Investigators had unravelled my criminal network and closed in on my accomplices and partners in crime. It was a matter of self-preservation for them: they were hoping to save their asses by taking the stand against me.

A charge sheet the size of an encyclopaedia was thrown at me. Murders, robberies, illegal guns; it was all there. I had become the incarnation of evil.

My sole defender was Mom, who sat every day like a purple or pink rock behind me. In her bag was a Tupperware dish of roast beef or frikkadelle or some other home-made delicacy. Whenever anybody asked her about her son, she said: 'Innocent until found guilty.'

Paul Williams' girlfriend was witness number one and, my God, did she set the scene for my inevitable demise! She wailed and bawled so much that the judge had to adjourn the court twice.

Then it was Johnnie's turn. He didn't look at me once but in a clear voice and wearing an expression that suggested butter wouldn't melt in his mouth he condemned me to eternity in a bottomless pit. He didn't stop at the murder of Paul Williams but for the next day and a half he recounted murder after murder and robbery after robbery.

I'd instructed Rassie Roelofse not to cross-examine him extensively because I wanted him to get indemnity from prosecution. 'You're digging your own grave,' he warned me.

'My grave has been dug,' I responded, 'and there's nothing you or anybody else can do about it.'

Pietman Pretorius slunk into the witness box, pointed his finger at me and said I was the loose cannon who had assassinated Paul Williams without authority and then demanded money to keep my mouth shut. He said he had never given an order for the killing.

'Is that why your operatives indulged in the black prostitutes in your brothel?' my advocate asked him.

'That's a figment of your imagination,' Pretorius responded.

'And is that why you tried to kill the accused?'

'That is also a figment of your imagination.'

And then the state produced Sharné Labuschagne and, for a moment, she reminded me of the bewitching nymphet who had walked through the oak doors of the presidential suite of the

Landdrost Hotel many years before. Gone was the wizened slut with hollow eyes and rotting teeth. She'd sobered up in witness protection and was her comely self once more. She had even married one of the cops assigned to look after her. Her surname was now Arendse.

She smiled nervously and looked at the state prosecutor who was holding up three photographs. A court orderly gave one to her, one to my advocate and one to the judge.

'I want you to look at this picture, Missus Arendse.'

'Yes,' she said.

'Is that you?'

'Yes, it is.'

'When was this photograph taken?'

'Two days after Gideon Goosen's arrest.'

'And can you explain to the court what state you were in at the time?'

'I was addicted to crack,' she said.

'And what about the bruise on your cheek?' he asked. 'And the black eye?'

'The accused attacked me and hit me with his fists,' she said, 'and when I fell down, he kicked me.'

'Why did he do that?'

'Because I wasn't cooking the crack fast enough,' she said and looked me in the eye.

'What was the nature of the relationship between you and the accused?'

'I was his drug and sex slave,' she said. 'He treated me like dirt.'

From there on I wasn't going downhill. I was freefalling towards a rubbish heap of human offal. The witnesses after Sharné simply drilled the nails deeper into my coffin.

Gielie wobbled into court but didn't quite fit in the witness box. He looked at me, nodded once and then told the judge how I'd conned him into participating in the raid on Playmates.

'How did the accused behave after killing Mister Papadakis?' the prosecutor wanted to know.

'He was happy. He celebrated.'

Jakes, flaunting an ill-fitting cream-coloured suit and what looked like a krugerrand around his neck, told the judge that I was the mastermind behind the diamond robberies.

'How would you describe the accused, Mister Verster?' the prosecutor asked.

'We were all scared of him, your honour,' said Jakes and glanced at me. 'He wouldn't have hesitated to take us out if we didn't cooperate.'

By then I had been stripped naked and paraded to the world as the sadist, the villain, the brute, the animal, the savage. A newspaper tagged me The Brothel Butcher and for some reason the name stuck.

By the time Georgina du Toit took the stand, I was already in the darkest darkness. She was wearing the green dress that I'd seen her in before. Her hair was tied in a ponytail and there might have been a hint of lipstick on her mouth. I couldn't see her properly because she didn't look at me. In fact she almost turned her back on me, keeping her eyes on the judge.

At some point, the prosecutor asked her: 'How would you describe your feelings towards the accused?'

'He fills me with contempt,' she said. 'I had to undergo therapy after our meetings.'

I wasn't listening. I only looked up again when she concluded her evidence and walked out of the witness box. My eyes were fixed on her round calves and her bum cheeks that moved in perfect unison as she walked towards the door.

What a beautiful fucking ass, I thought.

Twenty-One

The first sign of spring arrived at my window late yesterday afternoon. For just a few seconds, a ray of sun lifted its head high enough to tumble through the window high up on the wall and for a moment or two the gloom in my barricaded cocoon lit up. It was the beginning of a new season, and in the days and weeks that followed a green cloak would cover the jacaranda trees. Before long a swallow would land on my window sill and sing to its new mate.

I've spent fourteen winters in prison, each one of them as bleak as the one before. The cold penetrates every corner of this place and the chill seems to cling to you and permeate every bone in your body. There are no happy times in prison, but the coming of spring at least signals the end of another dreary winter and the onset of light and warmth. The mood in prison lifts. Inmates are less inclined to slice their wrists or tie sheets around their necks and hang themselves from the bars in their windows.

Spring is also a time for love, for holding hands and losing oneself in the warm embrace of another. When my dearest Debbie visited me this morning, she gave me a card. She must have spent hours decorating it with red hearts, blue butterflies and yellow daffodils. In the middle of the card, a heart surrounded the words: 'To my only love.'

When I opened it, I read: 'A lover is the one who sees the first tear in your eyes, catches the second and makes sure the third one never appears.'

As you know, I'm not one for tears but I had to swallow once or twice before I looked up into her gentle eyes. I leaned forward, put my arms around her and kissed her mouth. She giggled once or twice like a mischievous teenager and whispered in my ear: 'Be careful, darling. You're going to hoist the flag!'

'It's already flying half-mast and lifting off!' I responded and gently bit her neck.

It was a happy hour. We spoke about everything but The Bomb. Debbie was contemplating buying a smallholding on the other side of Honeydew and wanted my mother and Charmaine to move in with her. My mother was becoming increasingly frail and had difficulty disciplining my daughter, who seemed to have inherited her father's hard-arsed attitude. She needed a firm, unwavering hand.

When the hour was over, I pressed Debbie against me to absorb her warmth; enough warmth to sustain me for another week until I saw her again. I held her for a long time and kissed her on her forehead, her cheeks, her nose and, finally, on her lips.

I had to tear myself away from her. She was my lifeline and my salvation. I wanted to stay alive so that I could be with her one day; I wanted to wrap her in my arms and breathe her into my soul. But I'm trapped in a dungeon of brick and concrete and steel with psychopaths and sociopaths and hoods and hooligans and murderers. I'm more aware of that now than ever before. My back has never been as exposed as it is right now.

I'm convinced that somewhere in the bowels of The Bomb a home-made dagger with my name on the blade is being sharpened. My life is worth nothing. It might take a day or a week or a month or even longer, but eventually the crazies are going to come for me. It might be a blade concealed in a toothbrush that glides across my throat in the bathroom, glass in my porridge, a dagger in my ribs in the gym, or my cell door swinging open in the middle of the night. If I am lucky, I'll sustain a slash on my cheek or broken ribs or a hole in my head; but I could also suffer a punctured heart or a severed aorta and leave this concrete dungeon in a body bag.

This all started with the arrival in The Bomb of a nineteen-year-old white boy. The boy was delivered to a communal cell somewhere in this labyrinth of confinement. I saw him for the first time when, late one night, long after lights-off (that's around ten o'clock), I heard the steel gate opening at the end of the passage. The sound of hollow footsteps drifted towards my cell and I peered through the peephole in my door to try to see what was going on. It was Warder Van Deventer and a white lad. I saw the birdie, in orange uniform, for only a moment: clean-shaven, a mop of black hair, his eyes glancing from side to side. I knew what was in store for him.

He was being delivered to Auschwitz, the communal cell across the passage that is home to *Veggeneraal* Taliep Carstens and his mob of gangsters. The boy was destined to become a *wyfie*. All it took was a few blue notes and a friendly warder to deliver him into a pit of ravenous and deranged hyenas. I don't know if the lad knew what awaited him on the other side of the steel door as Van Deventer unlocked it and shoved him in.

He locked the cell door again, turned around and saw the movement at the peephole in my door as I pulled my face away. I was too late. He had seen me.

He pushed his face against the peephole. 'Goosen!' he hissed.

'Yes?' I said. By then I was back lying on my bed.

'You must sleep, you bugger! Mind your own business!'

I didn't respond and he didn't wait for a reply. I didn't sleep much that night. I kept thinking about the boy. I didn't hear a sound from Auschwitz but I had a good idea what was happening in there. Taliep would be the first to feast on the young carcass. When he had had enough, he might be generous and pass it on to his lieutenants to tuck in as well. They would rip him apart, devour him and leave him bleeding and injured.

Welcome to The Bomb. Welcome to a world where the crazies hover on the edges of insanity, stop at nothing, and feel no remorse or pity.

The next morning at four, just before the wake-up call, Van Deventer fetched the boy – or what was left of him – and took him back to his cell.

The thing with the white boy had been coming for some time. Birdies have little to do in C Section except check out newspapers for rumours about amnesties and early releases, and they also try to find out who is about to make his grand entrance into The Bomb.

Taliep was rubbing his paws in anticipation of The Menlopark Three – that's what the newspapers had dubbed them – setting foot in his lair. We all followed the case eagerly: three offspring of Pretoria's elite up for bumping off a black hobo. They were seventeen years old, at a party and pissed out of their skulls when they decided to engage in a good old *boere*-sport – kaffir-bashing! Jesus Christ, I thought when I read it, who hadn't when they were young? I certainly did and I can't say it bothered me too much. But that was then and this is now.

According to the newspaper, the three boys found this oke sleeping on a bench in a park and fucked him hard and good. Well, too hard and too good, because unfortunately he passed on. That should have been the end of it, but then one of the boys bonked his girlfriend's best friend and was caught in the act. The scorned girl – who witnessed the assault on the hobo from the comfort of daddy's four-by-four – turned on her boyfriend and started spreading the story. Before long, the cops were on to them. The judge was black and although the prosecutor was white, he obviously felt he had something to prove to his political masters. The boys denied everything and laughed and joked, not realising that they were going down.

I remember talking about the case during exercise in the courtyard. Taliep looked at a picture of the three youngsters in *Beeld* newspaper and exclaimed loudly: 'Check them out! They make me so fucking broody!'

His goons – he is always surrounded by them – just about cracked up with laughter. Everyone else, anxious not to piss the general off, hooted.

The judge saw right through The Menlopark Three and found them guilty of murder. Somehow they still didn't believe they would see the inside of prison. They had a very larney advocate – never believe those fuckers; they're just in it for the money – who argued that they were young and drunk when it happened and how sorry they were for precious life lost, and that sort of bullshit.

The judge didn't buy any of it and sentenced the principal accused, whose father is a stinking rich businessman, to fifteen years inside. The others got twelve years each and the smirks on their faces disappeared very quickly. They launched appeal after appeal but finally reached the stage where there was fuck all to appeal against. The main oke headed straight for The Bomb – and into the arms of Taliep. I don't know what happened to the others.

Ironically, it was jailer Van Deventer who reported the next morning that a bird was injured and couldn't get out of bed. They took the boy to the sickbay and from there to a hospital. The doctor who examined him informed the prison commander about the nature of his injuries. The boy would say nothing about what had happened because Taliep had warned him that he'd get a blade if he ever opened his mouth. Those numbers can nab you, no matter where you are. Even if they send you to Putsonderwater or Hotazhel or Pofadder, the numbers will get you.

A day or two later all hell broke loose when the bird's wealthy father went to court and asked for his son to be transferred to a safer facility or even that he be considered for early parole. Can't blame him, I would have done the same. It was all over the newspapers. Big headlines about the boy being raped, the prospect of his contracting Aids, unsafe prison conditions and shit like that.

And then some heavy brass from Correctional Services and a bunch of journos marched into The Bomb for an 'inspection in loco'. The culprits would be hunted down and would face the full might of the law, promised the Minister – a fat slob who looked as though he was permanently pissed.

The next day a team of coppers tasked to nail the miscreant arrived in C Section. It was a joke from the word go. Guess who was appointed to assist the police? None other than jailer Van Deventer! He marched up and down the passages like a *paraat* army recruit yelling orders to the birds.

On the first day of the cop investigation, Taliep and two of his goons swaggered into The Three Ships and made their way towards my table. The general's prison trousers hung loosely on him and I couldn't help thinking that maybe the rumour that the virus had nabbed him was true. He plonked down in the chair opposite me with his lieutenants on either side. It's not often that you see them in the eating hall because they usually get Nando's or Kentucky in their cells, but with all the coppers all over the place and Van Deventer busy assisting them, Auschwitz was forced to nosh in The Three Ships.

Taliep stared at me for a long time through his half-open eye. Then he said: 'So how're you, my china?'

All I saw when I looked up from my plate of chicken neck and beetroot were the two gold nuggets in his mouth and a bloodshot eye. 'Jesus Christ, Taliep,' I tuned the goon, 'you're an ugly fuck!'

He just cracked up as though it was the funniest thing he'd ever heard. His lieutenants chortled along with him and so did everyone else around us.

'*Jirre*, china, you're no fucking oil painting yourself!' he said. By now everyone was just about pissing themselves and rolling on the floor.

'What the fuck do you want, Taliep?' I asked him.

'I've been looking at the shit you're grazing and thought I should invite you over for Nando's and a Klippies and Coke.'

When I didn't answer him and went back to sucking the scraps of chicken flesh off the bone, he said: 'I know you like it with extra piri-piri. And your Klippies and Coke with more Klippies than Coke.' It's true. As much as I hate to admit it, now and then I pop in at Auschwitz for chicken and brandy. I knew, however, that there had to be another reason behind Taliep's offer of hospitality.

'What the fuck do you want, Taliep?' I looked him straight in the eye.

He leaned forward and whispered: 'China, you didn't see or hear anything the other night, did you, *broer* ?'

I wanted to say: Of course I did, you filthy fuck! I know exactly what happened and, what is more, I'm about to make a statement to the coppers that will send you so deep into this pit that you'll never see the sun again. But obviously I didn't. I'll never see the sun again either.

'I saw fuck all,' I told him.

'And did you hear anything?'

'I heard fuck all.'

Taliep leaned even closer. I could smell his vile breath. His closed eye opened for a moment and he said: 'That's strange, china, because at some point he squealed like a stuck pig.'

I continued to stare at the beetroot and chicken scraps on the tin plate. When I looked up again, Taliep was smirking. 'What a juicy piece of meat he was!' he said.

At that moment I ached to kill the dog. A baseball bat would do very nicely, I thought as I measured him up. One single blow to his skull. He's a tiny weasel and I'm sure if I hit hard enough I'd behead the miserable fuck. I know I'm supposed to have mended my ways, but the goon doesn't deserve to live and he's going to make many more lives a misery. That's if the virus doesn't mercifully whack him soon.

Everyone in C Section knew what had happened, but nobody said a thing.

Butter wouldn't melt in Taliep's mouth and his goons looked as innocent as choirboys. They shook their heads when the coppers asked them if they had seen or heard anything.

Van Deventer's night register showed that he had dutifully performed his rounds throughout the night and the investigators eventually reached the conclusion that the crime must have been committed inside the boy's cell. There were thirty jailers in the prison that night, so it was thought that it must have been one of them. That's as far as they got.

The boy returned to The Bomb after a week or so in hospital. By then what had happened was all over the newspapers and everyone knew who he was: Brendan de Klerk. The judge had rejected his father's application for parole but ordered that the youngster should be kept apart from hardened criminals who might do him harm. He was supposed to be given a single cell but The Bomb was so crowded that most single cells held two men, and the double cells four, and so on. That's of course except for deviants like me who are supposed to pose a threat to others.

The boy was thrown into a cell with a habitual criminal who had spent most of his adult life behind bars. The poor sod had contracted lung cancer from decades of puffing cheap raw tobacco. He had one foot in the grave and was forever hacking and spitting, but his condition was apparently not severe enough to justify his permanent transfer to the sickbay or to hospital to kick the bucket. His cell was only a few metres from mine and I woke up every morning to the sound of the most excruciating cough ripping through The Bomb.

Prison generally wakes up to a cacophony of coughs and the sour smell of farts slithering from beneath grey prison blankets. This is followed by a flurry of talking, the blaring of radios, the clatter of doors and the rude barking of jailers. Then there is roll-call when each bird confirms his identity and his status as state-owned property.

Imagine starting every day like this! Problem is that like everything else, you get used to it. That's the biggest danger of incarceration: you get used to it. It's not the goon in the bathroom with a blade hidden in his mouth creeping up behind you that poses the biggest threat to your survival. It's the fact that you get used to it.

Brendan was about to become a marked man in The Bomb. He was branded a kaffir-basher and would face a torrid time from black birds and jailers. His romantic encounter with Taliep Carstens in Auschwitz was destined not to be his last. Many a *sif* bandit dick was yearning for a romp with a piece of wealthy white Waterkloof ass.

Brendan was ordered to work in the prison library – where I was posted as well. When a jailer escorted him into the place, I decided that I was just going to ignore him. It was part of my keep-your-dick-to-yourself survival strategy.

'Are you Gideon Goosen?' said a voice behind me.

Without looking at him I answered: 'And so what if I am?'

'My father has warned me about you.'

I swung around, looked into his crystal clear eyes and said: 'Fuck your old man.'

He walked away and we didn't speak for a day or two. It took time but eventually I warmed to Brendan. I had no option but to shelter the boy because he clung to me like baby shit to a woollen blanket. He followed me like a motherless puppy to the eating hall, the library, the outside exercise square and, especially, to the bathroom.

He stood amid hungry stares on the sopping cement floor in black shorts and a white T-shirt and waited for me to get under the shower. Only then did he rip off his shirt and shuffle under the lukewarm stream. He never took his pants off. I watched him soaping his smooth, white body.

He made a beeline for wherever I was sitting in The Three Ships. 'Can I sit here?' he asked and before I could answer he had slammed down his tin plate and placed himself opposite me.

'So tell me,' he said, 'how do you survive in here?'

'I do my own time,' I said. 'And in here you forget everything you've learned out there.'

'What do you mean, "you do your own time"?'

I looked up from my porridge and bread, took a sip of weak lukewarm tea, and said: 'I don't see anything, I don't ask anything, and I don't want anything.'

I looked at the boy – believe me, he was nothing more than a boy – staring at the tin plate he had left virtually untouched. I continued: 'Even if you hear that your buddy's arse is about to be fucked, you keep it to yourself. Nothing that happens in here is any of your business.'

'Why then,' he asked, 'did you make *me* your business?'

I looked at his angelic features. His skin was pale and smooth, his nose was straight and his turquoise eyes were bright. They were almost the same colour as Debbie's.

He was from the other side of town; from a leafy suburb where moms wore gold crosses between their tits, drove to their beauticians and shrinks in four-by-fours, had hysterectomies by the age of forty, clasped their legs at the thought of their personal trainers, and guzzled Valium and Prozac as though they were Smarties.

Dads acquired off-shore bank accounts and blue-chip shares at the rate that our side of town popped bastard offspring and produced criminal records. And in the cubbyholes of their Mercs and Landcruisers were season tickets to Loftus and packets of rough riders for those unfortunate moments when, on their way to Broederbond meetings or charity dinners at the country club, worn-out hookers with heroin habits and Nigerian pimps stepped in front of the headlights.

Kids grew up with nannies in pink uniforms, play-stations, Nokias plastered to their ears, braces on their teeth, bank cards in their pencil pouches, after school maths or piano lessons, and torn Levi's in their cupboards. Brendan de Klerk was one of those snotty, hoity-toity brats we despised and pissed on as kids.

I became aware of increasing glances in our direction, most

of them from Taliep Carstens and his goons who had suddenly started frequenting The Three Ships. Taliep's functioning eye never left Brendan, and whenever the boy looked vaguely in his direction, he fluttered his fingers in the air and beamed from ear to ear.

'He's looking at me,' said Brendan.

'He wants your body,' I said.

'Oh my God,' he said, 'please help me.'

'Try to ignore him.'

'It's difficult,' he said. 'He's always sending me messages.'

'Like what?'

'He says if I visit him now and then he'll make sure I live like a queen.'

'Don't be fucking mad.'

He looked up at me. 'I'm not. But you know what?' he said. His eyes were wet and his voice was thin. 'He's going to get me again.'

I didn't answer him because he was right. We'd never discussed what happened to him that night in Auschwitz, but I have no doubt that it's a scar he'll carry all his life. I can't imagine what it must be like to be savaged by Taliep Carstens. I once asked Brendan if he knew what his Aids status was.

'They tested me when I was in the hospital,' he said. 'I'm negative.'

'I'm glad,' I said, 'but next time you might not be so lucky.'

A young prisoner has virtually no chance of escaping the deviant lust of a well-connected inmate. Many young birds feel it's safer to submit to one sugar daddy and seek his protection because you might get a few privileges thrown in.

Prison is no different from the world outside. Money rules, finish *en klaar*. Warders earn a pittance and usually have a team of brats to feed and a missus who wants a new rag for the year-end function. They're always looking to supplement their income. Sometimes a twenty or, at most, a fifty is enough for a quick bang in the shower. For a hundred you can have your turtle-dove delivered to your cell and have hours of uninterrupted canoodling under a blanket.

Some will say I exaggerate, but on Saturday nights The Bomb resembles a downtown Johannesburg brothel. There is only a skeleton staff on duty and many birds have managed to smuggle in money after their family visit earlier in the day. As the jailers flip the switch at about ten and the dark animal shuts its eyes and comes to a standstill, the soft shuffle of socked feet and the slow crunch of cell locks are the only indication that Mister Delivery is hustling sweethearts to their lovers.

'Can you fight?' I asked Brendan. Those birdies who managed to escape or avoid Taliep's clutches had to fight for their lives and left prison with scars on their backs and faces and gaps in their teeth.

'Not really,' he said. 'I've never used my fists.'

'That's apart from the *houtkop* you clobbered to death.'

'It was an accident,' he said. 'We were pissed out of our skulls.'

'You'd better learn to fight,' I said, 'and the sooner the better.'

The next morning, I dragged him to the gym and ordered him to start pumping iron. This daily ritual has helped me for years to dilute the anger that prison injects into my blood. It neutralises the poison and keeps me strong, calm and focused. I told him to hope for nothing, to trust no one, to talk to no one, to listen to no one, to need no one, and to piss no one off. 'And most important,' I added, 'is to keep your fucking dick to yourself.'

Brendan had one advantage: daddy's bottomless pocket. A well-greased and therefore happy jailer would help to keep his cell door locked or prevent him from being ushered into a steam-filled shower where Taliep, his gold teeth glistening in the hazy light, awaited his delivery.

I was on a collision course with Taliep. It wasn't long before the goon came creeping into my cell. 'Howzit, china, can I sit down?' he asked.

'No,' I said. 'I'm busy.'

'With what?'

'I'm writing,' I said. 'Can't you see?'

'Writing what?'

'None of your fucking business.'

'A saucy love letter to the old auntie?'

'Fuck off, Taliep.'

'Does she know her lover boy is fucking with the white laaitie?'

I looked him up and down. 'You know what, you miserable fuck?'

'What, china?'

'Even if I fancied him,' I said, 'I won't go anywhere you've been because I'd be infected by your *sif* cock.'

Taliep looked as though I'd stuck a dagger in his heart. Then he threw his head back and burst out laughing. When he had regained his composure, he said: 'At least it's fucking working, china. Ask your pansy; he'll tell you.'

He turned around and walked out. The battle lines had been drawn. Things came to a head a day or two later. Brendan's presence in the library generated a flood of new customers, most of whom had never opened a book before. One of them was Taliep. Surrounded by four of his goons, he swaggered into the room and banged his fist on the reception desk where I was standing. 'Howzit, china,' he said. 'Where's the apple of my eye? Isn't he working here?'

'He's at the back compiling an index,' I said. 'What do you want, you ugly fuck?'

Taliep cracked up. His goons joined in, hooting and howling with mirth. After Taliep had wiped the tears from his eyes, he continued: 'Hey, china, man, don't you have a nice gangster book for me?'

'I've got lots,' I said, 'but I'm not going to give you one.'

'And why not?' he wanted to know. 'I thought we were buddies?'

'Because you can't read, you dumb fuck!'

The goons' hooting echoed again through the library. 'But I thought,' sniggered Taliep, 'that *he* could read it to me at bedtime.'

At that moment, Brendan peered around a bookshelf. He froze when he saw Taliep, who spotted him at the same time. He pointed his finger at Brendan and said: 'Hey *bra*, come here!'

Brendan looked at me. He had a bewildered, pleading expression on his face. When he didn't move, Taliep continued: 'I'm talking to you, white boy! Come and give your Oom Taliep a hug.'

I looked at Brendan and said: 'Get on with your work.'

'*Jissus fok!*' snarled Taliep. 'Come here!'

A thickset black warder was standing at the entrance to the library. He glanced once or twice at the commotion unfolding behind him. He knew he was dealing with a goon who could send him home on a stretcher. He shuffled away quietly.

'Come on, Brendan,' I said again, 'go finish the indexing.'

Brendan turned around and walked away. I pretended I was filling in the library register but the goons remained planted in front of me like pillars of salt. After a while, I looked up. Taliep's cherry-coloured lips were pressed tightly together, the scar under his right eye bulged like an earthworm and his functioning eye was wide and bloodshot. The other eyelid trembled as he attempted to open it.

'Call your *wyfie*,' he spat. 'I want to see that piece of ass.'

I contemplated my next move. Keep your dick out of it, I said to myself. It has helped you to survive for more than a decade. Don't fuck it up. Don't cross swords with this goon. Although I could polish Taliep off with a single blow to his skull, I knew what the consequences would be.

I squared up to him. His creased face was flushed and his eye was blazing. He was a demented loony, courtesy of thousands upon thousands of white pipes that had eaten away at his sanity, an assortment of viruses frolicking in his brain and an array of thumps to his skull. He was already a lethal customer but his condition was compounded by his lust for Brendan which seemed to have ignited a torrent of testosterone in him. There was murder raging in his head, and it was directed at me.

My next words spilled out of my mouth like a waterfall. I wished I could snatch them back and swallow them. But it was too late. 'Fuck you, you miserable weasel!'

'What're you saying, china?' said Taliep. He bent forward, put his hand behind his ear and turned his head towards me. He reeked of sweet deodorant and cheap tobacco. 'I don't think I heard you too well.'

'Fuck off,' I hissed. 'If you're not out of here in a second, I'll break your fucking budgie neck!'

He pulled himself upright, lowered his chin and lifted his eyes. His voice was cold. 'China, you can't talk to your Taliep like that.'

'Get out!' I repeated. I was poised to leap over the counter and wring every molecule of air out of his lungs.

He moved back a metre, waved his hand at his goons and said: 'Come, guys. We're not wanted here.'

When he got to the door, he turned around, grinned at me and said: 'You're fucking with the wrong guy, china.'

'Fuck off, Taliep,' I said. 'Just get out of here!'

He shook his head and before he disappeared out the door, he said: 'You must watch your back, china. It's not safe in here.'

When I got back to my cell I sat down on my bed and waited for dusk to creep through my window and fling a cloak of darkness around me. I wanted to be with Debbie. I wanted my precious butterfly to float into this colourless, loveless, hopeless world of lewd faces, orange uniforms, brick walls, iron bars and barbed wire and transform it into our own little retreat. I fell asleep with her fragrance around me.

Early the next morning, I wrote her a letter.

Last night, I clung to the bars, stared at the sky and the stars and hugged your kind and generous heart to mine. I send you my tender love, my warm embrace, and my most passionate kiss. I will cherish you and love you forever and ever. If something should happen to me, I want you to know that I would never have known love if you hadn't extended the love in your heart to me. There are things in life that are inevitable. The sun will rise and set, the tide will come in and go out, the seasons will change and the birds will return for the summer. It is also inevitable that you and I and all those we love and cherish are one day going to die. In fact, if I can never touch you again then I might as well be dead. I don't fear death. I only fear living without you.

Twenty-Two

Brendan de Klerk leaned forward, touched the scar on my shoulder, rubbed his finger up and down the shrivelled piece of skin and wanted to know: 'Is this where the bullet went in?'

'And here,' I said, lifting up my vest. A few inches lower down was another bullet scar. 'That's the one that almost nailed me.'

'What did it feel like?'

'Pretty shit,' I said, 'although I can't remember much. The doctor reckoned the bullet kind of curled around my heart. Otherwise I would have pegged.'

'I'm glad it didn't get you,' he said and looked up at me with his earnest face. 'I'd be fucked in here without you.'

'And I'm fucked in here *with* you,' I countered.

We were both sweating after a workout in the prison gym. His sinewy upper arms glistened in the light that shone through the barred window. A drop of sweat trickled down his forehead and lingered for a second or two on his eyebrow before falling to the ground.

'Shall we go and shower?' he asked.

'Yeah,' I said. 'It's a good time so let's do it quickly.'

We followed our usual ritual. He shuffled under the lukewarm stream of water while I stood a few metres away watching his back. When he had finished, we switched places. It wasn't much, but it was at least some barrier against the perils that prowled The Bomb.

A few metres from us one of Taliep's goons was standing at a washbasin, pretending to wash his hands. His name was Rashied and he was easily one of the most terrifying inmates of Auschwitz. His mouth was a pot of gold teeth and a dagger scar stretched from underneath one watery brown eye all the way to his chin. Every visible square centimetre of his skin – hands, feet, neck, face – was covered in tattoos. He was one of those Auschwitz sewerage plumbers who fucked boys; his whole existence in Pretoria Central revolved around getting his grimy paws on male meat.

Taliep had obviously instructed Rashied to follow us wherever we went. Since the bad blood between us had been spilt in the prison library, he was making sure that he had eyes tracking us wherever we went. His men checked us out in the eating hall, the bathroom, the library, the gym, the outside exercise square, everywhere. He had spun a cobweb around us and every day the threads were getting tighter.

Rumours have been circulating about a lovey-dovey liaison between Brendan and me. I've never touched the boy. The merciless fucking God Almighty Lord Jesus Christ is my witness, I've never sampled male pussy in my life; neither Brendan's nor anyone else's.

It's common for birds to turn into poofters and the longer they're inside, the better the chance that they'll become homo. Your memory of the outside world fades after a few years inside and it gets harder and harder to reconstruct the faces of your girlfriends or the muff you've dived. Suddenly, there are new sex pictures in your head: the bums and cocks of your fellow birds.

Many inmates who were straight on the outside venture into the sewerage pits when the steel doors slam behind them. In their eyes, I suppose, any hole is better than no hole. Not me. I have Debbie in my life. My fantasies are built around the softness of her lips, the warmth of her hands and the swell of her breasts.

Prisons are their own little universes with their own peculiar smells and sounds. Take a clattering steel door, for example. It's like no other sound and for the first year or two it tore through my flesh but, like everything else, it becomes normal. The same with Auschwitz.

Auschwitz is not just the criminal capital of The Bomb, but also a love parlour and wedding venue. On the outside, the shenanigans that take place in there would be regarded as an abomination from Armageddon. In here, it's sort of normal. Believe it or not, in Auschwitz there are men and women. Well, not real women, but men who have been cast in that degrading role.

Every inmate of Auschwitz is either a butch, a *wyfie*, a punk or a queen. The butches are members of the 28s and Taliep's trusted soldiers. They are real men and they are the fuckers. A butch selects one of the inmates as his *wyfie*, and he becomes his property. A prospective *wyfie* has the option of either handing himself over to the butch and to submit willingly to his deviancy, or to be captured, raped and forced into submission. *Wyfies* are prison chicks and they can never be gang members. It's common for these lovebirds to get married in Auschwitz, with Taliep conducting the ceremony!

Then there are the punks, who are at the bottom of the pecking order. They're sluts and service anyone who wants a shag. And don't forget the queens, the true homosexuals, who are treated like ladies. They're held in slightly higher esteem than the punks but have an equally torrid time.

Taliep wants Brendan as his *wyfie*. His previous (fe)male companion had become a bit worn out and Taliep had sold him/

369

her on to another gangster. He often laments that he's lonely and in his mind a fresh, unsoiled Waterkloof arse befits a man of his stature.

Taliep's infatuation with Brendan is becoming an obsession and I have no doubt that he's prepared to kill in order to possess the boy. I'm the only obstacle that's preventing him from fulfilling his erotic fantasies. The only reason why he hasn't ordered one of his hitmen to slide a blade into my back is that he is scared of me. I'm a multiple killer with a reputation for savagery and he knows that if he fails, I'll come for him with every grain of strength and loathing I possess. I'll pop him with a song in my heart. At night I roll around on my cramped prison bed, my head on a straw pillow and think about killing him. I know that I've forsworn my old life, but a hit on him would be about self-preservation and nothing else.

Maybe there was something in what Sousie van den Berg said about the beauty of watching your prey's eyes go blank as life exits his body. I want to press my hands around his throat and watch his eyes go dull and blurry until they were motionless.

Problem is how to get to Taliep. His goons form an impenetrable iron curtain around him and he also has several warders in his pocket. Every inmate knows that there is a small arsenal of blades and daggers – and maybe even a gun – in Auschwitz, and if there's one thing these hooligans know how to do, it's slicing, cutting and stabbing.

Although Taliep doesn't dirty his own hands, he's The Bomb's prosecutor, judge and executioner. He holds court in Auschwitz, usually late at night and in the sombre glow of candlelight. I don't know the details, but I've been told that his men address him as 'judge' and that at the end of the sitting, he broods for a minute or two, clears his throat and pronounces a sentence that is as diabolical as his rotten brain can conjure.

It can be anything from a hiding in the workshops, a glistening blade in the library or the most infected hood ravaging you in the showers while the others hold you down. I've heard of inmates condemned to burn injuries in the kitchen, or having their heads shoved down dirty toilets.

More often than not, the sentence is one of death. In the days that follow, a dagger is sharpened in the workshops or a new blade inserted in a toothbrush. The execution is usually swift and efficient, but if you do happen to sidestep your fate, they'll simply come for you again and again. Taliep doesn't tolerate failure.

Irony is that this human jungle operates a bit like an exclusive resort. There's just about one keeper for every animal. But don't be fooled because I've seen countless warders turn their backs and walk away as punishment commences. For example, there's always a jailer on duty in the bathrooms, but you can't expect the shitty sod who's paid a shitty wage to put his shitty life on the line for some shitty bird whose life is in any case not worth a shitty cent. He'd much rather walk away and claim he didn't see anything. Check out the records and you'll be astonished to find how few prison crimes are solved.

I don't think Taliep has held court over me yet but I know that if Brendan's arse is not delivered on a plate to Auschwitz soon, I'll be the next to face his judgement somewhere in the bowels of this yellow-brick beast. I wonder if it's worth putting my arse on the line in order to protect Brendan's. Chances are good that I'll land up six feet under while he'll spend an awful long time on his knees and stomach in Auschwitz. That's unless I can whack the psychotic cunt first.

Up to now Brendan has managed to evade Taliep's claws by becoming my shadow. His greatest fear is that his cell door will mysteriously swing open at the dead of night – exactly as it happened before – and that he will be carried off and dumped in Auschwitz. To prevent this, Daddy de Klerk is depositing substantial amounts of legal tender into the bank accounts of jailer Van Deventer and three of his cronies. Can you imagine: greasing warders in order to keep prison doors locked!

An incident a few days ago confirmed that this will be a duel to the bitter end. I had tickled the lion's testicle and he was about to pounce. The Bomb is too small for both of us. There's going to be only one survivor: it's him or me.

Brendan came to my cell to fetch me for breakfast. He was clutching a box of chocolates in one hand; a note in the other. 'You want chocolate fondant with hazelnuts for breakfast?' he asked.

'What's this all about?' I asked him.

He handed me the piece of paper. I read it: 'Be my sweetheart and I will be forever yours.'

'Do you think Taliep sent me this?' he asked. He was shaking with anger.

'Without a doubt, but the poor fuck can't write,' I said. 'So someone else must have written it for him.'

Brendan had found the gift on his bed the previous afternoon. Birds get locked up for the night at around five (dinner is between three and four). When he got back to his cell, the box of Cadbury's was lying on his bed. And it wasn't just any box of candy. The dark blue box was decorated with red roses and inside was a double layer of chocolates wrapped in silver and gold foil.

'What do I do?' he asked.

'Give it back to him,' I said. 'Unless you intend becoming his bitch.'

'You know what?' he asked.

'What?'

'I've had enough of this fucking shit!'

He looked at me for a few seconds, shook his head, turned around and marched down the passage towards Auschwitz. I followed him. The gangsters' cell was empty but for a few of Taliep's soldiers having a smoke or munching cornflakes. Auschwitz kept their own pantry stocked with supplies brought in by friendly, kept warders.

'Where's Taliep?' he asked a gangster who was sitting on his bed smoking. The bird looked a bit fagged out. He was probably one of the cell sluts and had had a hell of a night. There was a layer of make-up on his face and light lipstick on his mouth. He had a Bible on his lap.

He looked up at Brendan. 'And what do you want to do if you know?'

'Shove this shit up his arse,' Brendan snapped, turned around and walked down the grey passage towards The Three Ships.

The birds were lining up for breakfast. They looked like a waving snake, its orange body slowly edging and curling forwards. I glanced across the sea of stony, coarse faces. Guards barking instructions and abuse stood on either side of the curving, human serpent. The stale sickening reek of a porridgy sludge permeated the air. After you've joined the snake and stared blankly into the orange back of your fellow degenerate, you finally reach the head of the snake where you wait for a heap of the shitty-coloured salt-less sludge to plop down on your tin plate. You gobble the shit down with weak black tea amid a cacophony of yelping jailers and chattering birds and banging doors and spoons scraping tin plates.

Taliep and his henchmen weren't in the line; they were sitting at a table having tea with another group of gangsters. Taliep was deep in conversation and didn't see Brendan entering The Three Ships. It was only when the boy stood in front of the table that he looked up. I was just behind him.

An almost coy smirk appeared around the corners of Taliep's mouth and he pried his droopy eye open, maybe to have a better view of his pet boy. He opened his mouth as though he wanted to say something, but before any sound could escape his throat, Brendan had lifted the box as high as he could above his head. The Three Ships suddenly froze into silence. The orange snake ground to a halt and those dishing up the bowls of porridge were paralysed, their spoons in the air.

'Take your fucking chocolates, sweetheart,' screamed Brendan at the top of his voice, 'and stick them up your dirty fucking arse!'

The next moment, the box thudded down in front of Taliep. The force with which Brendan had smashed it down on the steel table ripped it apart and chocolates flew in every direction. Taliep looked bewildered, almost as though someone had unexpectedly stuck a baseball bat up his arse.

The hooligan sitting next to him leapt to his feet. It was Rashied, the goon who had been following us around. He reached in his pocket and pulled out something shiny. My body reacted automatically. Without thinking, I launched myself off my feet. I soared like a sky-rocket through the air and crashed into Rashied and Taliep simultaneously. Most of these goons are stunted weasels. They don't eat much because of all the narcotics they pop and most of them have been nicked by that nasty virus. Taliep flew in one direction; his bodyguard in the other.

The dagger in Rashied's hand, a spoon with a sharpened handle, skidded along the polished floor and came to a standstill at the feet of a warder. I had knocked myself almost senseless when I collided with the table behind the one where Taliep was sitting.

As I tried to get to my feet the warders descended on me. Batons rained down on me and I fell to the ground again, holding my head in my hands. The whole eating hall was howling and whistling and punting for one or the other until a howling siren cut through the noise.

I peered through my fingers. A few metres away, warders were trying to separate Brendan and Taliep, who was howling like a stuck pig. A burly jailer was pinning Rashied to the ground with one hand while clobbering him with a baton with the other.

'This fucking thing wants to kill me!' Taliep howled as a warder dragged him away from Brendan, his spindly legs kicking in the air.

More shitty-coloured warders with batons joined in the fracas. It felt as though a mountain of human flesh had collapsed on to me, and a few seconds later my hands were tightly cuffed behind my back. A jailer grabbed my collar and pulled me to my feet.

Taliep stood a metre away from me, his watery eyes boring into me. His purple lips were pressed tightly together and his olive complexion had turned florid. The commotion in the eating hall had died down, although several of the birds were shouting at Taliep.

'*God Jissus*, Taliep,' yelped one, 'you said I was your sweetheart. Why didn't I get chocolates?'

'*Ja sies!*' shouted another. 'The only present I got from you is fucking *vrot-siekte!*'

The four of us were dragged out of The Three Ships and down another grey passage even deeper into the innards of Pretoria Central. Taliep was shaking his head and clicking his tongue and mumbling: 'This fucking china wanted to kill me.'

'Shut up, Carstens!' barked the warder. 'You're in enough shit as it is.'

Two gates opened and slammed behind us before we were ordered to stop in front of a row of grey steel doors. These were the isolation cells; hellholes two metres by one metre and bare except for a thin mattress, a blanket and a bucket in the corner.

The warders unlocked the first door and beckoned Rashied into the black hole. At that moment, Taliep turned to me and said in a low voice: 'And you, china, I hope you know what shit is waiting for you.'

I didn't say a word. The gold nuggets gleamed in his mouth as he whispered: 'A slow puncture. A very fucking slow puncture.'

I still didn't say anything, although a cold shiver trickled down my spine.

'And then, china,' he continued, his face shrivelled with delight, 'we're gonna cut your dick off with a very blunt fucking knife.'

A warder pushed me into the next hole and the bolt slammed behind me. I lay down on the mattress and for a few seconds my head was blank. Then it slowly dawned on me. Taliep Carstens had condemned me to the prison gangs' ultimate retribution, known inside as a slow puncture.

I have a good idea how it will work. At one of their court hearings, Taliep will select the most diseased gangster, someone who has one foot in the grave and is about to be transferred to the prison hospital, to rape me. The poor fuck will obviously be too weak to nab me himself so a squad of 28s will be assigned to hunt me out, pin me in a corner and hold me down. As I understand it, the rape has to be so savage that it draws blood in order to ensure infection. The family of the Aids goon will be looked after and the hit squad will be showered with boys, steak, Mandrax and brandy. And Taliep, of course, will claim his Waterkloof arse for himself.

I'm not sure how long I lay on my mattress with my head in my hands. My heart was beating in my throat and I wondered how long it would go on beating. I was exhausted. A gnawing sense of anxiety filled my mind and a terrible dread gripped my heart. I felt utterly alone. It was as though I was buried under the stone, bricks and steel that towered on both sides of my mattress. Tonnes of concrete pressed down on me.

I thought about Debbie and the serene glow of her green eyes. I wanted to taste her velvety mouth. And I wanted to feel the delicate fingers that she buried in mine and feel her flour-soft breasts against my chest. I'd seen her only two days earlier, sitting in the visitors' section of Pretoria Central, waiting for me. But she wasn't alone. Mom was with her, and Charmaine, my delectable little one who was budding into a gorgeous princess.

I see Mom and my daughter every month or so. Mom is not well and finds the journey to Pretoria long and arduous. For some reason, she's always dressed in her Sunday best when she comes to visit me. Her hair is always neatly coiffed, purple tinted, and her face is covered in a layer of powder in an effort to hide the furrows that are etched there. Her eyes are sombre and purple veins criss-cross the hand that she puts in mine. It always feels dry and papery.

Charmaine has recently turned fourteen and every time I see her I'm astonished by how much she resembles her mother: the same Arctic pools, a mane of reddish-brown hair and a lithe and supple frame. Her only flaw is the sprinkling of freckles on her nose but to me that makes her even more adorable. After all these years, Charmaine still stares at her long-lost daddy with a bewildered expression in her eyes. I'll always be consumed by guilt when I remember how Sharné and I abandoned her when she was a helpless bundle wrapped in a blanket with, probably, a wet, soiled nappy.

And yet, after all these years, she has extended her graceful pink fingers towards me and is nourishing me with the love that I've never offered her.

Charmaine doesn't really know the orange man sitting in front of her but is doing her childlike best to reconcile with me. It can't be easy to have a daddy in prison, especially not when he's been branded one of apartheid's most infamous thugs. She was still in nappies during my court case, but the rags still, from time to time, dig out my skeletons and remind everyone how fortunate they are that Gideon Goosen is rotting in the slammer.

Mom and Charmaine recently moved to Debbie's smallholding in Honeydew. I know that Debbie is doing her best to convince Charmaine that her father is not the debased cut-throat that everyone makes him out to be, but the victim of circumstances and bad friends and skewed political convictions and shit like that. It seems as though Debbie's therapy is working. For all practical purposes she is the mother that Charmaine has never had and she assures me that she'll protect my little one as though she is her own.

We were eating ice cream that Debbie had purchased at the tuck shop. At some point my cone broke and I tried to shove it into my mouth before it spilt on my orange prison uniform. I was only half successful. The shrill, almost happy shrieks of my daughter echoed through the hollow space as I attempted to wipe it from my mouth but emerged with an ice creamed face. My mother threw her head back and joined in the general merriment. I looked at her and thought that I hadn't seen her laugh for many, many years. For a moment, she looked almost cheerful. She pointed at me, chortled again and said: '*Boytjie*, you know what this reminds me of?'

'What, Mom?'

'Margate,' she said. 'It reminds me of the holidays in Margate.'

'Oh, come on, Mom,' I countered. 'That was such a long time

ago.'

Charmaine, wiping the tears from her eyes, asked: 'And what happened in Margate?'

'Your father was such a sweet little boy,' said Mom, 'that he always had two ice creams in his hand.'

'How come?' she asked.

I shook my head and said: 'Oh, Mom, don't start again.'

'He walked around the beach looking for the ice cream man,' Mom said, 'and when he found him he threw such a tantrum that everyone bought him a cone. He once had three ice creams at the same time.'

'No way!' shrieked Charmaine with a smile around her mouth. 'Is it true, Daddy?'

I looked at my daughter. My heart was pounding in my throat and I took a deep breath. It was the first time she'd called me Daddy! Fucking imagine: Daddy! As far as I know a daddy is someone who keeps you safe and warm and showers you with love and affection. I've done fucking sweet zero of any of that, and yet, I'm Daddy!

I looked at Debbie and her eyes were wet. I swallowed my own tears and said: 'Your granny is exaggerating. In any case, I don't remember it.'

'Oh yes, it's true,' said Mom looking at Charmaine. 'That's why your father will always be my little ice cream boy.'

'That's so cool!' she exclaimed, her eyes wide and smiling. 'That's really cool, Daddy.'

It is because of them that I must live. Every bird dreams about that day when, like any other, you wake up with coughs and farts and noisy movement around you. You sit on the edge of your bed and wait for the heavy footsteps approaching down the hollow passage to stop at your door.

The steel door of your cell swings open, and after that another and another and another until suddenly there are no more. After a lifetime in the guts of the yellow-brick beast it has finally puked you out into the arms of your beloved who embraces you under the purple jacarandas and takes you back to live again.

That's what you do. You try to stay alive so that you can live again one day.

I don't want to die now.

Especially not from a bug that will consume my body until I lie wasted and empty-eyed in my own shit and piss in a hospital bed, with Pastor van Heerden by my side, praying for my lost soul.

Charmaine has been through hell. The last thing she needs is to have to say goodbye to her daddy as the bug finally gobbles him up.

I simply have to stay alive.

For her, for Debbie, for Mom.

Epilogue

I spent three days in isolation before the door swung open. I had to shut my eyes tightly for a few moments to get used to the light. I was hauled out of my tomb and escorted through the innards of the prison back to The Bomb. The birds we passed stopped in their tracks and stared at me. The talk in the prison was of the brawl in The Three Ships and there was bound to be speculation about Taliep Carstens' response. Everyone knew that his revenge would be ruthless and lethal. That's how he keeps his control over the inmates.

Before we marched through the steel door leading to C Section, I was taken to an office with a 'Duty Officer' sign on the door and confronted by a black prison official with shiny things on his shoulders and an attitude from hell. He was holding a cup of Five Roses in one hand and a Romany Cream in the other.

He slowly dipped the cookie into his cup of tea. Then with one precise movement he stuffed it into his mouth.

He put his cup neatly back on to the saucer, looked me up and down, and then announced in a formal voice that he had decided not to institute any charges against me. When I didn't erupt with gratitude, he continued: 'You're very fortunate, Prisoner Goosen. We have, however, decided to suspend your visiting rights for four weeks.'

No! no! no! I clenched my fists and ground my teeth. Fuck, fuck, fuck! Cancelling an inmate's visits is like withholding morphine from a patient dying of cancer. It's that one hour every week that keeps you from raving lunacy, that turns your desperation into hope.

'Why?' I asked him. He swivelled his rotund body around in his chair and looked at me with a smirk on his face. The fact that he was black might have been his sole qualification for the job, but there was no difference between him and the white bureaucrats of yesteryear. I've been treated like shit by each and every one of them. Blacks despise me because they think I hate them and whites shun me because I remind them of what they might have been.

On the faded white wall behind him was a poster of the Correctional Services mission statement. It promised honesty and integrity and respect for human rights. It meant fuck all because after all these years I'm still apartheid assassin Gideon Goosen and I sometimes feel as though I'm paying for every sin ever committed by my white countrymen. Maybe this dude had once upon a time been a mean ANC fighting machine who had been captured and *klapped* by someone like my father. He'd never forgotten the white hand that strangled him and I'm a convenient whipping boy.

'We can't allow you to disturb the good order in this prison,' he said. 'Don't push your luck.'

'And Brendan de Klerk?' I asked. 'What about him?'

'Ah, Prisoner de Klerk!' he said with a smile. 'I'm afraid I have bad news for you, Goosen.'

He paused to let me to stew for a second or two before he continued: 'Your good friend is not with us any longer.'

He waited for me to say something and when I didn't, he said: 'We have decided to transfer him to another facility for his own safety.'

Brendan was the first real friend I'd made in fourteen years of incarceration. He was the only human face in this garbage dump. And now he was gone at the stroke of this cunt's pen. Sent from one garbage dump to another. Just like that.

It immediately crossed my mind that Brendan's departure would further infuriate Taliep. I knew he would blame me for it.

I bit my lip and asked: 'And why did you do that?'

'We don't believe the conditions in C Section are conducive to his rehabilitation,' he said, shaking his head. 'The two of you seem to have forged an unhealthy alliance.'

'What do you mean by that?'

He smiled as he said: 'I don't have to explain my decisions to you, Prisoner Goosen.'

I turned around to leave but he stopped me. 'Another thing,' he said, opening a file on his desk. 'Prisoner Carstens has instituted a charge against you.'

'Who? Taliep?'

'Yes,' he said. 'He claims that you've threatened to kill him.'

'When?'

'Several times, apparently. He says he's got witnesses.'

'That's a lie,' I said. 'He's threatened to kill *me*.'

'Do you want to institute a counter charge?'

'What happens then?'

'I'll have it investigated.'

'And how long will that take?'

'Difficult to say,' he said. 'Until it's finished.'

'Forget it,' I said. 'I'll be dead by then.'

'What do you mean by that?'

'Can I please go back to my cell?'

I know now that I am on my own.

Glossary and abbreviations

ANC – African National Congress, major liberation movement during apartheid

anderskleuriges – people of colour

'Apostolie stink na olie' – 'Apostolics stink of oil'

AWB – Afrikaner Weerstandsbeweging (Afrikaner Resistance Movement, a white neo-Nazi movement)

bakkie – South African word for a pickup truck

bliksem – bash; *bliksemmed* – bashed (slang)

bobotie – Cape Malay dish of curried minced meat baked with apricots and egg custard

boep – paunch (abbreviation of *boepens*)

boerboontjies – green beans cooked with onion and potato

boerestaat – homeland for ultra conservative whites, mostly Afrikaners, who opposed the end of apartheid

boerewors – traditional South African sausage containing ground beef and pork seasoned with spices (literally, farmer's sausage)

boet – brother

boetie – little brother

bosbefok/bossies – slang term to describe someone with combat fatigue or suffering from the Vietnam Syndrome

boytjie – little boy

bra – slang for 'brother'

braai/braaiing/braaivleis – South African word for barbecue, barbecuing

broer – brother

dagga – South African word for cannabis

domkop – blockhead

dônner – clobber, beat (slang)

dop – South African word for a drink, especially of brandy or other spirits

draadtrek – masturbation

ducktail – young hooligan of the 1950s

'*En dan sal ek mooi sit vir jou*' – literally 'And then I'll sit pretty for you'

finish *en klaar* – South African expression meaning 'that's the end of it' or 'that's how it is'

Fok-kop – Fuck Hill

frikkadelle – South African word for spicy meatballs, rissoles

gabba – friend, mate (slang)

gatvol – sick and tired

genotgrotte – 'pleasure caves'. Vulgar reference to women's genitals

gogga – South African slang for insect or creepy-crawly

grensvegter – border warrior

groeps-woeps – slang for group sex

grootbaas – big boss

grootseun – big boy

hensop – surrender (literally 'hands up')

hotnot – derogatory term for person of mixed blood

Huisgenoot – South African family magazine (literally 'home companion')

indaba – South African word for discussion or conference

jirre – exclamation of astonishment/horror derived from *Here*, which means God

jislaaik – exclamation of astonishment/horror

Jissus God – Jesus God (expression of astonishment/horror)

kafferboetie – literally 'kaffir brother'. Derogatory term for those who opposed racial segregation

kaffir – derogatory term for a black African

kak – shit

kakked out – literally 'shat on', slang for a telling-off

kêrel – chap, fellow

klap – a slap or cuff

kleinbaas – little boss, young sir

kleinboet – younger brother

kleinkoppie – literally 'small head'. Slang expression referring to the penis

Klippies – South African abbreviation for Klipdrift brandy

koeksister – South African word for a plaited doughnut dipped in syrup

kom binne – come in

laaitie – informal South African word for a male child, adolescent or young adult (also spelled 'lighty')

larney – South African word referring to wealth and high status, something that is smart and elegant

Leeutande – lion's teeth

lekker – South African word used informally to mean good or pleasant

lokasies – locations, former term for black townships

meid – derogatory term for a black woman

moer – hell

moffie – derogatory South African word for a man regarded as effeminate, male homosexual

nogal – informal South African word meaning 'what is more'

oke – informal South African word for a man

oom – South African word for an older man, respectful/affectionate form of address

oranje-blanje-blou – apartheid South Africa's official flag until 1994

ouboet – older brother

PAC – Pan Africanist Congress, one of the liberation movements during apartheid

pap – porridge (usually maize meal porridge)

pap-en-sous – maize meal porridge and sauce

paraat – prepared

platpoot – slang for policeman, flatfoot

poes – vulgar slang for woman's genitals, cunt

pomping – literally 'pumping'. Vulgar slang for copulating

pynkamer – literally 'room of pain'

rooinekke – Englishmen (literally 'red necks')

SACP – South African Communist Party

SAP – South African Police. Renamed South African Police Service after the 1994 election

seun – son/boy

siestog – shame (sympathetic exclamation)

sif – abbreviation for *sifilis* = syphilis

sis – South African informal expression of disappointment, disgust, contempt

sjoe – exclamation of astonishment/horror

skewetiet – literally 'skew breast'

skyf – joint (of dagga)

slymslote – 'slime gutters'. Vulgar reference to women's genitals

sousie – sauce

South West – short for South West Africa, present day Namibia

spoedvark – literally 'fast pig'

sterkte – strength

stinkvingertjie – literally 'stinking finger' (vulgar slang)

strooppampoen – sweet pumpkin

Swapo – acronym for South West Africa People's Organisation

takhaar – a lout, rough type

tannie – South African word for an older woman, respectful/affectionate form of address terr/terrie – abbreviation for terrorist

tickey – informal South African word for a small silver three-penny piece, withdrawn from circulation in 1961

tickey box – informal South African term for a public telephone

Tiertrane – literally 'tiger's tears'

tik – crystal methamphetamine

tjoekie – prison

veggeneraal – field general, combat general (military)

verraier – traitor

vlei – South African word for a shallow natural pool of water

Vierkleur – flag of the former South African (Transvaal) Republic. It has four colours: green, orange, white and blue

Volk en Vaderland – Countrymen and Country

Volksie – abbreviation for Volkswagen

vrot-siekte – literally 'rotten sickness', venereal disease

wrede – cruel

wyfie – bitch

Ystergarde – literally 'Iron Guard', military wing of the AWB

zol – South African word for a hand-rolled cigarette, especially of cannabis

Refresh yourself at www.penguinbooks.co.za

Visit penguinbooks.co.za for exclusive information and interviews with bestselling authors, fantastic give-aways and the inside track on all our books, from Penguin Classics to the latest bestsellers.

BE FIRST ▼

first chapters, first editions, first novels

eNEWSLETTER ▼

subscribe to receive our free weekly newsletter

EXCLUSIVES ▼

author chats, video interviews, biographies, special features

BLOG ▼

post your comments, chat with other readers

EVERYONE'S A WINNER ▼

give-aways, competitions, quizzes

BOOK CLUBS ▼

exciting features to support existing groups and create new ones

NEWS ▼

author events, bestsellers, awards, what's new

ABOUT US ▼

advice for writers and company history

Get Closer To Penguin ... www.penguinbooks.co.za